Domestic Revolutions

A Social History of American Family Life

Steven Mintz and Susan Kellogg

THE FREE PRESS
A Division of Macmillan, Inc.
NEW YORK

Collier Macmillan Publishers
LONDON

The Free Press
A Division of Macmillan, Inc.
866 Third Avenue, New York, N. Y. 10022

Collier Macmillan Canada, Inc.

Printed in the United States of America

printing number
1 2 3 4 5 6 7 8 9 10

Library of Congress Cataloging-in-Publication Data

Mintz, Steven
  Domestic revolutions

  Bibliography: p.
  Includes index.
  1. Family—United States—History. 2. United States—Social conditions—To 1865. 3. United States—Social conditions—1865–1918. 4. United States—Social conditions—20th century. I. Kellogg, Susan. II. Title.
HQ535.M46 1988   306.8'5'0973   87–27551
ISBN 0–02–921290–1

To Seth Kellogg Mintz and Sean Tomas Mintz

Marriage and the family are undergoing a change, nay, passing through a crisis. To close your eyes to it, to say that all is for the best in the best of matrimonial worlds, would be as shallow and as unscientific as to prophesy the downfall of the family. Some changes are necessary, but these will not affect the essential constitution of the family.

—Bronislaw Malinowski, *Marriage, Past & Present*

Contents

Acknowledgments

———————•———————

OVER the past twenty years, scholars have engaged in a far-reaching effort to reconstruct the texture of American family life in the past. These researchers have tapped new sources of evidence, particularly aggregate data derived from manuscript censuses and divorce and probate records. They have applied new methods of inquiry, such as the technique of "family reconstitution"; have closely examined diaries and family papers; and have reached into areas that were previously the domains of such disciplines as cultural anthropology, law, and demography. This book could not have been written in the absence of this body of scholarship. Our debts are recorded in every footnote.

A number of friends and colleagues deserve special acknowledgment. James H. Jones encouraged us to take on this project and offered important reassurance at every stage of our research and writing. Linda Auwers, Robin Stevens, and Kevin Sweeney gave us valuable advice and criticism and helped us avoid many errors of fact and interpretation. Charlotte and Julie Mintz helped us collect the book's illustrations. Our editor at Free Press, Joyce Seltzer, gave thorough and detailed criticism of the manuscript and offered expert assistance in transforming our early drafts into a book.

Our sons Sean Tomas Mintz and Seth Kellogg Mintz are our happiest collaboration—and also our link to a future in which the family will continue to perform its essential tasks, although its demographic characteristics, its form and composition, and its social functions and internal dynamics will certainly continue to change.

Introduction

UNTIL quite recently, most Americans subscribed to a common conception of a "proper" family life—a set of beliefs so widespread that it was largely taken for fact. These were some of the givens of that conception:

A family comprises a married couple and their minor children living together in a common residence

The father, as head of household, should single-handedly earn the family's income and determine the family's residence, and his surname will become that of his wife and children

The mother's primary responsibilities should be to serve as her husband's companion and helper and as facilitator of her children's education and development, staying home and devoting herself full-time to the tasks of child rearing and homemaking

Marriage is a lifelong commitment and sex should be confined to marriage

Parents have exclusive responsibilities for their children's care until the children enter kindergarten and, that even after that time, parents are free to discipline and care for their children as they see fit, without outside interference

Families that fail to conform to one or more of these givens may be regarded as "troubled" or "problem" families.

Over the past two decades, these givens have been subjected to profound inquiry and attack in light of contemporary mores. Today the term "family" is no longer attached exclusively to conjugal or nuclear families comprising a husband, wife, and their dependent children. It is applied to almost any grouping of two or more people domiciled together. These family groupings include single-parent households, blended families made up of stepparents and stepchildren or adoptive parents and their children, and couples cohabiting outside wedlock, including gay couples.

American family life today is markedly different from what it was even two decades ago. Over the past fifteen years, the divorce rate has doubled, as has the number of female-headed families. Today more than half of all mothers with school-age children work outside the home, more than a quarter of all families with children have just one parent, and more than half of all three-to-five year olds are enrolled in nursery schools or day-care centers. Over the course of a generation, the number of children per family has declined by half.

These dramatic changes constitute a fundamental reorientation in American family patterns. But as sudden and far-reaching as they are, they have precedents. Over the past 300 years, American families have undergone a series of far-reaching "domestic revolutions" that profoundly altered their familial life, repeatedly transforming their demographic characteristics, organizational structure, functions, conceptions, and emotional dynamics.

Although the family is seen as the social institution most resistant to change, it is, in fact, as deeply embedded in the historical process as any other institution. The claim that it is essentially a conservative institution—an island of stability in a sea of social, political, and economic change—is largely an illusion.If the family is a conservative institution in the sense that it transmits the moral and cultural values of one generation to the next, it is not conservative in the sense of being static. In structure, role, and conception, the American family has changed dramatically over time.

Three centuries ago the American family was the fundamental economic, educational, political, and religious unit of society. The family, and not the isolated individual, was the unit of which church and state were made. The household was not only the locus of production, it was also the institution primarily responsible for the education of children, the transfer of craft skills, and the care of the elderly and the infirm.

During the early colonial era, the family performed many functions that have since been relegated to nonfamilial institutions. The family was an integral part of the larger society. It was a "little commonwealth," governed by the same principles of hierarchy and deference as the larger society. During the seventeenth century, a sharp division between economics, religion, law, and politics and family life was unimaginable. All these aspects of life were part of a single, unitary, mutually reinforcing matrix.

Compared to seventeenth-century families, today's families are much more isolated from public life and specialized in functions. The family has not only ceased to be a productive unit, but its roles in caring for the aged, providing relief for the poor, and educating the young have increasingly been assumed by public institutions, ranging from government social agencies to insurance companies, banks, public charities, hospitals, and schools. As many of its traditional economic, educational, and welfare functions were transferred outside the home, the family ceased to be a largely autonomous, independent, self-contained, and self-sufficient unit. Instead the family has tended to concentrate on a small number of remaining functions—the socialization of children and the provision of emotional support and affection.

In the pages that follow we trace the shift from a society in which the family was the fundamental unit to a society in which the functions of the family are narrower—a transition from a society in which individuals were nothing apart from their family identity to a society in which the individual is of central significance and in which the family has been stripped of much of its legal meaning. These changes did not begin in the last decade or even the last half-century; they have been 300 years in the making.

By the time Alexis de Tocqueville visited the United States in 1831 and 1832, he found family patterns vastly different from those of the settlers who had left England in the seventeenth century. The older conception of the family as a "little commonwealth," a microcosm of the larger society, had receded and been replaced by a new image of the family as a "haven in a heartless world," a bastion of morality and tender feeling and a refuge from the aggressive and selfish world of commerce. The family had become a private place, a shelter for higher redeeming values and a shelter from the temptations and corruptions of the outside world. Relations within this new "democratic" family were less formal and hierarchical than they had been in the seventeenth- or eighteenth-century household. Marriages were more and more based on romantic love, relations between husbands and wives had grown increasingly affectionate and egalitarian, children stayed at home longer than before, and parents devoted increased attention to the care and nurture of their offspring. In this family, relations were organized around the principle of "separate spheres," according to which each family member had a special role, or sphere, appropriate to his or her age and gender.

During the early years of the twentieth century, a host of educators, legal scholars, social workers, and academic social scientists created a new ideal of family life that they termed the "companionate family." Responding to an alarming rise in the divorce rate, the falling birthrate, the revolution in morals and manners, and the changing position of women, these experts extolled a new ideal of family life in which spouses would be friends and lovers and parents and children would be pals. According to the new companionate ideal, relations within the family would not be based on patriarchal authority but on affection and mutual interest. The traditional conception of marriage as a sacred duty or obligation gave way to a new ideal of sexual satisfaction, companionship, and emotional support. To achieve this ideal, influential groups recommended liberalized divorce laws; programs of marriage counseling, domestic science, and sex education; and permissive child-rearing practices stressing freedom and self-expression over impulse-control.

Although the intellectual roots of the companionate family lay in the 1920s, the impact of this new ideal of family life was delayed by the depression and World War II, only to resurface dramatically after the war. By the mid-1950s, the ideal of the companionate family seemed well on the way to fulfillment. Family "togetherness" became a cultural watchword. Couples married earlier than their parents had, and women bore more children, had them at younger ages, and spaced them closer together. The increase in the divorce rate was lower than in preceding years. And rising real income permitted a growing majority of the nation's families to buy their own homes. At the same time, outside institutions continued to take on traditional family functions. As the proportion of the population over the age of sixty-five grew, the economic burden of supporting the elderly was increasingly assumed by public and private pensions. Similarly, more responsibility for the training of young people fell to separate age-segregated institutions.

Since the late 1950s, confidence that the American family is growing progressively stronger has eroded. The family, once viewed as the deepest source of affection and emotional support, increasingly came to be seen as an impediment to individual self-fulfillment. In those years the relationship between family values and the values of individualism and personal autonomy has grown ever more problematic. One source of strain lies in a continuing escalation in the expectations of what marriage can and ought to fulfill. Rising expectations have proved difficult to meet, and the result has been mounting divorce rates. A further source of strain has been individuals' increased desire for personal fulfillment, especially the middle-class belief that happiness can only be achieved through a successful, independent career. Career expectations frequently come into conflict with a more traditional view of marriage as an institution in which the spouses, particularly the wife, must sacrifice for the good of the family unit. Increasingly, this desire for greater personal freedom and fulfillment has been met by a proliferation of nonmarital relationships—most notably, a sharp rise in the number of couples cohabiting outside of marriage.

The distinguishing characteristic of American family life since 1960 has been increasing diversity in family arrangements. Today, as a growing number of young adults defer marriage and more and more elderly live by themselves, nearly a quarter of all American households consist of just a single member. As the divorce rate climbed, the number of stepfamilies increased, and now more than a tenth of the nation's children live with one stepparent and one natural parent. Higher divorce rates coupled with a sharp increase in the number of children born to single women have led to a marked upturn in the nuimber of female-headed families. Female-headed families now account for 13 percent of white families and 44 percent of black families.

Today the United States is a society without a clear unitary set of family ideals and values. Many Americans are groping for a new paradigm of American family life, but in the meantime a profound sense of confusion and ambivalence reigns. One consequence of this confusion has been deep social division over which responsibilities the individual family should shoulder and which should be assumed by other, nonfamilial institutions. As a society we vigorously debate the pros and cons of institutionalized child care, the emotional and psychological costs of divorce, and the advantages and disadvantages of placing seriously ill older persons in nursing homes or the severely mentally ill in custodial institutions, but the nation has found it increasingly difficult to agree on a plan of action.

Since the 1960s America has become a permissive society, not merely in the superficial sense of becoming more open and tolerant, but in the more profound sense of becoming reluctant to accept responsibility for the economic and social consequences of social change—most notably for such phenomena as increasing numbers of divorces, working mothers, and teenage pregnancies. Individuals, families, and society as a whole have been hesitant to accept full responsi-

bility for the care of young children, the elderly, the poor, the handicapped, or the mentally ill or for sex education or questions of birth
control. Responsibility has been splintered, and as a result many family-related problems are dealt with in a piecemeal or makeshift manner.
Unable to decide whether further to encourage the transfer of traditional family functions to public institutions or to help families to
become more capable of handling these problems on their own,
Americans have responded with a pervasive sense of uncertainty.

How are we to explain the extraordinary evolution of the American family over the past four centuries? The causes of familial change
cannot be reduced to any simple formula. The critical transformations
that have occurred in the family are aspects of broader demographic,
economic, social, and philosophic transformations that have reshaped
all aspects of American life. Three fundamental factors, however,
stand out.

Changes in the economy have been a principal force for change in
all other areas. Three centuries ago most American families were
largely self-sufficient agricultural units. Few families sought to maximize their income by producing specialized goods destined for distant
markets; their goal was to build up family farms or family enterprises
in order to maintain familial independence, to protect family property
and status and produce dowries or an inheritance for their children.
Although specialized craftmen made shoes, saddles, hats, iron implements, and men's clothing, most families produced most of the goods
they needed, including food, furniture, cloth, soap, candles, and
leather. Parental authority was reinforced by control of property
(land) or a craft skill that could be transmitted to the children. The
family was not merely an emotional unit; it was also an interdependent unit of labor in which all family members contributed to a collective "family economy."

By the late eighteenth century, a marked loosening of the economic
relationships among family members had taken place—a transition
marked by parents' diminishing control over their children's choice
of marriage partners. Household self-sufficiency declined as a growing
number of farm households began to specialize in the production of
cash crops and to use the proceeds to purchase household goods produced outside the home. Domestic industries that had employed large
numbers of women and older children gradually disappeared as an
increasing proportion of goods were produced in factories or other
businesses. For the middle class, older children ceased to be economic
assets, no longer employed in household industries or fostered out as
servants or apprentices. Instead they became economic dependents

requiring significant investments in the form of education. The effect of these changes was to transform the family from a public unit serving as workplace, a school, and a welfare agency into a more private, specialized unit.

Another potent force for change in American family life has been demography. Such fundamental characteristics of a population as age distribution and the proportion of the sexes exert strong influences on the size and composition of families, the marriage rate, the death rate, the birthrate, and other attributes of family life. Two key demographic changes have had especially far-reaching consequences for family life. The first is a gradual reduction of fertility within marriage. Beginning in the last quarter of the eighteenth century, American women began bearing fewer children, spacing children closer together, and ceasing childbearing at earlier ages. Smaller families meant that parents could invest more emotion and financial resources in each child, while closer spacing of children meant that mothers could expect to devote fewer years to bearing and rearing young children.

A second fundamental demographic change has been a gradual aging of the population. Some 150 years ago the average age in the United States was just seventeen, a figure comparable to the youngest populations in the world today. Now the median age has climbed to nearly thirty, giving the United States one of the oldest populations in the world. This shift means that a growing proportion of the American population now experiences aspects of family life less well known in the past, such as a period of marriage when children are no longer responsibilities, grandparenthood, and prolonged widowhood.

A third basic force for familial change lies in a series of profound transformations in women's roles. During the early nineteenth century, as production was increasingly transferred outside the home, married women lost many traditional "productive" economic roles. Many middle-class women concentrated on motherhood and household management. According to a new conception of sex roles, women's task was to shape the character of the children, make the home a haven of peace and order, and exert a moral and uplifting influence on men.

Especially since World War II, this process of privatizing the role of women has been reversed as the number of married women participating in the labor force has dramatically increased. A massive influx of wives and mothers into the work force has, in turn, made wives less financially dependent on their husbands and called into question traditional assumptions about the sexual division of roles in housekeeping and child rearing.

For over three centuries, Americans have worried about the future of the family. Within decades of the Puritans arrival in Massachusetts Bay Colony, Puritan jeremiads were already decrying the increasing fragility of marrige, the growing selfishness and irresponsibility of parents, and the increasing rebelliousness of children. Despite nearly four centuries of fears that the family is decaying, the institution has, of course, survived. But it has—for better and worse—changed in important ways.

Clearly, on the positive side of the ledger, families today are far less likely than those in the past to lose children as a result of high rates of infant mortality, and children are far less likely to be orphaned while growing up. Unlike parents in the past, parents now can anticipate seeing all of their children reach adulthood. Since mothers no longer bear children every two years after marriage until menopause or death, they can expect to spend a far smaller proportion of their adult lives rearing young children and can more easily combine family life with a career. And, finally, longer life expectancies and closer spacing of children mean that married couples can anticipate a period together after their children have ceased to be responsibilities.

At the same time, however, today's families are more isolated than their predecessors from the worlds of work, kinship, and community life, and there can be no doubt that the structural isolation of the contemporary family has made it in certain respects a more fragile institution. Shorn of traditional educational and productive functions, the stability of today's families rests on the tenuous basis of affection, compatibility, and mutual interest. Family members today are no longer tied together by their mutual participation in a collective family economy. As a result of smaller families and closer spacing of children, parents devote less time to the rearing of young children and have more time to ponder the quality of their interpersonal relations. Parental authority is no longer reinforced by control of property or craft skills or by the supervision of the surrounding community. Nor is authority buttressed by common sets of values held by large groups of people. Given the erosion of these earlier kinds of supports, it is not surprising to find that while families today are less likely to be disrupted by premature death, they are more vulnerable to divorce. The paradox of the modern American family is that while we attach far greater psychological and ideological significance to a happy family life than did our ancestors, our work lives, our emphasis on personal fulfillment, and our political behavior all conflict with strong, stable family bonds.

Elizabeth and Mary Freake (1670-1675).
Painted in Boston by an unknown artist.
Courtesy of the Worcester Art Museum.

CHAPTER I

The Godly Family
in New England
and Its Transformation

ON NOVEMBER 11, 1620, after an arduous nine-week voyage, 102
weary passengers aboard the *Mayflower* reached the rocky coast of
Cape Cod. "They had no friends to welcome them," wrote William
Bradford, one of the original Pilgrims, nor did they have "any houses
or much less towns to repair to." All they could see before them was
a "hideous and desolate wilderness full of wild beasts and wild men."
If they looked behind, all they could see "was the mighty ocean which
they had passed and was now as a main bar and gulf to separate them
from all the civil parts of the world." By spring, half of the *Mayflower*
passengers were dead.[1]

For the Pilgrims, and for other, later, English settlers, one social
institution was more important than any other in helping them to
adapt to New World conditions. That institution was the family, and
it performed many more functions than does its present day counterpart. It raised the food and made most of the clothing and furniture
for the early settlers. It taught children to read, worship their God,
and care for each other in sickness and in old age. It was a workplace,
a school, a vocational training agency, and a place of worship, and it
carried the heavy burden of responsibility for maintaining social order
and stability. It was the cornerstone of the larger society, a "little commonwealth," "a school wherein the first principles and grounds of
government and subjection are learned; whereby men are fitted to
greater matters in church and commonwealth." It was a patriarchal
institution, ruled by the father, who exercised authority over his wife,
children, and servants much as God the Father ruled over his children
or a king—the "father" of his country—ruled his subjects.[2]

1

A particularly full and vivid description of seventeenth-century family life is recorded in the diary of Puritan merchant and magistrate Samuel Sewall. During the seventeenth century, Calvinist theology inspired many religious persons to keep personal diaries, in which they recorded their spiritual self-examinations, inscribed their intimate thoughts and feelings, and took stock of the state of their soul. Samuel Sewall's diary describes in minute and telling detail what one particular family's life was like, from his first entry in 1673 to his final comments fifty-six years later, three months before his death.[3]

To read Sewall's diary is to enter a period alien to Americans today; a period in which even newborn infants were regarded as embodiments of sin; an era in which parents were expected actively to intervene in such decisions as their children's choice of a career or marriage partner. Sewall lived in a society in which life was colored by the inescapable presence of death—an environment still deeply affected by premature death, especially that of young children. In the late twentieth century, only fourteen of every thousand infants die during the first year of life, but in the seventeenth-century New England, one in ten died in healthy areas and nearly one in three in less healthy climes. Although one would think that under such circumstances parents might defend against the pain of infant mortality by distancing themselves from their children, Puritans were deeply attached to their infant children. Throughout his adulthood, Samuel was tormented by the very real possibility of losing a child. When a two-year-old daughter died, the family's grief was manifest in "general Sorrow and Tears," and Sewall reproached himself for not having been sufficiently "carefull of her Defence [sic] and preservation as I should have been." After seeing seven of his fourteen children buried before they reached their second birthdays, Sewall was haunted by a recurrent nightmare that most of his children would die. As it was, only three of his offspring would survive him.[4]

Sewall's diary reveals a society that believed that even newborns were innately sinful and that parents' primary task was to suppress their children's natural depravity. Seventeenth-century Puritans cared deeply for their children and invested an enormous amount of time and energy in them, but they were also intent on repressing what they perceived as manifestations of original sin through harsh physical and psychological measures. Aside from an occasional whipping, Sewall's primary technique for disciplining his children was to provoke their fear of death, sin, and the torments inflicted in hell. After a neighbor's nine-year-old child died of smallpox, Sewall tried to arouse his eight-year-old son's conscience by reminding him of the "need to prepare for death." Although the boy continued to chew on an apple, he later "burst out into a bitter cry and said he was afraid he should die." And, after hearing sermons on Puritan religious doctrine, his fifteen-year-old daughter "burst out into an amazing cry," convinced that "she should go to Hell," since "her sins were not pardoned." Months later Sewall records that his daughter was still subject to recurrent outbursts of tears, a consequence of fear that she was doomed to eternal damnation.[5]

The father in early New England felt free to intervene in his children's lives and to control their behavior. This included the right and duty to take an active role in his child's selection of a spouse. He had a legal right to determine which men would be allowed to court his daughters and a legal responsibility to give or withhold his consent from a child's marriage. When a suitor wanted to woo one of Sewall's daughters, the young man had to have his father write to secure the magistrate's consent, for fear that Sewall would sue him for inveigling his daughter's affections. Sewall openly expressed dismay when one daughter refused several suitors, and he did not hesitate to scrutinize one prospective husband to determine if he had courted other women. Even after they had married, achieved economic independence, and set up homes of their own, Sewall felt it was still his right and duty openly to criticize his children. When one son was thirty-nine years old, Sewall was still warning him against spending his time in taverns and was interfering in his son's domestic arrangements.[6]

Sewall, like other seventeenth-century colonists, viewed marriage as a property arrangement rather than an emotional bond based on romantic love. He prided himself on his industry in bargaining over marriage settlements for his children, and after one daughter's death, he proceeded to haggle with her father-in-law over the return of her dowry. When Sewall himself chose a wife, he took a calculating, mercenary approach to marriage. Less than four months after his first wife's death, he had already decided to marry again. He courted a certain Widow Denison, and the two proceeded to bargain over the size of the allowance Sewall would give her. "I told her I was willing to give her Two [one hundred] and Fifty pounds per anum during her life," he recorded, but the widow preferred the more generous allowance made in her husband's will. Subsequently the jurist courted and married another widow, who died after less than a year of marriage, and speedily searched for a third wife. The most persistent object of his affection was another widow, Mary Gibbs, and in their love letters financial bargaining plays a conspicuous role. He demanded that she "give Bond to indemnify me from all debts contracted by you before the Marriage," and in return he promised her "40 pounds per anum during the terms of your natural Life in case of your survival."[7]

Samuel Sewall's diary provides us with a window on early colonial American family life. The colonial family differed profoundly from the contemporary family in its definition of family functions and responsibilities, its conception of childhood, its attitude toward love and marriage, and its division of domestic roles. It is impossible fully to understand this early American family without closely examining the ideas of the people who most clearly defined its ideals, the New England Puritans.

Structure and Development of Puritan Family Life

In 1629, eight years after the Pilgrims arrived in Plymouth, an advance guard of four hundred English Puritans set up a self- governing commonwealth in Salem, Massachusetts. They undertook this "errand into the wilderness" in order to create a pure and godly commonwealth, "a Modell of Christian Charity," which would serve as an example for the reformation of England. In New England—a barren wilderness without such relics of Catholicism as bishops, ecclesiastical courts, priestly vestments, and elaborate rituals—they hoped to create a new and undefiled social order that conformed strictly to the teachings of the Bible.

In 1630 seventeen ships carried another thousand passengers to Massachusetts Bay Colony, and within the year, Puritans had established settlements at Boston, Cambridge, Charlestown, Dorchester, Roxbury, and Watertown. By 1640, when the English Civil War cut off further Puritan emigration, an additional fifteen or twenty thousand colonists had journeyed to New England.

The roughly twenty thousand Puritan men, women, and children who sailed to Massachusetts between 1629 and 1640 carried with them ideas about the family utterly foreign to Americans today. The Puritans never thought of the family as purely a private unit, rigorously separated from the surrounding community. To them it was an integral part of the larger political and social world; it was "the

Mother Hive, out of which both those swarms of State and Church, issued forth." Its boundaries were elastic and inclusive, and it assumed responsibilities that have since been assigned to public institutions.[8]

Although most Puritan families were nuclear in structure, a significant proportion of the population spent part of their lives in other families' homes, serving as apprentices, hired laborers, or servants. At any one time, as many as a third of all Puritan households took in servants. Convicts, the children of the poor, single men and women, and recent immigrants were compelled by selectmen to live within existing "well Governed families" so that "disorders may bee prevented and ill weeds nipt."[9]

For the Puritans, family ties and community ties tended to blur. In many communities, individual family members were related by birth or marriage to a large number of their neighbors. In one community, Chatham, Massachusetts, the town's 155 families bore just thirty-four surnames; and in Andover, Massachusetts, the descendants of one settler, George Abbott I, had by 1750 intermarried into a dozen local families. The small size of the seventeenth-century communities, combined with high rates of marriage and remarriage, created kinship networks of astonishing complexity. In-laws and other distant kin were generally referred to as brothers, sisters, aunts, uncles, mothers, fathers, and cousins.[10]

Today spousal ties are emphasized, and obligations to kin are voluntary and selective. Three centuries ago the kin group was of great importance to the social, economic, and political life of the community. Kinship ties played a critical role in the development of commercial trading networks and the capitalizing of large-scale investments. In the absence of secure methods of communication and reliable safeguards against dishonesty, prominent New England families, such as the Hutchinsons and Winthrops, relied on relatives in England and the West Indies to achieve success in commerce. Partnerships among family members also played an important role in the ownership of oceangoing vessels. Among merchant and artisan families, apprenticeships were often given exclusively to their own sons or nephews, keeping craft skills within the kinship group.[11]

Intermarriage was also used to cement local political alliances and economic partnerships. Marriages between first cousins or between sets of brothers and sisters helped to bond elite, politically active and powerful families together. Among the families of artisans, marriages between a son and an uncle's daughter reinforced kinship ties.[12]

In political affairs the importance of the kin group persisted until the American Revolution. By the early eighteenth century, small groups of interrelated families dominated the clerical, economic, military, and political leadership of New England. In Connecticut and Massachusetts, the most powerful of these kinship groups was made up of seven interrelated families. The "River Gods," as they were known, led regional associations of ministers, controlled the county courts, commanded the local militia, and represented their region in the Massachusetts General Court and Governor's Council. Following the Revolution, most states adopted specific reforms designed to reduce the power of kin groups in politics by barring nepotism, establishing the principle of rotation in office, prohibiting multiple officeholding, providing for the election of justices of the peace, and requiring officeholders to reside in the jurisdiction they served.[13]

Unlike the contemporary American family, which is distinguished by its isolation from the world of work and the surrounding society, the Puritan family was deeply embedded in public life. The household—not the individual—was the fundamental unit of society. The political order was not an agglomeration of detached individuals; it was an organic unity composed of families. This was the reason that Puritan households received only a single vote in town meetings. Customarily it was the father, as head of the household, who represented his family at the polls. But if he was absent, his wife assumed his prerogative to vote. The Puritans also took it for granted that the church was composed of families and not of isolated individuals. Family membership—not an individual's abilities or attainments—determined a person's position in society. Where one sat in church or in the local meetinghouse or even one's rank at Harvard College was determined not by one's accomplishments but by one's family identity.[14]

The Puritan family was the main unit of production in the economic system. Each family member was expected to be economically useful. Older children were unquestionably economic assets; they worked at family industries, tended gardens, herded animals, spun wool, and cared for younger brothers and sisters. Wives not only raised children and cared for the home but also cut clothes, supervised servants and apprentices, kept financial accounts, cultivated crops, and marketed surplus goods.[15]

In addition to performing a host of productive functions, the Puritan family was a primary educational and religious unit. A 1642 Massachusetts statute required heads of households to lead their households in prayers and scriptural readings; to teach their children, servants, and apprentices to read; and to catechize household members in the principles of religion and law. The family was also an agency for vocational training, assigned the duty of instructing servants and apprentices in methods of farming, housekeeping, and craft skills. And finally the Puritan family was a welfare institution that carried primary responsibility for the care of orphans, the infirm, or the elderly.[16]

Given the family's importance, the Puritans believed that the larger community had a compelling duty to ensure that families performed their functions properly. The Puritans did not believe that individual households should be assured freedom from outside criticism or interference. The Puritan community felt that it had a responsibility not only to punish misconduct but also to intervene within households to guide and direct behavior. To this end, in the 1670s, the Massachusetts General Court directed towns to appoint "tithingmen" to oversee every ten or twelve households in order to ensure that marital relationships were harmonious and that parents properly disciplined unruly children. Puritan churches censured, admonished, and excommunicated men and women who failed to maintain properly peaceful households, since, as minister Samuel Willard put it, "When husband and wife neglect their duties they not only wrong each other, but they provoke God by breaking his law." In cases in which parents failed properly to govern "rude, stubborn, and unruly" children, Puritan law permitted local authorities to remove juveniles from their families "and place them with some master for years . . . and force them to submit unto government." Men who neglected or failed to support their wives or children were subject to judicial penalties. In instances in which spouses seriously violated fundamental duties—such as cases of adultery, desertion, prolonged absence, or nonsupport—divorces were granted. In cases of fornication outside marriage, courts sentenced offenders to a fine or whipping; for adultery, offenders were punished by fines, whippings, brandings, wearing of the letter *A*, and in at least three cases, the death penalty.[17]

The disciplined Puritan family of the New World was quite different from the English family of the sixteenth and seventeeth centuries that had been left behind. In fact, it represented an effort to re-create an older ideal of the family that no longer existed in England itself.

English family life in the era of New World colonization was quite unstable. Because of high mortality rates, three-generational households containing grandparents, parents, and children tended to be rare. The duration of marriages tended to be quite brief—half of all marriages were cut short by the death of a spouse after just seventeen to nineteen years. And the number of children per marriage was surprisingly small. Late marriage, a relatively long interval between births, and high rates of infant and child mortality meant that just two, three, or four children survived past adolescence. Despite today's mythical vision of stability and rootedness in the preindustrial world, mobility was rampant. Most Englishmen could expect to move from one village to another during their adult lives, and it was rare for an English family to remain in a single community for as long as fifty years. Indeed, a significant proportion of the English population was denied the opportunity to *have* a family life. Servants, apprentices, and university lecturers were forbidden from marrying, and most other young men had to wait to marry until they received an inheritance on their father's death.[18]

The English migrants who ventured to New England sought to avoid the disorder of English family life through a structured and disciplined family. They possessed a firm idea of a godly family, and they sought to establish it despite the novelty of American circumstances. Puritan religion had a particularly strong appeal to these men and women who were most sensitive to the disruptive forces transforming England during the sixteenth and seventeenth centuries—such forces as an alarming increase in population, a rapid rise in prices, the enclosure of traditional common lands, and the sudden appearances of a large class of propertyless men and women who flocked to the growing cities or took to the woods. To the Puritans, whose spiritual community was threatened by these developments, establishment of a holy commonwealth in New England represented a desperate effort to restore order and discipline to social behavior. And it was the family through which order could most effectively be created.[19]

Migration to the New World wilderness intensified the Puritan fear of moral and political chaos and encouraged their focus on order and discipline. In the realm of economics, Puritan authorities strove to regulate prices, limit the rate of interest, and fix the maximum wages—at precisely the moment that such notions were breaking down in England. And in the realm of family life, the Puritans, drawing on the Old Testament and classical political theory, sought to reestablish an older ideal of the family in which the father was endowed with patriarchal authority as head of his household. Their religion taught that family roles were part of a continuous chain of hierarchical and delegated authority descending from God, and it was within the family matrix that all larger, external conceptions of authority, duty, and discipline were defined.[20]

Puritans organized their family around the unquestioned principle of patriarchy. Fathers represented their households in the public realms of politics and social leadership; they owned the bulk of personal property; and law and church doctrine made it the duty of wives, children, and servants to submit to the father's authority. The colonies of Connecticut, Massachusetts, and New Hampshire went so far as to enact statutes calling for the death of children who cursed or struck their fathers.[21]

Patriarchal authority in the Puritan family ultimately rested on the father's control of landed property or craft skills. Puritan children were dependent upon their father's support in order to marry and set up independent households. Since Puritan fathers were permitted wide discretion in how they would distribute their property, it was important that children show a degree of deference to their father's wishes. The timing and manner in which fathers conveyed property to the next generation exerted a profound influence upon where children decided to live and when and whom they decided to marry. In many cases fathers settled sons on plots surrounding the parental homestead, with title not to be surrendered until after their deaths. In other instances fathers conveyed land or other property when their sons became adults or were married. Not uncommonly such wills or deeds contained carefully worded provisions ensuring that the son would guarantee the parent lifetime support. One deed, for example, provided that a son would lose his inheritance if his parents could not walk freely through the house to go outdoors.[22]

Such practices kept children economically dependent for years, delayed marriage, and encouraged sons to remain near their fathers during their lifetimes. In Andover, Massachusetts, only a quarter of the second-generation sons actually owned the land they farmed before their fathers died. Not until the fourth generation in mid-eighteenth-century Andover had this pattern noticeably disappeared. In Plymouth, Massachusetts, and Windsor, Connecticut, fathers gave land to children on marriage. Among Quaker families in Pennsylvania, fathers who were unable to locate land for sons in the same town bought land in nearby communities. In order to replicate their parents' style of life, sons had to wait to inherit property from their fathers. In most cases ownership and control of land reinforced the authority of fathers over their children.[23]

A corollary to the Puritan assumption of patriarchy was a commitment to female submission within the home. Even by the conservative standards of the time, the roles assigned to women by Puritan theology were narrowly circumscribed. The premise guiding Puritan theory was given pointed expression by the poet Milton: "God's universal law gave to man despotic power/Over his female in due awe." Women were not permitted to vote or prophesy or question church doctrine. The ideal woman was a figure of "modesty" and "delicacy," kept ignorant of the financial affairs of her family. Her social roles were limited to wife, mother, mistress of the household, seamstress, wet nurse, and midwife. Although there was no doubt that she was legally subordinate to her husband, she had limited legal rights and protections.[24]

Puritan doctrine did provide wives with certain safeguards. Husbands who refused to support or cohabit with their wives were subject to legal penalties. Wives, in theory, could sue for separation or divorce on grounds of a husband's impotence, cruelty, abandonment, bigamy, adultery, or failure to provide, but divorce was generally unavailable, and desertion was such a risky venture that only the most desperate women took it as an option. Colonial statutes also prohibited a husband from striking his wife, "unless it be in his own defense." Before marriage single women had the right to conduct business, own property, and represent themselves in court. Upon marriage, however, the basic legal assumption was that of "coverture"—that a woman's legal identity was absorbed in her husband's. Spouses were nevertheless allowed to establish antenuptial or postnuptial agreements, permitting a wife to retain control over her property.[25]

For both Puritan women and men, marriage stood out as one of the central events in life. Despite their reputation as sexually repressed, pleasure-hating bigots, the Puritans did not believe that celibacy was a condition morally superior to marriage. The only thing that Saint Paul might have said in favor of marriage was that it is "better to marry than to burn," but the Puritans extolled marriage as a sacrament and a social duty. John Cotton put the point bluntly: "They are a sort of Blasphemers then who dispise and decry" [women as a necessary evil,] "for they are a necessary Good; such as it was not good that man should be without."[26]

For the Puritans love was not a prerequisite for marriage. They believed that the choice of a marriage partner should be guided by rational considerations of property, religious piety, and family interest, not by physical attraction, personal feelings, or romantic love. Affection, in their view, would develop after marriage. This attitude reflected a recognition of the essential economic functions of the colonial family. Marriage was a partnership to which both bride and groom were expected to bring skills and resources. A prospective bride was expected to contribute a dowry (usually in the form of money or household goods) worth half of what the bridegroom brought to the marriage. Artisans tended to choose wives from families that practiced the same trade precisely because these women would be best able to assist them in their work. In New England the overwhelming majority of men and women married—and many remarried rapidly after the death of a spouse—because it was physically and economically difficult to live alone.[27]

According to Puritan doctrine, a wife was to be her husband's help-mate, not his equal. Her role was "to guid the house &c. not guid the Husband." The Puritans believed that a wife should be submissive to her husband's commands and should exhibit toward him an attitude of "reverence," by which they meant a proper mixture of fear and awe; not "a slavish Fear, which is nourished with hatred or aversion; but a noble and generous Fear, which proceeds from Love."[28]

The actual relations between Puritan spouses were more complicated than religious dogma would suggest. It was not unusual to find mutual love and tenderness in Puritan marriages. In their letters Puritan husbands and wives frequently referred to each other in terms suggesting profound love for each other, such as "my good wife . . . my sweet wife" or "my most sweet Husband." Similarly, the poems of Anne Bradstreet refer to a love toward her husband that seems deeply romantic: "To my Dear and loving Husband / I prise thy love more than whole Mines of gold." It is also not difficult, however, to find evidence of marriages that failed to live up to the Puritan ideal of domestic harmony and wifely submissiveness. In 1686, a Boston spinster, Comfort Wilkins, publicly spoke out about the "Tears, and Jars, and Discontents, and Jealousies" that marred many Puritan marriages.[29]

Puritan court records further reveal that wife abuse is not a recent development. Between 1630 and 1699, at least 128 men were tried for abusing their wives. In one case a resident of Maine kicked and beat his wife with a club when she refused to feed a pig; in another case an Ipswich man poured poison into his wife's broth in an attempt to kill her. The punishments for wife abuse were mild, usually amounting only to a fine, a lashing, a public admonition, or supervision by a town-appointed guardian. Two colonists, however, did lose their lives for murdering their wives.[30]

Even in cases of abuse, Puritan authorities commanded wives to be submissive and obedient. They were told not to resist or strike their husbands but to try to reform their spouses' behavior. Some women refused to conform to this rigid standard. At least thirty-two seventeenth-century Puritan women deserted their husbands and set up separate residences, despite such risks as loss of their dower rights and possible criminal charges of adultery or theft. Another eight women were brought to court for refusing to have sexual relations with their husbands over extended periods. Seventy-six New England women petitioned for divorce or separation, usually on grounds of desertion, adultery, or bigamy.[31]

Women who refused to obey Puritan injunctions about wifely obedience were subject to harsh punishment. Two hundred seventy-eight New England women were brought to court for heaping abuse on their husbands, which was punishable by fines or whippings. Joan Miller of Taunton, Massachusetts, was punished "for beating and reviling her husband and egging her children to healp her, biding them knock him in the head." One wife was punished for striking her husband with a pot of cider, another for scratching and kicking her spouse, and a third for insulting her husband by claiming he was "no man." How widespread these deviations from Puritan ideals were, we do not know.[32]

Within marriage, a woman assumed a wide range of responsibilities and duties. As a housewife she was expected to cook, wash, sew, milk, spin, clean, and garden. These domestic activities included brewing beer, churning butter, harvesting fruit, keeping chickens, spinning wool, building fires, baking bread, making cheese, boiling laundry, and stitching shirts, petticoats, and other garments. She participated in trade—exchanging surplus fruit, meat, cheese, or butter for tea, candles, coats, or sheets—and manufacturing—salting, pickling, and preserving vegetables, fruit, and meat and making clothing and soap—in addition to other domestic tasks. As a "deputy husband," she was responsible for assuming her husband's responsibilities whenever he was absent from home—when, for example, he was on militia duty. Under such circumstances she took on his tasks of planting corn or operating the loom or keeping accounts. As a mistress she was responsible for training, supervising, feeding, and clothing girls who were placed in her house as servants.[33]

Marriage also brought another equally tangible change to women's lives: frequent childbirth. Childlessness within marriage was an extreme rarity in colonial New England, with just one woman in twelve bearing no children. Most women could expect to bear at least six children and delivered children at fairly regular intervals averaging every twenty to thirty months, often having the last child after the age of forty. The process of delivery was largely in the hands of women and took place within the home. Labor was typically attended by a large number of observers. When one of Samuel Sewall's daughters gave birth in January 1701, at least sixteen women were in attendence in the lying-in room to offer encouragement and give advice. Often a midwife would intervene actively in the birth process by breaking the amniotic sac surrounding the infant in the uterus, steering the infant through the birth canal, and later removing the placenta.[34]

Death in childbirth was frequent enough to provoke fear in many women. It appears that almost one delivery in thirty resulted in the death of the mother. Among the complications of pregnancy that could lead to maternal death were protracted labor, unusual presentation of the infant (such as a breech presentation), hemorrhages and convulsions, and infection after delivery. The sense of foreboding that was felt is apparent in the words of a Massachusetts woman, Sarah Stearns, who wrote in her diary, "Perhaps this is the last time I shall be permitted to join with my earthly friends."[35]

After childbirth, infants were commonly breast-fed for about a year and were kept largely under their mother's care. Not until a child reached the age of two or three is there evidence that fathers took a more active role in child rearing.[36]

Unlike marriages in contemporary England—where a late age of marriage and short life expectancy combined to make the average duration of marriage quite short—colonial unions tended to be long-lived, even by modern standards. A detailed study of one New England town found that an average marriage lasted almost twenty-four years. The extended duration of New England marriages gave such unions a sense of permanence that contrasted sharply with the transience characteristic of English marriages. In contrast to the pattern found today, however, the death of a spouse did not usually lead to the creation of households composed of a widow or widower living alone. Single adults of any age living alone were very unusual, and lifelong bachelors and spinsters were a rarity. Remarriage after the death of a spouse was common, particularly among wealthier men, and even individuals of very advanced ages (into their seventies or eighties) often remarried. Among those least likely to remarry were wealthy widows. If these women did remarry, they generally made an antenuptial agreement allowing them to manage their own property. The remarriage of a spouse often led to the rearrangement of families; the fostering out of children from an earlier marriage was not uncommon.[37]

The experience of widowhood did give a small number of colonial women a taste of economic independence. Legally, a widow in seventeenth-century New England was entitled to at least a third of her husband's household goods along with income from his real estate until she remarried or died. Actual control of the house and fields— and even pots and beds—usually fell to a grown son or executor. But, in a number of cases, widows inherited land or businesses and continued to operate them on their own, assuming such jobs as blacksmith, silversmith, tinsmith, beer maker, tavernkeeper, shoemaker, shipwright, printer, barber, grocer, butcher, and shopkeeper—occupations and crafts usually monopolized by men.[38]

Of all the differences that distinguish the seventeenth-century family from its present-day counterpart, perhaps the most striking involves the social experience of children. Three centuries ago, childhood was a much less secure and shorter stage of life than it is today. In recent years it has become fashionable to complain about the "disappearance of childhood," but historical perspective reminds us that— despite high divorce rates—childhood is more stable than it was during the colonial era. For a child to die during infancy was a common occurrence in colonial New England; more deaths occurred among young children than in any other age group. In Plymouth, Andover, or Ipswich, Massachusetts, a family could anticipate an infant death rate of one out of ten; in less-healthy towns such as Salem or Boston, three of every ten children died in infancy. It cannot be emphasized too strongly that high infant death rates did not necessariy make parents indifferent toward their young children. Cotton Mather, who lost eight of his fifteen children before they reached their second birthdays, suggests the depth of feeling of parents: "We have our children taken from us; the Desire of our Eyes taken away with a stroke."[39]

Not only were children more likely to die in infancy or to be orphaned than today, they were raised quite differently. In certain respects young children were treated, by our standards, in a casual way. Child rearing was not the family's main function; the care and nurture of children were subordinate to other family interests. In colonial New England newborn infants of well-to-do families were sometimes "put out" to wet nurses who were responsible for breast-feeding, freeing mothers to devote their time to their household duties. As in Europe, new babies were sometimes named for recently deceased infants. In contrast to Europeans, however, New Englanders did not wrap infants in tightly confining swaddling clothes, and carelessly supervised children sometimes crawled into fires or fell into wells.[40]

The moral upbringing of Puritan children was never treated casually. The Puritan religion taught that even newborn infants were embodiments of guilt and sin (traceable to Adam's transgression in Eden), who, unless saved by God, were doomed to writhe in Satan's clutches for eternity. This belief in infant depravity and original sin exerted a powerful influence on methods of child rearing. In their view the primary task of child rearing was to break down a child's sinful will and internalize respect for divinely instituted authority through weekly catechisms, repeated admonitions, physical beatings, and intense psychological pressure. "Better whipt, than damned," was Cotton Mather's advice to parents.[41]

Although Calvinists could be indulgent with very small children, among many parents their religious faith led to an insistence that, after the age of two, any assertion of a child's will be broken. A Pilgrim pastor eloquently defined a parent's responsibility to combat the inherent evil of a child's nature: "Surely," he affirmed, "there is in all children (though not alike) a stubbernes and stoutnes of minde arising from naturall pride which must in the first place be broken and beaten down so the foundation of their education being layd in humilitie and tractablenes other virtues may in turn be built thereon." A child's willfulness could be suppressed through fierce physical beatings, exhibition of corpses, and tales of castration and abandonment—techniques designed to drive out "the old Adam" and produce traits of tractableness and peaceableness highly valued by Calvinists. The Puritans would strongly have rejected the twentieth-century "progressive" child rearing advice that the goal of parents should be to draw out their children's innate potentialities.[42]

Without a doubt the most striking difference between seventeenth-century child rearing and practices today was the widespread custom of sending children to live with another family at the age of fourteen or earlier, so that a child would receive the proper discipline its natural parents could not be expected to administer. Children of all social classes and both sexes were frequently fostered out for long periods in order to learn a trade, to work as servants, or to attend a school. Since the family was a place of work and its labor needs and its financial resources often failed to match its size and composition, servants or apprentices might temporarily be taken in or children bound out.[43]

If childhood is defined as a protected state, a carefree period of freedom from adulthood responsibilities, then a Puritan childhood was quite brief. Childhood came to an end abruptly around the age of seven when boys adopted adult clothing (prior to this both boys and girls wore frocks or petticoats) and were prevented from sleeping any longer with their sisters or female servants. By their teens most children were largely under the care and tutelage of adults other than their own parents. They were fostered out as indentured servants or apprentices or, in rare cases, sent to boarding schools.[44]

While childhood ended early and abruptly, adulthood did not begin right away. Around the age of seven, young Puritans entered into a prolonged intermediate stage of "semi-dependency" during which they were expected to begin to assume a variety of productive roles. Young boys wove garters and suspenders on small looms, weeded flax fields and vegetable gardens, combed wool and wound spools of thread, and were taught to be blacksmiths, coopers, cordwainers (shoemakers), tanners, weavers, or shipwrights. Teenage girls received quite different training from their brothers. They were taught "housewifery" or spinning, carding, sewing, and knitting. Girls customarily helped their mothers or another mistress by hoeing gardens, spinning flax and cotton, tending orchards, caring for domestic animals, and by making clothing, lye, soap, and candles. Like their mothers, teenage girls might also assist their fathers in the fields or in a workshop.[45]

For both young men and women, marriage, economic independence, and establishment of an independent household would come much later. For young men, the transition to full adulthood only occurred after they had received a bequest of property from their father. Marriage took place relatively late. The average age of marriage for men was over twenty-five years, and few women married before the age of twenty.[46]

For New Englanders, migration across the Atlantic gave the family a significance and strength it had lacked in the mother country. In the healthful environment of New England, family ties grew tighter than they had ever been in the Old World. The first settlers lived much longer than their contemporaries in England and were much more likely to live to see their grandchildren. Marriages lasted far longer than they did in contemporary England, and infant mortality rates quickly declined to levels far below those in the old country. Migration to the New World did not weaken paternal authority; it strengthened it by increasing paternal control over land and property.

Even when individuals did move around in New England, they almost always migrated as part of a family group. Few sons moved father than sixteen miles from their paternal home during their father's lifetime. Contrary to an older view that the New World environment dissolved extended family ties, it now seems clear that the family in early-seventeenth-century New England was a more stable, disciplined, and cohesive unit than its English counterpart in the Old World.

Transformation of the Godly Family

The first settlers of New England had sought to create a family unit that would conform strictly to the teachings of the Bible. Within forty years of their arrival in the New World, however, the colonists feared that their families were disintegrating, that parents were growing ever more irresponsible, and that their children were losing respect for authority. Ministers repeatedly lamented the fact that parents were neglecting to convert their children to God's religion and that children of the Puritans were "frequenting taverns," keeping "Vicious company," and "tending to dissolutnes."[47]

The colonists responded to creeping nonconformity by enacting ever-more-stringent laws charging children with obedience to their father and mother and parents with the duty to properly discipline their offspring. In Connecticut, New Hampshire, and Massachusetts, authorities adopted severe penalties, including death, for children who struck or cursed their parents. Laws enjoining parents to catechize and enforce discipline upon their children were also authorized, as were statutes requiring towns to appoint selectmen to supervise discipline within the family. And when these measures seemed insufficient, local towns were assigned full responsibility for such functions as education, which had originally been vested in the family.[48]

While the colonial family was certainly not disintegrating, it was changing. Over the span of 150 years, the Puritan family adjusted to changing circumstances and challenges. The New World environment, with its rapid rate of population growth, its readily available land, and its shortage of labor, demanded a new flexibility from the family. And by the time of the American Revolution, the shape of a new family unit had emerged. A "silent revolution" had taken place, one that diminished parental control over children's marriages, differentiated family patterns across social classes, and produced a new conception of childhood in which children were viewed not as embodiments of sin but as innocent and malleable creatures whose characters could be molded into any shape.[49]

By the end of the seventeenth century, a significant erosion of fathers' control of landed property and productive skills had taken place. Land was increasingly being replaced by more portable forms of capital as a major source of wealth. New opportunities for nonagri-

cultural work allowed many children to live farther away from their
parents and permitted greater freedom from parental authority. At
the same time, rapid population growth, coupled with the practice of
partible inheritance, which divided family lands among all sons and
resulted in plots too small to be farmed viably, weakened paternal
control over heirs. In many older settlements the number of children
born was so great that it gradually outstripped the amount of cultiva-
ble land available. In the healthful environment of New England, the
population grew at an astonishing rate. Some communities grew by
five or six percent annually, and the number of surviving sons proved
to be greater than the resources necessary to establish viable farms.
Older towns such as Kent, Connecticut, and Andover and Dedham,
Massachusetts, ran out of land to distribute to children.[50]

Families adopted a number of specific strategies to meet this dilemma. In some instances family homesteads were simply subdivided
among all sons. In others fathers encouraged sons to migrate to newer
communities where fresh land was available or else converted inheritances into some form other than real estate, such as a formal education, an apprenticeship, or a gift of money. In still other cases, such
as Andover and Dedham, partible inheritance tended to give way to
primogeniture—the bequest of land to the eldest son. And in other
instances whole families moved to areas with abundant land.[51]

In Chebacco, a little village on the Massachusetts north shore, families combined a variety of strategies. First and second sons typically
remained in the community, while younger sons migrated to newer
areas. To balance the conflicting desires to preserve the family's estate,
to allow most children to remain in the village, and to provide a legacy for each child, families adopted a complex system of inheritance.
Widows received only a life interest in the family's landholdings. All
daughters, regardless of age, received a small but equal share of the
family's estate, usually in the form of money or household goods,
since it was assumed that they would depend on their husbands for
financial support. One son would receive the bulk of the father's land;
in turn, he acquired any debts incurred by his father, he assumed
liability for paying his brothers' and sisters' inheritance portions, and
he had the responsibility of caring for his widowed mother.[52]

The declining ability of fathers to transmit land to their sons undermined the traditional basis of paternal authority. In the seventeenth century, fathers—supported by local churches and courts—had
exercised close control over their childrens' sexual behavior and had
taken an active role in their choice of a marriage partner. But during
the first half of the eighteenth century, the ability of fathers to enforce

obedience diminished. A symptom of this decline in paternal control was a sudden upsurge in the mid-eighteenth century in the number of brides who were pregnant when they got married. During the seventeenth century, parents in New England had kept premarital intercourse at extremely low levels. The percentage of women who bore a first child less than eight-and-a-half months after marriage was below 10 percent. By the middle of the eighteenth century, this figure had shot up to over 40 percent.[53]

Another indicator of a decline in paternal authority was an increase in children's discretion in deciding whom and when to marry. Up to the mid-eighteenth century, family considerations continued to play an important role in determining marital circumstances. Until the late eighteenth century, fathers were able to delay the age at which their sons married until their late twenties. The sons of fathers who were alive married significantly later than sons whose fathers had died. By the middle of the eighteenth century, well before the onset of the American Revolution, the ability of fathers to delay their sons' marriages had eroded. There was also a gradual breakdown in a sevententh- and early-eighteenth-century pattern in which the order of a son's birth was closely connected to the economic status of his future spouse. Although most families in early New England did not practice strict primogeniture—the right to inheritance belonging exclusively to the eldest sons—many families practiced a more limited form of primogeniture by assigning eldest sons a larger share of resources than younger children. Receiving larger inheritances themselves, eldest sons tended to marry daughters of wealthier families. By midcentury, the close connection between birth order and a spouse's economic status had gradually declined.[54]

By the middle of the eighteenth century, other signs of weakening parental control over marriage were visible. In Plymouth during the seventeenth century, the brothers and sisters of one family frequently married the sisters and brothers of another. After 1760 this pattern gave way to marriages based on individual choice. In Hingham, Massachusetts, greater freedom in marriage was evident after 1741 in the growing number of women electing not to marry at all and the growing ease with which younger daughters were able to wed before their older sisters.[55]

The key to the decline in paternal control was the breakdown of the conception of marriage as a property settlement involving the division of family land. Marriage was in large measure seen as an economic agreement between a couple's parents. Most colonies required paternal consent for first marriages so that the parents of an engaged couple could reach a satisfactory agreement over the distribution of family property. Parental permission was necessary precisely *because* marriage involved something more than the love between two individuals—it also involved the transmission of family land and property. But, during the early eighteenth century, children depended less and less on their fathers' land in order to establish economic independence. The emergence of new sources of income—such as the rise of household industries, which permitted a couple to earn a cash income spinning wool or fabricating clothing—allowed young people to resist parental authority, to engage in premarital sex, and to marry early if pregnancy should result.[56]

Paternal authority had not disappeared; it had merely been weakened. In the communities that have been most closely studied, it is clear that most sons had to wait until their father's death to gain economic independence. In older settlements like Andover, Massachusetts, 70 percent of sons in the mid-eighteenth century only inherited land on their father's death. And yet, change had occurred. In each generation fewer fathers withheld land from their sons. By the end of the eighteenth century, fathers were more and more willing to accept the earlier age of independence for their children.[57]

The weakening of paternal authority was accompanied by the emergence of a new attitude toward children. Although few New Englanders would go so far as the English poet William Wordsworth or the French philosopher Jean-Jacques Rousseau in celebrating children's innocence, by the late eighteenth century there is clear evidence of a decline in the belief in childhood depravity. Gravestones reveal a progressive shift from the grim and terrifying death's-head or winged skull, replete with blank eyes and a grinning visage in the seventeenth century, to the winged cherub and urn of the eighteenth century. The stylistic shift in gravestones from grim death's-head to smiling cherubs signaled a softening and decline of the harsh orthodox Puritan view of infant depravity. The doctrine of the innate sinfulness of children was furiously debated in the mid-eighteenth century and gradually diluted. Death was increasingly perceived not as an object of dread, after which one might suffer eternal torment, but as an occasion for salvation when one would be released into eternal life. In heaven earthly burdens would be shed, and families would be rejoined permanently. The changing view of death is evident in a subtle shift in the wording of epitaphs. Instead of, "Here lies buried the body of," inscriptions began to read, "Here rests the soul of," suggesting that while the corporeal body might decay, the soul survived. By the end of the eighteenth century, this wording had been replaced by inscriptions reading "In memory of," and the smiling cherub was replaced by symbols of remembrance, the urn and willow. Death was increasingly regarded as merely a temporary separation of loved ones.[58]

By the end of the eighteenth century, children were increasingly viewed as special creatures with unique needs. One sign of this new sensibility was a proliferation of books and games and toys aimed specifically at children. Another was a marked decline in the seventeenth-century custom of requiring children to stand while their parents took their meals. Evidence of increasingly close and affectionate relations between parents and children, especially among the well-to-do, multiplies during the late eighteenth century. Fewer parents named children for a deceased brother or sister, and the practice of fostering out children became less common. A growing number of parents gave their adolescent sons and daughters forms of freedom previously inconceivable. Sons were allowed temporarily to hire out their labor during the fall and winter months, thereby helping them to achieve a measure of financial independence while still in their teens or early twenties. Daughters, too, received new opportunities to attend school and to work outside the home.[59]

The increasing indulgence shown toward children was partly a by-product of New England's prospering economy. Well before the end of the seventeenth century, New England's flourishing and expanding trade economy had begun to undermine the Puritan ideal of a closely circumscribed hierarchical society. Rising living standards encouraged a growing appreciation of privacy inside and outside the home. Public supervision of family relations gradually declined, and the punishments imposed by church or secular authorities for such offenses as fornication or adultery were reduced. At the same time that close community and patriarchal regulation of the family weakened, an increasing emphasis was placed on privacy inside the home. Work spaces were clearly marked off from areas devoted to eating, sleeping, and entertaining, and the preeminent position of the father in the household was diminished.[60]

Changes in domestic architecture and household furnishings provide particularly revealing evidence of a profound and pivotal transformation in the way New Englanders thought about the family. The typical dwelling around 1650 was sparsely furnished, afforded little personal privacy, and failed to make specialized use of space. It usually consisted of just four rooms, a "hall" and a "parlor" on the main floor flanking a central fireplace, and two "chambers" upstairs, with perhaps a wooden lean-to added on, serving as a kitchen. Sleeping, eating, and work space were not sharply separated. The parlor, which contained the most expensive bed, served not only as the bedroom of the head of the household but also as a room for dining and entertaining. The other major room on the ground floor, the hall, was where a family prepared and ate meals and where some family members slept. Upstairs rooms, which were reached by a ladder rather than stairs, were rarely used as bedrooms; more commonly, they provided storage space for textiles and grain. The most striking characteristic of such a house was that it was largely devoid of furnishings. Typically, it contained just two beds, one or two chests, a few stools, a bench, and a few wooden chairs. What furniture there was was usually movable, reflecting the varied functions of the house's rooms. The head of the household sat on a chair, while other family members sat on benches, chests, stools, or stood, symbolizing the father's central authority and the social distance separating him from other household members. Conspicuous by their absence were mirrors, upholstered or padded chairs, or desks. Ornaments were largely limited to pillows, bolsters, sheets, and coverlets decorating the father's great bed.[61]

A century later, in 1750, the typical dwelling contained three times the amount of furniture found in a house of the same social status a hundred years before. It now had three beds, twelve chairs, three or four chests, three or four tables, one or two mirrors, and a chest of drawers and a bureau. Luxury items like framed pictures and quilts were apparent for the first time. Personal comfort was still not highly valued: Easy chairs were still uncommon, and chair bottoms, even of the affluent, were still unpadded.[62]

The specialization of space, however, was increasingly evident, and as living space was more and more subdivided, it provided family members greater privacy. Food was increasingly prepared in separate kitchens, and the hall had evolved from a room for dining, sleeping, and entertaining into a family sitting room, a special place for family prayers or reading aloud. Sleeping arrangements had also changed. Increasingly, children had their own distinct place to sleep, apart from adults or servants. Beds were located in rooms devoted exclusively to sleeping and were partially or fully curtained in order further to enhance personal privacy. These changes in the domestic environment provide visual evidence of the decline in the authority of the father over his wife and children, the view of childhood as a distinct stage of life, the rising standard of living, and the increasing emphasis on privacy and domestic comfort.[63]

By the late eighteenth century, a revolutionary redefinition of the functions of the family had occurred. During the seventeenth century, families in New England were required to perform a wide range of roles and functions that we now think of as public responsibilities— functions since assumed by factories, schools, banks, insurance companies, and the government. They had to produce food, clothing, and furniture; care for the sick and aged; educate the young; and accumulate enough land or other property to provide the next generation with an adequate dowry or inheritance. In order to perform these roles and responsibilities, the welfare of individual family members at times had to be sacrificed to the familial good, and parents had to retain powers that were essential to their functions.

During the decades preceding the American Revolution, this "corporate" form of family life was already giving way to a new, fundamentally different kind of family. As parents lost the ability to pass on their "status position" to their children by distributing land to each of their sons, relations between parents and children were transformed and the emotional character of family life began to change. A new conception of parental responsibility appeared that centered on the care and proper nurture of children. Parents were becoming increasingly self-conscious about questions of child rearing. At the same time that adults began to show greater concern for child development, relations between spouses became increasingly intimate. In their correspondence, fewer husbands and wives referred to each other as "Madam" or "Sir"; increasingly, they used first names or such terms as "dear." Indeed, in Massachusetts the number of women petitioning for divorce rose sharply after 1764, suggesting an increase in the emotional expectations women were bringing to marriage, a shifting sensibility.

It was in the fast-growing commercial cities of the Atlantic seaboard that the transition from the godly family to a new form can most clearly be seen. By the middle of the eighteenth century, a variety of specialized public institutions had begun to absorb traditional familial responsibilities. To reduce the costs of caring for widows, orphans, the destitute, and the mentally ill, cities began to erect almshouses instead of having such people cared for in their own homes or the homes of others. Free schools and common pay schools educated a growing number of the sons of artisans and skilled laborers. Workshops increasingly replaced individual households as centers of production. But, as the family lost its earlier position as society's primary social and economic unit, it began to acquire new emotional significance as a place of peace and a repository of higher moral and spiritual values, a haven in a heartless world.

*The Washington Family (1796) by Edward Savage
(1761-1817). Courtesy of the National Gallery of Art,
Washington, D.C.*

CHAPTER II

The Roots of Diversity

IN 1787, John Jay, one of the authors of *The Federalist Papers*, expressed his thanks that Providence had given victory in the American Revolution "to one united people—a people descended from the same ancestors, speaking the same language, professing the same religion, attached to the same principles of government, very similar in their manners and customs." At the time the future first Chief Justice of the Supreme Court wrote those words, half of the colonial population may have been non-English in origin.[1]

In the early twentieth century, it was customary to describe America as a "melting pot" in which diverse cultural traditions melded into one. Today it is more common to think of America as a pluralistic society, composed of a variety of differing cultures and traditions. Even during the colonial era, America's most distinctive and significant trait was the diversity of its cultures. The early settlers included gentleman, merchants, yeoman and tenant farmers, artisans, indentured servants, and slaves. They settled in tightly organized villages and plantations, in growing cities, on small farms, and in isolated frontier settlements. In the early seventeenth century, English colonists—who came from Essex, Hampshire, London, Norfolk, and other English cities and counties—shared the Atlantic seaboard with a large Dutch population along the Hudson River, small colonies of Swedes and Danes inhabiting the Delaware River region, and more than forty Indian tribes. At the end of the seventeenth century, diversity increased greatly as large numbers of African slaves, and Scottish, Scot-Irish, and German immigrants added to the racial, ethnic, and religious heterogenity of the colonies. In one small mid-eighteenth century Pennsylvania village of three thousand persons, blacks,

Dutch, English, French Huguenots, Germans, Irish, Swedes, and Swiss were all represented in the population.[2]

Colonial Families

Any generalizations about the colonial family must necessarily be qualified by such variables as class, region, and ethnicity. The variety of social and ethnic settings of colonial family life can be seen more fully by examining just three distinct groups: Native Americans, Afro-Americans, and white families in the Chesapeake colonies of Maryland and Virginia. Each in their own way adapted to and triumphed over a perilous, hostile, and rapidly changing environment. Facing severe obstacles in seeking to create and maintain stable families, they eventually triumphed and established patterns of family life that provided stability, emotional support, and a sense of continuity with their past. At the end of 150 years, these people, like the Puritans, had successfully adapted their family patterns to the New World environment.

NATIVE AMERICAN FAMILIES

At the time of English settlement in the early seventeenth century, the Native Americans who lived north of Mexico numbered from 850,000 to 2,000,000 people. Although Europeans regarded the Indians as a single undifferentiated people, in fact the American Indian peoples were composed of 240 or more distinct groups, each with its own political structures, language, economy, and patterns of family and kinship.[3]

During the early years of European contact, the Indian peoples of North America were concentrated in seven major geographic and cultural areas: the Eastern Woodlands, the Southeast, Plains, the Southwest, the Great Basin and California, the Pacific Northwest, and the Arctic Coast. In each area Native Americans adapted their economic systems, their styles of housing, and their family arrangements to the differing demands of specific environments.[4]

Stretching from the Atlantic coast west to the Great Lakes and southward from Maine to North Carolina lie the Eastern Woodlands. At the beginning of the seventeenth century, 75,000 Native Americans divided into forty tribal entities lived in this region. Political organization varied from loosely organized bands and tribes to an elaborate political confederacy, the Iroquois League. The peoples of the Woodlands divided into two basic language groups, Algonquian speakers and Iroquoian speakers. Among Algonquian speakers, the basic social and economic unit was the wigwam, a dome-shaped structure usually containing one or two families. Among Iroquoian speakers, the basic social unit was the longhouse, a large rectangular structure that contained about ten families.[5]

South of the Eastern Woodlands, stretching across the southern Appalachian mountains to the Gulf of Mexico, lay the Southeastern cultural area. Here agriculture was more important, and the population was denser than in the northern Woodlands. The peoples of the Southeast lived in small villages or larger towns that might unite, for protection, into larger confederacies combining thirty or more settlements. In the Southeast the nucleus of social activity was the extended family. A husband, upon marriage, usually joined his wife's family's household.[6]

Beyond the Mississippi River, stretching westward to the Rocky Mountains and north and south from Alberta and Saskatchewan in Canada to Texas, lies a vast area of grassland known as the Great Plains. The introduction of the horse by Spanish explorers drew many farming families onto the Plains during the seventeenth and eighteenth centuries. Nomadic bands hunted antelope, bison, deer, and elk, while village dwellers cultivated corn, beans, and squash. Semi-sedentary tribes, such as the Iowa, Kansas, Missouri, and Pawnee, lived in earth- or sod-covered lodges with log frames. More nomadic peoples lived in portable tepees covered with buffalo hides. Most of the Plains Indians lived in extended families of two or three generations.[7]

South and west of the Plains, in what are now Arizona and New Mexico, lived the Southwestern Indians. Here village dwellers known as Pueblo Indians, such as the Hopi and Zuni, coexisted with nomadic hunters and gatherers like the Apache. Among the western Pueblo, the nucleus of social and economic organization was the extended household consisting of a group of female relations and their husbands, sons-in-law, and maternal grandchildren, living together in a multistoried communal structure.[8]

The densest concentration of Indians in North America was in California, where some 275,000 Native Americans lived. Living arrangements ranged from small single-family houses to large multifamily structures in which several families lived in adjoining units. These family units, in turn, were grouped into tribelets that varied in size from a few hundred to a few thousand people. Among many Califor-

nia Indians, a man's wife or wives resided with his family after marriage.[9]

North of California, along the Pacific coast, lived 129,000 Northwest Coast Indians. The basic economic and social unit was the simple
family made up of a man, his wife or wives, and their children or the
man's sister's sons, living in a plank house. Even further northward,
inhabiting the Arctic Coast from the Aleutian islands eastward to
Greenland and southern Labrador, were the Eskimo, who lived in
sizable villages and supported themselves by fishing and hunting cari-
bou, seal, walrus, and whale. For the Eskimo the basic unit of economic activity was the simple family, composed of a husband, wife,
and children, or the household, which usually contained two families.[10]

It was difficult for the European colonists to appreciate or comprehend this tribal diversity, and they tended to conflate the native
American peoples into a single undifferentiated group. They called
the vast native population "Indians," described their color as "red,"
and treated them as ignorant children whose religions were pagan,
languages incomprehensible, politics disorganized, and agriculture
and land use patterns primitive.[11]

Dimly, however, the European colonists perceived that Native
Americans had ideas about the family and the kin group that diverged
sharply from European patterns. Europeans were astonished to en-
counter tribes that had adopted communal housing arrangements,
other tribes in which men were absent for prolonged periods of time,
and still other tribes in which premarital sexuality was permitted and
even encouraged, in which polygamy was practiced, or in which a
wife was allowed to divorce her husband just by putting his belongings outside her home.

Although they differed in language, culture, political systems, and
religion, all Native Americans organized their societies according to
principles of kinship. Family ties—based on marriage or bloodlines—
formed the basis of their political, economic, and religious systems.
Succession to political office, religious positions, ownership and inheritance of property, and even whom one could or could not marry
were determined on the basis of membership in a kin group.

Indian kinship and family systems divided into an intricate variety
of forms, with regulations governing marriages, relations with in-laws,
and residence after marriage. In patrilineal societies like the Cheyenne, land use rights and membership in the political system flowed
through the father. In a matrilineal society like the Pueblo, membership in the group was determined by the mother's family identity.

In the Algonquian-speaking tribes of eastern North America, group membership was based on ties among siblings and cousins and other relationships.[12]

Most Indian families were small. Two factors contributed to small families: a high infant and child death rate and the fact that Indian mothers nursed their children for two or more years. Breast-feeding mothers generally abstained from sexual relations until the child was weaned, and lactation itself suppressed fertility.[13]

Children were usually born in a special birth hut, located some distance from the family's home. Newborn children were dipped into cold water or rubbed with animal oil. Several months later, newborns underwent a special initiation ceremony that marked their entrance into the tribe. In the presence of relatives, a child was given a name from a wealth of family names. Among some tribes, children also underwent a rite involving the piercing of the nose or earlobes. In many areas papooses were carried in a skin bag or strapped to a wooden cradleboard until they were a year old in order to straighten their bones.[14]

The young were encouraged to behave properly largely through praise and public reward for achievement. Indian parents seldom spanked their children—an absence of corporal punishment that shocked Europeans. Instead of relying on physical punishments, Indian parents praised children when they were good and publicly shamed or ridiculed them when they misbehaved. Indians believed that physical punishment made children timid and that their techniques produced independent and self-disciplined adults. Among some Indian peoples, child rearing was left to mothers or grandmothers, while among other groups, such as many Plains tribes, uncles, grandfathers, and other male relatives played active roles as mentors and disciplinarians. Among the Southeastern tribes, young boys received instruction and discipline from their father and their mother's brother.[15]

Participation in work began very early for Indian children. Children's play was modeled on their parents' work. Girls learned to sew by making clothes for dolls and to farm by raising corn, squash, and beans in small garden plots. Very young boys were encouraged to fish, hunt game, and gather wild nuts, fruits and berries.[16]

In Indian societies the process of growing up was marked off by a series of social rites of passage that demarcated the transition from one life stage to the next. Girls underwent a puberty ceremony, consisting of isolation at the time of first menstruation. During her isolation, which might last from several weeks to a year, an older woman would care for her and instruct her in her role as an adult. After her return the girl began to wear adult dress. Boys also underwent rites of initiation. A number of firsts, including the first tooth, first steps, and the first big game killed by a boy, were recognized in public ceremonies. Among many tribes, when a boy approached adolescence, he went alone to a mountaintop or into a forest to fast and seek a vision from a guardian spirit. On his return he assumed adult status.[17]

Indians married at an early age. Women married between the ages of twelve and fifteen; men between fifteen and twenty. Methods of choosing a spouse varied widely. Among the California Indians, marriages were arranged by the families of the bride and groom. Other tribes permitted young men and women to select their own spouse.[18]

Among some Indian tribes, the newly married husband moved in with his wife's family until the birth of the first child, when the couple established a separate household. In other societies a wife lived with her husband's family. Most Indian marriages were monogamous, but some tribes, including many Plains tribes, allowed husbands to have more than one wife. Some tribes also allowed men to have sexual relations outside of marriage when their wives were pregnant or nursing. In many societies divorce was easy, and either a husband or wife could dissolve a marriage. Many Indian societies practiced the levirate—in which a widow married a brother of her deceased husband—or sororate—in which a widower married a sister of his deceased wife.[19]

Even before the end of the seventeenth century, contact with Europeans brought dramatic changes to the American Indian family. The most obvious effect of contact was a sharp decline in the size of their population. Eastern Indians were decimated by Old World diseases, to which they were highly vulnerable. Native Americans had little immunity to, and died in staggering numbers from, such diseases as influenza, measles, smallpox, and typhus. Plymouth Colony was actually located in a deserted Indian village whose inhabitants had been devastated by epidemic diseases brought by Europeans. By the 1670s only 10 percent of the original Indian population of New England had survived. At least fifty tribes became extinct as a result of disease and massacre.[20]

The effects of contact were manifest in other ways. Among the consequences of the European "discovery" of the New World were the introduction of the horse, firearms, and metal knives. In the mid-sixteenth century, the arrival of the horse in the New World allowed many Plains peoples to become more nomadic as they pursued herds of buffalo. Guns and knives encouraged massive animal slaughter as well as more lethal human violence. Another consequence was an increased in the practice of polygamy in some regions. The trade in furs increased the economic value of wives, who were responsible for dressing hides, and particularly on the Northern Plains increasing numbers of hunters began to take more than one wife.[21]

For the Iroquois, contact wrought a profound transformation in family and kinship practices. Displaced from their traditional lands and suffering the effects of psychological and cultural disintegration brought on by epidemic disease, rampant alcoholism and dwindling land resources, the Iroquois reconstituted and revitalized their culture under the leadership of a prophet called Handsome Lake, who adapted the patterns of the new settlers to tribal life. The prophet endorsed the demand of Quaker missionaries that the traditional sexual division of labor emphasizing male hunting and female horticulture be replaced by a pattern in which men would farm and women would rear children and care for the home. He also called for modification of the Iroquois system of matrilineal descent, in which the tie between mothers and daughters had been strong and the bond between fathers and sons and spouses had been fragile. Handsome Lake placed heavy emphasis on the sanctity of the marriage bond, declared that divorce was a great sin, and said that marriage should take precedence over all other kinship ties. He called on mothers not to interfere with their daughters' marriages and held that sons should obey their fathers. The nuclear family, not the maternal lineage, was to be the central social and economic institution in Iroquois life.[22]

As a result of Handsome Lake's religious movement, the Iroquois would successfully adapt to changing economic, political, and social conditions. They abandoned their matrilineal longhouses and began to dwell in male-headed households in individual log cabins. They modified their system of matrilineal descent to allow fathers to pass land to their sons. And Iroquois men took up farming, even though this was traditionally viewed as women's work. By adopting those aspects of the encroaching white cultures that were relevant to their lives and fitting them into traditional cultural patterns, the Iroquois were largely able to maintain their culture, values, and rituals.[23]

AFRO-AMERICAN FAMILIES

In late August 1619, over a year before the *Mayflower* landed at Plymouth, a Dutch warship deposited twenty Africans seized from a Portuguese slave ship at Jamestown in Virginia. For the next fifty years, the

number of blacks in the English colonies remained low. At late as
1675 there were probably no more than 4,000 black slaves in the
mainland colonies, against more than 100,000 in the British West
Indies. But by the end of the seventeenth century, black slaves could
be found in each of the thirteen English colonies. During the early
eighteenth century, blacks made up almost 70 percent of the population of South Carolina, 40 percent of the population in Virginia, 8
percent in Pennsylvania, and 4 percent of the population in New England.[24]

Initially the status of colonial blacks was unclear. The first blacks
to arrive in the colonies were apparently sold to local planters as
indentured servants, not as slaves. Like white servants, they were
freed at the end of their term of service. Over the course of the seventeenth century, as the slave population grew, slaves and free blacks in
the Southern colonies were stripped of rights that they had shared
with white indentured servants. In Virginia as late as the 1660s, some
slaves were able to own property, hire out their own labor, and purchase their freedom. But already blacks' legal status had begun to
decline. In 1662 a statute declared that all children would have the
legal status of their mother; in 1667 the Virginia assembly established
that baptism would not bring freedom to slaves; and in 1670 free
blacks were deprived of the right to own white servants. A year later
the colony adopted a statute authorizing strict punishments for miscegenation inside or outside of wedlock. Other laws prohibited slaves
from testifying in court, owning property, making contracts, traveling
without permission, congregating in public places in groups of more
than two or three, or contracting marriage. Laws adopted in several
colonies in the early eighteenth century even prohibited owners from
freeing their slaves.[25]

The experience of colonial blacks was anything but uniform. Their
living arrangements, their kinds of work, their population density,
and their legal rights varied markedly from place to place. In the
North the black population was concentrated in port towns like Boston, New York, and Philadelphia, where they usually lived in the
homes of their masters. Slaves were employed as household servants,
as laborers clearing brush and erecting housing, and as artisans working as bakers, blacksmiths, shipwrights, mast makers, and sailors. Relatively few Northern slaves served as farmhands. In 1690 one Boston
family out of every nine owned slaves; in 1703, 42 percent of all households in New York City had at least one slave. In contrast to conditions in the South, slave marriages in New England were solemnized
and legally recorded in the same manner as those between whites,

and slaves were permitted to baptize their children in a church. Even in the North, however, it was legal for slaveowners to separate spouses or parents from children as a result of a sale or the settlement of a will.[26]

In the Chesapeake Bay colonies of Virginia and Maryland and in North Carolina, blacks raised tobacco on small farms and often worked, ate, and slept alongside white farmers and white indentured servants. In South Carolina, following the introduction of rice cultivation at the end of the seventeenth century, slaves labored on large rice plantations in the low-lying Sea Islands and coastal areas where few whites lived.[27]

During the seventeenth century, slaves had few opportunities to establish a stable and independent family life. Throughout the colonies, the chances of a slave finding a spouse were quite low. In the Chesapeake colonies and the Carolinas, most slaves lived on plantations with fewer than ten slaves. These units were so small and so widely dispersed, and the sex ratio was so skewed, that it was difficult for slave men and women to find a spouse of roughly the same age. In Northern cities most slaves lived with their masters and were restricted from associating with other slaves.[28]

A high death rate meant that many slaves did not live long enough to marry or that if they did, their marriages did not last very long. Overwork and susceptibility to epidemic and respiratory diseases such as pleurisy, influenza, pneumonia, yellow fever, malaria, and tuberculosis took untold lives. During the first years of the eighteenth century, when improvements in agriculture, clothing, and housing brought increases in white life expectancy in South Carolina, the slave death rate actually rose and the birthrate declined—apparently because slaveholders expanded and intensified production on rice plantations in order to purchase more slaves.[29]

Throughout the seventeenth and eighteenth centuries, only two slave women were imported for every three slave men. (In the first years after the settlement of South Carolina, the proportion was three males for every one female.) Individual farms or plantations could have even more sharply imbalanced sex ratios than more general estimates would lead one to expect. One consequence of this gross sexual imbalance was manifest in the inability of the black population in either Virginia or Maryland to reproduce its numbers naturally.[30]

At the end of the seventeenth century, however, two fateful developments gave an increasing number of black slaves the opportunity to establish a family life. The first momentous change was a sharp increase in the number of slaves imported into the Southern colonies.

As late as 1700, only 5,000 slaves had been imported into the Chesapeake colonies. During the first decade of the eighteenth century, the number of imported slaves climbed to 1,000 a year; by the 1730s the figure had reached 2,000 annually. Sixty percent of the 550,000 Africans forcibly imported into the American colonies arrived between 1720 and 1780. As the number of slaves increased, the average size of plantations grew, and on larger plantations slaves had a greater opportunity to find spouses.[31]

The other significant social change was a sharp upturn in slave fertility. In the late seventeenth century, the slave birthrate was so low and the death rate so high that their numbers would actually have declined in the absence of the slave trade. By the 1720s slaves in the Chesapeake region—unlike slaves in Brazil, the Caribbean, or even South Carolina—began to reproduce their numbers naturally. Slave fertility not only surpassed the growth rate of all other slave populations, it actually exceeded the European fertility rate. As slave births began to exceed slave deaths, the imbalance in the sex ratio of the slave population began to disappear.[32]

A variety of factors contributed to this shift toward a self-reproducing population. One factor was the increasing proportion of American-born female slaves in the black population. Because disease immunities develop during early childhood, American-born mothers had greater resistance to disease than did African-born mothers. They lived longer, subsequently bore more children, and began to bear them earlier and to space them closer together. African women newly arrived in the colonies and typically in their early twenties had a shorter period in which they could give birth than did their American-born counterparts, who usually bore their first children between eighteen or nineteen, thus permitting them to bear two or three more children than New England white females.[33]

Another reason for the transition to a higher level of fertility and a positive rate of natural growth for black Americans included the absence in the Chesapeake region of the tropical diseases that killed large numbers of slaves in Central and South America or the moist humid regions of coastal South Carolina as well as a relative abundance of food and land and the less physically taxing cultivation of tobacco. The desire of Chesapeake planters to establish self-sufficient plantations and reduce dependence on the African slave trade may also have led them to encourage a more stable family life among their slaves.[34]

The remarkable upsurge in slave fertility paralleled a similar fertility increase among Southern white women. It was not until 1700 that the white population in the Chesapeake region succeeded in reproducing itself by natural increase, just two decades before the black population achieved a similar rate of increase. During the eighteenth century, the demographic profile of white and black mothers was remarkably similar: Both began child rearing at approximately the same age; both spaced their children closely together; both breast-fed their children for a similar space of time. One difference, however, persisted over time: Even in the late eighteenth century, the proportion of unmarried black women was much higher than among whites, reflecting the fact that many slaves lived on small, scattered farms and plantations where potential husbands were not readily available. Given the small size and isolation of many farms, the high mortality rates among slaves, and imbalances in the distribution of slaves by sex and age, it is the high proportion of slaves who married that stands out.[35]

Well before the American Revolution, slaves had succeeded in fashioning a strong family and kinship system. Despite the fact that the Southern colonies refused to recognize the legality of slave marriages, many slaves, especially on larger plantations, established lifelong unions lasting twenty years or more. By the time of the Revolution, most slaves on larger plantations lived in two-parent households, in which parents resided together with their children. To sustain a sense of family identity, slave children were often named for a parent or other blood kin or given traditional African names. Family continuity was reinforced as parents passed down craft skills, such as barrel making, mechanics, or midwifery, to their children.[36]

Although slave marriages were not legally binding, slaves eschewed casual sexual relationships and placed a premium on marital stability. Typically, slave women in the late eighteenth century bore first children a little past puberty, usually between the ages of fifteen and twenty-three and sometimes out of wedlock, but they would proceed to establish stable and long-lasting relationships in their early twenties.[37]

During the first decades of the eighteenth century, slaves began to create a distinctive Afro-American system of family and kinship that would help sustain them against slavery's physical cruelties and its material deprivations. The family patterns that developed would be a mixture of African and white traditions and would balance strong nuclear family ties with loyalties to an extended kin group. This pattern, more than anything else, would provide slaves with the emotional resources necessary to make life under slavery bearable.

EUROPEAN IMMIGRANT FAMILIES IN THE SOUTH

Family life in the seventeenth-century Chesapeake colonies of Maryland and Virginia provides a dramatic contrast to the highly ordered
and structured patterns found in Puritan New England and to the
highly flexible and adaptive patterns found among Indians and
blacks. For colonists south of Chesapeake Bay, a high level of mortality, a short average life span, a low average duration of marriage, and
a sharply skewed sex ratio all contributed to an environment in which
family relationships were ephemeral. And yet, even though Southern
colonists lacked certain conditions conducive to order and discipline
that were found in New England, they did succeed in creating intricate networks of social relationships—based on blood, marriage, and
friendship—that provided a basis for social cohesion.[38]

The contrast in the population characteristics of the two regions
could hardly be starker or more significant. In seventeenth-century
New England, immigration by family groups, a healthful climate, and
a prospering economy permitted the family from a early date to serve
as a stabilizing force in society. In the Chesapeake colonies of Maryland and Virginia, a continuing heavy influx of new male immigrants
added to the imbalance of the sexes, and the prevalence of epidemic
diseases prevented the region from developing stable families.[39]

Compared to the Chesapeake, which remained a region of pioneers
throughout the seventeenth century, New England, by the middle of
the century, had already become a society with roots. In New England
rapid immigration ended at an early date. The English Civil War cut
off the flow of immigrants around 1640, allowing the social system to
begin to stabilize. During the seventeenth century, immigration to
Virginia and Maryland was seven times as high as that to New England. Until the last two decades of the century, the number of immigrants to Virginia never fell below a thousand a year, and the kinds
of immigrants who traveled to Virginia created an extraordinarily
youthful but unstable society.[40]

The overwhelming majority of immigrants to the Chesapeake colonies were young, unmarried indentured servants. As many as 70 to
85 percent of the immigrants to Maryland and Virginia during the
seventeenth century arrived as indentured servants. And in Virginia
the majority of servants were single males not over the age of sixteen.
Particularly during the first half-century of settlement, men consider-
ably outnumbered women. It is true that more Englishmen than
women migrated to all regions during the seventeenth century, but
in the Chesapeake, the lesser numbers of women lasted longer. In

New England two-fifths of all immigrants were females; in Virginia in the 1630s only one woman arrived for every six males. And even as late as 1704 in the colony, there were three males for every two females.[41]

Women were not the only ones in short supply in the Chesapeake region. Older people were also quite rare. In New England, males who survived infancy were likely to reach their seventies. Women survived almost as long. But in the Chesapeake, few inhabitants were over the age of sixty. During the seventeenth century, a Chesapeake man who reached the age of twenty could expect to live just another twenty-three years. Half of all women failed to reach their twentieth birthdays. As late as 1770, people over the age of sixty accounted for between 4 and 6 percent of the population. In the Chesapeake region, unlike New England, the paucity of older people meant that the society failed to divide along clear generational lines of grandparent, parent, and child.[42]

Unlike the colonists who settled New England and quickly achieved a level of health and length of life even greater than that found in England, the colonists who settled the South suffered almost unimaginable levels of mortality. Between 1607 and 1624, of the 6,000 settlers who had arrived in Jamestown, only 1,275 were still alive. Before 1640 a colonist in Virginia had a fifty-fifty chance of dying the first year, a death rate comparable to that reached in England during epidemics of plague.[43]

Standards of health and life improved during the second half of the seventeenth century but remained lower than those in England, France, and, above all, New England, where mortality was approximately half as great. In late-seventeenth-century Maryland, only 41 percent of those who reached the age of twenty were still alive at the age of forty, and just 15 percent lived to reach the age of sixty. In contrast to New England, which experienced no crop failures during the colonial era, many colonists in the Chesapeake region and the Carolinas suffered diseases suggesting malnutrition—including beriberi, infant cholera, diarrhea, dysentery, marasmus, pellagra, rickets, and scurvy. Drinking water contaminated with salt killed many settlers in low-lying coastal areas. And, unlike New England—which avoided such epidemic diseases as bubonic plague, malaria and typhus (though not diphtheria, measles, pneumonia, scarlet fever, smallpox, and tuberculosis)—the Southern colonies were ravaged by epidemics.[44]

Then, too, households were more widely separated in the Chesapeake and the South than in New England or the mother country.

Instead of clustering in villages, tobacco and rice farmers south of the Chesapeake located on widely scattered farms.[45]

The population characteristics of the Chesapeake colonies contributed to family patterns fundamentally different from those found in New England. The fact that many immigrants were committed to long terms of service as indentured servants meant that marriage was often delayed to relatively late ages. In Maryland the typical woman was twenty-four or older when first married. Delayed marriages, combined with high levels of infant mortality that saw a quarter of all children die before their first birthday, helped limit the number of children per family to an average of just two or three, compared to seven or eight in New England. The short average life expectancy meant that long marriages were extremely rare. Indeed, by the seventh wedding anniversary, as many marriages had been broken by the death of one of the partners as lasted beyond that point. The geographic dispersal of the population, the shortage of women, and the prevalence of recent immigrants contributed to a society in which traditional social controls were weak—evident in rates of illegitimacy far higher than those in New England. One-fifth of the female servants in one Maryland county bore children out of wedlock, despite stern punishments ranging from heavy fines to whippings.[46]

Other characteristics of the Chesapeake colonies in the seventeenth century included substantial numbers of orphans and bereaved parents, frequent remarriages, widows and widowers, stepparents and stepchildren. Two-thirds of all children lost one parent before their eighteenth birthdays; one-third lost both. All this might lead one to expect devastating consequences for family life, but this does not appear to have been the case. Marriages may have been short lived and unstable, parent-child ties fragile, bonds to extended kin tenuous, and yet reliance on kin and neighbors, far from being weak, was strong. And parents, far from treating their children with indifference, developed affectionate, loving relationships with their offspring.[47]

George Washington's upbringing suggests the strength and significance of these family ties. Augustine Washington, George's father, died in 1743, when his son was eleven. Scrupulously attentive to the welfare of his survivors, he left his sons from a previous marriage the bulk of his land and left George and his mother the family farmhouse. After his father's death, George went to live with his half-brother Lawrence, fourteen years his senior, who had been named his guardian. Lawrence married into the wealthy Anglo-American Fairfax family and secured George an appointment as a surveyor through his connections with the English Lord Fairfax. When Lawrence's only child died in 1752, George inherited his half-brother's estate. Family connections played a critical role in George Washington's rise to prominence.[48]

In Middlesex County, Virginia, located on the south bank of the Rappahannock River, parents had deep feelings for their offspring and created an intricate web of social relationships based on ties of friendship, blood, and marriage to ensure that their children would be cared for even if they themselves should die prematurely. By 1724 more than half the families in Middlesex County had family ties to five or more other families in the county. Indeed, the typical head of a household could count thirty-one relatives in Middlesex County; by the first quarter of the eighteenth century, kinship ties were augmented by social and community bonds. Friends would administer a deceased husband's estate or look after orphaned children or stand security for a bond. Networks of kinship, friendship, and neighborhood made up for the fragility and transience of individual attachments. Given this tight web of interdependence, it is not surprising that most marriages were contracted between neighbors living no more than five miles apart.[49]

Strong kinship ties provided a mechanism for maintaining a sense of cohesion and continuity in a precarious environment. Parents sustained a sense of family continuity by naming children for themselves and for their own parents. They also took great care to ensure that minor children would inherit property on reaching their majority. Overseers and executors were named to ensure that stepparents would not misuse estates; wills carefully specified the expenditures that executors could make from the inheritance.[50]

It is difficult not to be struck by the resilience and adaptability of these Southern families in the face of unstable frontier conditions. Nowhere is this more readily apparent than in responses to the death of a spouse. In seventeenth-century Maryland, most marriages lasted less than seven years, and only one-third lasted as long as a decade. In two out of three cases, the surviving spouse was the wife, and colonists in Maryland responded to this high death rate by assigning more rights and powers to widows than was the practice elsewhere in the colonies. Law and custom assigned widows primary responsibility for holding their farms and households together, and husbands' wills reflected this concern. Most husbands made their wives executors of their estates and entrusted their spouses with more land and property than the law required—reflecting their confidence in their wives' abilities to manage the estate and recognizing their spouses' economic contributions to the household, which included raising tobacco, milling corn, growing vegetables, milking cows, churning butter, making cheese, as well as spinning yarn and knitting clothing.[51]

By the end of the seventeenth century, family life in the colonies south of the Chesapeake had begun to stabilize. The death rate began to fall, life expectancy started to rise, and the imbalance in the sex ratio began to ease. Marriages lasted longer, fewer children died in infancy, families grew larger, and the birthrate rose sharply. Female children of the initial settlers underwent very different experiences than their mothers, who had had to delay marriage until they completed their term of indentured servitude. The second generation of Chesapeake women was free to marry at much younger ages—in one Maryland county averaging just sixteen and a half years old. Earlier marriage was accompanied by significant increases in family size. Instead of bearing four or five children, which was the pattern in the seventeenth century, Chesapeake women in the eighteenth century bore seven or eight, of whom five or six could be expected to reach adulthood.[52]

Despite a stabilization in the eighteenth century, the pattern of family life in the Chesapeake remained fundamentally different from the one prevalent in New England. Life expectancy remained much shorter in the Chesapeake throughout the eighteenth century. High mortality rates meant that most children still lost their parents before they reached adulthood. The Chesapeake also diverged from New England in the continuing ability of its parents to bequeath all their sons land. Because of the plentitude of land, wealthier planters were able to leave the eldest son the home plantation, while younger sons received land in outlying areas. Consequently, the Chesapeake colonies were distinguished by the early emergence of a wealthy intermarried group of planter families at the end of the seventeenth century and the beginning of the eighteenth. These families, which owned hundreds of slaves and controlled the region's most valuable land and its political offices, reflected the pattern of life enjoyed in Restoration England. The great planter families constructed estates, like Mount Vernon and Monticello, modeled on English country houses, which served as important public centers of activity. Within these "great houses," friends, relatives, children, and slaves came to conduct business, to socialize, or to make requests of the planters. During the first half of the eighteenth century, gentry families did not attach a high priority to domestic life. Life's greatest pleasures, they believed, came not from domesticity but from such public activities as hunting, entertaining, and political service.[53]

Inside the great houses, family life emulated Restoration ideals of moderation, balance, and restraint. Emotional display was discouraged. Family members were taught to mask and moderate their emotions behind a veneer of formal language and gesture. Emotional intensity between spouses and between parents and children was to be scrupulously avoided. This emphasis on moderation and restraint was not, however, always realized in practice. Surviving documents reveal that violent quarrels between parents and children took place, as did sexual exploitation of female servants and slaves.[54]

During the second half of the eighteenth century, family patterns in the Chesapeake increasingly came to resemble patterns found in the Northern colonies. Planters' children became more likely to select marriage partners without parental interference. Instead of asserting ties to a broad network of kin and friends, planter families began to focus their emotional affection on their immediate families. Open expressions of affection between spouses and parents and children became more common, and mothers tended to devote more time to the nurture of their children. In both Northern and Southern colonies, a new style of family life was beginning to emerge, emphasizing domestic intimacy, the care and nurture of children, and freedom in choice of a spouse.[55]

One hundred and sixty-nine years elapsed between the founding of the first permanent English settlement at Jamestown and the signing of the Declaration of Independence. A longer span of time separated the founding of Jamestown and the battles of Concord and Lexington than lies between Abraham Lincoln's election to the presidency and the present. Despite the length of the colonial era, however, the popular image is of a period in which little change occurred. The most typical representations of colonial America—peaceful New England farmhouses and elegant Virginia plantations—reinforce this image of a peaceful and unchanging era.

By the beginning of the nineteenth century, the families of Iroquois Indians, black slaves, and Chesapeake planters had all successfully met the challenge of establishing stable families in an unsettled environment. The families these groups created were not replicas of New England families; they retained distinctive rules and customs. Dramatic change had occurred in family structure and form. An earlier heritage had been drastically modified, and yet earlier traditions had not been entirely lost. It is the mixture of continuity and change that stands out as the most striking characteristic of family change during the colonial era.

The Sargent Family (1800) *by an unknown American artist.*
Courtesy of the National Gallery of Art, Washington, D.C.

CHAPTER III

The Rise
of the Democratic Family

In 1831, Alexis de Tocqueville, a twenty-six-year-old French noble-man, arrived in America, ostensibly to study the nation's new system of prisons. The young aristocrat used the occasion to develop a broader analysis of the forces that were transforming American soci-ety. As Tocqueville looked into the state of early-nineteenth-century America, he concluded that the spirit of "individualism" (a word he coined) was its distinguishing trait. Tocqueville believed that the American trend toward individualism had reshaped every social insti-tution and that the drift toward equality had redefined family life. He observed that marriage was becoming more intimate and more egalitarian. Fathers were granting more freedom to their children and greater control over the domestic sphere to their wives. And, as par-ents had come to regard children as unique individuals requiring love and nurture, family life was becoming increasingly child-centered.[1]

Despite some misconceptions and factual errors, Tocqueville pro-vides an indispensable insight into the transformations that took place in family life in the late eighteenth and early nineteenth centu-ries. Between 1770 and 1830, a new kind of middle-class family ap-peared. The democratic family, as Tocqueville called it, was character-ized by a form of marriage that emphasized companionship and mutual affection, by a more intense concern on the part of parents with the proper upbringing of children, and by a new division of sex roles, according to which the husband was to be the family's bread-winner and the wife was to specialize in child rearing and homemak-ing. Mutual affection and a sense of duty provided the basis for the democratic family's existence.[2]

Tocquevile shared the view of many foreign observers that the dis-tinguishing characteristic of the American family was its isolation and

43

detachment from society as a whole. By the 1830s Americans had come to define the family as essentially a private place, distinct from the public sphere of life. It was a shelter and a refuge, a contrast to the outside world.[3]

During the seventeenth century, the family had been seen as the foundation of the social order and the center of institutional life. It was "a little church," "a little commonwealth," "a school," the cornerstone of church and state and a microcosm of the larger society. This conception of the family reflected the fact that colonial conditions had broadened the family's functions and responsibilities. Not only was the colonial family responsible for the care of children, it was also the basic unit of economic production, the center of religious observance, and the institution charged with primary responsibility for education and for the care of the ill and the elderly.[4]

By the beginning of the nineteenth century, a radically new definition of the family had emerged. Instead of being viewed as an integral component of the network of public institutions, the family was beginning to be seen as a private retreat. The term "family" generally referred not to the household or kin group but to the smaller and more isolated nuclear, or conjugal, family—the unit made up of the father, mother, and their children. It was a place for virtues and emotions threatened by the aggressive and competitive spirit of commerce, a place where women and children were secure and where men could escape from the stresses of business and recover their humanity.[5]

The family, which seventeenth-century colonists believed to be governed by the same principles of hierarchy and subordination as the community at large, was, according to a flood of early-nineteenth-century books and articles celebrating the sanctity of hearth and home, governed by values fundamentally different from those that held sway in the outside world. The values of independence, self-reliance, and ambition were appropriate for the marketplace and government, but within the home, a wholly different set of values reigned supreme: love, mutuality, companionship, selflessness, sacrifice, and self-denial. No longer a microcosm of the larger society, the family was now a counterweight to acquisitive values and a refuge from materialistic corruptions.[6]

The new attitude toward the family was a reflection of a more general eighteenth-century shift in sensibility that sentimentalized the home as a bastion of harmony and higher moral and spiritual values. It was also a reaction to the nation's rapid material and geographic expansion, which led men and women to place a high premium upon the family, which worked for order and cohesion amidst vast social and economic change. An increasingly commercial and market-oriented economy demanded a new work discipline that required less emotionality on the job and more impersonal relations with other workers or customers. The home became the primary arena for feelings of affection, vulnerability, and belonging.[7]

By the end of the eighteenth century and the beginning of the nineteenth, the American family had been transformed from a public institution whose functions were primarily economic into one whose major role was to rear children and provide emotional support for its members. The family was changing in its emphasis from an institution in which all members were expected to contribute to an integral family economy to a unit in which individuals lived together for the sake of each other's emotional well-being and development. Unlike the Puritan family, whose main functions had been to carry on farming and domestic manufacturing, to transmit property or the skills of a family craft, and to care for dependent kin, the chief functions of the democratic family were psychological and ideological. Its purposes were to ensure individual happiness and to serve the political order by diffusing self-serving needs and instilling children with values of order, responsibility, and self-discipline—the values of good citizenship.[8]

Impact of the Revolution

The roots of the transformation that had taken place in the American family lay in enlightened philosophical, religious, political, and economic ideas about the rights of the individual. In the years just before the American Revolution, a flood of advice books, philosophical treatises, and works of fiction helped to popularize revolutionary new ideas about child rearing and the family. The most popular books in the colonies on the eve of the American Revolution were not political discourses, such as John Locke's *Second Treatise on Liberty*, but philosophical tracts on child rearing—such as his *Essay Concerning Human Understanding* and Jean-Jacques Rousseau's *Emile*—and novels, plays, and poems concerned with family relations, such as Samuel Richardson's *Clarissa* and *Pamela* and Oliver Goldsmith's *The Vicar of Wakefield*. Such works disseminated a radically new sensibility that was to transform American ideals about the family over the next century.[9]

In the fiction of Daniel Defoe, Henry Fielding, Samuel Richardson, Laurence Sterne, and numerous lesser-known writers, the patriarchal family came under attack as unduly repressive and incompatible with the spirit of the time. Readers learned that love was superior to property as a basis for marriage; that marriage should be based on mutual sympathy, affection, and friendship; that parental example was more effective than coercion in governing children; and that the ideal parent sought to cultivate children's natural talents and abilities through love.[10]

The burgeoning literature on the family explicitly rejected the older conception of marriage as an economic transaction between two families based on property considerations in favor of marriage as an emotional bond between two individuals. As such, neither parental permission nor parental approval were prerequisites for a happy marriage. Rather than choosing spouses on economic grounds, young people were told to select their marriage partners on the more secure basis of love and compatibility. In a survey of all extant colonial magazines published during the thirty years preceding the Revolution, one issue out of four contained at least one reference to "romantic love" as the proper basis of marriage; during the next twenty years, the number of references to romantic love would triple. Affection, compatibility, and reciprocated love, readers were told, were the only lasting adhesives that would bind spouses together. Personal happiness, not wealth or a desire to please parents, should be the primary motive behind decisions to marry. Indeed, so great was the emphasis attached to personal happiness that more than one pre-Revolutionary author advised young women that they should reject any feelings of "obligation" to be married if these should conflict with their desire for personal happiness.[11]

Within marriage the older ideals of patriarchal authority and strict wifely obedience were replaced by new ideals of "mutual esteem, mutual friendship, mutual confidence," According to one popular English guide published in 1762, in an ideal marriage, husbands regarded their wives not as "domestic drudges, or the slaves of our pleasures, but as our companions and equals." This shift to a new companionate conception of marriage was accompanied by an open recognition that personal happiness was a primary goal of marriage and a union's success or failure should be judged by its ability to provide love. It was a commonplace of the eighteenth-century novel that the choice of a spouse should be based exclusively on mutual affection and that loveless marriages lacked legitimacy. As Henry Fielding wrote in *Tom Jones*, "Love is the only foundation of happiness in a married state, as it can only produce that high and tender friendship which should always be the cement of the union." It needs to be stressed that the new ideal of marriage did not imply sexual equality or a blurring of gender boundaries. The new companionate ideal of marriage was based on the idea that husbands and wives were interdependent partners, joined in a "reciprocal union of interest."[12]

A new attitude toward children was an essential element in the emerging mid-eighteenth-century conception of the family. Childhood was depicted as a stage in the life cycle, and the child was described as a special being with distinctive needs and impulses. Drawing on Locke's view of the child's mind as a *tabula rasa*, or "blank slate" which could be imprinted in an infinite variety of ways, and on Rousseau's conception of children as naturally social and affectionate, novelists and child-rearing experts told their readers that the primary object of child rearing was not to instill submission to authority but to develop a child's conscience and self-government. Earlier in time, community leaders had held that the primary task of parenthood was to restrain children and make these innately sinful creatures obedient to external authority. Increasingly, however, parents were told that self-government was a necessity; it was, wrote Catharine Sedgwick in the early nineteenth century, "the only affective and lasting government—the one that touches the springs of action, and in all circumstances controls them." Even before the Revolution, parents were advised to train their children in independence. While still young and malleable, they had to develop a capacity for self-reliance, self-assessment, and self-direction, in the hope that this would prepare them for a world in which they would have to make independent choices of a career, of friends, and of a spouse. Childhood, previously conceived of as a period of submission to authority, was increasingly viewed as a period of growth, development, and preparation for adulthood.[13]

There can be no doubt that many pre-Revolutionary families failed to conform to this new "individualistic" ideal of family life. Private behavior frequently diverged from the models set forth in the prescriptive literature. In fact, Benjamin Franklin, the printer, revolutionary, diplomat, and experimenter in electricity whose aphorisms in *Poor Richard's Almanack* have served as guides to moral virtue for countless Americans, fathered an illegitimate son, took a common-law wife, lived apart from her for fifteen years of their marriage, and apparently dallied with other women. His marriage was not based on affection and mutual respect. He quite openly described his relationship with his wife as little more than a marriage of convenience that provided a channel for his sexual appetites, "that hard-to-be-governed passion of youth that had hurried me into intrigues with

low women that fell in my way which were attended with great ex-
pense and . . . a continual risk to my health by a distemper which of
all things I dreaded." Emotional distance characterized his relations
with his childen as well as his wife. He refused to attend the marriage
of either his son or daughter after they had chosen marriage partners
over his objections, saw his son just once during a period of thirty
years, and failed to return from Europe to visit his dying wife.[14]

Yet there can be little doubt that the long-term historical trend was
in the direction of increasing affection and equality between husbands
and wives and parents and children. During the early nineteenth century, life became more domestic than it had been in the past. In many
pious households, the day began with the family gathering for prayers
and Bible readings. In the evening, many families reassembled to read
aloud from the Bible, novels, or family magazines. On the Sabbath,
families attended church together. By the mid-nineteenth century, the
family vacation had appeared, as did a series of new family oriented
celebrations, such as the birthday party, Christmas, and Thanksgiving. The birthday cake, the Christmas tree, Christmas presents,
Christmas caroling, and the Thanksgiving turkey were all manifestations of the reorientation of daily life around the family. Heaven itself
was increasingly described as a "home" where family members would
be eternally united after death.[15]

Along with a growing emphasis on domesticity, a new attitude
toward marriage was characteristic of the nineteenth-century family.
By the middle of the nineteenth century, the marriage ceremony was
treated with greater solemnity than had been the case earlier. Church
weddings became more common and more elaborate, and bride-
grooms began to signify the permanence of their love by bestowing
wedding rings on their brides. Within marriage, there was a marked
decline in the formality and deference that had characterized relations
between husbands and wives earlier in eighteenth century. By the end
of the eighteenth century, many spouses had abandoned the earlier
practice of addressing each other as "Mister" and "Mistress." Fewer
husbands addressed their spouses with phrases like "dear Child,"
which betokened patriarchal authority, and wives became more likely
to address their husbands by their first names or to use pet names. In
their correspondence a growing number of husbands openly sought
out their spouses' advice and admitted that they loved and missed
their wives.[16]

Relations between parents and children also became somewhat less
harsh and distant. By the beginning of the nineteenth century, there
is significant evidence that children were increasingly being viewed as

distinct individuals with unique needs. Instead of referring to an infant as "it" or "the baby" or "the little stranger," parents began to refer to newborns by their first names. Stiffly posed portraits depicting children as miniature adults gave way to more romantic depictions of childhood, emphasizing children's playfulness and innocence. Furniture specifically designed for children, painted in pastel colors and decorated with pictures of animals or figures from nursery rhymes, began to be widely produced, reflecting the popular notion of childhood as a time of innocence and playfulness. A declining number of affluent mothers put their newborns out to wet nurses, while the custom of naming newborns after recently deceased siblings disappeared. The appearance of a profusion of toys and books specifically intended for children highlighted the new focus on, and respect for, the child.[17]

Economic Transformations

The early-nineteenth-century spread of a new conception of the family as a private and protected place was closely tied to a broad process of social and economic change that transformed the economic functions of the family. This economic process is usually termed "industrialization," but in fact, changes in the family's economic roles were already under way several decades before the significant growth of factories. This process would eventually deprive married women of earlier "productive" roles and transform them into housewives, prolong the length of childhood and produce a new stage of youth called "adolescence," and create the demographic transition through which families began to reduce their birthrates.[18]

Throughout the seventeenth and eighteenth centuries, more than 90 percent of the population lived on farms, and most farm households were largely self-sufficient. Craftsmen with specialized skills produced the small number of items difficult to make at home, such as hats, iron implements, men's clothing, saddles, and shoes, but most other necessities were produced in the home. Families, sometimes assisted by neighbors, erected their own houses, produced their own food, made their own furniture, dipped their own candles, tanned their own leather, spun their own wool, manufactured their own cloth, and sewed their own garments, but not men's. Even in the Chesapeake and Southern colonies, where from an early date many farms and plantations produced such cash crops as indigo and tobacco, most households were largely self-sufficient in the production of food and clothing.[19]

Inside the home, the husband, the wife, and their older children were all expected to play important productive roles. Typically a father and his elder sons took charge of the fields, while a wife and her daughters took care of dairy cows, the poultry, and spinning, knitting, weaving, and fabricating clothing. The wives of urban craftsmen might also manage the shop, keep accounts, and supervise apprentices. Because production was integrated with familial activity, servants, apprentices, and paid laborers usually lived in their master's house.[20]

The expansion of a market-oriented economy during the eighteenth century reinforced the older conception of the family as a cooperative economic enterprise. The need for a cash income led many households to participate in various "putting-out" systems of production. Urban merchants and village storekeepers supplied individual households with the raw materials to make such articles as thread, cloth, textiles, beer, cigars, and shoes. A wife and her older children might supplement the family budget by spinning yarn, making lace, sewing dresses, or setting up a tavern or inn in their home. Under these circumstances, married women and children had clearly defined economic functions and made a readily measurable contribution to the family economy.[21]

During the first decades of the nineteenth century, however, the family as a largely self-sufficient economic unit began to disappear. Instead of producing most of the items necessary for subsistence, a growing number of farm families began to specialize in the production of grain or cotton and use the cash proceeds they obtained from the sale of crops to buy necessities. Especially in the Northeast, fewer families produced their own food, cut their own clothing, or made their own candles and soap. Handstitching of garments or shoes at home was replaced by factory production using power looms and sewing machines. Economic specialization began to extinguish the domestic industries that had employed large numbers of married women and children. At the same time, an increasing number of apprentices and paid laborers moved out of rooms in their masters' homes into boardinghouses in working-class neighborhoods.[22]

By the middle of the nineteenth-century, the older pattern in which husbands, wives, and children worked together as participants in a common economic enterprise had been replaced by a new domestic division of labor. The middle-class husband was expected to be the breadwinner for the family. Instead of participating in domestic industries, the middle-class wife was expected to devote herself full-time to keeping house and raising children. Psychologically the daily lives of men and women became more separate and specialized. For a growing number of men, the place of work shifted away from the farm or household to counting houses, mills, factories, shops, and offices, where work was defined by wages and a clearly demarcated working day. Women's work, in contrast, was unpaid, unsupervised, and task-oriented. It took place in a segregated sphere of domesticity, which became dissociated from the masculine, more literally productive world of income-earning work. As a result, work and family life came to be viewed as two distinct and separate endeavors.[23]

The displacement of economic partnership from the matrix of family life contributed to a fundamental demographic change: a marked lowering of the birthrate. Before 1800 marriage was followed by a repeated cycle of pregnancy and childbirth. A woman might bear her first child at the age of twenty-three and continue to bear children at two-year intervals until she was forty-two. This twenty-year span of childbearing consumed more than half of a woman's married life, since a typical husband died at the age of forty-six. A woman devoted most of the years of her marriage to productive labor and to bearing or rearing children. As new children arrived, older children were often fostered out as servants or apprentices or sent out on their own on a seasonal basis to work as hired laborers or to attend school. Between 1800 and 1860, a drastically different pattern of family life gradually emerged. By the middle of the nineteenth century, women were bearing fewer children and lengthening the interval between births by birth control. Instead of bearing seven or eight chilren, most women were having five or six. By the end of the century, women had further reduced the number of children born to three or four, spaced them closer together, and ceased childbearing at earlier ages. At the same time, older children were staying at home with their parents longer. Increasingly, child rearing, not childbearing, became the most time-consuming aspect of a woman's life.[24]

The gradual imposition of limits on the birthrate is one of the defining characteristics of the "democratic" family that emerged in early-nineteenth-century America. During the seventeenth and eighteenth centuries, a typical white woman bore seven children, one or two more than her West European counterpart. By the late eighteenth century, before a comparable decline began in most Western European countries, some groups, like the Pennsylvania Quakers, were already making conscious and effective efforts at contraception. In all parts of the United States, fertility had begun a sustained decline by 1810, and by the end of the century, birthrates had been cut in half.[25]

The sharp decline in birthrates is a phenomenon easier to describe than to explain. The drop in fertility was not the result of sudden

improvements in contraceptive devices. The basic birth control techniques used before the Civil War—such as coitus interruptus (withdrawal), douching, and condoms—had been known about in earlier
times but had previously been employed haphazardly and ineffec-
tively. Nor was the imposition of limits on the birthrate a result of
urbanization. Although fertility fell earliest and most rapidly in the
urban areas of the Northeast, the decline in fertility occurred in all
parts of the country—in rural as well as urban areas and in the South
and West as well as the Northeast.[26]

In part the reduction in fertility reflected the growing realization
among parents that in an increasingly commercial and industrial society, children were no longer economic assets who could be productively employed in household industries or bound out as apprentices
or servants. Instead children required significant investment in the
form of education to prepare them for respectable careers and marriages. The emergence of a self-conscious middle class concerned
about social mobility and maintaining an acceptable standard of living encouraged new limits on family size.[27]

The shrinking size of families was not merely a matter of economics; it also related to a more enlightened view of women and children. The drop in fertility reflected the changing relationship between
husbands and wives and the growing concern with child development. So long as women were regarded essentially as chattel and child
rearing as simply a process through which children were taught to
submit to authority, there was little inpetus to reduce the number of
births. But when husbands took an increasing interest in their wives'
welfare and parents showed increasing concern about forming their
children's character and drawing out their latent abilities and potentialities, a reduction in fertility seemed not only desirable but essential.
Smaller families permitted parents to improve the quality of their
child's upbringing by allowing them to invest more time and energy
as well as more financial resources in each child.[28]

By 1831, when Tocqueville visited the United States, demographic,
cultural, and economic changes had converged to produce a new con-
figuration of roles within the middle-class family.[29]

Family Roles

Of all the images associated with the nineteenth-century American
family, none has proved stronger or longer-lasting than the picture of
the bewhiskered Victorian father presiding over his dutiful wife and
submissive children. Here, many believe, was a time when fathers

were Fathers, women were glorified as Victorian housewives and mothers, and children were to be seen but not heard. In fact, the realities of nineteenth-century family life were much more complicated than any stereotype would allow, varying according to class, ethnic group, and region. And yet, like many stereotypes, the public image of the nineteenth-century family—the father as breadwinner, the wife as full-time housewife and mother, the children as dependents—was based on a kernel of reality.[30]

During the late-eighteenth and early-nineteenth centuries, roles within the family were sharply redefined to meet the radically altered requirements of the workplace. The model husband and father was solely responsible for earning the family's livelihood; he was expected to earn the income that supported the family and to provide for his wife and children after his death. The ideal wife and mother devoted her life exclusively to domestic tasks; she was expected to run an efficient household, provide a cultured atmosphere within the home, rear moral sons and daughters, display social grace on public occasions, and offer her husband emotional support. And children, particularly in urban, middle-class homes, were expected to be dutiful dependents who were to devote their childhood and adolescence to learning the skills necessary for the demands of adulthood.[31]

Alexis de Tocqueville likened the differentiation of roles within the family to the broader process of specialization and differentiation taking place in the economy as a whole. In the economic sphere, specialization maximized efficiency and productivity. In the domestic sphere, role differentiation also served the function of efficiency; each family member had a proper "place" that was appropriate to his or her age and gender and contributed in his or her own way to the family's effective functioning. The father earned income outside the family, the wife ran the domestic sphere, and children might help around the house or supplement the family's income by taking on odd jobs. As in a factory, the roles assigned to each family member were interdependent, distinct but complementary.[32]

Today many people believe that the division of roles in the nineteenth-century family represents an ideal. But even in the nineteenth century, the family roles of father, mother, and child were already characterized by a series of latent tensions. Although the democratic family was idealized as a place of peace and a haven from the strains of modern life, it was not immune to internal stress and conflict. From its inception in the latter part of the eighteenth century, the family's roles were characterized by a series of underlying contradictions.[33]

In sharp contrast with the contemporary image of the early-nine-

teenth-century father as the patriarchal head of his household, nineteenth-century observers emphasized the relative weakness of paternal
authority in America. Foreign travelers and native commentators
shared the opinion that the paternal role was characterized by an
informality and permissiveness unknown in contemporary Europe or
in America itself earlier in time.[34]

During the seventeenth century, it had been an almost unquestioned premise that the father, as head of his household, had a right
to expect respect and obedience from his wife and children. A father's
authority over his family, servants, and apprentices was simply one
link in the great chain of being, the line of authority descending from
God. Fatherhood was associated with sovereignty. A king was the
father of his country, individual communitites were governed by town
fathers, and God was the father of all his children. This ideal of patriarchal authority found vivid expression in the realm of law. The prevailing attitude was that a father had an absolute right to custody of
and guardianship over his offspring and legal control over the property and earnings of his dependents.[35]

The centrality of the father's position within the colonial household was reflected in child-rearing manuals, which—up until the middle of the eighteenth century—were addressed to fathers and not to
mothers, and also in family portraits, which, prior to 1775, uniformly
showed the father standing above his seated family.[36]

By the middle of the nineteenth century, the scope of the father's
authority had, to a limited degree, been constricted—a transition
clearly evident in art, with family portraits, for the first time, showing
all family members on the same plane, and in child-rearing manuals,
which began to be addressed to mothers, not to fathers. In the realm
of law, the father's prerogatives began to be restricted as well. As early
as the 1820s, married women began to gain legal control over their
own personal property and earnings and the right to enter into legal
contracts and to bring lawsuits. A number of states gave courts discretion to grant mothers custody of younger children. The father's role
within the household was also circumscribed. Fathers increasingly
were expected to acquiesce in the early independence of their sons,
and child-rearing experts openly criticized those who persisted in med-
dling in their children's lives after they had grown up.[37]

The ability of a father to transmit his "status position" to his children declined. By the early nineteenth century, families were finding
it increasingly difficult to pass on their status by bequeathing land or
a family craft to their offspring. The practice of partible inheritance,
in which the paternal estate was divided into equal portions for all

the children, made it difficult for farm or artisan families to pass on farms or family shops over time. An increase in opportunities for non-agricultural work, and the replacement of land as a primary medium of value by more portable forms of capital, further reduced the dependence of grown sons upon their parents.[38]

As the father's economic role changed, a new set of images of fatherhood began to emerge. Instead of referring to a father's sovereign right to rule his household, the late- eighteenth- and early-nineteenth-century literature on the family spoke about a father's paternal duties. Foremost among these was responsibility for his family's economic well-being. But a father was expected to be more than an economic provider. He also had a duty to provide love and affection to his wife and moral and religious training to his children, and he had ultimate responsibility for putting down disobedience or disrespect on the part of his offspring. The father's authority, which had once rested on control of land and craft skills, had become increasingly symbolic. Where the mother represented nurturance, selflessness, and devotion to others, the father was the symbol of public and external conceptions of authority. He was referred to as a "moral force" or a "governor" because his role was to prepare a child for a life of disciplined independence.[39]

The early nineteenth century witnessed a radical redefinition of women's roles. A profusion of women's magazines, novels, poems, and sermons glorified the American woman as purer than man, more given to sacrifice and service to others, and untainted by the competitive struggle for wealth and power. This set of ideas, known as the "cult of true womanhood," extolled the American wife and mother as the personification of four primary virtues: piety, submissiveness, purity, and domesticity. A torrent of articles with titles such as "Woman, Man's Best Friend" and "The Wife, Source of Comfort and Spring of Joy" depicted women as inherently more virtuous and less selfish than men. This conception of womanhood was sharply at odds with the image that had held sway earlier. Well into the eighteenth century, womanhood was associated with deviousness, sexual voraciousness, emotional inconstancy, and physical and intellectual inferiority. Now, in a sudden reversal of opinion, there was a growing consensus that only women, through their uplifting influence over the home and children, could be a source of moral values and a counterforce to commercialism and self-interest.[40]

Years of revolutionary upheaval had given women unprecedented opportunities to deal with matters of finance, to operate farms, to take part in economic boycotts and petition campaigns, and to obtain an education (four-fifths of women could not write their names in 1700; four-fifths were literate a century later). A new ideal of "republican motherhood" celebrated the woman who served the country by shaping her child's character and instilling a capacity for virtue in her offspring. The experience of revolutionary ferment and republican fervor had contributed its share to a new conception of women's role.[41]

At the same time, during the first decade of the nineteenth-century, unmarried women between the ages of fourteen and twenty-seven received unprecedented opportunities to work outside the home as schoolteachers and as mill girls or to remain at home in their parents' increasingly affluent households. A growing number of women achieved leadership positions organizing religious revivals, engaging in missionary work, establishing orphanages and almshouses, and editing religious publications. Many middle-class women achieved a public voice in such reform movements as temperance and antislavery and succeeded in communicating with a wider public as journalists and authors. Rising living standards, increased access to education, and unprecedented opportunities to work outside the home increased women's expectations for self-fulfillment and contributed to a new outlook on marriage.[42]

Tocqueville and other European commentators were struck by a seeming paradox in American women's lives: Compared to their European counterparts, young American women experienced a high degree of independence and freedom. They had a much greater opportunity to attend school, to earn an independent income, to travel without a chaperone, and to choose a spouse free from parental interference. But the lives of American wives seemed more restricted. Their daily lives were largely circumscribed "within the narrow circle of domestic interests and duties" beyond which they were forbidden to step. European travelers were struck by the rigid social division between married men and women; they noted, for example, that at social gatherings women were compelled by public opinion to separate from men after dinner.[43]

This discrepancy between the relative independence of girlhood and the "extreme dependence" and heavy duties of wifehood would exert a direct effect on women's attitudes toward marriage. During the colonial period, marriage was regarded as a social obligation and an economic necessity, and few women or men failed to marry. But beginning in the mid-eighteenth century, the number of unmarried men and women increased and a growing number of women elected to remain single. Marriage became a far more deliberate act than it had been in the past. It was an enormous responsibility. As Catharine Beecher, an early-nineteenth-century educator and author of the nation's most popular book on household management, put it, "the success of democratic institutions" depended "upon the intellectual and moral character of the mass of people," and "the formation of the moral and intellectual character of the young is committed mainly to the female hand. The mother forms the character of the future man . . . the wife sways the heart, whose energies may turn for good or for evil the destinies of a nation."[44]

As new emotional and psychological expectations arose about marriage, marriage became a more difficult transition point than it had been in the past. The transition from the role of girl to the role of wife was so difficult that many young women experienced a "marriage trauma" before taking or failing to take the step. Many prospective brides who did eventually marry hesitated to leave the relative independence they had enjoyed in girlhood. In their correspondence many young women expressed fears about the loss of their liberty—often linking marriage with death or loss of self—and foreboding about the dangers of childbearing—often omitting children from their fantasies of an ideal marriage.[45]

After marriage a growing number of women expected to take a more active role in running the household than their mothers or grandmothers had and expected their husbands to be more than providers. Congeniality, companionship, and affection assumed a greater importance within marriage. Novelist Harriet Beecher Stowe, for example, chastized her husband repeatedly for hiding himself behind his daily newspapers and failing to pay sufficient attention to her needs, problems, and interests. In a letter written after eleven years of marriage, she contrasted the "unnumbered tenderness[es]" her husband had exhibited in the early years of their marriage with "the morbid brooding & jaundiced eye on my faults" he had since shown. She proceeded to remind her husband that such exacting criticism had no place within a true marriage. "You know as well as I," she wrote, "when both parties begin to stand for their rights & to suspect the other of selfish exaction there is an end of every delicate & refined affection & a beginning of coarse and brutal selfishness."[46]

Stowe was not alone in her expectation that marriage offer mutuality, companionship, love, and understanding. A growing number of women expected men to invest more time and emotional energies in their families. During the first half of the nineteenth century, centers of segregated male entertainment, such as taverns or houses of prosti-

tution, came under attack from militant reformers. Temperence reformers denounced alcohol on the grounds that it encouraged husbands to spend their time in saloons away from their families, to abuse
their wives and children, and to squander their family's financial resources, while Magdalen societies and Moral Reform societies crusaded against prostitution as a threat to the family.

By the middle of the nineteenth century, the expectations of marriage had grown far more demanding, and it was increasingly perceived not as a union in which a man provided financial support in
exchange for domestic service from his wife but as a relationship in
which two people lived together for the sake of each other's emotional
well-being.[47]

By 1830 a new conception of childhood began to emerge. The earlier pattern of children temporarily leaving and returning home began
to give way to a lengthening period of residence within the parental
household. Instead of sending their children off to work as servants
or apprentices at the age of eight or nine or permitting their children
to be hired out for months at a time, a growing number of parents,
particularly in the Northeastern middle class, began to keep their sons
and daughters home well into their teens and even their twenties. As
the economic role of children began to shift from producer to consumer, childhood began to be viewed as a distinct stage of growth
and development in which a young person was prepared for eventual
emergence into adulthood.[48]

Techniques of child rearing changed too. There was a growing consensus that the object of child rearing was not to break a child's will
through intense moral or physical pressure but to shape his or her
character in preparation for the temptations of life. The primary purpose of child rearing became the internalization of moral prohibitions,
behavioral standards, and a capacity for self-government that would
prepare a child for the outside world. According to innumerable
guidebooks, tracts, and domestic novels dealing with the "art and
responsibility of family government," the formation of character was
best achieved not through physical punishment or rigorous instruction in moral and religious precepts, but by emotional nurture, parental love, and the force of parental example. Obedience remained a
primary goal, but a growing number of experts believed that techniques designed to provoke guilt, such as confining children to their
rooms, withholding love, or expressing parental disapproval, would
be more effective in securing obedience than would physical punishment. As one popular writer put it, "Whatever the privation or other
token of your displeasure may be, the delinquent must, if possible, be

made to feel, that he has brought it upon himself. . . . " This writer considered exclusion of a child from the parents' presence an excellent way to teach him or her to assess the consequences of acts and to suppress instinctual desires, especially when accompanied by some such remark as, "Much as I love you, I cannot bear to see you, till you are sorry for what you have done, and will promise amendment."[49]

According to a growing number of writers, child rearing was a task for which women were uniquely suited. A reason for the shift from father to mother as primary parent was the belief that children were more effectively governed by persuasion than coercion and by rewards than by punishments (a belief that ties in with the growing conviction among laissez faire economists that laborers could be encouraged to work harder by rewarding rather than penalizing them). Women were perceived as more likely than men to entice obedience from their offspring. Physical discipline or corporal punishment, the province of fathers, was increasingly viewed as producing at best outward conformity; at worst it provoked obstinacy or a sense of bitterness. But persuasion held out the hope of bringing about a basic change in a child's character. The emphasis placed on moral influence tended to enhance the maternal role in child rearing, since mothers were believed to have a special talent for instilling self-control. Whereas paternal authority was associated with force and fear, female influence connoted love and affection.[50]

By the middle of the nineteenth century, the realities of a middle-class upbringing differed dramatically from the pattern prevalent half a century before. Instead of shifting back and forth between their parents' homes and work experiences as members of other households, a growing proportion of children were continuing to live with their parents into their late teens and twenties. One justification for this new practice of keeping children at home longer in life was the growing belief that "adolescence" (previously a rarely used term) was a particularly unsettled phase of life during which children were deeply in need of parental protection and supervision. Drawing on Rousseau, a growing number of educators and advice writers argued that the years surrounding puberty were a period of rapid physical growth and moral, sexual, and psychological upheaval during which youngsters were particularly vulnerable to the corruptions and temptations of the adult world. This was no time to send youngsters out on their own. As one expert put it, "Early departure from the homestead is a moral crisis that many of our youth do not show themselves able to meet. It comes at a tender age, when judgment is weakest and passion and impulse strongest.[51]

According to an emerging consensus, only a gradual process of maturation within the protected confines of the home could ensure a
smooth transition to adulthood. The prolongation of childhood dependency offered a further advantage: It encouraged parents to keep
their children in school longer, where they could learn skills increasingly necessary in order to enter the professions or business.[52]

As more and more young people over the age of fourteen remained
at home with their parents, emotional and psychological stresses, previously little noted, became more common in the middle-class home.
Foremost among these were adolescent struggles with their parents.
Middle-class children saw their financial dependence on their parents
prolonged and intensified, in part because of an increase in the duration of formal schooling and in part because of rising living standards,
which greatly increased parental expenditures on children's upbringing. Although a child might be anxious for the responsibilities of
adulthood, he or she remained subordinate to the parents. While
lengthened residence within the parental home provided a basis for
increased emotional intimacy between parents and children, it could
also be a source of potential strain.[53]

By the middle of the nineteenth century, childhood and adolescence were beginning to be defined in terms recognizable today—special stages of life, with their own unique needs and developmental
problems. Emotionally and financially, middle-class children were
dependent much longer on their parents than had been their eighteenth-century counterparts, and yet, at the same time, they were also
spending larger and larger portions of their daily lives away from
adults in specialized age-segregated institutions like Sunday schools
and common schools. Adulthood and childhood had been sharply
differentiated into two radically separate times of life.[54]

Family Law

The changes that took place in family ideals and roles were reflected in
the legal realm as well. During the years before the Civil War, in response to the nation's changing conceptions of the family, marriage,
and sex roles, a fundamental revision of family law took place. A companionate conception of marriage demanded that husbands and wives
be able to terminate unions that were not "true marriages" and that
married women be given limited control over their property and earnings. The veneration of women's child-rearing role required that
women be given new rights of custody over their children.[55]

During the early decades of the nineteenth century, more and more people came to believe that if the primary objects of marriage were the promotion of personal happiness and the welfare of society, then divorce and remarriage were justified in instances of adultery, physical abuse, or failure of a marriage partner to fulfill his or her proper role. Before the nineteenth century, divorce was exceedingly difficult to obtain and the number of divorces granted was minuscule. Massachusetts records reveal that it granted only twenty-seven divorces in the period it was a colony. In a number of colonies, especially those in the South, divorce was unavailable, and in those colonies where legal divorce was possible, it could only be on the limited grounds of adultery, nonsupport, and abandonment or prolonged absence (usually after a period of seven years). Even in colonies that made provision for divorce, the law did not generally permit an injured spouse to remarry. Remarriage was only allowed in instances in which the marriage could be annulled (such as impotence or bigamy); otherwise the spouse could only obtain a legal separation. In many colonies divorce was only available through a special act of the colonial legislature. Given the difficulty of obtaining a divorce, unhappy couples were more likely to separate formally; in eighteenth-century Massachusetts, only 220 couples divorced, but 3,300 notices of separation were printed in the newspapers.[56]

In the early nineteenth century, the availability of divorce as a remedy to intolerable marriages began to expand as states gave courts jurisdiction over divorce petitions. In the 1820s a growing number of reformers argued that the grounds for divorce should be expanded to include physical cruelty, willful desertion, intemperance, and temperamental incompatibility on the grounds that removing the barrier of indissolubility would promote individual happiness and discourage adultery. By the 1830s a number of states, led by Indiana, had adopted permissive divorce laws. Connecticut, for example, allowed a divorce to be granted for any misconduct that "permanently destroys the happiness of the petitioner and defeats the purposes of the marriage relation." But even in the states that did not liberalize divorce laws, the number of divorces began to rise after 1840. In 1867 the number of divorces granted in a single year reached 10,000.[57]

Of much greater importance than divorce in altering the position of women in the nineteenth-century American family was the adoption of laws guaranteeing married women's property rights. At the beginning of the nineteenth century, the basic principle guiding American law was that a husband was the natural guardian of his wife's interests. Her property, earnings, and services became his on marriage. A married woman was prohibited from bringing legal suits or being sued, from making contracts, and from owning property individually. She was not even permitted to control her own wages. By the Civil War, however, a crack had been made in the defenses of male prerogatives. Many states, beginning with those of the Deep South, adopted married women's property acts, which permitted married women to control their own property and earnings.[58]

The new domestic ideology was also recognized in legal changes involving child custody in divorces. English common law, on which most American law was based, had given fathers almost unlimited rights to the custody of their children, but by the 1820s in the United States, the growing stress on the special child-rearing abilities of women led judges in all parts of the country to limit fathers' custody rights. In determining custody, courts began to look at the "happiness and welfare" of the child and the "fitness" and "competence" of the parents. As early as 1860, a number of states had adopted the "tender year" rule, according to which children who were below the age of puberty were placed in their mother's care unless she proved unworthy of that responsibility.[59]

Banners, barricades, and bayonets are often thought of as the stuff of revolutions, but sometimes the most important revolutions take place more quietly—and so successfully that when they are over, few even realize that they ever took place. Such was the transformation that took place in American family life between 1770 and 1830—as profound and far-reaching as the political revolution then reshaping American politics. This period witnessed the emergence of new patterns of marriage, based primarily on companionship and affection; a new division of domestic roles that assigned the wife to care full-time for the children and to maintain the home; a new conception of childhood that looked at children not as small adults but as special creatures who needed attention, love, and time to mature; and a growing acceptance of birth control in order to produce fewer children.

In many respects the new patterns of middle-class family life that emerged in the late eighteenth and early nineteenth centuries represented a clear advance over family life in the past. A marked decline in childhood and adulthood mortality meant that family life was much less likely to be disrupted by the premature death of a child or a parent. Lower birthrates meant that parents were able to invest more material resources and emotional energies in their offspring. Rising living standards and a shrinking family size allowed many middle-class women to raise their expectations for self-fulfillment.

There can also be little doubt that the new patterns of family life were well adapted to the changing conditions of society. The inward-turning, child-centered middle-class family was well matched to the object of teaching children the complex tasks demanded by an increasingly urban and commercial society. Within the home, parents would instill skills that children would need as adults: qualities of independence and self-direction, a capacity for self-discipline, an ability to suppress instinctual desires, and sensitivity to the needs and feelings of others. The sharp separation of the husband's and wife's roles fitted well with the process of economic specialization that was separating "domestic" and "productive" tasks and taking production and the father out of the home. Finally, this new style of family was well suited to providing men with an emotional haven from the world of work.[60]

And yet, for all its many benefits, this new style of family life also involved certain costs. The patterns of family life that began to appear in the late eighteenth century often proved in practice to be a source of conflict and personal unhappiness. One underlying source of strain lay in the disparity between women's rising expectations for self-fulfillment and the isolation of married women within a separate domestic sphere. Young women were raised in a society that placed a high value on independence. Growing numbers of women attended school, earned independent incomes as mill girls, teachers, and household servants, and were allowed to manage courtship largely free of parental interference. On marriage, however, a woman was expected to "sacrifice . . . her pleasures to her duties" and derive her deepest satisfactions from homemaking and childbearing and rearing. The latent contradiction between woman's preparation for self-fulfillment and her role as the family's key nurturing figure often resulted in enormous personal tension, sometimes manifested in the classic nineteenth-century neurosis of hysteria.[61]

Another source of tension derived from the increasing isolation of the family. By the early nineteenth century, the American family had been deprived of a range of traditional economic, social, and ideological supports. The family had lost its economic autonomy and was increasingly dependent on the vagaries of the marketplace. Parental authority had lost the reinforcement of local churches and courts and a system of apprenticeship. The middle-class family existed in a society that rewarded independence and self-reliance and tended to isolate domestic ideals—deference, obedience, and loyalty—from broader economic and political values. Yet, at the very time that the family had been detached from traditional economic roles and external sup-

ports, it had acquired awesome new emotional and psychological responsibilities. It was charged with primary responsibility for properly
rearing children and providing its members with emotional sustenance. Even before the Civil War, men and women of diverse persua-
sions agreed that the family should be a source of affection, nurturance, and companionship. Already the family was beginning to
acquire an overload of expectations it often proved incapable of meeting—a failure apparent in the gradually rising divorce rates.[62]

One more source of stress grew out of the prolongation of childhood dependence. Middle-class children left home, married, and
entered the professions at later ages than had their eighteenth-century
counterparts. The erosion of traditional productive roles for young
people within the household further sharpened the split between
childhood and adulthood. It exacerbated the difficulties children
faced in asserting independence in the home and compounded the
difficulties they faced in transforming childhood emotional bonds
into acceptable adult forms. Prolonged residence with parents provided the basis for a previously unimaginable degree of emotional
closeness between children and parents, but it also increased dependence and resentment.[63]

While this new domestic ideology became prevalent especially in
the northeastern United States, there were notable utopian experiments which explicitly rejected the tenets of middle-class family life.
Their critiques of conventional family life indicate some of the real
problems confronting early-nineteenth-century families. By the 1840s
and 1850s, hundreds of religious and secular communities in Massachusetts, New York, Ohio, Indiana, Tennessee, and Texas experimented with alternate forms of familial and sexual practices. While
some of these efforts were rooted in a religious faith that Christ's
return was imminent and that the righteous should prepare for his
reign by living according to biblical principles, and others were the
product of an Enlightenment faith in reason, all were united by a
belief that the nuclear family posed a threat to a harmonious society.
Utopian critics of the middle-class family argued that conventional
conceptions of sex roles stultified women's intellect and constricted
their development; that monogamous marriage distracted individuals
from broader social obligations; and that children needed to have
contact with more than two adults and to take part in the world of
work.[64]

Many communities tried to emancipate women from traditional
household and child-rearing responsibilities and to elevate them to

positions of equality with men. A number of these experimental societies, such as the Shakers, the Rappites, and (for a time) the Separatists at Zoar, practiced celibacy; other communities retained "traditional" families while adopting liberal divorce practices and communal childrearing; a third group experimented with more communal forms of marriage and sexuality, such as polygamy, complex marriage, eugenics, and free love.

The most revolutionary early-nineteenth-century experiment in restructing family life was Mormon polygamy. In the early 1840s, Joseph Smith, the founder of the Mormon church, declared that he received a revelation justifying polygamy as a way of overcoming the extreme individualism in American life and reestablishing the patriarchal Old Testament family. Critics denounced polygamy as "a slavery which debases and degrades womanhood, motherhood and family," but in fact polygamy was not envisioned as a sexually licentious arrangement. It served the practical social function of absorbing the many single and widowed women who migrated to the Mormon Zion in Utah and of increasing the Mormon birthrate. Contrary to popular belief, polygamy was not widely practiced. No more than 10 to 20 percent of Mormon households involved plural marriages, and two-thirds of these unions involved a man and two wives.[65]

Respectable middle-class Americans, shocked by Mormon polygamy, the growth of urban prostitution, and the philosophy and practice of free love, insisted ever more strongly on the new ideals of domesticity and stigmatized families that failed to conform to these new domestic ideals as deviant and disorganized. Emphasizing purity, romantic love, and the glorification of motherhood and childhood, they sought to sustain moral values in the face of an alarming increase in urban density, diversity, novelty, and vice.[66]

In his appraisal of the transformations that had taken place in the American family, Alexis de Tocqueville had little doubt that the changes had contributed to human happiness. According to him, while democracy had loosened traditional social ties, it had strengthened the natural bonds of affection within the family. Ironically, however, the privacy and isolation of the "democratic" family—which Tocqueville regarded as the source of intimacy and affection between family members—could also prove, in less pleasant circumstances, to be bases for frustration, conflict, and unhappiness.

A black couple in Virginia. Photograph by Frances B.
Johnston. Courtesy of the Museum of Modern Art, New York.

CHAPTER IV

The Shaping
of the Afro-American Family

SHORTLY after the Civil War, a Northern visitor asked a freedman if his master had been kind. "Kind!" the freedman replied. "I was dat man's slave; and he sold my wife, and he sold my two chill'en. . . . Kind! yes, he gib me corn enough, and he gib me pork enough, and he neber give me one lick wid de whip, but whar's my wife?—whar's my chill'en?[1]

According to early-nineteenth-century abolitionists, the "worst abuse of the system of slavery [was] its outrage upon the family." Slavery, critics of the institution argued, devastated black family life. Slave sale separated husbands from wives and parents from children. Slave masters undermined the authority of slave parents. Sexual exploitation, slave breeding, and illegitimacy thrived on Southern plantations.[2]

And yet, despite the frequent breakup of marriages and families by sale, Afro-Americans managed to forge strong and durable family and kinship ties within the institution of slavery. Despite legal prohibitions on slave marriages, most slaves established de facto arrangements that were often stable over long periods of time. In spite of the dissolution of many marriages by sale, most slaves lived in two-parent households headed by a father and a mother. Ties to an immediate family stretched outward to an involved network of extended kin. In large measure because of the strength and flexibility of their kinship ties, black Americans were able to sustain themselves despite the psychologically debilitating effects of discrimination, material privation, and physical violence. Indeed, the kinship system developed under slavery would continue to serve positive functions for poorer rural and urban blacks well into the twentieth century.

The nation's first census in 1790 showed that 750,000 blacks lived in the United States, nine-tenths of them as slaves, accounting for a fifth of the population. By 1820 there were approximately 1,500,000 slaves in the United States, and by 1860 the slave population had climbed to nearly 4,000,000. During the last years of the eighteenth century and the first years of the nineteenth, at the same time that the Northeastern middle class was developing the family patterns that Tocqueville called the "democratic family," black Americans just a generation or two after enslavement were creating their own distinctive Afro-American system of family and kinship that helped them survive the dehumanizing effects of slavery. Their family system represented one of a number of alternatives to the middle-class family ideal that was gaining influence in pre–Civil War America.

The roots of the Afro-American family were planted in the mid- and late eighteenth century, when slaves combined African and American cultural beliefs and practices into a distinctive Afro-American system of family and kinship with its own rules of courtship, sexual behavior, and marriage. It was during the forty-year period between 1740 and 1780 that more than half of all Africans brought to the American colonies arrived. Few were bought by wealthy plantation families. Most were purchased by whites of lesser means—small planters, tavernkeepers, sailors, horse traders, small-time speculators, and minor government officials—many of whom had themselves first come to the American colonies as voluntary or involuntary bound servants. As a result, most eighteenth-century Africans and first-generation Afro-Americans did not live on large plantations with lavish big houses but on relatively small farms with fewer than twenty slaves.[3]

On these small farms, slaves created their own distinctive Afro-American kinship system, largely free of interference from white masters. The system they developed was not simply a continuation of African patterns nor was it merely an imitation of the patterns typical of Southern white families. Rather, it was an adaptation of African and English beliefs and practices to the specific circumstances of enslavement. The distinctiveness of slave family practices is apparent in an absence of first-cousin marriages, which slaves regarded as incestuous. Marriages between first cousins, common among Southern whites, were generally prohibited by West African peoples. American slaves perpetuated this West African custom.[4]

A taboo against first-cousin marriages was one indication of the importance that slaves, even in the eighteenth century, attached to the extended kinship group. Strong feelings of kinship were also evident in naming practices. To sustain a sense of family identity over time, slave parents often named their children after parents, grandparents, recently deceased relatives, and other kin. For example, a Maryland slave known as Old Anthony named his daughter Molly for his own mother. When Molly had a son, she named him Isaac, after the child's great-great-grandfather. Slaves also passed down family names to their children, usually the name of an ancestor's owner rather than their current owner's.[5]

Over the course of the eighteenth century, debt, the death of a master, or merely the prospect of economic gain led many slaveowners to separate slave families. But family destruction and dispersal did not erode family and kinship ties. Instead, the breakup of slave families created extended kinship networks stretching across whole counties—networks slaves drew on in times of need. The extended kinship network played a particularly important role in helping slaves adapt to family breakup. Whenever children were sold to neighboring plantations, grandparents, aunts, uncles, and cousins often took on the functions of parents. When blood relatives were not present, strangers cared for and protected children. Slave parents taught their children to call all adult slaves "aunt" and "uncle" and to refer to all younger slaves as "brother" and "sister." In this way slave culture taught young people that they were members of a broader community in which all slaves, whether related or not, had mutual obligations and responsibilities.[6]

The strength of the slave family is nowhere more evident than in the advertisements eighteenth-century slaveowners posted for runaway slaves. The advertisements reveal that apart from physical punishment, the attempt to find relatives was the major reason why slaves fled their masters' plantations. Over a third of all such advertisements indicate that fugitives left an owner to visit a spouse, a child, or other relatives.[7]

Despite the oppressions of slavery, the stable two-parent nuclear family was the norm among pre–Civil War black Americans. Most slaves married and lived with the same spouse until death, and most slave children grew up in households containing both a slave father and a slave mother. This was true despite the fact that slave marriages had no legal sanction, that many slave owners allowed slave husbands and wives to separate freely, and that owners dissolved nearly one marriage in six by sale.[8]

To say that stable two-parent households predominated under slavery is not to imply that slavery did not inflict severe hardships on slave family life. Children were frequently sold away from parents, and husbands and wives were often torn apart. During the Civil War, nearly 20 percent of ex-slaves reported than an earlier marriage had been terminated by "force." A letter written by a Georgia slave named Abream Scriven in 1858, after he had been sold away from his family, suggests the deep anguish caused by the forced breakup of slave families: "Give my love to my dear father and mother and tell them good bye for me. . . . My dear wife for you and all my children my pen cannot express the grief I feel to be parted from you. I remain your true husband until death."[9]

Children were even more likely to be sold away from their parents than husbands were to be sold away from their wives. The sale of teenagers was particularly common; but even young children were auctioned away from their loved ones. Records from the New Orleans slave market—the South's largest—indicate that nearly 10 percent of all sales were of children twelve years or younger. Fewer than 1 percent of these young children were likely to be orphans. Nancy Gardner, a former slave, remembered what it was like to be sold as a child: "Well, dey took us on up dere to Memphis and we was sold jest like cattle. Dey sold me and ma together and dey sold pa and de boys together. Dey was sent to Mississippi and we was sent to Alabama."[10]

The threat of family breakup hung over the head of every slave family. Over the course of a thirty-five-year lifetime, the average slave had a fifty-fifty chance of being sold at least once and was likely to witness the sale of at least several members of his or her immediate family.[11]

Even when marriages were not broken by sale, slave husbands and wives often resided on separate farms or plantations and were owned by different individuals. On large plantations one slave father in three had a different owner than his wife and could only visit his family at his master's discretion. On smaller holdings, divided ownership was even more common. A former South Carolina slave described the hardships that slave spouses faced when they lived on separate plantations: "A man dat had a wife off de place, see little peace of happiness. He could see de wife once a week, on a pass, and jealously kep' him 'stracted de balance of de week, if he love her very much." Some slave fathers tried to visit their families without their owners' permission. If caught, they faced severe punishment. Miller Barber, whose parents lived five miles apart, recalled what happened to his father when he was caught visiting his family: "Patrollers catch him way up de chimney hidin' one night; they stripped him right befo' mammy and give him thirty-nine lashes, wid her cryin' and hollerin' louder than he did."[12]

The typical farm or plantation was so small that it was difficult for many slaves to find a spouse at all. As one ex-slave put it, men "had a hell of a time getting a wife during slavery." One indication of the difficulty slaves faced in establishing a "normal" family life was the large number of slave marriages with unusual age combinations. Nearly two-fifths of the marriages registered by slaves in Alabama and Mississippi in 1864 and 1865 involved a husband more than ten years older than his wife.[13]

Other obstacles stood in the way of an independent family life. Many slaves had to share their single-room cabins with relatives and others who were not related to them. On larger plantations food was cooked in a common kitchen and young children were cared for in a communal nursery while their parents worked in the fields. Even on model plantations, children were taken from their parents and sent to live in separate cabins between the ages of seven and ten.[14]

Slavery severely circumscribed the authority of slave parents. One ex-slave recalled being whipped "because I said to missis, 'My mother sent me.' We were not allowed to call our mammies 'mother.' It made it come too near the way of the white folks." Slave children quickly learned that the prohibition against refering to their own mothers as "mother" was only one way that parental authority was limited. Nearly every slave child went through an experience similar to one recalled by a young South Carolina slave named Jacob Stroyer. Jacob was being trained as a jockey. His trainer beat him regularly, for no apparent reason. Jacob appealed to his father for help, but his father simply said to work harder, "for I cannot do anything for you." When Jacob's mother argued with the trainer, she was whipped for her efforts. From this episode Jacob learned a critical lesson: that the ability of slave parents to help their own children was sharply limited.[15]

Despite the constraints imposed by slavery, slave parents succeeded in holding their families together and providing their children with love and wisdom. By raising vegetables on small garden plots and hunting small game, slave families asserted their independence. Slave fathers communicated a sense of competence by passing on craft skills to their sons. Through the teachings of folklore and religion, slave parents gave their children the will and skills necessary to endure slavery and transmitted a sense of history, morality, and identity.[16]

Each slave family passed through a series of clearly defined phases or family life stages. The family life cycle began with courtship and marriage. Men initiated courtship but could only marrry after securing the permission of the slaveowner. Although Southern state laws denied slaves the legal right to contract marriages, slaves nevertheless held ceremonies that revealed the seriousness with which they regarded married life. Many slaves had their weddings performed by black or white preachers, and thousands of slaves had church weddings. As many as two-fifths of all Episcopal weddings in Alabama, Georgia, Louisiana, Mississippi, North Carolina, South Carolina, and Virginia in 1860 involved slaves.[17]

Slaves celebrated marriages by holding revelries during which the couple would ritually jump over a broomstick. Many masters marked off the wedding ceremony by declaring a holiday and giving the married couple a separate cabin and a gift of household goods or a cash bonus. Yet, even during these joyous occasions, the vulnerability of slave marriages was grimly apparent. Slave wedding ceremonies often referred to the contingent nature of the marriage bond. As one slave noted, "Dey neber would say . . . 'what God done jined, cain't no man pull asunder.'" One slave preacher in Kentucky married brides and grooms with the words: "until death or distance do you part."[18]

The next stage of slave family life was devoted to childbearing and child rearing. Around the age of twenty or twenty-one, either shortly before marriage or soon afterward, a slave woman would bear the first of six or seven children. She might then have to face the loss of one or more of her young children; more than a third failed to reach the age of ten.[19]

Around the age of six, slave children were inducted into the labor force—a transition symbolically marked off by a change in clothing. Instead of wearing shapeless knee-length smocks known as "split-tail shirts," boys began to wear pants or breechcloths and girls, short petticoats. Young boys and girls helped to spin thread, pick seeds from cotton, churn butter, gather eggs, pluck chickens, and light fires. Young girls might sweep and milk cows, while young boys might chop wood, hoe weeds and fetch water. Between the ages of seven and ten, the children left their parents' cabin and went to live in a barracks-like structure with other unmarried young people.[20]

Relatively few slaves reached old age. In 1850 just 10 percent of slaves were fifty or older. Slave women too old to work in the field prepared meals for other slaves, cared for slave children, nursed the sick, or worked as seamstresses. Elderly men were put in charge of livestock, cared for farm implements, or served as gardeners or household servants.[21]

Deprivation and physical hardship were the hallmarks of life under slavery, and slaves lived in conditions roughly comparable to those of the lowest-paid manual laborers in the poorest urban slums of the Northeastern United States and Western Europe. Although the material conditions of slave life improved greatly in the nineteenth century, slaves were much more likely than Southern whites to die prematurely, to suffer malnutrition or dietary deficiencies, and to lose a child in infancy.

A slave's life expectancy under slavery was short—just twenty-eight to thirty-six years, or up to twelve years less than that of American whites. The infant mortality rate among slaves was twice as high as among white newborns.[22]

The slaves' diet was meager and monotonous, consisting largely of cornmeal and salt pork or bacon. Only rarely did slaves drink milk or eat fresh meat or vegetables. This diet provided enough bulk calories to ensure that slaves had sufficient strength and energy to work as productive field hands. But it did not provide adequate nutrition, and as a result slaves suffered from vitamin and protein deficiencies and such ailments as beriberi, kwashiorkor, and pellagra.[23]

The physical conditions in which slave families lived were truly miserable. Lacking privies, they had to urinate and defecate in the cover of nearby bushes. Lacking any sanitary disposal of garbage, slaves lived surrounded by decaying food. Chickens, dogs, and pigs lived next to the slave quarters, and in consequence animal feces contaminated the area, attracting swarms of flies. Such squalor contributed to high rates of dysentery, typhus, diarrhea, hepatitis, typhoid fever, and intestinal worms.[24]

Slave quarters were cramped and crowded. The typical cabin—a single, windowless room, with a chimney constructed of clay and twigs and a floor made of dirt or of planks resting on the ground— ranged in size from ten feet square up to twenty-one feet square. These small cabins often housed five, six, or more occupants. On some plantations slaves lived in single-family cabins; on others two or more families shared the same cabin. On the largest plantations, unmarried men and women were sometimes lodged together in dormitory-like structures.[25]

Slave housing was ill protected from the elements. One slave said that "In the winter time we had to stop in the cracks in the wall and in the floor with old rags and pieces of paper. This kept the wind out." Josiah Henson, the Kentucky slave who served as the model for Harriet Beecher Stowe's Uncle Tom, described his cabin this way: "We lodged in log huts. . . . Wooden floors were an unknown luxury. In a single room were huddled, like cattle, ten or a dozen persons, men, women, and children. . . . There were neither bedsteads nor furniture. . . . The wind whistled and the rain and snow blew in through the cracks, and the damp earth soaked in the moisture till the floor was muddy as a pig sty." The crowded, drafty, poorly heated conditions of the slave quarters in turn contributed to the prevalence of respiratory diseases, mumps, measles, rheumatic fever, diphtheria, whooping cough, and chicken pox.[26]

But of all the evils associated with slavery, abolitionists most bitterly denounced the sexual abuse suffered by slave women. Abolitionists claimed that slaveholders adopted deliberate policies to breed slaves for sale—"like oxen for the shambles"—and kept "black harems" and sexually exploited slave women. Abolitionists also charged that sexual life under slavery was casual and promiscuous.[27]

Some aspects of the abolitionist indictment of the sexual side of slavery were true. The sexual abuse of slave women was a problem of enormous severity. The autobiographies of runaway slaves provide graphic examples of sexual abuse. Henry Bibb, for instance, recorded that a slave trader forced his wife to become a prostitute, and Solomon Northrup declared that his owner took a slave woman as his concubine. One ex-slave remembered that his master, Sam Watkins, a Tennessee planter, "would ship their husbands out of bed and get in with their wives. One man said he stood it as long as he could and one morning he just stood outside, and when he got with his wife he just choked him to death." A survey of former slaves conducted by the Works Progress Administration revealed that 4.5 percent said that one of their parents had been white. If the actual proportion of slaves fathered by whites was 4 percent, as many as 160,000 slave women may have been exploited by white men or otherwise compromised.[28]

Some slaveowners tried systematically to breed slaves for sale. A Charleston advertisement of slaves for sale stated that "they were purchased for stock and breeding negroes, and to any planter who particularly wanted them for that purpose, they are a very choice and desirable gang." In selling female slaves, planters often emphasized their childbearing capabilities. Read one notice: "For Sale—a Girl about twenty-nine years of age. . . . She is very prolific in her generating qualities, and affords a magnificent opportunity to any man who wishes to raise a family of healthy niggers for his own use." For the most part, slaveowners did not try to maximize reproduction by manipulating the sex and age composition of their labor force. Many slaveholders, however, did adopt a variety of incentives designed to encourage slave women to bear children. They gave bounties, in the form of cash or household goods, to mothers who bore healthy children and increased the rations and lightened the workload of pregnant and nursing women. Beginning in the fifth month of pregnancy, the fieldwork requirement of expectant mothers was cut in half, and in the last month, they were assigned to such chores as child care or spinning and sewing. Nursing mothers were allowed three to four hours a day to breast-feed their infants.[29]

In one important respect, the abolitionist critique was clearly incorrect. Contrary to what the nineteenth-century abolitionists charged, slave women did not become mothers at particularly early ages or engage in promiscuous sex. Some slave mothers, like some Southern white mothers, never married or had children by more than one father. The mother of fugitive slave William Wells Brown bore seven children by seven different black and white men. But, in general, slave sexual behavior was not casual, a point underscored by the fact that the incidence of illegitimacy or venereal disease among slaves was not particularly high.[30]

Slave sexual behavior followed a set of clearly defined standards, which deviated in certain respects from prevailing white norms. The owner of a Georgia plantation described the standards that she believed slaves adhered to: "The Negroes had their own ideals of morality, and held to them very strictly; they did not consider it wrong for a girl to have a child before she married, but afterwards were extremely severe upon anything like infidelity on her part." Premarital intercourse and childbirth were more common among slaves than Southern whites. A sizable minority of young women became sexually active as soon as they began to menstruate. But most unmarried slave mothers later took husbands and remained with them until death, and most slave women bore all their children by the same father. The slave community itself discouraged early sexual activity and early marriage and attached great value to marital fidelity. Although as many as three slave women in ten may have had one or more children prior to marriage, black preachers vehemently opposed premarital intercourse, and churches frequently punished offenders found guilty of fornication.[31]

The strength of the black family was revealed most clearly after the abolition of slavery. At the end of the Civil War, Union chaplains found not the hordes of orphaned children and abandoned mothers they had expected but a vital kinship network through which, as one white minister put it, "all indigent or helpless people are supported by relatives, parents or friends." The Civil War inflicted severe hardship on the slave family. Even before the outbreak of war, restrictions prevented many slave husbands from regularly visiting their wives and children. More were separated as growing numbers of slave men were impressed into the Confederate cause, serving as bakers, blacksmiths, boatmen, butchers, iron makers, machinists, nurses, shoemakers, and teamsters. During the fighting, 500,000 slaves flocked to the Union lines, and nearly 180,000, who had escaped from slavery or been liberated by Northern troops, enlisted in the Union Army.[32]

After emancipation thousands of freedmen roamed the South, struggling desperately, but largely unsuccessfully, to reunite families that had been forcibly separated by sale. A Northern journalist met an ex-slave in North Carolina, "plodding along, staff in hand, and apparently very footsore and tired," who had walked 600 miles searching for his wife and children who had been sold four years before. Some were fortunate enough to find their loved ones. Ben and Betty Dodson had been sold apart twenty years earlier; they were reunited in a refugee camp. "Glory! glory! halleluja," Ben shouted. "Dis is my Betty, shuah. I foun' you at last." Other reunions were bittersweet. One couple encountered each other near Norfolk, Virginia. "Twas like the stroke of death to me," the woman later recalled. She threw herself into her former husband's arms and cried, only to discover that he had since taken another wife.[33]

Many couples, forbidden to marry during slavery, took the opportunity to formalize their unions. One woman, who had lived with her husband for fifteen years, declared, "We wants to be married over again now." Mildred Graves, a former Virginia slave, had married her husband under slavery. Nevertheless she, too, decided to have "a real sho' nuff weddin' wid a preacher."[34]

Many ex-slaves, who had lived apart from their families during slavery, were finally free to reside with their spouses and children. As soon as he heard that he was free, Exter Durham of North Carolina gathered up his belongings and moved to his wife's plantation. Explained Tempie Herndon, his wife, "kaze den me an' Exter could be together all de time 'stead of Saturday and Sunday."[35]

After emancipation, slavery was gradually replaced by new systems of labor, the most common of which was known as sharecropping. Instead of cultivating land in gangs supervised by overseers, land-owners divided plantations into twenty- to fifty-acre plots suitable for farming by a single family. A share of the crop was kept by the tenant family, another share went to the landlord, and a third share went to whomever provided the farm family with agricultural implements, seed, and other supplies. As a symbol of their newly won independence, freedmen had teams of mules drag their former slave cabins away from the slave quarters into their own fields.[36]

Ex-slaves preferred sharecropping to wage labor because it allowed them to have an independent family life. Black wives and daughters sharply reduced their labor in the fields and instead devoted more time to child care and housework. Many former slaveowners complained of "ingratitude" and "betrayal" when the ex-slaves refused to work according to the old rules. One Alabama planter said that he lost a quarter of his work force because the ex-slaves as a "matter of pride" would not allow their wives to do fieldwork. Mary Jones, a Georgia plantation owner, described the changes that took place on her plantation: "Gilbert will stay on his old terms, but withdraws Fanny and puts Harry and Little Abram in her place and puts his son Gilbert out to trade. Cook Kate wants to be relieved of the heavy burden of cooking for two and wait on her husband." For the first time, black families could divide their time between fieldwork and housework in accordance with their own family priorities.[37]

Free Black Families

Although most antebellum black Americans labored as slaves in agricultural fields, tobacco factories, ironworks, sawmills, and quarries, a small minority of blacks were free. Their family lives, like those of many poor Afro-Americans in twentieth-century America, were heavily influenced by the effects of poverty and urban patterns of life.

Before the Civil War, 250,000 free blacks occupied an uneasy middle ground between the dominant whites and the mass of slaves. After the American Revolution, slaveholders freed thousands of slaves, while countless others freed themselves by running away. In Louisiana a large free black and Creole population evolved under Spanish and French rule and in South Carolina a Creole population arrived from Barbados. The number of free blacks increased greatly with the arrival of thousands of light-colored refugees from the black revolt in Haiti.[38]

Free black families varied profoundly in status. Most led a marginal economic existence, but in a few cities such as New Orleans, Baltimore, and Charleston, free blacks worked as skilled carpenters, shoemakers, tailors, and millwrights. In the lower South, a few free blacks actually bought slaves.[39]

Legally the free people of color were denied the right to serve on juries or to testify against whites. Throughout the South, laws restricted their freedom of movement and forbade them from fraternizing with slaves, holding meetings, purchasing liquor, or smoking in public.[40]

In addition to the 150,000 free blacks who lived in the South, another 100,000 free blacks lived in the North. Although free blacks made up no more than 3.8 percent of the population of any Northern state, they faced intense legal, economic, and social discrimination. They were prohibited from marrying whites, relegated to separate jails, cemeteries, asylums, and schools and, in all but five states, denied the right to vote.[41]

Free black families in the North typically lived in lofts, garrets, and cellars or in back alleys and narrow courts at the rear of white-owned dwellings. Many unmarried free blacks and urban slaves and a significant portion of married women resided in boardinghouses or worked as live-in servants in white residences, hospitals, or hotels. In Philadelphia an 1847 visitor described the typical black dwelling as "a desolate pen," six feet square, without windows or bed or furniture, possessing a leaky roof and a floor so low in the ground "that more or less water comes in on them from the yard in rainy weather." According to the *New York Express*, the principal dwelling place of blacks in that city was located in "a small narrow, and exceedingly dirty court. . . . with a row of shabby three story brick houses on one side, and dilapidated brick and wooden hovels on the other." A house generally had eight or ten rooms, "and in these are crowded not infrequently two or three hundred souls."[42]

The available demographic evidence suggests that free black family life, like slave family life, was organized around two-parent households. In Boston, Cincinnati, Cleveland, Louisville, New Orleans, Pittsburgh, and several smaller towns located in the Ohio River valley, two-parent households predominated in the 1850 and 1860 censuses. Only in Philadelphia was the proportion of single-parent, female-headed households conspicuously high.[43]

Nevertheless a significant number of urban blacks lived in female-headed households or outside a family unit. A study of Philadelphia found that during the nineteenth century between a quarter and a third of the city's blacks lived in female-headed families, two to three times the rate among the city's German, Irish, or native whites. This high rate of female-headed households was not caused not by high rates of divorce, desertion, or illegitimacy. It was the result of two key demographic facts. The first was the fact that particularly in the South, the free black and urban slave populations were largely female. In many cities slave women outnumbered slave men by more than 50 percent and free black women outnumbered men by more than 25 percent. A number of factors contributed to this skewing of sex ratios, including the tendency of slaveowners to manumit females and superior employment opportunities for women in urban areas, mainly as live-in domestic servants, cooks, laundresses, nurses, and seamstresses. The second major source of family instability was a level of adult mortality roughly twice that of whites. In Philadelphia at least a quarter of married women were widowed by their forties. The causes of family dissolution were economic, not racial. When property holdings among ethnic groups were held constant, racial variations in family composition largely disappeared.[44]

For free blacks before the Civil War, as for many blacks who live in poverty today, low income, chronic unemployment, and a high death rate combined to produce relatively high levels of family instability.

Thirty-five years after the end of the Civil War, Virginia's largest black newpaper, the *Richmond Planet*, continued to receive letters from former slaves seeking information about the whereabouts of parents, spouses, siblings, and children who had been separated from them during slavery. Requests for information were so frequent that the paper established a regular column in which it printed the letters, entitled "Do You Know Them?" Although fifty and sometimes sixty years had passed since these husbands had been torn from their wives and mothers had been forcibly separated from their children, they vividly recalled personal details about their relatives and still clung to hopes of reunion.[45]

During the first half of the twentieth century, a long line of historians and sociologists argued that one of the long-term legacies of slavery was the weakening of the black family. Slavery, it was said, destroyed the African family and kinship system and emasculated slave fathers. With the exception of a few privileged house slaves, black family structure under slavery was forced into a matriarchal structure in which women played the dominant role in the household. Slave sexual life was random and promiscuous.[46]

This viewpoint, we now know, was entirely incorrect. Most slaves lived in two-parent households that were often stable over long periods of time. The nuclear family, in turn, received support from an involved extended kinship network. Despite the harshness and misery of life under slavery, enslavement did not destroy the slaves' ability to develop a distinctive life and culture. Even under the weight of slavery, slaves developed a vital family life, religion, and culture. Through their families and cultural traditions, slaves were able to fashion an autonomous culture and community, beyond the direct control of their masters.

Today the kinship system forged under slavery continues to function as a source of mutual assistance and support. In present-day urban ghettoes, networks of kin or "fictive" kin often share resources and responsibilities. Similarly, in many rural black communities, enlarged kinship groups still frequently form the core of local communities and continue to function as protective networks for individual family members. Though familial and kinship connections have experienced enormous strain across the twentieth century—as a result of the stresses of migration and high rates of unemployment—they continue to function as they did under slavery: as a source of solace and support, of collective identity, and a vehicle of generational and cultural continuity.[47]

Women garment workers in Detroit around 1900. Courtesy of the Burton Historical Collection, Detroit Public Library.

CHAPTER V

Industrialization and the
Working-Class Family

SEVEN miles downstream from Pittsburgh, on the banks of western
Pennsylvania's Monongahela River, stands a small town named
Homestead. At the beginning of the twentieth century, Homestead,
a community of 25,000 people, was a mill town in the Carnegie Steel
Company empire best known as the site of a violent 1892 strike.
Homestead was a drab and unsightly place, covered by gray plumes
of smoke that stunted the growth of trees and withered the foliage.
Yet as recently as 1870, two farms had stood on the site occupied by
the town.[1]

In many respects Homestead was a rather typical turn-of-the-
century mill town. Its population, like those of most mill towns, was
ethnically diverse, with a high proportion of recent immigrants. More
than 161 separate ethnic and nationality groups toiled in Homestead's
mills, and nearly a third of the town's population had been born
abroad. Also like those of other such towns, its population was
sharply skewed sexually. Because the steel industry only employed
male workers, there were six men in the town for every four women.[2]

Steel company policies involving wages, work schedules, and employment levels shaped the lives of Homestead's families, determining
their living standards and daily patterns. The hours of work in
Homestead's mills were extraordinarily long. A typical steel worker
would arrive at work at 7:00 A.M. and toil in front of a blazing open-
hearth furnace until 5:30 in the afternoon, six days a week. On alternate weeks, he would start work at 5:30 P.M. and work until 7:00 the
next morning, a thirteen-and-a-half-hour day. A fifth of the workers
actually toiled seven days a week inside the mills, working long hours
for miserably low wages. Despite steel's image as a high-paying indus-

try, most of Homestead's workers made less than the $15.00 a week that local charities defined as a minimum subsistence budget. Half of all mill workers earned less than $12.00 a week, or just $1.65 a day.[3]

How did industrialization in the mill towns across America affect workers and their families? In Homestead the typical family of a mill worker lived below the poverty line, spending eight dollars a month for one or two rooms in an alley residence. After budgeting for food (twenty-three cents a day for each adult male and less for women and children) and deducting for clothing, fuel, and insurance, the family was left just forty-one cents at the end of the month, a sum that had to cover health care, furniture, education, recreation, church contributions, and savings. To supplement their weekly paychecks, families took in washing or boarders (who contributed, on average, a quarter of a family's income) and depended on the earnings of older sons, who typically contributed nearly a third of the family's income.[4]

Living conditions were abysmal. Half of all Slavic and black families in Homestead inhabited one- or two-room shanties located in tin-can-strewn alleyways. Lacking running water, families had to use outdoor pumps, and lacking indoor toilets, groups of twenty families shared the use of wooden outbuildings with ten compartments opening onto a vault. In these alleyways two of every three children died before their second birthdays.[5]

In the second half of the nineteenth century, industrialization and urbanization transformed the nation's workplaces, whether factories, mills, mines, or farms. The result was difficult new working and living conditions for America's working-class families. Although the toll was high and family life was strained and oppressed, family strategies and support were often all that one could depend on.

Up until World War I, working-class Americans—who earned a livelihood in the nation's steel mills, rail yards, textile and clothing factories, coal mines, and farms—made up a majority of the nation's population. Because of their diverse origins and their economic struggles they evolved patterns of family life strikingly different from those of middle-class Americans. The men and women who made their livings with their hands came from a variety of religious, cultural, and national backgrounds, and these ethnic differences helped shape attitudes toward marriage, family roles, child care, and woman or child labor distinct from those touted in the popular literature of the time. A high degree of transience diluted the effects of middle-class norms on working-class life. Extraordinarily few working-class families were able to settle down in a community permanently. Most working-class families moved frequently, seeking work and subsistence wherever they could be found. Earnings and employment were unstable, making for a marginal economic existence. A job might be lost as a result of an economic downturn, changes in consumer demand, inclement weather, or technological displacement. Full-time year-round employment was a rarity, and most working-class families depended on supplementary income from more than one wage earner. At a time when most middle-class families had only one breadwinner, relatively few working-class families could support themselves without the economic contribution of other family members, including children.[6]

During the course of the nineteenth century, many American families lived amid poverty, filth, stench, and disease difficult for many middle-class Americans to fathom. In New York in 1850, over 18,000 people lived in damp, ill-lit, unventilated cellars containing from six to twenty persons in each room. In Boston, the Committee on Internal Health reported that in the slum districts, residents were "huddled together like brutes without regard to sex, age or a sense of decency, grown men and women sleeping together in the same apartment, and sometimes wife, husband, brothers and sisters in the same bed." Especially after the Panic of 1837, vivid descriptions of impoverished families; of ragged children begging for pennies; of small girls selling nuts, fruits, and toothpicks; and of teenage hoodlums stealing goods from piers, junk shops, and warehouses appeared frequently in American newspapers and popular literature. Many middle-class observers feared that the families of the laboring classes were disintegrating and that child neglect, cruelty, and drunkenness were spreading.[7]

A number of writers echoed Friedrich Engel's observations of workers in England in the 1840s that when parents worked in factories, infants and younger children suffered neglect and ill treatment, older children repudiated parental discipline, and sexual immorality was widespread. Declared Carroll D. Wright in the tenth United States Census in 1880: "The factory system necessitates the employment of women and children to an injurious extent, and consequently its tendency is to destroy family life and ties and domestic habits, and ultimately the home." It was argued that the growing number of working wives lacked the time to cook and care for their families. And it was charged that many working-class parents exploited their children's labor, forcing them to work long hours at an early age instead of attending school. Complained one cotton manufacturer: Often parents "were disposed to live upon the labor of their children rather than upon their own. . . ."[8]

Despite the disruptions and dislocations caused by urbanization and industrialization, the strains of adjustment to demanding and adverse conditions often strengthened family bonds and encouraged a return to earlier patterns of mutual assistance and dependence on family and kinship ties. Migration to urban areas, poverty, and integration into industrial economies uprooted, threatened, and tested family ties dramatically. However, among the nation's expanding number of industrial immigrants, family and kinship relations remained the familiar and flexible core of a dynamically changing environment, thereby easing the stresses of migration and facilitating the adjustment to a modernized urban and industrial way of life.

Immigration and the Emergence of a New Working Class

In 1849, when Patrick Kennedy, the great-grandfather of President John F. Kennedy, boarded the American ship *Washington Irving* to emigrate to Boston, he was part of one of the greatest movements of people in history. In that year 159,398 Irish people came to the United States because of crop failure or famine. Kennedy was luckier than many of the immigrants who traveled on the "coffin ships": More than one voyager in ten died of typhus or cholera before reaching the New World. In Boston, Kennedy found work on the docks as assistant to a stevedore and eventually supported his family by making barrels and wagons.[9]

Beginning in the late 1830s, a new class of manual laborers appeared in the growing cities of the Northeast, increasingly composed of immigrants and their children. Pushed out of Europe by economic distress and attracted to the United States by the promise of jobs and land, members of immigrant families increasingly replaced native-born women and children in the nation's factories. As early as 1855, virtually all shoemakers and tailors in New York had been born abroad. By mid-century, the distinguishing characteristic of the urban working class in the North was its immigrant and ethnic character.[10]

The number of immigrants that arrived in the United States is staggering. At the beginning of the nineteenth century, just 5,000 immigrants arrived in the United States each year. But during the 1830s, the number of newcomers climbed to 600,000; in the 1840s the number reached 1.5 million, and in the 1850s the figure rocketed to 2.8 million. Between 1877 and 1890 another 6 million arrived and in the quarter century before World War I, another 18 million immigrants entered the country. Prior to the Civil War, most immigrants came from northern and western Europe, particularly from England,

Germany, Ireland, and Scandinavia. After 1890 most newcomers were from southern and eastern Europe, especially Austria-Hungary, Italy, Russia, and Spain.[11]

Some immigrants planned to work temporarily in the United States and then return to Europe. Many Italians and Poles and people from other Slavic countries did not emigrate as families, and a high proportion returned to the Old World. Others, including the Irish, Jews, and Czechs fleeing economic and political oppression, came with their families intending to settle permanently. But whether they arrived as individuals or as members of families, the immigrants sought out family, friends, and ethnic communities to sustain them in the frightening novelty of the new world.[12]

Far from destroying relationships among kin and reducing immigrants to rootless individuals, migration across the Atlantic strengthened family and kinship ties. Families were the basic resource in effecting the immigrants' transition to their new environment. Most immigrants made use of kin and friends in traveling and settled in neighborhoods already populated by people from the same home village or community, who provided information about urban life, offered temporary housing, and assisted in finding work.[13]

Even when men and women emigrated alone, they often did so for family reasons. Unaccompanied fathers or sons customarily sent money to relatives back home or accumulated savings in order to bring their families to the New World. Many young men saved their wages in order to purchase farms in their native villages, while many young women from farm families entered mills in order to acquire dowries.[14]

The heavy reliance on one's "own people" was a response to shared adversities. Immigrant families encountered a host of problems, including the language barrier, difficulties in obtaining jobs, inadequate income, frequent unemployment, and trouble finding housing. They faced the possibility of losing their own customs and values to American ways. The American stress on mobility and independence threatened Old World adherence to family solidarity and deference to parental authority.[15]

Working-Class Family Economy

Around 1900, two anonymous southern Italian brothers arrived in New York City, where they boarded with fifteen other men in a single third-story room in a wood-frame house. To support themselves, the brothers picked up rags, mattresses, umbrellas, clothes, hats, and boots from the garbage on the streets of wealthier neighborhoods and cleaned and restored them. To save money, they ate a plain and monotonous but cheap diet, consisting of a breakfast of bread, cheese, onions, garlic, and herring; a lunch of soup and bread; and a dinner of meat purchased for four cents a pound. By scavenging and by polishing shoes for a nickel a shine, the brothers succeeded in accumulating $700 hoping that when they had accumulated $1,000 they could buy a farm in Italy.[16]

To accumulate a savings account or maintain a family required multiple incomes from several family members. Like the two southern Italian brothers, kin often pooled their resources and provided each other with support. For many immigrants the kinship network provided day-to-day assistance with housing, child care, and loans. During critical life situations—illnesses, unemployment, injury, housing shortages, or old age—individuals often turned to kin for support. Given the inadequacy of private and public assistance, the family and kin group offered the only reliable source of mutual assistance and support.[17]

The strategies families adopted to acquire a home or to provide care for younger children or aging relatives often required individual family members to subordinate their personal wishes to larger family considerations. Key decisions—regarding emigration, whether women or children should work, and when sons and daughters should marry—tended to be based on family needs rather than individual choices. Among many ethnic groups, it was common, for example, for daughters to leave school at an early age and enter work so that sons could continue their education. It was also customary for at least one daughter to remain unmarried so that she could care for younger siblings or her parents in their old age. The concept of the "family economy" describes this pattern, in which decision making was a by-product of collective needs rather than individual preferences.[18]

During the nineteenth century, the families of blacks, immigrants, and the American-born working class, all accepted the necessity of a cooperative family economy, in which all household members contributed to the material support of the family. In the middle class, women and children were deprived of many of their earlier productive roles, but in the working class, the notion of a collective family economy persisted, since it was absolutely essential to family survival. In Massachusetts in 1882, family living costs exceeded the earnings of the household head by almost a third. The difference had to be made up by other sources of income, including child labor and working wives.[19]

Wives and mothers contributed to the working-class family economy in diverse ways. In most working-class households, the housewife was the manager of the family finances and was therefore responsible for seeing that the family's limited income was used productively. Often this necessitated taking in boarders or lodgers. Today fewer than one family in twenty shares its home with a boarder. One hundred years ago, the situation was far different. On average, 15 to 20 percent of familes took in boarders. In the industrial town of Holyoke, Massachusetts, in 1880, over a third of all households contained non-related persons, and among the largely immigrant industrial working class in Pennsylvania's steel towns, between a quarter and a half of all families took in nonrelatives as boarders. Usually boarders were unmarried men or women between the ages of twenty and thirty-five, of the same ethnic affiliation as the household head, and their payments supplemented a family's income and provided support in a couple's old age. The households most likely to take in boarders or lodgers were female-headed and older. At a time when children had left home or a family member had died, leaving rooms vacant, taking in kin or boarders helped families to maintain their standard of living.[20]

Many women added to the family income by doing piecework in the home, such as making embroideries, producing artificial flowers, tailoring garments, or doing laundry. Called "outwork" because it took place outside a shop or factory, this kind of low-paid household labor was the most common form of employment for immigrant women in the nation's largest cities, permitting them to earn a cash income while caring for their households.[21]

Women's primary work remained caring for the family and the home. Within the working-class household, housework was onerous and time consuming. Although industrialization tended to make certain household tasks—such as emptying chamberpots, hauling water and wood, carding wool and spinning cloth, or grinding grain—increasingly obsolescent—other domestic duties were actually expanded, such as time spent cooking, cleaning, or doing laundry. The many traditional household crafts that were eliminated were quickly supplemented by the pressures of time, filth, and crowding in factory towns and urban slums that women now confronted.[22]

Standards of cleanliness rose, and as a result women devoted increased amounts of time to cleaning, dusting, scrubbing, and launder-

ing. The growing availability of washable cotton fabrics increased the
amount of laundering housewives performed. Oil and gas lamps,
which began to replace candles early in the nineteenth century, produced heavy soot that had to be cleaned away every day. Cooking,
which had tended to be simple and monotonous in the eighteenth
and early nineteenth centuries—composed primarily of pancakes and
stews (since it was necessary to boil meat to dilute the taste of the salt
used to preserve it)—became increasingly time consuming. At a time
when most food was sold unprepared, housewives had to devote significant amount of their time to plucking feathers from chickens,
soaking and blanching hams, roasting coffee beans, and grinding
whole spices and sugar. Technological innovation did little to cut a
housewife's workday. At the end of the century, a typical housewife
spent six hours a day on just two tasks: meal preparation and cleaning. Women spent an hour a day simply maintaining the family's cast-
iron cooking stove, disposing of ashes, kindling the fire, adding coal,
cleaning the flue, and blacking the oven to keep it from rusting.[23]

Child labor provided a major contribution to family earnings.
Children worked not because their parents were heartless but because
children's earnings were absolutely essential to the family's standard
of living, particularly in times of economic distress. As one observer
noted, a girl was expected to work "to relieve her hard-working father
of the burden of her support, to supply [her] home with comforts and
refinements, [and] to educate a younger brother."[24]

Child labor was not new. Before the nineteenth century, however,
children had worked as part of a family unit or as participants in a
system of apprenticeship which provided at least minimal training in
a skilled trade. During the early decades of the nineteenth century,
however, as rural life increasingly gave way to urban environments,
traditional obligations on the part of masters toward apprentices were
diluted. Instead of a master watching over an apprentice in his own
home, customary obligations for room and board were converted into
cash payments to a boy's parents.[25]

Boys were more likely to work than girls, older children were more
likely to work than younger children, and Southern children were
more likely to work than Northern children. In 1900 more than half
of the nation's child laborers lived in the South, where they performed farm work or labored in textile mills. Wherever they lived,
however, children made a critical contribution to their families' income. In a Massachusetts survey of working-class families in 1875,
children under fifteen contributed nearly 20 percent of their family

income. During economic slumps, children might be their family's primary source of support.[26]

Children's obligation to help support their family did not end with adolescence. At times when economic stress was most acute, children were expected to defer marriage, remain at home, and contribute to the family's income. Young men or women generally worked for perhaps seven years before marrying and were frequently unable to establish households of their own until their early thirties.[27]

Living Standards

In 1851, Horace Greeley, editor of the *New York Tribune*, estimated the minimum weekly budget needed to support a family of five. Greeley calculated that essential expenditures for rent, food, fuel, and clothing amounted to $10.37. Noting that the budget contained no items that could be regarded as luxuries, Greeley asked: "Have I made the workingman's comforts too high? Where is the money to pay for amusements, for ice-creams, his puddings, his trips on Sunday up or down the river in order to get some fresh air, to pay the doctor or apothecary, to pay for pew rent in church, to purchase books, musical instruments?"[28]

In fact, in 1851 most urban workingmen were unable to earn enough to sustain even this minimal standard of living. A shoemaker or a printer received just four to six dollars a week; a cabinet maker made five dollars a week; textile workers averaged just six and a half dollars a week for men and less than three and a half dollars for women. Unskilled laborers—who constituted two-thirds of the workforce in most cities—earned just a dollar a week. Only blacksmiths, engineers, machinists, and skilled building tradesmen earned enough to achieve Greeley's weekly budget.[29]

While the popular press spoke of a "family wage" sufficient for a father to support his entire family, large numbers of black, immigrant, and native-born white working-class families found it impossible to live on the father's income alone. Although real blue-collar wages rose sharply in the decades following the Civil War (between 10 and 20 percent in the 1870s and 25 percent in the 1880s), most industrial workers still did not earn enough money to support a family decently. The growth in real wages was punctuated by wage cuts and unemployment experienced during economic contractions, which were severe in this period. To make matters worse, a worker's wages peaked early and subsequently declined. Even in good times, few could afford to save anything very significant to meet temporary losses in income, so even short or comparatively minor crises caused severe destitution.[30]

Families faced particularly acute financial stress at two points in the life cycle. Especially vulnerable were familes with young children. During the early years of a marriage, when children were too young to work and contribute directly to the family's income, many working-class couples lived with parents or boarded with another family. Families were also vulnerable at later ages of the family life cycle. Since strength and manual dexterity were important qualifications for unskilled or semiskilled jobs, wages were highest for men in their twenties and thirties. A manufacturing worker might reach his peak earnings at the age of twenty-five and see his earnings fall off as he grew older.[31]

Working-class families devised a number of imaginative strategies to maintain a degree of economic security. Ownership of property, such as a house or agricultural land or even a garden, provided protection against the financial insecurity caused by temporary unemployment, illness, or old age. At a time when bad weather, a drop in prices, or machinery breakdown threw many workers out of their jobs (for instance, in Massachusetts in 1877, two-thirds of all workers were out of work an average of ninety-four days), ownership of property offered at least minimal financial security. On New York City's East side, Irish immigrants kept goats and pigs. Upwardly mobile working-men in Newburyport, Massachusetts, frequently bought farm property on the edge of town.[32]

Ownership of a house was a particularly valuable source of security, since a family could always obtain an extra income by taking in boarders and lodgers. City workers went to enormous lengths to buy a house. In Newburyport, where more than two-thirds of the working-class men who lived in the city for twenty years acquired a house, parents had to sacrifice their children's education and assume onerous mortgages to make the purchase. Immigrants, in particular the Irish and Slavs, were actually more likely to purchase a house than were native-born families, perhaps because of their peasant background or because of their concern about economic security. But significant numbers of every ethnic and income group owned a house. Even families with few children or with low-paying, unskilled jobs purchased homes as a way of accumulating capital and establishing a future source of income. Renters who could not afford to buy a house frequently subdivided and sublet their rooms and shared meals with lodgers in order to obtain extra income.[33]

The Copley Family (1776–1777) by John Singleton Copley (1738–1815). In this early portrait of genteel family life, male dominance is reflected in the stark formality of the two adult men (the artist and his father-in-law Richard Clarke, a prominent merchant), which contrasts sharply with the warm emotions displayed by the artist's wife and daughters. *Courtesy of the National Gallery of Art, Washington, D.C.*

The Haight Family (c. 1848). Attributed to Nicolino Calyo (1799–1884). Although family members were increasingly portrayed on the same plane, hierarchy remained an important element in family portraiture. Beginning in the second half of the eighteenth century, differences in age and sex were reflected in subtle distinctions in dress. Children wore loose frocks and knickers. In this portrait, the toddler is still wearing a skirt, while the middle son is adorned with a lace collar and the eldest son does not yet wear the father's rigid neckwear. The mother's full skirt contrasts with her daughter's short one. *Courtesy of the Museum of the City of New York.*

Childrearing in a Utopian Community. This photograph, taken in the 1850s, shows older children tending infants at Zoar, a German separatist community in Ohio, which was one of hundreds of utopian communities that launched experiments in marriage, sexual practices, and childrearing. Because women were expected to share in fieldwork, childrearing responsibilities fell on older girls. *Courtesy of the Ohio Historical Society.*

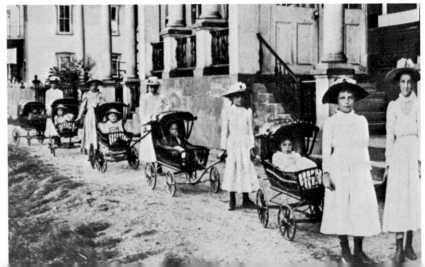

A Slave Mother. Each year in the antebellum era, approximately a thousand slaves fled northward to escape bondage. Most walked on foot, traveling at night, and slept in barns or woods. Margaret Garner, a fugitive slave, killed two of her children rather than permit them to be returned to slavery. After her capture by slavecatchers, she drowned herself in the Ohio River. *Courtesy of the Schomburg Center for Nineteenth Century Research in Black Culture, The New York Public Library, Astor, Lenox, and Tilden Foundations.*

The Strength of the Black Family. Despite the fact that slave marriages were not legally binding, slave family ties remained strong and many slave marriages lasted twenty years or more. This photograph, which was taken on a plantation near Beaufort, South Carolina, in 1862, shows five generations of a slave family. *Courtesy of the Library of Congress.*

A Sense of Loss. The Civil War left a scarring impact on the lives of thousands of families. At least 540,000 Americans lost their lives during the war. Here a widow and her orphaned children grieve for a husband and father killed in the war. *Courtesy of the Library of Congress.*

Pioneering the Great Plains. The story of pioneer families on the Great Plains is a tale of poverty, unremitting toil, and ceaseless effort, but a story too of successful innovation and adaptation to new and challenging circumstances. In the process, the most potent resource pioneers were able to draw upon was the family. This photograph shows the Tidwell family, who homesteaded a farm in Sunnyside, Utah. *Courtesy of the Utah State Historical Society.*

Pioneers along the Overland Trail. Between 1840, when the first company of one hundred pioneers crossed the Missouri River, until the 1870s, nearly a half million Americans crossed the overland trails to California and Oregon. For up to eight months they traveled fifteen or twenty miles a day, sixteen hours a day by covered wagon. For most pioneers, the journey was undertaken in the company of parents, children, and grandchildren, who provided the only security and familiarity in a harsh environment. *Courtesy of the Denver Public Library.*

The Sod House Frontier. As the pioneers set out across the Great Plains, they encountered an environment that severely tested their determination. Without trees, families were unable to get logs for cabins or planks for fences or kindling for fires. Without streams, pioneer families lacked water for drinking or washing or irrigating crops. Many early Nebraska families built their homes out of sod. This photograph, taken during the 1880s, illustrates the sod home of the Chrisman sisters, daughters of a Nebraska rancher. *Courtesy of the Nebraska State Historical Society.*

A Cheyenne Family. For the Cheyenne, as for many other Plains peoples, the buffalo provided food, clothing, and shelter. Beginning in the 1860s, buffalo herds began to dwindle and many Plains Indians were forced to live on reservations, where they were dependent on the federal government for food. A Cheyenne family dries meat for the winter. Photograph taken in July, 1895. *Courtesy of the National Anthropological Archives, Smithsonian Institution.*

Cooking with a Cast-Iron Stove. While the industrial revolution tended to make certain household tasks obsolescent, such as emptying chamberpots, hauling water, and spinning cloth, other domestic duties expanded, such as time spent cooking, cleaning, or doing laundry. Coal-burning stoves and oil and gas lamps produced heavy soot that clung to walls and draperies. *Courtesy of General Foods.*

A Victorian Parlor. The nineteenth-century home was regarded as a "secular temple" and a retreat from the world of commerce and trade. Unlike the twentieth-century home, with its vast expanse of windows opening up on the outside world, the Victorian home was oriented inward. The exterior world was hidden by an elaborate series of draperies and wall coverings. *Courtesy of the Museum of the City of New York.*

The Hatch Family (1871) by Eastman Johnson (1824–1906). During the second half of the nineteenth century, family portraiture began, for the first time, to depict extended, multigenerational family groups. This group portrait depicts fifteen members of a prominent New York family in the library of their elegant Fifth Avenue residence. *Courtesy of the Metropolitan Museum of Art, New York.*

Ethnic Diversity

Although most nineteenth-century American families resembled each other in their nuclear structure, consisting of two parents and their children, family behavior and style varied drastically according to ethnicity and social class. Despite the popular image of America as a melting pot in which diverse cultural traditions dissolved into distinctly American patterns, in actuality, economic and cultural pressures made for different family styles. Immigrants tended to have higher birthrates than both native-born whites and blacks; they were also more likely to take in boarders or lodgers, and their children were more likely to work than their native born counterparts. In their allocation of family roles, their internal dynamics, their housing arrangements, their attitudes toward female and child labor, and their kinship patterns, immigrant and native-born families differed profoundly.[34]

Each ethnic group adapted to the challenges of American life in its own distinct way. Jewish families tended to rent larger apartments and share their residences with lodgers. Italian families, in contrast, resided in smaller and cheaper single-family apartments. Urban blacks often rented space in another family's household.[35]

Some immigrant groups, like the Irish and Slavs, were willing to forgo their children's education rather than send married women into the work force. Other groups, particularly Jews and blacks, tended to keep their children in school despite the lost earnings. Italian families, more than almost any other ethnic group, discouraged women from working outside the home. Italian girls, for example, were rarely permitted to work unsupervised by relatives or friends, and Italian mothers tended to work outside the home only intermittently, when required by family illness or emergency. When Italian mothers did work for wages, they preferred homework to factory work, and often turned to such tasks as millinery, garment finishing, and handcrafting artificial flowers—jobs which did not conflict with an intense family life. Polish women preferred domestic service to factory work; Jewish women, in contrast, rarely took employment as domestic servants and were more likely to work in factories.[36]

Some of the distinctions between the family structures of different ethnic groups diminished with a single generation. The fertility rates of immigrant families began to decline rapidly after a single generation. Marriages within the ethnic group also tended to decline in frequency after the first generation. Among the second generation, men and women were two to three times as likely to marry outside the group. Although only 3.5 percent of second-generation southern Italians and 8 percent of Jews married outside their group, 30 to 50 percent of northern Italians, Irish, Slovaks, Czechs, and Poles did so. Scandinavians, Hungarians, British, and Canadians had even higher rates of intermarriage.[37]

The marginal economic situation of urban working-class families was often a source of conflict and insecurity, but it also produced a strong sense of cohesiveness and intense family loyalty. Each family member was expected to subordinate his or her personal ambitions and contribute to the family's support. Familial values, not individualistic values, lay at the heart of working-class family life.

Factory Work and the Working-Class Family

The January 14, 1828, edition of the Providence, Rhode Island, *Manufacturers' and Farmers' Journal* carried an advertisement that read as follows: "Families Wanted—Ten or Twelve good respectable families consisting of four or five children each, from nine to sixteen years of age, are wanted to work in a cotton mill, in the vicinity of Providence."[38]

For many working-class families, particularly during the early phases of the Industrial Revolution, the movement of work into the factory did not seem to have a revolutionary impact on family life because many employers felt it necessary to adapt the organization of their primitive factories to the familial values of their employees. To dispel the impression created by English factories that factory work was degrading and exploitive, many early textile manufacturers hired whole families for their mills, while others hired young women and set up special dormitories and boardinghouses to provide their employees with surrogate families.[39]

In many early textile mills, factory owners permitted employees to select their children as assistants or apprentices, and parents were able to work alongside their children. Since child labor was supervised by parents, traditional relations between family members were not radically altered. Elsewhere, in the textile mills of Lowell and Waltham and in northern New England, the early mill hands were unmarried women, mainly between the ages of fifteen and twenty-five, who worked temporarily before marriage. Even for these women, work did not constitute a major break with their families or their families' values. Many women interrupted their work periodically for trips home, and in many cases more than one family member worked in the mills.[40]

Although many contemporary observers feared that factory employment would undermine family cohesion, because children who earned independent wages could repudiate parental control and leave home, industrial work in fact allowed many sons and daughters to live in their natal homes far longer than had been the case in the past. Until the middle of the nineteenth century, leaving home had been a normal part of growing up. A family farm could only support one son so others had to seek farm employment elsewhere or enter an apprenticeship, while many girls served temporarily as domestic servants. By the mid-nineteenth century, however, most working-class children continued to live at home or in the homes of relatives until their late teens or early twenties and to contribute part of their income to their family. The availability of factory work allowed a degree of family cohesion that had previously been an inconceivable luxury on the family farm. It was now possible for all family members to work in the same community.[41]

Although working-class parents and children were able to live together longer than in the past and in the same community, fewer families worked in the same workplace. During the second half of the century, fewer industries employed whole families or permitted workers to select their own assistants. Nevertheless, the family-based pattern did not completely break down. Many employers, particularly in the textile industry, continued to respect kinship ties in recruiting and promoting workers and allocating work.[42]

It would not be until the early twentieth century, when many companies began to introduce elements of scientific management into the workplace, that the role of the extended kinship group in factories was severely circumscribed. The centralization of hiring, promotions, and firing; the introduction of the time clock; and other methods introduced to gain a tighter control over the work process and reduce labor turnover had the practical effect of weakening the importance of the extended family group in the workplace.[43]

Rural Families

The most common image associated with industrial America is of steelworkers casting molten metal in front of roaring open-hearth furnaces or of rows of garment workers tending sewing machines in crowded sweatshops, amid scattered remnants of fabric. But during the nineteenth century, more families made their livelihood farming, digging coal from the earth, laying rails, or cutting timber than worked in all of the nation's factories.

As late as 1870, just three Americans in ten made their homes in a city or town with as many as 2,500 inhabitants. The other seven lived in small rural villages or farms. Pioneer families moving westward during the two decades following 1870 settled 430 million acres of land west of the Mississippi, more than doubling the area under settlement. Mining families inhabited "company towns" in remote rural areas far from traditional centers of population. Farm families raised crops and grazed livestock in New England, the South, the Midwest, the Great Plains, and the Far West. Not until 1920 would more than half the nation's population live in small towns or cities.[44]

MOVING WESTWARD: FAMILIES ALONG THE OVERLAND TRAILS

Between 1840, when the first company of 100 emigrants crossed the Missouri River, until the 1870s, from a quarter to half a million pioneers traveled the overland trails westward toward California and Oregon. For eight months they traveled fifteen or twenty miles a day, sixteen hours a day, in a wagon trains made up of 50, 100, or even 150 Conestoga wagons. These pioneers were mostly farm families from such Midwestern states as Illinois, Indiana, Iowa, and Missouri, seeking richer and more productive farmland. They tended to come from families of "habitual movers" who had migrated before in search of prosperity and now were on the move again. Fully four out of five pioneers had previously moved in search of a better life.[45]

Pioneering was not an option for urban laborers, however, since their earnings of a dollar or less a day were inadequate to meet the cost of westward travel. To make the trek, a family had to raise a minimum of $400 to purchase a wagon and oxen plus another $140 for food and cooking utensils plus a sum sufficient to buy tools, clothing, and other supplies.[46]

At Independence and St. Joseph, Missouri, and Council Bluffs, Iowa, the pioneers gathered each spring to begin the two-thousand-mile trek. With the exception of the fortune hunters seeking gold in California, most pioneers traveled with their familes and relatives. For nearly half the pioneers, the journey was undertaken in the company of parents, children, children's spouses, and grandchildren, who provided the only security and familiarity in a harsh environment. Even many unattached men sought the mutual support and stability that came with being a part of a family group—as many as a third of the unattached single men hired into family parties.[47]

In virtually every recorded case, it was the husband, and not the wife, who made the decision to set out on the overland trail. In their diaries or recollections, only a quarter of the wives said they agreed with the decision to emigrate and recorded their reluctance to leave parents and lifelong friends. Along the trail, women strove desperately to maintain a semblance of domesticity. Even on the harshest parts of the trek, fording streams or climbing the Rocky Mountains, women were reluctant to shorten their hemlines, to throw away daguerreotypes or other family mementos, or to dispose of stoves or rocking chairs.[48]

Once on the trail, the pioneers tried to maintain a firm sexual division of labor. Men's work included driving and maintaining the wagons and livestock, standing guard duty, and hunting buffalo and antelope for extra meat. Women's trail work began at four in the morning, half an hour before the men rose, to collect fuel, haul water, kindle campfires, begin breakfast, knead dough, and milk the cows. At the end of the day, women were expected to fix dinner, make beds, air out the wagons to prevent mildew, launder, mend, knit, and tend the children.[49]

As the pioneers set out across the Great Plains they encountered an environment that severely tested their determination. Accidents, disease, and sudden disaster were constant threats. Children fell out of wagons, wagon-hauling oxen grew exhausted and died, and such diseases as typhoid, dysentery, and mountain fever killed many pioneers. Migrant parties also suffered devastation from buffalo stampedes, prairie fires, and floods. The stalwart men and women who set out on the western trails had to cross arid plains, rushing streams, and dangerous mountain passes. At least 20,000 were buried along the overland trails. But they were willing to risk their lives because of a thirst for adventure and a chance to better themselves.[50]

To venture westward was to enter a foreign land. As late as the Civil War, the area on maps west of the Missouri River and east of the Rocky Mountains bore the inscription "the Great American desert." West of the ninety-eighth meridian, annual rainfall is less that thirty inches a year, and such a low amount of precipitation, especially when it is uneven and readily evaporates, is only barely sufficient to raise crops. Woodland was rare, streams were uncommon, and rainfall was erratic and unpredictable. Without large numbers of trees, where was a farm family to get logs for cabins or planks for fences or fuel for fires? Without streams, where was a family to get water for drinking or washing or irrigating crops? Without even rainfall, how was a family to raise corn?[51]

In spite of these impediments, beginning in the late 1850s, covered wagons and steamboats took pioneers along the Missouri River into Kansas and Nebraska, across the Red River into North and South Dakota, and across the Sabine into the central Texas hill country. The great rush to settlement took place in the 1870s and 1880s, when the railroads began to provide transportation of crops to markets, new kinds of wells and windmills began to provide water, barbed wire offered cheap fencing, and the federal Homestead and Timber Culture acts provided cheap land. Farm families were attracted by the vast expanses of level land carpeted by native grasses, which did not have to be cleared of tree stumps.[52]

Quickly, however, farmers learned how ill adapted techniques suited to the eastern woodlands were to conditions in this new environment, where hot winds called chinooks withered crops, clouds of grasshoppers darkened the skies and feasted on growing vegetation, and prairie fires jumped creeks to destroy fields.[53]

Houses, even in cities such as Lawrence or Topeka, Kansas, had to be constructed of whatever materials were available, such as cottonwood boards covered with hay, sod, or thatch. Further west, where timber was especially scarce, homes were customarily made of sod or dug out of the side of a hill or ravine, much like the home of a prairie dog and, in the words of one pioneer, made "without mortar, square, plumb, or greenbacks." One such dugout in Nickolls County, Nebraska, had a single room nine feet by twelve feet, housing six family members as well as a bed, a stove, a table, and several boxes. In 1876 nine-tenths of the settlers of Butler County, Nebraska, lived in houses made of dirt. These dugouts and sod houses allowed little light or air to enter, but they did keep cool in the summer heat and warm during the winter. Beds were made of rough boards threaded with cord and covered with a mattress stuffed with hay. Greased paper substituted for glass in windows, and the original doors were often made of old carpets or buffalo skins.[54]

The story of pioneer families on the Great Plains is a tale of poverty, unremitting toil, and ceaseless effort, but a story too of successful innovation and adaptation to new and challenging circumstances. In the process, the strongest and most potent resource pioneers were able to draw on was the family. Life on the prairies was harsh and monotonous, characterized by brutally long hours of work, unvarying scenery, the threat of drought, and the burdens of mortgages and debt. Yet adversity tended to reinforce family cohesion by requiring all members to cooperate in order to survive.[55]

Nothing prepared a pioneer family for the drudgery and toil of farm life. Although mechanization—by automating threshing and harvesting—helped to ease some of the burdens confronting men, women's work was unrelieved by technological change. A farm wife spent long days toting loads of firewood and buckets of water to the house, scrubbing soiled clothes against zinc washboards, and making soap and candles out of bacon, lard, and bone marrow. As late as the 1920s, a typical farm wife could expect to devote nine hours a day to such chores as cleaning, sewing, laundering, and preparing food. An additional two hours a day were spent cleaning the barn and chicken coop, milking the cows, caring for poultry, selling eggs and butter, and gardening. In addition farm women carried primary responsibility for saving and scrimping. One boy vividly remembered how his mother sought to economize on meals, to raise petty cash by selling butter and eggs, and improvise furniture and wall coverings out of boxes and yellowing newspapers. Childbirth was perhaps the greatest trial of all, since it often took place without either a midwife or a doctor in attendance.[56]

The pioneer families who ventured onto the Great Plains went with a strong spirit of optimism and enthusiasm. Unfortunately for many families, high hopes were soon dashed. Of the four hundred thousand families that took advantage of the Homestead Act to start a farm, two-thirds failed. During the late nineteenth century, drought, grasshoppers, fire, hail, blizzards, and floods devastated farms from Texas to the Dakotas, leaving many families absolutely destitute. A Minnesota girl described her family's plight to the state governor: "We have no money now nothing to sell to get any more clothes with as the grasshoppers destroyed all of our crops what few we had for we have not much land broke yet. . . . We . . . almost perish here sometimes with the cold."[57]

Thousands of families of agricultural pioneers lost their crops and were thrown into poverty. In 1894 an elderly Nebraska woman informed her grandson that she was subsisting on a diet of boiled weeds and bread and butter. A farm wife who lived in western Kansas informed her governor that her family was on the verge of starvation: "My husband went away and told me that we would have to starve. . . . I haven't had nothing to eat today and it is three o'clock."[58]

Although many pioneers stayed on and eventually succeeded in sustaining farms, many others abandoned their dreams and headed back eastward. During five months in late 1874, one Kansas official counted the wagons of 600 families leaving a six-county area in the north-central part of the state. For these families, the dream of building a farm was over.[59]

Still, despite hardships and tragedies, few emigrants ever regretted the decision to move west. As one pioneer put it: "Those who crossed the plains . . . never forgot the ungratified thirst, the intense heat and bitter cold, the craving hunger and utter physical exhaustion of the trail. . . . but there was another side. True, they had suffered, but the satisfaction of deeds accomplished and difficulties overcome more than compensated and made the overland passage a thing never to be forgotten."[60]

FAMILIES ON THE FARMING FRONTIER

It is common to think of the Industrial Revolution as exclusively an urban phenomenon. But beginning in the late 1850s, an agricultural revolution began that would reshape farm life and cause changes as dramatic and far reaching as those taking place in the nation's factory towns. Between the Civil War and 1900, the nation's farms experienced more rapid change than during the preceding two centuries. Farmers' traditional sense of independence began to diminish as farm families began to sell an increasing share of their crops in commercial markets, as absentee land ownership increased, and as a growing number of farm families began to farm land that they did not own. At the same time, farmers' traditional ways of using the soil became increasingly obsolescent, as hand power was increasingly replaced by animal power and wrought-iron plows and mechanical reapers sharply reduced farm labor requirements.[61]

One consequence of this agricultural revolution was a sharp decline in birthrates. In those areas most committed to commercial farming, many parents began to limit the number of births and hire wage labor instead of putting their own children to work on the farms. In contrast, in those areas where subsistence farming was most prevalent, fertility levels remained high because children continued to be viewed as economic assets who would contribute to household production.[62]

The agricultural revolution accelerated the movement of young people—particularly young men—away from Midwestern agricultural communities. As a result, after the second or third generation of settlement, many Midwestern farming communities were composed of closely knit female kin, since many daughters married neighbors and set up farms near their parents' homes. These kinship networks offered many Midwestern farm women companionship and the opportunity to share such tasks as child care, spinning, sewing, and quilting.[63]

A strong orientation toward family and kinship was a defining characteristic of farm life. Throughout the nineteenth century, many farm children followed their fathers and mothers into farming and relied heavily on parents and other relatives for assistance and land. Farm communities, in turn, were knit together by bonds of kinship. Farm children tended to marry neighbors, and over time rural communities in such states as Vermont and Illinois became increasingly intertwined as a result of intermarriage.[64]

Simply to assure farm operations over time required cooperation among family members. In many farming communities, legal mechanisms were adopted permitting parents to grant control of the family farm to one of their sons, on the condition that he care for his parents and any unmarried brothers and sisters. In the rural township of Chelsea, Vermont, for example, older farmers let a younger son take over operation of a farm only if he agreed to assume his father's debts and not to sell the land without parental consent. Frequently a Chelsea son was also required to maintain his parents and any unmarried siblings, provide dowries for any unmarried sisters, and even build an "ell" onto the family homestead so that parents and son could live in the same house. Often noninheriting siblings would remain in neighboring areas or nearby towns and provide assistance in times of need.[65]

For nineteenth-century farm families, the commercial revolution and migration westward, far from weakening family ties, actually strengthened family bonds and obligations.

FAMILIES ON THE MINING FRONTIER

No portrait of family life in industrial America would be complete if it ignored the families that lived in the isolated mining villages of northeastern and western Pennsylvania, southern West Virginia, and the Midwest. During the late nineteenth century, as many families made their livelihoods from mining coal from the earth as from working in iron and steel mills. (In eastern Pennsylvania alone, this involved more than a hundred thousand families.)[66]

Coal-mining families endured a particularly harsh existence. Employment was short and erratic, and annual earnings were low. At the turn of the century, when one state survey estimated that it took a yearly income of $754 to provide food, clothing, and shelter for a family of five, 60 percent of the adult miners in northeastern Pennsylvania's anthracite fields earned less than $450. Nominal wages often exaggerated the income of mining families, since many employers paid in "scrip" that could only be redeemed in company-owned stores, where a barrel of flour typically cost $8.50 compared to $6.50 at a cash store and two pounds of bacon cost twenty cents against fifteen cents at a grocery.[67]

Miners' incomes were often inadequate to meet ordinary needs. One miner who lived in Belleville, Illinois, was able to find work just thirty weeks in 1883 and earned only $250. After paying for rent, heat, and clothing, he had only $80 left to feed his wife and five children. In 1877 in eastern Pennsylvania, coal miners—who had to support their families on yearly wages of $200—lived in unpainted wooden shacks and subsisted on potatoes and mush. In most cases it was difficult for a coal-mining family to live solely on the earnings of a single breadwinner. To supplement the father's income, it was necessary for sons to enter the mines at an early age.[68]

To make matters worse, employment in the coalfields was highly irregular. Since mining operations regularly shut down for as long as six months of the year, miners were often idle. To maintain steady employment, it was necessary for families to move frequently; a central reality of coal-mining life was intense physical mobility. Mining families in western and northeastern Pennsylvania, southern West Virginia, and the Midwest led, in one miner's words, "a gypsy's life." They moved from one company town to another in search of regular employment. At the beginning of the twentieth century, the U.S. Immigration Commission estimated that one-third of miners moved every two years.[69]

Living quarters tended to be cramped and dilapidated. At the end of the nineteenth century, a typical Slavic miner's dwelling in eastern Pennsylvania's anthracite coal region was rented from a coal company for $1.75 to $3.00 a month and consisted of two or three unpainted rooms, twelve by thirteen feet in area, illuminated by a single window.

Such houses had no cellars, and the walls were neither plastered nor ceiled but consisted of rough boards and roof joints. Household furnishings generally consisted of a few strips of carpeting, a used cooking stove, a table, and one or two beds. It was not unusual for six to eight boarders to live in each house. In one such dwelling, there resided a husband, wife, two children, and ten boarders; in another there were fourteen boarders.[70]

Life in the coalfields was characterized by particularly acute levels of mortality. Work-related accident rates were miserably high. One of twelve miners died annually, and one of every three was injured. Mortality rates outside the mines were also high. In the coal districts of northeastern Pennsylvania, the death rate of children under the age of five was about 35 percent.[71]

In the isolated coal-mining villages of northeastern and western Pennsylvania, southern West Virginia, and the Midwest, coal miners tended to marry at an unusually early age and to have large numbers of children. A low marriage age was encouraged by the fact that coal miners reached their peak earnings at an early age, usually in their late teens or early twenties. Strength and dexterity were the most important skills in the coalfields, making youth a period of high wages. Independent wages permitted sons to set up their own households at a relatively early age. A low marriage age also contributed to an extraordinarily high birthrate. In eastern Pennsylvania, birthrates actually increased between 1850 and 1880, during a time when fertility declined for all other occupational groups. As late as 1900, a typical coal miner's wife gave birth to more than eight children—two or three more than other American mothers.[72]

To keep a mining family at or above the subsistence level, all members of a household had to contribute to the family economy. In spite of laws forbidding child labor, sons helped their fathers in the mines as soon as they were physically able. More than one mining family in four reported earnings from sons' children. This heavy reliance on child labor meant that few children could stay in school very long. Most children had no more than five years of formal education, and half were out of school by their twelfth birthdays.[73]

Women in coal-mining regions were particularly unlikely to work outside the home and instead devoted substantial energy to tasks in the home such as manufacturing handicrafts or taking in laundry or boarders (more than one household in six took in boarders). Daughters and mothers devoted a great deal of energy to gardening and raising livestock. As late as 1924, over half of West Virginia's mining families planted gardens and kept cows, pigs, and poultry. As one miner recalled, "Our garden saved us during all those depressions, and when I was out of work." "Miners couldn't always depend upon the mine," said another, "therefore we would have to raise a garden to make sure we always ate."[74]

It is important not to romanticize working-class family life. Although ties to the immediate family and the wider kinship network tended to be strong, family cohesion stemmed in large measure from the marginal economic existence of many working-class families. The frequency of premature death, irregular employment, disabling accidents, and wages at or below the subsistence line, coupled with the inadequacy of public welfare mechanisms, required individuals to rely on the family and the kinship network for assistance and support.[75]

Even at the beginning of the twentieth century, conditions of working-class life remained bleak. Death rates remained extraordinarily high. Infant mortality, orphanhood, and early widowhood affected a distressingly high proportion of families. Ten of every hundred white infants—and one out of every five black newborns—died by the age of one. High rates of infant mortality were matched by similarly high rates of childhood and adolescent mortality: One child out of every five was dead before reaching an age at which he or she could marry. A similarly high adult death rate meant that many children were orphaned and many husbands and wives were prematurely widowed. High mortality rates tore at the very fabric of family life. Altogether, early death would disrupt between 35 and 40 percent of all American families before all the children had left home.[76]

The physical conditions of working-class life remained horrific. Work hours were nearly as grueling in 1900 as they had been a century before. At the beginning of the twentieth century, a typical industrial worker labored fifty-nine hours a week for just twenty-two cents an hour; a coal miner, fifty-two hours a week for twenty cents an hour; a typical farm wife, ten hours a day in winter, and thirteen in summer. Maiming accidents were probably more frequent than they had been fifty years before. On the railroads, one worker in twenty-six lost a limb, and one worker in almost four hundred lost his life each year. Living conditions were still abominable. At the turn of the century, a third of all black farmers lived in windowless one-room cabins with dirt floors; a third of the residents of Seattle slept on rows of wooden bunks in temporary labor camps or rooming houses; and half of New York City's population inhabited tenement apartments where seven, eight, or more adults and children crowded into 250 square feet, often without windows and indoor toilets.[77]

It would not be until the 1920s that a more stable form of blue-collar family life would begin to appear. Outside agriculture and the New England textile industry, the trend in unemployment rates until 1929 was downward, aided by restrictions on foreign immigration and by a shift in employment away from temporary jobs in such seasonal fields as construction. Also contributing to family stability was the establishment of the first seniority systems governing promotion, lay-offs, and rehiring, which helped reduce the number of arbitrary dismissals of older workers. An even more important contributor to family stability was increased real wages, particularly after 1914, coupled with shorter work hours.[78]

Unfortunately, in 1929, this seemingly ever-rising tide of prosperity came to a crashing end.

An Italian immigrant family arriving at Ellis Island in New York Harbor. Courtesy of the Library of Congress.

CHAPTER VI

The Rise of the Companionate Family, 1900–1930

IN 1926, Claude H. Harman, a railroad locomotive engineer from San Francisco, sued his wife, Jessie Harman, for divorce. His divorce petition charged her with causing him "grievous bodily injury and grievous mental suffering," rendering him unfit to perform his job. His wife had, he maintained, told him on many occasions that she did not love him but only lived with him because he was a good provider. She had frequently called him "vile names, too opprobrious to be set out in this complaint" and said that his mother was "no good" and that his sister was a "whore." In addition she had often threatened to commit suicide and had said that her husband would be "branded as her murderer."[1]

Although California law stipulated that divorce could be granted only for acts "so grave and weighty . . . as to show an absolute impossibility for the duties of married life to be discharged," such as adultery, desertion, and physical cruelty, the court decided to interpret the statute liberally to include mental cruelty and awarded Claude H. Harman a divorce. For the first time, jurists were beginning to take cognizance of vast changes occurring in American family life, particularly in marital relations.[2]

Over the course of the nineteenth century, a momentous transformation had taken place in the functions and expectations assigned to the middle-class American family. By the beginning of the twentieth century, middle-class families had been shorn of many traditional economic, educational, and welfare functions. The family's role in education, in health care, and in care of the aged, poor, and the mentally ill had increasingly been assumed by specialists and institutions outside the family. At the same time, however, the family had acquired new burdens and expectations. The middle-class family was assigned primary responsibilities for fulfilling the emotional and psychological needs of its members. Along with providing economic security and a stable environment for children, family life was now expected to provide romance, sexual fulfillment, companionship, and emotional satisfaction.[3]

Many turn-of-the-century Americans believed the family to be in a unique state of crisis. Psychologist John B. Watson predicted, "In fifty years there will be no such thing as marriage." Critics denounced the family as "illimitably selfish, psychologically egocentric, spiritually dwarfish and decivilizing" and declared it a "factory of feeble-mindedness and insanity." Even defenders of the family were fearful of its future.[4]

Concern was provoked by a number of factors, one of which was a rapid upsurge in the number of divorces. Despite the efforts of late-nineteenth-century moral conservatives to make it difficult for couples to divorce, the divorce rate rose sharply after 1870. By 1916, in San Francisco, one out of every four marriages ended in divorce; in Los Angeles, one out of five; in Chicago, one out of seven.[5]

At the same time, a sharp decline in the birthrates of native-born, old-stock whites elicited deep concern. Birthrates had so decreased that the educated classes were failing to reproduce themselves, while the rate of childbearing among immigrant women was nearly twice that of native-born women. In 1903, Theodore Roosevelt expressed fear that the old-stock middle class was committing "race suicide."[6]

The drop in the nation's birthrate was merely one symptom of a dramatic change in traditional sex roles. More women were pursuing higher education, joining organizations, and working outside the home, and fewer young women seemed content to accept their traditional roles—caring for their homes, and tending their children. Many books, newspapers, and magazines bristled with alarm over this so-called revolution in morals and manners. Young women danced the fox-trot, smoked cigarettes openly and defiantly, read sex and confession magazines, watched lurid motion pictures, and, to an unprecedented extent, engaged in premarital sex. Alarm was expressed about how such radical changes would affect the cherished ideal of the family.[7]

The turn-of-the-century family was clearly an institution in flux, buffeted by stresses and pressures that have continued to confront twentieth-century families to this day. A rapidly rising divorce rate, an alarming fall in the birthrate, a sexual revolution, and a sharp increase in the numbers of women continuing their educations, joining women's organizations, and finding employment—each of these worked to transform the middle-class family. Many Americans believed that the family was being destroyed, but in fact a new kind of family was emerging from these demographic and cultural revolutions: It was the "companionate family," a new model and ideal of family function and behavior, which remains with us today.

Signs of Crisis

Beginning in 1889, following the discovery that the United States had the highest divorce rate in the world, and continuing until 1906, state legislatures across the country sought to tighten divorce statutes to discourage marital separation. The statutory grounds for divorce were reduced from over four hundred to fewer than twenty, and only three states continued to allow courts to grant divorces on any grounds they deemed proper. New Jersey allowed divorce only on the grounds of adultery and desertion; New York only in cases of adultery; South Carolina prohibited divorce altogether.[8]

Not only was divorce granted on fewer grounds, but the process of applying for divorce was made more stringent. A number of states prolonged the waiting period between divorce and remarriage, prohibited the guilty party from remarrying for a period of time, imposed longer residency requirements before divorce could begin, and required more adequate notice to the defendants in divorce cases and more adequate defense of divorce suits. In most states, divorce laws were rewritten around the concept of "fault" or moral wrongdoing. To obtain a divorce, it had to be shown that one party had transgressed seriously against the other. The innocent party was to be rewarded economically, in many instances through the provision of lifelong alimony, while the guilty wrongdoer was to be punished.[9]

Despite their intent these restrictions made surprisingly little difference in the prevalence of divorce proceedings. In the half-century between 1870 and 1920, the number of divorces granted nationwide increased fifteen fold. By 1924 one marriage out of every seven ended in divorce. Legal restrictions made little difference when many couples were willing to participate in a charade to meet legal requirements for divorce in order to liberate themselves from unsatisfying marriages.[10]

At the same time that the divorce rate was rising, the birthrate was falling. During the nineteenth century, average family size was reduced by 50 percent. In 1800 the average number of children born to a white woman was more than seven; by 1900 the figure had fallen to 3.56 children; and by 1929 the birthrate had declined by another third. Not only were women having fewer children, they were also spacing children closer together and ceasing childbirth at an earlier age. Instead of bearing children into their late thirties, most women stopped giving birth by their early or mid-thirties. As a result of falling birthrates, fewer years devoted to childbearing, and longer life expectancy, in 1900 a typical woman had half her life ahead of her after her last child was born—and at least a decade more than her mother had experienced free of child-rearing responsibilities.[11]

Many late-nineteenth-century Americans were convinced that the fall in the American birthrate was concentrated among old-stock native-born Protestant women and that, as a result, "the ignorant, the low-lived and the alien" would eventually take over the country by outreproducing "our own population." The number of educated Americans remaining single was high. A 1914 survey of women graduates of Barnard, Bryn Mawr, Cornell, Mount Holyoke, Radcliffe, Smith, Vassar, Wellesley, and Wells showed that fewer than 40 percent married. Of men who graduated from Harvard during the 1870s, nearly a third were still single between the ages of forty and fifty.[12]

To encourage population growth among the American-born, "nativists" (nineteenth-century organized opponents of immigration) opposed any birth control measures for Americans. In 1873 antiobscenity crusaders, led by Anthony Comstock, head of the New York Society for the Suppression of Vice, persuaded Congress to adopt "an Act for the Supression of Trade in and Circulation of, Obscene Literature and Articles of Immoral Use" that prohibited the sale of contraceptives, the publication of abortion-related advertising, the distribution of abortion-inducing drugs, and the dissemination of birth control information. Between 1880 and 1900, a loose coalition of physicians and nativists also successfully persuaded state legislatures across the country legally to prohibit the practice of abortion in order to encourage a higher birthrate.[13]

To moralists the most alarming symbol of change was the newly identified "restlessness" of the nation's women—the most conspicuous sign being a shift in their appearance. Before the turn of the century, most women, regardless of class, wore highly formal clothing designed to exaggerate their sexual distinctiveness. Irrespective of season, middle-class women covered their bodies with up to twenty-five pounds of petticoats, bustles, hats, and ankle-length skirts. Even before World War I, however, growing numbers of young women had begun to raise their hemlines; bob their hair; shed their bulky undergarments; and wear powder, rouge, lipstick, and eyeliner in public. A slender, boyish form quickly replaced the large breasted, wide-hipped, nineteenth-century feminine ideal. By 1928 the amount of material used in a typical woman's dress had declined from nineteen yards to just seven. Women were shedding a familiar but cumbersome image.[14]

The symbol of the new woman was the flapper, the independent, assertive, pleasure-hungry young woman, "making love lightly, boldly, and promiscuously." Much more than her mother or grandmother, this new woman was likely to have attended high school or college, to be a member of a women's organization, or to hold a job in which she worked in the company of men. From 1890—when just one college-age woman in fifty continued her education—until 1910, female college enrollment tripled (doubling again during the teens). Extraordinary growth also took place in the membership of women's organizations. New women's organizations sprouted in large numbers during the last years of the nineteenth century, including the National Council of Women, founded in 1888; the General Federation of Women's Clubs and the Daughters of the American Revolution, formed in 1890; the National Congress of Parents and Teachers, established in 1897; and the National Consumer's League, set up in 1899. Membership in the leading woman suffrage organization shot upward from a few thousand members in the late nineteenth century to a hundred thousand members in 1910 and then to two million members in 1917. Women were seeking their own organizational outlets for their energies and aims, rather than using men's vehicles.[15]

Women's participation in the paid labor force in the late nineteenth century rocketed upward, doubling between 1880 and 1900 and then increasing by another 50 percent between 1900 and 1919. By the latter year, for the first time in the nation's history, more than a fourth of all women in the work force either were or had been married. Although most women continued to work in the traditional sectors of the economy, growing numbers of women were beginning to work in clerical, sales, and other service occupations, for the first time in the company of men. Clearly the boundaries of "woman's sphere" were shifting. During the first decades of the twentieth century, the educational attainments of women began to approximate those of men; growing legitimacy was extended to female activity outside of the home; and, most importantly, new realms of work opened up to women.[16]

The clock had struck "sex o'clock in America," declared a notorious 1913 magazine cover, and many feared that the magazine was

right. America's revolution in morals, commonly associated with the
Roaring Twenties, had begun at least a decade earlier. Even before
the beginning of World War I, growing numbers of young women
had begun to shorten their skirts, roll their stockings below their
knees, carry their own latch keys, take part in "petting and necking"
parties, drink alcohol, demand the right to vote, and smoke in public.
Vice films, with suggestive titles like *Trapeze Disrobing Act* (1901),
What Demoralized the Barber Shop (1901), *How They Do Things on the
Bowery* (1902), and *The Physical Culture Girl* (1903), played the movie
theaters.[17]

Ironically, among the forces that had produced the revolution in
morals, one of the most important was the "purity crusade" of the
1880s and 1890s against prostitution, syphilis, gonorrhea, and the
double standard of sexual morality. This crusade—which enlisted the
support of many physicians, educators, municipal reformers, psychologists, sociologists, and social workers—broke the veil of silence that
had surrounded discussions of sexuality during the nineteenth century and inspired pioneering efforts at sex research and sex education.
For the first time, women's sexuality was publicly acknowledged.[18]

The revolution in manner and morals was accompanied by a revolution in sexual conduct. Women who came to maturity after the
turn of the century were much more likely than their forebears to
have sex both before marriage and outside it. A study found that of
fifty women born before 1890, seventeen had intercourse outside of
marriage; of fifty born after 1890, thirty had. Other studies also pin-
pointed 1890 as a watershed. Sex researcher Lewis M. Terman found
that nearly 90 percent of the women surveyed born before 1890 were
virgins at marriage, compared to 74 percent born between 1890 and
1899, 51 percent born between 1900 and 1909, and just 32 percent
born after 1910. Alfred Kinsey would also detect a momentous shift
in sexual behavior among women born around 1900 who came to
sexual maturity around 1916. These women were two to three times
as likely to have premarital intercourse compared to women born before 1900 and were also more likely to experience orgasm. Premarital
sexual experience among men did not increase, but it occurred less
often with prostitutes and more frequently with other women. Taken
together, these studies suggest that fewer and fewer women regarded
sex as something dirty and disgusting and instead were beginning to
regard it as a normal part of life.[19]

By the second decade of the twentieth century, the upsurge in divorce, the declining birthrate among the "better classes," the rise of
the "New Woman," and the revolution in morals had combined to

produce a profound sense of crisis. Most observers agreed that the family was undergoing a profound transformation, but few had any idea about the direction of change. Family roles, methods of child rearing, relationships between spouses, and the relationship of the family to larger social institutions were all visibly changing, but many feared that these changes were simply signs of the breakdown or death of the family. So widespread were such fears that the leading historian of the American family declared that the future of the institution was "problematic." A central question dominating social debate was whether marriage and the family could be modified sufficiently to adjust to the conditions of modern life.[20]

New Ideal of the Family

Some defenders of the family responded to the revolutionary changes taking place in family life with a reassertion of Victorian values. To restore respect for traditional values, the forces of conventional morality launched a crusade to discourage indecent styles of dancing, immodest dress, and impure books and films. Religious journals denounced popular styles of dancing as "polluting, corrupting, debasing, destroying spirituality, [and] increasing carnality." A bill was introduced in the Utah state legislature to fine and imprison women who wore skirts on the streets "higher than three inches above the ankle"; a bill introduced in the Ohio legislature sought to limit decolletage to two inches and prohibit the sale of any "garment which unduly displays or accentuates the lines of the female figure." Four states and many cities established boards of censorship to regulate films. Police in many cities arrested birth control activists like Margaret Sanger for disseminating contraceptive information and opening birth control clinics. Other cities required licenses for dance halls where "lurid" dances like the turkey trot were performed.[21]

Instead of idealizing the family as a sacred refuge in a corrupt world, a small but influential group of psychologists, educators, and legal scholars gave shape to a new conception of a "companionate family" in which husbands and wives would be "friends and lovers" and parents and children would be "pals." Convinced that the "old-style" family, based on sexual repression, patriarchal authority, and hierarchial organization, was "unsatisfactorily adjusted to twentieth century conditions," these "experts" on the family sought to facilitate the transition to a new kind of family better suited to "modern society and industrial conditions."[22]

In the eyes of a growing number of family experts, the crisis of marriage and the family was a manifestation of a painful economic and social transition that the larger society had undergone and that required new life-styles. According to the studies of Joseph Kirk Folsom, Ernest W. Burgess, and other figures associated with the Chicago school of urban sociology, "the present instability of monogamous wedlock" reflected the collapse of the material conditions that had supported the traditional family. The decline of farming and the shift of production outside the home had undermined the traditional basis of paternal authority. Urbanization and the growth of industrial society had deprived the family of its traditional economic, educational, religious, and welfare functions. The decline of the family's role in production combined with rising standards of living had encouraged parents to limit births.[23]

Far from abandoning marriage and the family, Americans had simply rejected a series of older family ideals that were ill suited to modern realities. Patriarchal authority, which had deprived women of an equal role in the household, had begun to give way to a new ideal of sharing rights and responsibilities. Marriage, which was romanticized by Victorian morality as a way of overcoming man's "animal nature," was instead to be a source of romance, emotional growth, and sexual fulfillment. The ideal of motherhood, which sentimentalized the woman as a pious and virtuous figure, the guardian of domestic morality, was to be replaced by a new ideal of woman emphasizing mutuality in sexual gratification. And finally, the Victorian ideal of childhood, emphasizing innocence and insulation from the corruptions of the adult world, was to give way to a "democratic" ideal offering children greater freedom from parental control, greater latitude in expressing their feelings, and increased interaction of adolescents with peers.[24]

Vocal debate over the proper nature of marriage shocked the nation during the early twentieth century. Well before the twenties, radical as well as conservative ideas about marriage were publicized and debated. Swedish feminist Ellen Key preached a scheme of "unwed motherhood." Edith Ellis, wife of British sex researcher Havelock Ellis, advocated trial marriage and "semi-detached marriage," in which each spouse occupied a separate domicile. Still others advocated "serial marriage" and easier divorce as solutions to marital incompatibility. Sexual modernists, including Havelock Ellis, G. Stanley Hall, and, of course, Sigmund Freud, attacked older Victorian notions that denied women sexual feelings and argued for greater sexual self-awareness for both men and women.[25]

The phrase "companionate marriage" first came to public notice in an influential 1925 book, *Revolt of Modern Youth*, by Denver Juvenile Court Judge Ben B. Lindsay and Wainright Evans. Sociologists had previously used the concept of "companionate marriage" to refer to childless marriages. Lindsay and Evans referred to something quite different. Their ideal was marriage unions held together not by rigid social pressures or religious conceptions of moral duty but by mutual affection, sexual attraction, and equal rights. In their view the achievement of companionate marriage required a series of social reforms, including access to birth control information, availability of divorce by mutual consent for childless couples, and training in the skills of marriage and parenthood.[26]

Popularized by a growing number of psychologists, educators, and social service professionals, the ideal of companionate marriage came to dominate discussions of marriage in twentieth-century America. It inspired efforts to legalize birth control and to permit marriages to be terminated on grounds of incompatibility, and it inspired programs of sex education, marriage counseling, and sex research. Exerting a powerful influence on marital expectations, it elevated anticipation of achieving emotional, sexual, and interpersonal fulfillment in marriage. The goal of marriage was no longer financial security or a nice home but emotional and sexual fulfillment and compatibility. Though marriages were not expected to be conflict and tension free, it was hoped that disagreements could be overcome if husbands and wives talked about their feelings, recognized the existence of conflicts, and worked out their problems through close "communication."[27]

The companionate marriage placed an unprecedented emphasis on the importance of sexual gratification in marriage. By the beginning of the 1920s, a sharp shift had occurred in public attitudes toward sex. In the first scientific statistical study of marriage in 1922, Dr. Katherine B. Davis found that only a small minority of married men and women (15.3 percent) believed that the only legitimate purpose of sex was procreation. Most of those surveyed said that sex was also justified "as an expression of love, because it is a natural relation, because children might for many reasons be undesirable, because desire is strong; for pleasure, satisfaction, development; because the intimacy of married life necessitates it; for physical and mental health." According to an emerging consensus, a "vigorous and harmonious sex life" was one of the cornerstones of happiness in marriage, while sexual disagreements were a major source of marital conflict. "Coitus," declared Robert Latou Dickinson, America's most prominent gynecologist, "is an index to marriage. . . . Satisfactory sexual relations are necessary to fully adjusted and successful union."[28]

One serious impediment to the realization of sexual fulfillment within marriage was many women's lack of instruction in sex. Katherine Davis's 1922 survey revealed that before marriage, nearly half of the educated women interviewed had never received any instruction whatsoever about sex and most of the rest considered their knowledge of sex inadequate. Sex education was the answer, and it initially gained support from the Social Hygiene Movement, which united many prominent physicians, clergy, educators, social workers, and philanthropists in a crusade against prostitution, venereal disease, and the double standard of sexual maturity. Courses in sex education, these people believed, offered a way of protecting the family and reshaping the nation's sexual morality. Beginning in 1909, the veil of silence surrounding sex and reproduction was broken by the appearance of the first modern textbooks and pamphlets discussing human reproduction. This was followed in 1914 by the establishment of the first birth control clinic and in the mid–1920s by the first marriage counseling centers.[29]

The achievement of a new ideal of sexual fulfillment within marriage depended in part on the availability of effective methods of contraception. As early as 1906, one physician noted that there was "hardly a single middle-class family" that did not expect him to help them "prevent conception." Between 1915 and 1921 a movement to legitimize and spread contraceptive practices, spearheaded by Margaret Sanger, succeeded in promoting the use of condoms, pessaries, and diaphragms as birth control devices. The drive to disseminate birth control information sprang from a variety of motives, including a desire to promote happier and more stable marriages, to increase women's autonomy, to improve infant and maternal health, and to reduce the birth rate of the poor and "unfit." By the time Katherine Davis conducted her survey in 1922, nearly three-quarters of the women questioned acknowledged using contraceptives to prevent conception. In their famous study of Muncie, Indiana, during the 1920s, sociologists Robert and Helen Lynd found that the use of contraceptives was practically universal among women of the professional and business classes but rare among working-class wives.[30]

The same wife who sought sexual fulfillment in marriage in the early twentieth century had become the central and dominant figure within the home. When the Lynds examined family patterns in Muncie, Indiana, in the mid–1920s, they were struck by the psychological gulf separating husbands and wives. The husbands' main preoccupation was with earning an income and taking care of such practical matters as car repairs. They felt little involvement in their families' day-to-day concerns. Wives, in contrast, were wholly responsible for organizing household affairs, caring for and disciplining children, and arranging the family's social life. Few fathers any longer anchored their identities in their role as domestic patriarch responsible for shaping the moral character of their children. Fathers who came of age at the turn of the century tended to associate fatherhood with being a reliable provider and breadwinner. Primary responsibility for the guidance and discipline of children had clearly shifted to the mother. No longer did the social definition of fatherhood emphasize the father's disciplinary role as "governor" and "moral force."[31]

The narrowing definition of fatherhood was due in part to the fact that more and more middle-class men were employed some distance from their residence. The time spent commuting to and from work greatly reduced the amount of time they spent in the presence of their families. Yet the contracting definition of the father's role also reflected increased male resistance to traditional domestic responsibilities. Major themes of popular culture at the turn of the century supported and reinforced this resistance by their glorification of competitive athletics, physical prowess, virility, and intense scorn for effeminacy and frailty. Masculine humor disparaged marriage and family responsibilities. In one example, H. L. Mencken defined marriage as an occasion for a man "to yield up his liberty, his property, and his soul to the first woman who, in despair of finding better game, turns her appraising eye on him." The new genres of cowboy and adventure fiction, written by such authors as Owen Wister and Jack London, celebrated the man who had escaped the confines of domesticity. Spokesmen for the rising business culture preached that the highest levels of personal accomplishment could only be achieved outside the home in the world of business.[32]

The most striking example of this shift away from a patriarchal father was apparent in immigrant families, most notably Jewish ones. The skills and character traits that had been most highly prized in the Old World, such as Torah study and rigid orthodoxy in religious practice, were viewed by members of the second generation as irrelevant in a dramatically altered social environment. In the New World, the father's traditional sources of authority were weakened, and the mother became the most important figure in helping her children adjust to new conditions. In the voluminous first-generation Jewish-American literature—including Sholom Asch's *The Mother*, Henry Roth's *Call It Sleep*, Anzia Yezierska's *Bread Givers*, and Abraham Cahan's *Yekl*—the mother, and not the father, is identified as the chief source of approval and emotional support for the immigrant child.[33]

It was the conduct of sons and daughters, however, more than that of parents that prompted concern about the family in the early twentieth century. The anthropologist Bronislaw Malinowski gave a pointed example of why parents were suddenly worried. His five-year-old daughter ended a family argument with a phrase that reduced him to silence: "Daddy, what an ass you are." Malinowski could not even imagine how his father, forty years before, would have responded to such impudence.[34]

According to Malinowski, his daughter's words epitomized a series of changes that had taken place within the middle-class family in the course of a generation. The rigid role hierarchy characteristics of the nineteenth-century family had begun to break down. Children had increasing latitude to express their feelings. And relations between children and parents had grown more democratic.[35]

Relationships between parents and children in the post World War I middle-class home were increasingly characterized by a fundamental paradox. Interaction between parents and children was more intimate than it had been in the past, and affection was more openly demonstrated. At the same time, however, adolescents were given greater freedom from direct parental supervision and their behavior was more and more heavily influenced by the peer group and popular culture, including advertising, movies, and popular music. Nor was this new social freedom of teenagers confined solely to the middle class. By the 1920s fewer working-class families expected working children to hand over their entire paychecks to their parents and instead simply permitted their children to pay board and to spend the remainder of their earnings in any way they liked.[36]

When Robert and Helen Lynd contrasted Muncie, Indiana, in 1894 and 1924, one of the most striking developments noted was the emergence of a distinct youth subculture, with its own status hierarchy, institutions, customs, modes of dress and language, and sexual mores. By the 1920s teenagers in Muncie were much more likely to attend high school and participate in athletics, clubs, sororities, and fraternities and take part in dances and parties. Throughout the country, more and more of the time of adolescents was spent outside the family and in the company of people their own age. The hallmarks of teenage life were school attendance, dating, bull sessions, proms, bonfires, driving, and moviegoing. For young people, friends were coming to play an ever increasing role in the process of socialization. It was through the peer group, and not parents, that young people were introduced to new styles of dress and behavior, new fashions of music and entertainment, and changing attitudes toward sex and glamour.[37]

The breaking away of adolescents into their own milieu aroused public concern for the diminution of parental authority. Popular magazines like *Atlantic Monthly, Literary Digest, Ladies' Home Journal*, and *New Republic* expressed anxiety about young peoples' rejection of genteel manners, their defiant clothing and hairstyles, their slang-filled language, and their "lewd" pastimes. Many middle-class homes were torn with dissension about teenagers smoking or attending "petting parties" or driving the family automobile or going out on school nights. Young people seemed to be achieving unprecedented freedom from parental control. One juvenile court judge reported instances of girls carrying contraceptives in their vanity cases, while another declared that the automobile had become a "house of prostitution on wheels" and cited nineteen instances in which young women had committed sex crimes in a car. Public condemnation and moral outrage were widespread.[38]

Progressive Reform and the Family

During the period from 1890 to 1930, "progressive" educators, psychiatrists, social workers, penologists, sociologists, and lawmakers initiated a variety of reforms intended to help the family adapt to modern conditions. To improve the quality of homemaking, educators and social welfare professionals instituted special programs to train mothers in the new science of parenting plus home economics and domestic science. To reduce mortality in childbirth, gynecologists and obstetricians transformed the birth process by introducing anesthetics and antiseptics and transferring deliveries to hospitals. To improve the quality of family life, psychologists and social workers launched ambitious programs of parent education and marriage counseling. To protect society against the family's failures, legal reformers crusaded for new laws relating to marriage and divorce and extending control over homeless and ill-treated children and juvenile delinquents. And finally, to provide assistance to needy families, lawmakers enacted the first state and federal programs in American history to provide health care for infants and pregnant mothers and financial aid to families with dependent children.[39]

Tying these diverse efforts together was a distinctive political and moral climate that might loosely be labeled "progressivism." Between 1890 and 1930, the watchwords of reform were "education," "social science," "government regulation," and professional expertise. Progressive reformers were convinced that government institutions, social welfare agencies, and schools, guided by knowledgeable professionals, could prevent or remedy social problems. Inspired by this faith in reform, they transformed the processes of childbirth, child rearing, and housework and assigned the government new authority to intervene in family problems.[40]

Transformation of Childbirth and Child Rearing

Childbirth was one of the first areas of family life to feel the effect of progressive reform. Male doctors replaced female midwives, anesthetics replaced natural childbirth, and hospital delivery replaced home delivery. The process of childbirth, presided over by "experts," was supposed to become safer and less painful. As late as 1910, half of all births in the United States were still attended by midwives, but increasingly the clientele of midwives was limited to black and immigrant women. By the start of World War I, the number of women using midwives had fallen sharply. Only 16 percent of white women in Mississippi and Wisconsin had babies delivered by midwives, and just 38 percent of the women in New York City, despite its high proportion of immigrants.[41]

The demand for delivery by physicians was accompanied by growing insistence on the use of anesthesia in childbirth. The assumption that pain was a necessary part of childbirth was challenged, and the introduction of anesthetics to deaden pain during delivery was called for by a number of women. One of the more popular drugs was scopolamine, or "twilight sleep," a cerebral depressant developed by German doctors. In spite of the fact that many anesthetics—such as ether and chloroform—impaired the alertness of both mother and newborn, caused a loss of control over contractions, and could even cause death if improperly given, their use became widespread by the 1920s.[42]

Perhaps the most dramatic change in childbirth after the turn of the century involved the shift from childbirth at home to childbirth in the hospital. Before 1900 only poor and unwed mothers gave birth in hospitals. By 1935, 37 percent of all American women delivered their babies in hospitals, and by 1945 the figure had reached 79 percent. The explanation lay in part in a fear that infection was more likely to be contracted at home than in the antiseptic hospital setting. But more important was the belief that childbirth in hospitals permitted doctors trained in obstetrics to conduct deliveries, thus curbing the use of forceps by undertrained physicians and midwives. The shift toward hospital delivery was accompanied by a marked increase in cesarean births—surgical delivery of babies through the abdomen—in instances where complications threatened either the mother or infant's life. The increased professionalization of childbirth contributed to a long-term decline in maternal mortality in childbirth from 60.8 per 10,000 live births in 1915 to 37.6 in 1940.[43]

As women demanded that childbirth become more safe, scientific, and systematic, they came to apply more modern methods to the rearing of their children. The first three decades of the twentieth century witnessed a series of profound changes in American child-rearing advice and practice. At the turn of the century, experts began to argue that the thoughtless and haphazard methods of child rearing characteristic of the past needed to give way to a more systematic approach to child care. Professionals advocated strict feeding and sleeping schedules and early toilet training and admonished mothers against fondling or playing with their children. This emphasis on procedure and detachment was part of a larger cultural movement at the turn of the century to rationalize, organize, and control the complexities of modern life. Beginning in the 1920s the rigidity and futility of such strict theories began to be remedied and replaced by more permissive child-rearing techniques, emphasizing delayed weaning and toilet training, attentiveness to a child's needs, and an awareness of the need to foster a secure and well-adjusted personality. Once more a broader cultural shift away from inflexible rationalization and scientific planning and toward an emphasis on self-fulfillment and self-gratification was influencing families to be less authoritarian and more responsive to their children.[44]

As late as the 1890s, most child-rearing advice assumed that children would surely grow up to become responsible adults if their mothers provided a proper model for emulation. Most child-rearing manuals said that the primary object of child rearing was to shape a child's moral character and that the procedure through which the values of courtesy, honesty, orderliness, industriousness, duty, and self-discipline were best instilled was one of maternal example.[45]

By 1900 the traditional emphasis on character formation was already supplanted by a new ideal of "scientific mothering" based on the study of child development. Inspired by the growth of child psychology as an academic discipline that sought to trace the psychological and physiological stages of child development, proponents of scientific mothering explicitly rejected the notion that the child was an essentially passive creature whose character was to be molded by the mother. Instead the child was seen as an active entity with special needs requiring special nurture. According to a growing number of experts, a parent's responsibility was to furnish, through a child's environment, the stimuli and cues that would encourage proper growth and orderly development.[46]

Prevalent advice rejected the seeming sentimentality of Victorian child-rearing practices and replaced them with a more detached and supposedly more scientific approach. Writers discouraged mothers from spoiling their children with overattention or catering to their every whim and advised them to let their infants cry out their frustrations without succor. Mothers were also warned against playing with their infants or encouraging them to laugh, lest such spontaneous shows of affection encourage a desire for sensual gratification and place undue strain on the children's undeveloped nervous systems. Guided by an assumption that faulty child-rearing techniques lay at the root of such larger social problems as poverty, delinquency, and even class antagonism, proponents of scientific mothering hoped to instill habits of regularity through the establishment of rigid schedules of eating, sleeping, and bowel movements.[47]

An infant-care bulletin issued by the federal government's Children's Bureau in 1914 provides a vivid summary of emerging assumptions about child rearing. According to the bulletin infants were born with strong autoerotic, masturbatory, and thumb-sucking impulses that had to be suppressed if they were not to "grow beyond control." To prevent masturbation mothers might tie their children's feet to opposite sides of the crib so that they could not rub their thighs together; to stop thumb sucking, a mother could sew a sleeve over the fingers of the offending hand. In the same vein, another popular child-rearing tract advised mothers to train their infants to have a bowel movement into a container at the age of one month by holding the infant over it and "inserting about two inches into the rectum, a tapered soap stick . . . for three to five minutes." The demand for regularity and conformity was strong.[48]

During the 1920s this stern and regimented line of advice received support from the behaviorist psychology of John B. Watson. "Children," Watson wrote in his influential 1928 text *Psychological Care of Infant and Child*, "are made not born," and he sought to show parents how to mold children's behavior through a process of positive and negative reinforcement. By rewarding behavior they wanted to encourage and punishing behavior they hoped to discourage, parents could produce a properly socialized child. The unsystematic methods used by earlier parents, who coddled their children and smothered them with kisses, had taught their offspring a variety of unfortunate lessons, to remain dependent on their mothers, to expect to be the center of attention, and to express themselves by having tantrums whenever their desires were frustrated. As an alternative Watson proposed that parents adopt a regimen of strict feeding, sleeping, and toileting on the grounds that they conditioned a child to adopt standards of "politeness and neatness and cleanliness" demanded of adults.[49]

Watson's behaviorist theories coexisted with a growing body of advice on child rearing stressing personality development. During the 1920s, two decades before the appearance of Dr. Benjamin Spock's *Infant and Child Care*, an increasing number of experts maintained that the primary goal of child rearing was to produce a secure, well-adjusted personality, not to instill carefully conditioned patterns of behavior. A series of strikingly modern themes began to appear in manuals for the first time. One author argued that if a child's psychological and emotional needs were frustrated during early childhood, the scars would last throughout life. Another author warned that mothers could "warp the lives of their children" through smothering affection. The one common theme was the significance of raising children properly.[50]

The new prominence placed on personality formation was evident in a shift away from tight scheduling and a renewed stress on physical cuddling and responsiveness to a child's needs. The influence of Freudian psychology and its criticism of undue repression of children; theories of psychological development, which stressed the gradual unfolding of a child's personality; and the educational theories of John Dewey and Maria Montessori, which sought to encourage curiosity and independence in children, all worked against an inflexible scientific approach to children and in favor of a more humanistic and empathetic approach.[51]

Greater permissiveness in child rearing was apparent by the early 1930s in the advice of such experts as Arnold Gesell, who recommended that mothers adopt more flexible schedules for feeding and sleeping based on the principle of "self-demand" and recommended delayed weaning and toilet training on the grounds that these were conducive to the development of a well-adjusted personality. Temper tantrums and thumb sucking were seen not as behavior problems requiring discipline but as phases children would pass through and grow out of. The child was coming to be seen as an active and feeling individual in need of respect and love as well as discipline.[52]

TRANSFORMATION OF HOUSEWORK

Along with far-reaching changes in childbirth and child rearing, the early twentieth century witnessed profound shifts in housework and women's domestic roles. Today a live-in servant is a rarity. This was not the case a century ago, when many middle-class families hired live-in servants to assist with such household chores as lighting stoves and fireplaces, preparing meals, making beds, diapering babies, serving meals, dusting, sweeping, laundering, and ironing. In Boston in 1870, one family out of every three had a live-in servant; in New York and San Francisco, one in every four had a full-time live-in servant; in Philadelphia and Chicago, one family in every five. Domestic architecture reflected the prevalence of domestic servants. To separate employers from servants, architects incorporated back entrances, back stairways, and servants apartments into the design of middle-class homes, permitting servants to perform their chores without disturbing the family.[53]

After the turn of the century, as alternative employment opportunities opened up for women, the availability of servants fell off sharply. Between 1890 and 1920, the ratio of domestic servants to the general population fell by half, thereby greatly affecting the life-style of many middle-class families. The servants that remained tended not to be young immigrant or native-born whites who lived with their employers but older black day workers, who returned to their own homes at the end of the day. The absence of household help 24-hours a day meant a veritable revolution in the life of the mistress of the household. Household designs changed to reflect the growing unavailability of servants. The "servantless" kitchen, which placed sink, stove, cupboards, and drawers within convenient reach of the homemaker, and which was located with easy access to other rooms in the house, characterized the architectural adaptation to social changes.[54]

Inspired in part by the declining availability of servants, a mass-based "mother's movement" sought to restructure women's domestic roles in terms of the principles of efficiency, expertise, and professionalism. Since the 1840s such experts as Catharine Beecher had called on women to apply rational business principles to housekeeping, but in the late nineteenth century, home economics and domestic science became specific courses of study in the nation's schools and universities. Spearheaded by such groups as the Congress of Mothers and the Society for the Study of Child Nature, and such key figures as Ellen Swallow Richards, an MIT-trained chemist, the movement sought to introduce young women to the relevant teachings of biology, chemistry, bacteriology, and child psychology. Menu planning would be placed on a scientific basis through an understanding of dietetics, shopping would be guided by the principles of economics, and housecleaning would be governed by a thorough understanding of germs. Wrote home economist Helen Campbell: "To keep the world clean, this is the great task for women."[55]

The Mother's Movement gained public notice in 1909 when the first White House Conference on Child Welfare was convened by President Theodore Roosevelt, and it gathered further momentum with the establishment in 1912 of the federal Children's Bureau, the adoption in 1914 of Mother's Day, and the enactment that same year of the federal Smith-Lever Act, providing funding for two thousand home demonstration agents to train housewives in proper methods of homemaking, budget management, and child rearing. And Congress appropriated money for teaching vocational home economics courses in secondary schools for the first time.[56]

If homemaking was to become a female equivalent to other professions, housewives had to have access to the proper kinds of professional equipment. The first years of the twentieth century saw the introduction of a vast array of new electric appliances, ranging from washing machines and dryers to vacuum cleaners, ranges, and refrigerators. Although these appliances were advertised as "labor saving," there is little evidence to suggest that they actually reduced time spent on housework. The long-term effect of the domestic science movement was to elevate standards of hygiene and cleanliness and make greater demands on women. Mothers were encouraged to launder clothes more frequently, to clean floors and rugs more often, and to devote more time to menu planning and shopping. Studies conducted in the mid-1920s showed that the time spent by urban housewives preparing meals, making clothes, and preserving and canning foods had declined from six hours a day to one, but that the amount of time devoted to cleaning and child care had risen even more sharply.[57]

Public Policy and the Family

As scientific methods were applied to the study of the family in the early twentieth century, explanations of the causes of family breakdown began to emphasize the consequences of societal and economic change on the family unit and environment. Industrialization had eroded the economic functions of the family; urbanization had weakened the extended family; birth control and advanced education had facilitated greater independence for women; and economic prosperity, the automobile, and the movies had encouraged a revolution in morals. Convinced that the problems of the family reflected underlying social problems, reformers of the Progressive Era sought to use social legislation and education to stabilize marriage and the family. Through new laws regulating marriage, programs of marriage counseling and family education, the creation of family courts, and welfare legislation to assist needy women and children, early-twentieth-century Americans hoped to address the sources of family instability.[58]

Many turn-of-the-century lawmakers held to the conviction that marriage laws could be devised that would discourage marriages of "the immature, the reckless, and the unfit." To accomplish these ends, many state legislators proposed laws to raise the age of consent; to impose physical and mental health requirements; and to forbid common-law marriages, interracial marriages, and polygamy.[59]

Between 1887 and 1906, unprecedented steps were taken to prevent the formation of bad marriages and thereby diminish the possibilities of divorce. During those two decades, eight states raised the age at which minors were allowed to marry; twelve states prohibited marriages on grounds of miscegenation, mental defectiveness, venereal disease, addiction, or drunkenness; and eighteen states imposed restrictions on the remarriage of divorced persons.[60]

Such efforts to regulate marriages met substantial resistance in some states. As late as 1930, twelve states permitted boys to marry at fourteen and girls at twelve (with parental consent), and only twelve states required as much as five-day waiting period between application for a marriage license and performance of the ceremony. Only seven states required a medical certificate showing freedom from venereal disease.[61]

Efforts to reform marriage laws were accompanied by far-reaching changes in divorce laws. Before 1900 the nation's divorce courts strongly reinforced Victorian notions of wifely and husbandly behavior. In order to obtain a divorce, it was necessary to show either that a man had violated his husbandly duties by failing adequately to support his family or by abusing his spouse or that a wife had violated her domestic duties to care for her family and house.[62]

By 1920 reformers, convinced that the law's adversarial approach to divorce was harmful for both spouses and children, recommended a variety of changes in divorce proceedings, including mandatory counseling of parties seeking divorce, nonadversarial divorce proceedings, and greater availability of divorce on grounds of mental cruelty and incompatibility. Although few jurisdictions instituted these specific reforms, the stringent rules governing divorce during the late nineteenth century were being modified in many states.[63]

In an effort to stifle the upsurge in divorce rates, many states intervened with the establishment of separate family courts, specifically charged with resolving a variety of family-related problems, including desertion, parental neglect or maltreatment of children, adoption, and juvenile delinquency as well as divorce. Proponents believed that separate family courts, dedicated to the welfare of families and children, would offer a less formal and less adversarial mechanism than the regular courts for settling domestic disputes. Many sponsors of family courts were inspired by the example of divorce proctors, who had been hired by a number of jurisdictions prior to World War I to investigate petitions for divorce, make recommendations to the court, and try to achieve reconciliation between the parties. In practice, however, a lack of funds and overcrowded dockets prevented family courts from conducting careful investigations of petitions for divorce or reconciling differences between spouses. However, they did assert the state's special interest in family welfare.[64]

The main tendency in divorce legislation was correspondingly toward greater stringency. Most states lengthened residence requirements for petitioning for a divorce and imposed longer waiting periods before parties were allowed to remarry, in order to discourage hasty marriages, encourage reconciliation, and deter hasty remarriages. The trend in judicial interpretation, however, was to dilute stringent legal statutes. In 1931 only seven states specifically permitted divorce on the grounds of mental cruelty, but judges in most other jurisdictions broadly reinterpreted laws permitting divorce on grounds of physical cruelty to encompass such conduct as constant nagging, humiliating language, unfounded and false accusations, insults, and excessive sexual demands. As the Indiana appellate court ruled in 1910: "Anything that tends to humiliate or annoy may as effectively endanger life and health as personal violence and affords grounds for divorce." Two states—New Mexico and Oklahoma—went even further and allowed divorce on grounds of incompatibility, and three other states—Arkansas, Idaho, and Nevada—shortened residency requirements in order to attract couples seeking divorce.[65]

In an effort to better protect the interests of children in divorce, the nation's courts elaborated new doctrines regarding custody. In questions of custody, the courts increasingly held that the decisive factor should be the "best interests of the child." The courts also held that any decisions on custody were open ended; that is, custody decisions could be reconsidered in the event of any changes in circumstances, moral transgression, or the increased age of the child.[66]

The economic impact of divorce, a topic of enormous public interest today, elicited surprisingly little debate in the courts during the first third of the century. Awards of alimony and property division were relatively rare. Few spouses requested alimony (just 20.3 percent in 1916), and even fewer were awarded such payments (just 15.4 percent in 1916), perhaps because most divorces were granted to families of semiskilled laborers who lacked real property to divide or the income to pay alimony awards. Stringent enforcement of awards was rare. Only five states made imprisonment the punishment for nonpayment of court-ordered alimony awards.[67]

Convinced that the major problem confronting the twentieth-century family was not divorce but a breakdown of love and companionship within marriage, a number of social workers, physicians, and psychologists joined together during the 1920s to promote new marriage counseling programs. These authorities maintained that marriage required special instruction in the art of personal interaction and that, contrary to older Victorian ideals of romantic love, conflict and tension were normal parts of married life. They believed that the major source of marital instability included a lack of communication and cooperation, unsatisfactory sexual relationships, and psychological maladjustments that might be prevented by sex education, counseling, and clinical therapy. By the early 1930s, courses in marriage counseling and family relations had spread throughout the country, treating such topics as dating, courtship, reproduction, birth control, and divorce.[68]

These changes in marriage and divorce law were accompanied by the efforts of states and localities to assume certain "parental" functions over children, by enacting laws mandating compulsory education and prohibiting child labor, establishing programs to provide care for homeless and ill-treated children, and creating special courts and reform schools to deal with juvenile offenders. New legislation, drawing on the old legal doctrine that the state had an obligation to protect children from "imminent harm," gave public agencies the power to remove neglected and vagrant children from their parents, to construct industrial-training and reform schools, and to invoke criminal penalties against parents for abandonment, nonsupport, and contributing to the dependency or delinquency of a minor.[69]

The changes that took place in the realm of family law during the early years of the twentieth century constituted a revolution in public philosophy. The nation's courts and state legislatures declared that government had not merely a right but a duty to promote family welfare. To this end, courts upheld state laws regulating the right to marry, liberalized the interpretation of divorce statutes, and undercut the older notion that the relationship between parents and children was one of almost absolute parental authority. Courts increasingly took the position that the state has the power to intervene in family life, punishing parents who failed to support their children and even depriving parents of custody if it could be determined that the relationship was harmful to the child. In all these ways, the legal system had begun the process of bringing family law into line with the new ideal of the companionate family.[70]

Changing social and economic conditions due to urbanization and industrialization after 1900 led to a sharp increase in the number of working mothers. Poverty forced a sizable proportion of mothers to work for wages. In 1900 just 6 percent of married women worked outside the home, but a third of all widowed and divorced women were employed. Many of these women were the mothers of young children, often working at night so that they would be able to care for their children during the day. Others sought employment at home or work with short or flexible hours. Most working mothers, however, had to make special arrangements for their children's care. Usually care was provided by an older child, a relative, a neighbor, or a lodger who baby-sat in exchange for room and board. In many cases child care arrangements were haphazard, supervision was casual, and the care provided children was perfunctory. An investigation of children of working mothers in Philadelphia concluded that "for one quarter of the children not twelve years old the time spent at school was the only period during which they were supervised."[71]

Concern over the lack of supervision of children led to the launching of pioneering efforts to provide day nurseries for the children of working mothers. By 1910, 450 charitable day nurseries had been opened in working-class neighborhoods, supplemented by a small number of for-profit centers. Public investigations found many of these nurseries overcrowded, unsanitary, understaffed, and lacking in toys, games, and playrooms. Concluded a 1917 study of Chicago's thirty-five charity nurseries: "Apathy and boredom would seem to have no place in the group life of normal children, yet they are to be found frequently among nursery groups." In most municipalities no provision was made for licensing or inspection in day nurseries, but public concern had been aroused and family professionals added another barrier to child welfare to their agenda.[72]

The fact the most mothers worked primarily out of financial need encouraged public debate about the problems of poor families. The early twentieth century witnessed the first public efforts to provide financial and medical assistance to the families of the poor. Stimulus for these efforts came from a White House conference convened by President Theodore Roosevelt in 1909, which took the position that state and local governments should provide financial aid to needy mothers so that they could afford to care for their children at home. The first state to provide public aid to mothers of dependent children was Missouri in 1911, and by 1913, eighteen states had enacted aid-to-mothers laws. These laws initially restricted aid to widows with dependent children but were eventually broadened to provide aid to needy families in which the father was physically or mentally incapacitated or in which the mother was divorced, deserted, or unmarried. But it would not be until 1935 that the federal government, under the Social Security Act, would provide federal grants to mothers with dependent children.[73]

These aid-to-mothers laws provided assistance to only a small fraction of needy female-headed families, in part because of strict eligibility standards and partly because few eligible women applied for assistance. A study of widowed mothers in Philadelphia in 1924 indicated that two-thirds of the women where ineligible for assistance and that a third of all potentially eligible widows failed to apply for aid. The inadequacy of public and private charities is apparent from the number of children placed into custodial care because their widowed mothers were unable to support them. In 1913 alone, 2,817 New York City children were institutionalized or placed in foster homes because of the death of a father or the illness of a mother. However, the state had begun to acknowledge its obligation to care for disadvantaged children and in doing so had become a partner in the raising of America's children and the stabilizing of its families.[74]

Not only did states legislate to prevent inadequate care of children, but government also took the first steps to protect the unborn through improved prenatal and obstetrical care. As late as 1924 in Wyoming, 40 percent of women were not attended by a doctor, nurse, or midwife during childbirth. In 1921, to combat infant mortality, Congress enacted the Sheppard-Towner Act to promote the health and welfare of infants and mothers. The act provided for the establishment of child health and maternity consultation centers and "health-mobiles" to educate mothers in prenatal care and furnished funds for hospital facilities for problem pregnancies and deliveries. Congress refused to extend the act beyond 1929, however. These early efforts to provide public assistance to families at risk sparked the first rumblings of a long-lasting debate in American politics over the proper role of the state and federal governments in helping families.[75]

By the 1930s, optimists viewed the evolving American family as a success story. Compared to families in the past, it was much less likely to be disrupted by the premature death of spouses or children. Couples were likely to live to see their grandchildren and to experience a period in which their own children were no longer their responsibility. Declining death rates meant that fewer children experienced the loss of a parent or sibling and fewer parents experienced the loss of a child or spouse. Rising life expectancies meant that the duration of marriages was far longer than in the past. The chances of a marriage lasting forty years or more rose from just one in three to one in two between 1900 and 1940. A sharp decline in the number of boarders and lodgers after 1920 meant that more families were able to minister exclusively to family members' emotional needs.[76]

The improvements that had occurred in family life were not simply demographic. Contraceptives allowed sex to become an increasing source of mutual gratification within marriage. Housework had become less onerous. Childbirth had become safer and less painful. And relations within the home had become less formal and hierarchial and more democratic and companionate.

Pessimists, however, could see a darker side to family life. Many changes in family life pointed to disintegration and disorganization. Signs of instability seemed rampant—the rising divorce rate; the increasing numbers of working mothers; the rebelliousness of youth; the falling birthrate; and the growing incidence of illegitimacy, adultery, and premarital sex.

Ironically, the very factors that the optimists pointed to as evidence of improvement also proved to be the sources of the family problems that pessimists deplored. The increased duration of marriage and the new emphasis attached to companionship and emotional fulfillment may have encouraged divorce as a solution to unhappy marriages that did not afford intimate relations. Similarly, the continuing decline in birthrates, the extended time that young people spent in their natal homes, and the new expectations about children's needs may have combined to produce greater public consciousness about the problems of adolescence. Instead of regarding these developments as alarming signs of the family's demise, however, they should be viewed as challenges American's families faced as they adapted to changing demographic circumstances.[77]

Freight car used as a house. Illinois, 1937. Photograph by Arnold Rothstein. Courtesy of the Library of Congress.

CHAPTER VII

America's Families Face the Great Depression

LATE in 1930 a crisis occurred in the life of five-year-old Russell Baker. His thirty-three-year-old father died suddenly of an acute diabetic coma, leaving Russell, his mother, and two sisters with only an aging Model T Ford, a few dollars of insurance money, and several pieces of Sears-Roebuck furniture. Having no way of making a living and no prospects for the future, Russell's mother decided to leave her home in rural Morrisonville, Virginia, and move in with a younger brother who lived in Belleville, New Jersey, a commuter town on the outskirts of Newark. But before she packed up the family's meager belongings, she did something that would haunt Russell for the rest of his life. To make herself and her children less of a burden, she gave up her dimpled, blond-haired, ten-month-old baby Audrey to a childless aunt and uncle.[1]

Stories like Russell Baker's were commonplace during the Great Depression. Many families were unable to protect themselves against adversity. In Pennsylvania, coal-mining families crowded three or four families together in one-room shacks and lived on wild weeds. In Arkansas, families were found living in caves. In St. Louis, adults and children dug through garbage dumps for rotten food. In Oakland, California, whole families inhabited sewer pipes. And in Harlan County, Kentucky, families subsisted on dandelions and blackberries. President Hoover declared, "Nobody is actually starving. The hoboes are better fed than they have ever been." But in New York City in 1933 at least twenty-nine people died of hunger, and in 1934 official statistics indicated 110 deaths caused by starvation.[2]

After more than half a century, the images of the Great Depression remain etched in the American psyche—breadlines and soup kitchens, tin-can shanties known as "Hoovervilles," penniless men and women selling apples on street corners, and gray battalions of Arkies and Okies packed into Model A Fords heading to California. The depression confronted families with economic crisis and uncertainty, with loss of support and sustenance. The economic disaster caused a major revolution in the lives and welfare of families in America and the government's role in securing them. It produced a new recognition that the federal government had an obligation to intervene to provide security against the risks of hunger and destitution. The economic collapse of the 1930s created a new and more threatening kind of poverty as well as a federal response that permanently changed the meaning and experience of poverty.

"Mass unemployment," a depression-era journalist observed, "is both a statistic and an empty feeling in the stomach. To fully comprehend it, you have to both see the figures and feel the emptiness." The economic collapse of the 1930s was terrifying in its scope and impact. By 1933, 50 percent of the labor force in Cleveland and 80 percent of the work force in Toledo were out of work. A million were jobless in New York. The unemployment rate was higher and the duration of high unemployment was longer in the United States than in Britain, France, or Germany. Unemployment jumped from less than three million in 1929 to four million in 1930, eight million in 1931, and twelve-and-a-half million in 1932. The unemployment rate climbed from just 3.2 percent in 1929 to 8.7 percent in 1930, 15.9 percent in 1931, and 23.6 percent in 1932, and before 1941 never fell below 14.3 percent. Worse yet, few of the jobless found new work quickly. A sixth of the unemployed were out of work for more than two years, and a third walked the streets looking for employment for at least one year.[3]

The collapse was staggering in its dimensions. By 1933 Americans had only 54 percent as much income as they had had in 1929 to purchase food and clothing, pay taxes, or repay debts. Average family income tumbled 40 percent from $2,300 in 1929 to just $1,500 four years later. During 1932, the worst year of the depression, 28 percent of the nation's households, containing thirty-four million men, women, and children, did not have a single employed wage earner. But even those fortunate enough to hold jobs suffered drastic pay cuts and reductions in hours. Only one company in ten did reduce wages, and by mid-1932, three-quarters of the nation's workers were on part-time schedules.[4]

The depression not only created poverty, it also brought preexisting poverty to public notice. As the economy contracted, it revealed poverty that had been largely ignored during the boom years of the 1920s. In 1929 the Brookings Institution estimated that just 8 percent of American families had incomes of more than $5,000 a year, that more than 60 percent of the nation's families earned less than $2,000 a year, and that 42 percent lived on less than $1,500 annually. "At 1929 prices," the Brookings Institution calculated, "a family income of $2,000 may be regarded as sufficient to supply only basic necessities." Hence, prior to the depression, nearly 60 percent of American families lived at or below a basic subsistence level.[5]

During the first few years of the twentieth century, a combination of social developments had contributed to an increase of poverty. Growth in the number of "broken" families—fractured by death, divorce, and desertion—had been under way throughout the 1920s. A rapid increase in the number of older Americans over the age of sixty-five, from 4.9 million to 6.6 million, also contributed to the growing incidence of poverty. Joblessness was on the rise even before the stock market crash, climbing from 1.5 million in 1926 to perhaps 2.86 million in 1929. Tenant farming had been climbing since the start of the century, and soil depletion, farm mechanization, boll weevils, and deflated crop prices pushed a million Americans off farms during the 1920s.[6]

Economic hardship and physical want were not new. Immigrants, the unskilled, and female-headed families had long faced the threat of destitution. Before the 1930s the loss of employment for several months a year was a normal event for industrial and unskilled workers. In pre-Depression Massachusetts 25 percent of workers were unemployed for three months a year in prosperous times, and more than 40 percent were jobless for periods of four months or more in bad years.[7]

What was new after 1929 was that the trauma of joblessness and loss of property began to affect families that had previously felt immune from such fears. Families that had spent a lifetime accumulating a savings account or acquiring a farm or house suddenly found themselves penniless or unable to pay off mortgages. A fifth of the nation's commercial banks closed their doors, and nine million families lost their savings. By 1934 more than half of all homeowners in Indianapolis, Indiana, and Birmingham, Alabama, had defaulted on their loans, as had two-fifths of all homeowners in twenty other cities.[8]

The spread of poverty to previously untouched families created two discernible groups of poor. There were the traditional poor, including the families of tenant farmers (numbering 8,500,000 in 1930), members of single-parent families (10,500,000), the disabled (1,000,000), and the elderly (6,500,000), whose economic insecurity predated the depression and whose numbers had been on the rise before 1929. And there were the "new" poor, comprising thousands of formerly middle-class and working-class families who had been thrown out of work or off farms by industrial shutdowns or bankruptcy, their savings accounts exhausted and hopes of being able to meet mortgages and automobile payments steadily diminishing.[9]

The upsurge in unemployment and poverty after 1929 created new political pressures to force the federal government to assume an active role in alleviating the sufferings caused by unemployment, dependency, and old age. But even then, as bold as its initiatives were, the social safety net erected by Franklin Roosevelt's New Deal established a two-tiered system of social provision that would treat the "old" poor and the "new" poor differently.[10]

To some Americans during the 1930s, the depression seemed to have a salutory effect on the family. It encouraged members of the family to turn "toward each other with greater, more intelligent interdependence." Despite fears that the family would disintegrate, optimists noted, the depression sharply curtailed activities outside the home and forced families to pool their resources and find comfort in each other. Divorce rates actually declined during the depression, and in popular magazines a new emphasis on familial "comradeship, understanding, affection, sympathy, facilitation, accommodation, integration, [and] cooperation" was apparent. Families began to play new games like Monopoly together and to listen to the radio or go to the movies together. As a Muncie, Indiana, newspaper editorialized, "Many a family that has lost its car has found its soul."[11]

Others, however, believed that the economic downturn had an essentially destructive impact on the family. Unemployment, part-time work, reduced pay, lowered living standards, and the demands of needy relatives tore at the fabric of family life, devastated men's self-esteem, and undermined a family's self-respect. The rate of increase in divorce declined, to be sure, but rates of desertion soared, and by 1940 there were over a 1,500,000 married women living apart from their husbands. Family disintegration was dramatically evident in the facts that the number of children placed in custodial institutions rose 50 percent during the first two years of the depression and that more than 200,000 vagrant children wandered about the country as a result of the break-ups of their homes. The destructive impact of the depression was especially apparent in the growing numbers of children suffering acute undernourishment and contracting such diseases as pellagra and rickets, which indicated nutritional deficiencies. Many young people, reported the Children's Bureau, found themselves "going for days at a time without taking off their clothes to sleep at night, becoming dirty, unkempt, a host to vermin. They may go for days with nothing to eat but coffee, bread and beans."[12]

The Great Depression would leave an indelible mark on American family life. Not only did it throw breadwinners out of jobs and impoverish families, it forced many Americans to share living quarters with relatives, delay marriages, put off having children, or tolerate unhappy marriages for financial reasons. In many cities, particularly in the South, as many as one-sixth of all families "doubled up" in apartments in order to cut expenses. As the economy contracted, the marriage rate declined. In 1932 there were 250,000 fewer marriages than in 1929, and altogether 800,000 marriages were postponed by the depression. The fall in the marriage rate was accompanied by a sharp decline in the birthrate, as economic uncertainty forced people to have fewer children than they wanted. For the first time in American history, the birthrate dropped below the replacement level, and Americans had nearly three million fewer babies than they would have had at the 1929 birthrate. The divorce rate also fell for the simple reason that fewer families could afford one. Between 1930 and 1935, there were 170,000 fewer divorces than would have occurred had predepression trends continued.[13]

The gravest effects of the depression on family life were largely invisible to the casual observer. The most common response to its harsh disruptions was denial of economic realities. Many families sought desperately to maintain their social status by postponing payments on loans and mortgages, taking second mortgages on real estate, depleting savings accounts, or borrowing against insurance policies before being willing to pare luxuries or other expenditures. "Status" expenditures persisted as families sought to disguise their economic straits by painting the exteriors of their houses or purchasing new shutters in order to impress neighbors. Unable to confront the loss of income and the loss of social position it entailed, they tried to forestall disaster for as long as possible.[14]

Other families sought to cope by adopting more labor-intensive household practices, including planting gardens, canning foods, making clothing, and doing their own household repairs. Sales of electric toasters, mixers, percolators, and washing machines slumped, as many families attempted to pickle, preserve, and cure food, bake bread, and dye cloth. In 1931 sales of glass jars reached an eleven-year high even though demand for store-bought bottled and canned foods declined. Falling back on their own resources, many Americans tried to return to an earlier state of self-sufficiency. Unemployed Massachusetts textile workers set up looms in their living rooms. Wives and mothers throughout the nation tried to earn supplementary income by taking in sewing or laundry or by dressmaking, performing manicures for a dollar, setting up parlor groceries, or feeding and housing boarders.[15]

Pooling family incomes provided another buffer against loss of work. The 1930 census indicated that one-third of all American families had more than one wage earner and that a quarter had three or more income earners. Part-time jobs for children—running errands, mowing lawns, baby-sitting, and selling newspapers and magazines, shining shoes, carting groceries, or returning pop bottles for two cents apiece—supplemented their father's income. Altogether, half of the nation's unemployed lived in a household in which someone was working.[16]

People turned to creative economies to meet the exigencies of the depression. They bought day-old bread, handed down old clothing, reused razor blades, used cardboard and cotton for shoe soles, and relined coats with old blankets. To cut expenses and avoid embarrassment, social interaction with friends and neighbors was sharply restricted. In New Haven, Connecticut, just 3 percent of the adults questioned said they still attended parties, and only 25 percent continued to visit neighbors. Club memberships and extracurricular school activities were also restricted, and fewer family members went to pool halls, bowling alleys, or boxing rings.[17]

Given the inadequacy of public and private charity, individuals relied on kinship ties to provide financial support to relatives outside their immediate family, particularly elderly parents. Forty percent of the working wives in Cleveland, Ohio, and 50 percent of those in Utah contributed income to relatives living outside their home.[18]

The economic dislocations caused by the depression had a powerful effect on the father's stature as economic provider and disciplinarian. Many fathers were overwhelmed by guilt because they were unable to support their families. One father told a *New York Daily News* reporter in 1932: "I haven't had a steady job in more than two years. Sometimes I feel like a murderer. What's wrong with me, that I can't protect my children?" And in truth, unemployment often significantly lowered the status of the husband within the family and undermined his role as primary decision maker. The inability to support their families proved to be psychologically debilitating for many men, who lost their sense of self-respect and were unable effectively to look for work. One wife commented "they're not men anymore, if you know what I mean."[19]

The father's diminished stature was mirrored by a great increase in the money-saving and -earning roles of mothers inside the family. Sociologists Robert and Helen Lynd were impressed by the profound changes that took place in women's roles during the depression in contrast to the fixity of men's roles. Despite widespread public hostility—evident in a Gallup poll indicating that 80 percent of men opposed employment for their wives under almost any circumstances—growing numbers of married women entered the paid labor force during the depression. Among families of high economic and educational attainment there was a marked relaxation in husbands' attitudes toward the employment of their wives. In Berkeley, California, nearly 40 percent of all wives worked at some point during the depression, and in rural Mississippi, two-thirds of all female textile workers were married.[20]

In most cases women's occupational opportunities were narrowly circumscribed, hours exceedingly long, and pay low. In 1930 out of every ten working women, three were engaged in domestic service, two worked in textile or apparel factories, and one worked as a schoolteacher or nurse. In black families the economic contributions of married women were particularly great. Forty percent of black women were in the labor force at any time, against just 20 percent of white women.[21]

Although economic loss and hardship visited all sections of the country, the effects of the depression varied widely according to region, class, race, gender, and age. All groups suffered. Between 1929 and 1933, doctors and lawyers saw their incomes fall as much as 40 percent; salaries of the most highly skilled New York stenographers tumbled from $40 a week to just $16; in Chicago, a majority of working women toiled for less than twenty-five cents an hour. Even among the privileged, some suffered. One-third of the Harvard class of 1911 confessed that they were hard up, on relief, or dependent on relatives. But the most severe economic hardship fell on those groups already trapped in poverty or in low-paid, unskilled jobs.[22]

The plight of the elderly became increasingly desperate during these years. A Long Beach, California, physician looked out his window and saw three haggard old women bending over garbage cans, "clawing into the contents." Eighty-seven percent of older Americans had been self-supporting in 1910; this figure had declined to 67 percent in 1922 and 60 percent in 1930, even before the full impact of the depression had been felt. By 1940 two-thirds of all older Americans were dependent wholly or partly on public relief, private charity, or friends and relatives.[23]

The depression also brought new hardships to the lives of younger Americans. Many families were so needy that their children went hungry. A fifth of New York city's children suffered from malnutrition, and in coal-mining areas of Illinois, Kentucky, Ohio, Pennsylvania, and West Virginia malnutrition was said to be over 90 percent. When a teacher told a young girl to go home to eat, the child replied, "I can't. This is my sister's day to eat."[24]

Many children also lacked the opportunity to pursue an education. In 1932, a third of a million children could not attend school because their classrooms were closed for lack of funds. Schools in Dayton, Ohio, were open just three days a week, and more than three hundred Arkansas schools were shut for ten months or more.[25]

To help their families make ends meet, many children were expected to find some sort of job. A Los Angeles family subsisted on a teenage daughter's earnings as a five-and-ten cent store clerk. Russell Baker was forced to go to work at the tender age of eight. In Oakland, California, 50 percent of all teenage boys and 25 percent of all teenage girls took up part-time jobs as baby-sitters, janitor's assistants, store clerks, and delivery boys.[26]

Midwestern and Southern farmers were in particularly desperate straits. Take the example of the Gudgers, a white southern Alabama cotton sharecropping family of six. From their landlord, they received twenty acres of land, seed, an unpainted one-room house, a shed, a mule, and fertilizer as well as ration money of ten dollars a month. In return, they owed him half their corn and cotton crops, half their cottonseed, and 8 percent interest on their debts. By 1934, they were eighty dollars in debt; by 1935, their debts had risen another twelve dollars.[27]

Few images have left a deeper imprint on the nation's historical memory than the picture of Midwestern or Southern farm families piling their meager possessions into an aging Ford jalopy and heading off to California. During the Great Depression, as many as a million Dust Bowl refugees and tenant farmers took to the nation's highways and railroads. Railroad officials in Kansas City counted 1,500 transients a day hitching rides on freight trains, and municipal officials in towns in Arizona, New Mexico, and Texas witnessed an influx of as many as 200 migrants a day. The Southern Pacific Railroad boasted that it threw 683,000 vagrants off its trains in 1931. Free public flophouses and missions in Los Angeles provided beds for 200,000 of the uprooted.[28]

Many of the migrants were farmers and farm laborers, lured away from debt-ridden farms by the hopes of jobs and a better life in the nation's cities but also pushed off the land by farm mechanization, shifts in consumer demand, and a drought that turned fertile land to dust. The trend toward mechanized farming was disastrous for small farmers and tenant farmers. Particularly in the South, draft animals were replaced by tractors, trucks, and combines, allowing a single farm family to perform the work formerly done by a dozen members of a threshing and harvest crew. Mechanization permitted many farmers to substitute their sons and daughters for hired help. As a result, 514,000 farm workers lost their jobs.[29]

Displaced farmers and farm workers headed westward to California or northward to the industrial Midwest. Noted one observer: "They roll westward like a parade. In a single hour from a grassy meadow near an Idaho road I counted 34 automobiles with the license plates of states between Chicago and the mountains." Whole counties were depopulated. In 1936 seven counties in southeastern Colorado reported only 2,078 houses still occupied; 2,811 houses were abandoned and another 1,522 homes had disappeared.[30]

Black Americans suffered during the depression with particular intensity. A year after the stock market crash, 32 percent of adult blacks were jobless in Baltimore; 38 percent in Pittsburgh; 70 percent in Charleston; and 75 percent in Memphis. In Chicago, 58 percent of black women were unemployed; in Detroit, 75 percent.[31]

Hardship was particularly acute in the South, where three-fourths of the black population lived. In Macon County, Alabama, the site of Booker T. Washington's famous Tuskegee Institute, thirty miles east of Montgomery, black families lived in abysmal conditions of poverty. Their diet consisted almost entirely of salt pork, hominy grits, corn bread, and molasses. Red meat, fresh vegetables, fruit, and even milk were almost unknown luxuries. Most dwellings had dirt floors, no windows or screens, and almost no furniture. A fifth of the homes had no water; three-quarters had no sewage disposal. Privies were only constructed when underbrush was not nearby. Black income in Macon County averaged less than a dollar a day.[32]

Before the depression, rural black Southerners suffered extreme poverty, but the economic crisis of the 1930s greatly worsened their position. Payment for picking a hundred pounds of cotton fell to twenty cents, a rate that amounted to sixty cents for a fourteen-hour day. Many sharecropping families were given cash advances of as little as ten dollars a month to support families of six or eight. Throughout the South the depression eliminated substantial numbers of jobs traditionally held by blacks in the building trades, street cleaning, garbage collecting, and domestic service.[33]

Conditions were equally distressed in the North, where three million black Americans made their home. In Chicago and in other large cities, the bulk of the black residents made their homes in what were euphemistically called "kitchenettes." Six-room apartments, previously rented for $50 a month, were divided into six kitchenettes renting for $8 a week, assuring landlords of a windfall of an extra $142 a month. Kitchenettes typically contained an icebox, a gas hot plate, and a single bed. A bathroom that once served a single family was now shared by six. A typical building that previously held sixty families now contained three hundred.[34]

Northern blacks lived at the very bottom of the economic scale. During the depths of the depression, when the Works Progress Administration estimated that a family of four needed an income of $973 per year to support a minimum subsistence budget, more than 70 percent of Chicago's black families had annual incomes of less than $1000 and a third earned less than $500.[35]

The dissolution of lower-class black family life was one of the most distressing consequences of the depression. In Chicago two out of every five adult black women were without husbands, mainly because of early widowhood. In one neighborhood on Chicago's west side, half of all households lacked a husband or father. The underlying causes of family instability were high mortality rates and the precarious economic status of black men. High rates of unemployment, lack of stable jobs, and low wages all made it difficult for lower-class black men to function effectively as breadwinners.[36]

The full brunt of depression hardship was felt by black Americans, but the public response was woefully inadequate. Even though black unemployment rates were consistently one-and-a-half times higher than the rates for whites, just 3 million black Americans—one out of four—received any public relief during the depression. Even when relief was given, black families often received less than their white counterparts. In Texas rural black familes received a quarter less aid than white families on relief. In Jacksonville, Florida, whites received thirty cents an hour on work relief; blacks, only twenty cents. In

Harlem three-fourths of all jobless black families received no relief payments at all. To survive the depression the nation's black families had to rely largely on their own financial and emotional resources.[37]

The nation's Mexican American families also suffered greatly during the depression. Their plight is illustrated by an incident that occurred in San Antonio, Texas, in February 1930. Approximately five thousand Mexican Americans gathered at the city's railroad station to depart the United States for resettlement in Mexico. In August of that year a special train carried another two thousand to central Mexico. Most Americans are now familiar with the forced relocation in 1942 of 112,000 Japanese Americans from the West Coast to internment camps. Far fewer are aware that during the Great Depression the Federal Bureau of Immigration (after 1933, the Immigration and Naturalization Service) and local authorities rounded up naturalized Mexican American citizens and shipped them to Mexico to relieve U.S. welfare rolls. In a shameful episode in U.S. history, more than 400,000 *repatriados*, many of them American citizens by birth, were sent across the Mexico–U.S. border from Arizona, California, and Texas.[38]

Large-scale Mexican migration to the Southwest dates back to the 1880s when western railroads, construction companies, steel mills, mines, and canneries recruited Mexicans as manual laborers. Immigration increased still further early in the twentieth century as a result of rapid population growth in Mexico, the social upheaval caused by the Mexican revolution, and the growth of large-scale commercial agriculture in Arizona's Salt River valley, Texas's lower Rio Grande valley, and California's Imperial and San Joaquin valleys. Increasingly, during the 1920s, Mexican Americans moved into urban areas, where they established themselves in neighborhoods called *colonias*.[39]

Typically, life in a *colonia* was divided into subunits of one or two blocks called *barrios*, made up largely of extended families. Customarily second-generation Mexican Americans tended to cluster around the home of the husband's father; children of the third generation, in contrast, increasingly lived adjacent to the wife's father. In other words the extended family remained important as an organizing principle even though individual households tended not to consist of three generations of a family.[40]

Even before the stock market collapse, there was intense pressure, spearheaded by the American Federation of Labor and municipal governments, to reduce the number of Mexican immigrants. Opposition from local chambers of commerce, economic development associations, and state farm bureaus stymied efforts to impose an immigration quota, but rigid enforcement of existing laws slowed legal entry. After President Herbert Hoover appointed William N. Doak as Secretary of Labor in 1930, the Bureau of Immigration launched intensive raids designed to identify Mexican aliens liable for deportation. These were accompanied by city and county efforts to repatriate destitute Mexican American families. Altogether approximately 82,400 Mexican Americans were involuntarily deported by the federal government. Many more left because of the threat of unemployment, deportation, or loss of relief payments.[41]

New Deal

The plight of the nation's families on March 4, 1933, the day Franklin Roosevelt assumed the presidency, was truly miserable. Philadelphia had exhausted all available funds for poor relief. Detroit had been forced to strike a third of the families receiving aid from its relief rolls; St. Louis dropped half its families from relief. New Orleans refused new applications for relief, and Dallas and Houston refused to aid black and Mexican American families. More than a hundred cities provided no relief at all.[42]

The economic crisis of the 1930s called into question two key tenets of American political life. First, the depression threw into disrepute the nation's faith in limited government and generated a conviction that the federal government had a positive duty to intervene to rescue families from poverty. Second, it toppled the notion that public assistance could be left to private charity and local government and created a consensus that the federal government had a responsibility to support the aged, provide jobs for the unemployed, and protect families' savings. Debate still rages over how successful Franklin Roosevelt's programs were in dealing with the problems posed by the depression. But there can be no doubt that the New Deal was a critical watershed in the history of the American family, because for the first time the federal government became a major guarantor of family welfare.[43]

During the Progressive Era, coalitions of reformers, progressive business associations, trade unions, and farmers had limited success in establishing a small number of social insurance schemes. Between 1911 and 1919, thirty-eight states adopted workers' compensation laws, and another thirty-nine instituted pensions for needy mothers with dependent children. In 1920 the federal government enacted a program of compulsory old age and disability insurance for its half-million civil servants. Six states followed suit before 1929, and most cities established limited pensions for police officers, fire fighters, and teachers. Private retirement plans remained extremely unusual, and private companies provided pensions to fewer that 50,000 beneficiaries.[44]

The Great Depression revealed the total inadequacy of the nation's existing welfare programs. Local resources quickly proved inadequate to meet the growing need. In Chicago in 1931, 624,000 men and women—40 percent of the city's work force—walked the streets looking for jobs. Each day, these people lost $2 million in wages, but the city could provide only $100,000 in relief. In Philadelphia, private and public charities distributed $1 million a month in poor relief, providing families with only $1.50 to $2.00 a week for groceries. By June 1932 even these meager funds were exhausted. The same story was repeated throughout the nation. In south Texas the Salvation Army was forced to reduce its allocation for feeding each client to a penny a day. By early 1932, 20,000 children had been placed in institutions or foster homes because their parents could no longer support them. Total public and private expenditures on relief in 1932 amounted to only $317 million, less than $27 for each of the twelve million jobless.[45]

Virtually every domestic government program enacted during the depression decade touched the nations' families. To reduce unemployment among the young, the Roosevelt administration created the Civilian Conservation Corps in April 1933. To fund state-run welfare programs, the New Deal established the Federal Emergency Relief Administration in May 1933. To provide jobs for 4 million jobless families, the Civil Works Administration was set up in November 1933, followed by the Works Progress Administration in May 1935.

Washington would enact several thousand pieces of legislation that would directly affect the welfare of the nation's families. Rural electrification programs meant that for the first time Americans in Appalachia, the Texas hill country, and elsewhere would have an opportunity to share in the benefits of electric light and running water. New Deal farm relief programs provided assistance to many family farmers but also had the ironic effect of accelerating the flight of poor farm families from the land by concentrating ownership. Social Security, the nation's first national retirement program, not only established a system of assistance for many of the elderly but also welfare programs for many of the needy. State government-assisted family-planning programs disseminated birth control information among the poor.

No New Deal initiative brought more dramatic improvement to the lives of common families than rural electrification. In 1935, 6 million of the nation's 6.8 million farm families lacked electricity. Thirty million Americans were still without washing machines, electric irons, vacuum cleaners, indoor plumbing, radio, and electric lights. These families had no electric pumps, and water was still carried by hand from wells. They lacked gas or electric ranges, and cooking was still done on stoves that required housewives to haul wood from a pile outside. They lacked refrigerators, and they had to keep their milk on ice and can fruits and vegetables as soon as they were ripe. They had no washing machines, and clothes had to be scrubbed by hand on washboards and boiled in huge vats.[46]

The beginning of change would come in 1936 with congressional passage of a law authorizing the establishment of a Rural Electrification Administration (REA) to provide electricity to farmers. During the first seven years after its founding, the REA increased the proportion of farms supplied with electricity from 11 to 35 percent. In the areas where electrification took place, the REA revolutionized family life by bringing housework techniques into the twentieth century.[47]

To try to restore prosperity to the nation's farm families, the New Deal initiated a vast system of farm relief. At the start of the depression, a fifth of all American families still lived on farms. But farm families were in deep trouble. By 1931 one-quarter of all farmers who had borrowed from the federal government were delinquent on their debts. By the beginning of 1932, farm foreclosures were averaging 20,000 a month, and by 1934, 30 percent of the total value of farmland in the plains states was owned by creditors. Farm tenancy increased sharply, until more than two of every five farmers owned no land. Farm family income fell by a staggering two-thirds during the first three years of the depression. Before the depression three bales of cotton had been enough to send a child to college for a year; by 1931 eight bales were needed. To meet farm debts in 1932, it was necessary to grow 2.5 times as much corn as in 1929, 2.7 times as much wheat, and 2.4 times as much cotton.[48]

Ironically and sadly, many of the government relief policies designed to alleviate the plight of farmers worsened conditions for tenants and other small farmers. New Deal farm policies had multiple objectives that often proved incompatible. They sought to supplement farm income, retire marginal soil, reforest worn land, mechanize farm work, and limit farm output. Measures to accomplish these ends included production controls, acreage reduction, marketing quotas, and paying farmers not to produce. These policies did raise farm income, which doubled between 1932 and 1939, but the benefits were not evenly distributed. In 1937, for example, larger operators received direct government payments of $833; the families of tenant farmers received just $27.[49]

Many large landholders used government payments to purchase tractors and combines, allowing them to mechanize farm operations and reduce farm labor. One large Mississippi planter used his government payments to buy 22 tractors and 13 cultivators and subsequently evicted 160 tenant families. An unintentional consequence of New Deal farm relief policies was to encourage the flight of smaller farmers from the land.[50]

Not only did the government bring electricity to rural areas and try to assist the nation's farm families, it also encouraged efforts at family planning. In the face of widespread joblessness and economic distress, public opposition to contraception eased. At the beginning of the depression, there were just twenty-eight clinics in the entire nation offering birth control advice. Six years later there were 288, located in forty states and the District of Columbia. Ten years later there were 746, one-third of them publicly supported. Federal laws forbidding the sale or dissemination of contraceptive information were weakened as public opinion increasingly favored "planned parenthood." A 1936 Gallup poll showed two-thirds in favor of allowing doctors to provide birth control information. Federal restrictions on prescription of contraceptives by physicians were struck down by a 1936 court decision, and the next year the American Medical Association recognized birth control as an area of legitimate professional practice. By the end of the depression decade, every state except Massachusetts and Connecticut permitted doctors to provide birth control advice.[51]

One factor motivating public support for birth control was a growing recognition that poorer families were bearing more children than wealthier families. During the depression half of all births were in families on relief or making less than $1,000 a year. The birthrate of Southern farm women was three times the national average, and many of these women were eager to limit the number of children. When one sociologist visited tenant farm women in the Carolina piedmont, Georgia, and Alabama, she found that "every one of the mothers with babies of two or under, either explicitly or by inference expressed the attitude, 'I hope this is the last one.'" Only 2 percent of the tenant women questioned used contraceptives of any kind, but virtually all declared themselves in favor of birth control. The common attitude was, "I think it's a bigger sin to have children you can't provide for (or haven't the strength to take care of) than to do something to keep from having them." By 1941 state-sponsored birth control clinics in North Carolina were providing contraceptive advice in seventy-five counties, and rural outreach programs sponsored by the Birth Control Federation reached 23,500 rural mothers.[52]

The centerpiece of the New Deal's system of social welfare provision was the Social Security Act of 1935, which set the pattern for future programs of public assistance. The law set up two separate systems of social provision. It established a contributory system of old-age insurance paid out of special funds accumulated from the payroll taxes of potential recipients. This part of the law covered all workers except civil servants, domestics, merchant seamen, farm laborers, casual laborers, and employees of charitable, religious, and educational institutions, and provided monthly annuities based on previous earnings. It also provided federal grants-in-aid to help support state-administered, need-based programs for the nation's unemployed, 50,000 blind Americans, 900,000 handicapped Americans, dependent children lacking a wage-earning parent, and the indigent poor not covered by the old-age insurance program.[53]

From its inception the old-age insurance system set up under the Social Security Act was criticized on a number of counts: for its failure to include health insurance; its reliance on regressive payroll taxes that exacted a heavier burden on the poor than the rich, its exclusion of the poorest of the poor, who worked in agriculture or domestic service; and for the inadequacy of its financial payments, which initially ranged from just $10 to $85 a month. In fact, up until the 1950s, more of the elderly received assistance from Social Security's welfare programs than from the old-age insurance program.[54]

Social Security's critics accused it of initiating a sharp, invidious distinction between old-age insurance and welfare for the needy. One of the legacies of Social Security was the establishment of a sharp separation between the beneficiaries of old-age insurance and a separate system of federally subsidized, state-administered, need-based welfare programs for the dependent poor, with widely uneven eligibility requirements and benefit levels across the states.[55]

Despite this drum fire of criticism, Social Security remains the single most popular government program. As costly and controversial as the program has been, there is little doubt that it succeeded in its major task: reducing the proportion of older Americans living in poverty.

The Great Depression left America's families many bequests, ranging from Social Security and Aid to Families with Dependent Children (AFDC) to federal home mortgage insurance and insured bank deposits. But the depression's greatest legacy was not any specific program or policy but a major shift in public philosophy. It revealed the inadequacy of the traditional family means of coping with economic disaster in an increasingly complex and bureaucratic society and underscored the fact that families were no longer able to protect themselves against adversity without government aid. Because of the depression, the federal government was induced, for the first time, to take active responsibility for alleviating the loss of earnings caused by unemployment, disability, sickness, and old age. It is this precedent for growing governmental involvement in the lives and welfare of the nation's families that is the central legacy of the New Deal.

A Nisei family at the Manzanar Relocation Center in California. Courtesy of the National Archives, Washington, D.C.

CHAPTER VIII

Families on the Home Front

IN the spring of 1942, a twenty-one-year-old Kentucky woman named Frankie Cooper decided to leave her family's chicken farm and move to a city. Frankie had a husband and a two-year-old daughter, and the three migrated to East St. Louis, Illinois, where Frankie found a job at an American Steel Company foundry. Like many other Americans who moved during the war years, Frankie's decision to leave home involved a mixture of patriotic and economic motives. By moving to East St. Louis, she and her husband hoped to contribute to the war effort, to earn some money, and to make a better life than they had managed on their hill-country farm.[1]

Life in East St. Louis differed enormously from life in Kentucky. On her farm Frankie had lived without electricity, a telephone, or indoor plumbing, and she had worn clothing made from chicken-feed sacks. In East St. Louis, for the first time, Frankie shopped in a grocery store, drove a second hand car, attended movies, and ate out in restaurants. East St. Louis was filled with luxuries unimagined by a woman who had spent her life in a pre–Civil War cabin, lacking an indoor sink or toilet. Migration brought excitement and a startling improvement in Frankie's standard of living.[2]

But adjustment to life in East St. Louis was not easy. Frankie felt isolated from her relatives and her roots. Fellow workers poked fun at her Kentucky accent. She had never worked for wages before, and her foreman was frequently irritated because she was slow to understand his instructions.[3]

Finding decent housing was a particularly difficult problem. East St. Louis, like many other wartime boomtowns, was ill equipped to deal with the sudden influx of war migrants. Housing was in such short supply that one landlady divided a five-car garage into five apartments, while a local store owner had converted his shop into apartments simply by hanging sheets from the ceiling. Frankie was much more fortunate than many newcomers in that she was eventually able to find a two-room apartment for her family.[4]

Even though Frankie Cooper never served in the armed forces and lived thousands of miles from the nearest battlefield, World War II left an indelible mark on her life. For Frankie and for millions of other Americans on the home front, the war was a powerful instrument of social change. The war spurred an unprecedented tide of migration. More than fifteen million people were wartime migrants, searching for jobs in industrial areas or following loved ones from one military base to another. Hundreds of boomtowns sprouted up in the South and West, and acute shortages of housing, schools, and other essential social services plagued the nation's cities. The wartime boom in industrial and financial activity ushered in a massive revival of the nation's economy. The gross national product—the measure of goods and services produced by the economy—soared from just $90 billion in 1939 to $213 billion in 1945. Depression unemployment virtually disappeared, wages climbed dramatically, and large economic gains occurred among the poor, sharply reducing income inequality. A growing labor shortage forced industry to turn to groups that had been excluded from manufacturing before the war—women, teenagers, blacks, Southern white migrants, retirees, and the handicapped.[5]

These developments had far-reaching implications for American family life. Wartime prosperity contributed to a sudden upsurge in the marriage rate and a sharp rise in the birthrate. Young people who had delayed marriages and postponed childbearing during the depression married and had children in record numbers. Wartime families confronted severe problems of adjustment as they moved from one community to another. Housing was in short supply, educational and health facilities were overburdened, and child care facilities were inadequate. Other families suffered prolonged separation from husbands and fathers, provoking shifts in family roles and relations. The widespread employment of women and teenagers during the war, to fill in for the men at the fighting front, drastically changed their perception of themselves and their place in the family.[6]

The Great Depression and World War II were seminal experiences in the lives of twentieth-century Americans. Each experience profoundly affected an entire generation, and each brought irrevocable changes in family life. The legacy of the depression was to reinforce a long-term trend toward growing government involvement and responsibility in American family life. The legacy of World War II was no less important. A shared sense of danger and privation drew families closer together and infused family and community bonds with new strength. At the same time, conditions tested families with novel economic and psychological strains whose effects remain with us today.[7]

The Rush to the Altar

One day a corporal asked his duty officer, Lieutenant Elliot Johnson, for help. "I did something stupid," explained the corporal. "I got drunk last night and when I woke up and looked down there was ninety-eight pounds of woman flesh beside me, and she . . . reminded me that we had gotten married. But I don't want to be married."[8]

The war years brought a number of hasty, impulsive marriages. In sharp contrast to World War I, when the number of marriages and births actually declined, the number accelerated during the early years of World War II, continuing a trend that had begun in the last years of the 1930s. As unemployment fell and the level of wages rose, the marriage rate marched with it. With congressional passage of the Selective Service Act in September 1940, the rate jumped upward as men across the country confronted military service and separation from loved ones. J. R. Woods and Sons, a large manufacturer of wedding rings, reported a 250 percent increase in sales after the Selective Service Act was passed. In the three months after the military draft was initiated, marriage rates climbed 25 percent over the preceding year and remained at the new higher level throughout 1941. Then came Pearl Harbor. In the month after the surprise attack, the marriage rate was 60 percent higher than in the same month the year before.[9]

Quick weddings were the rage. Young people, who had asked parents for permission to marry and entered into prolonged courtships before the war, now ceased to wait. Private Mickey Rooney, based at Camp Siebert, Alabama, proposed to a seventeen-year-old on their first date and married her seven days later. "I married Betty Jane because I was determined to marry someone," the actor later wrote. "I'd had some drinks, was hurt and lonely, reached and grabbed."[10]

Newspapers and magazines celebrated whirlwind romances and marriages, giving front-page headlines to marriages involving stars and celebrities, such as Judy Garland and Vincente Minnelli. Popular films, like the 1945 romance *The Clock*, also celebrated quick courtships. Reflecting young people's rush to have it all before marching off to war, this film depicts the meeting between a corporal on a two-day leave before going overseas and a young woman. Separated on a crowded subway, they fear that they will never see each other again. When they find each other, they marry at once, even though they know nothing about each other's background or family.[11]

Unsettled wartime conditions spawned a host of rapid marriages. Many young people rushed to marry in a desperate attempt to find something to hang onto amid the uncertainties of wartime life. One young woman described the pressures that she felt when a young pilot asked her to marry him. "I've told him I don't love him," she said. "But he's an aviator and he says I should marry him anyhow and give him a little happiness. He says he knows he'll be dead in a year."[12]

Some married to avoid the draft, since men with dependents were deferred until 1942. Others rushed to marry for a taste of marital intimacy before the husband shipped off overseas. Still other quickie marriages were more avariciously provoked by "Allotment Annies" who married in order to receive the $50 monthly allotment checks and $10,000 life insurance policies given to the wife of each GI.[13]

Whatever the cause, the marriage rate skyrocketed. Between 1940 and 1946 3 million more Americans married than could have been expected if marriage rates had remained at prewar levels. Servicemen wed during the course of the war came to 1.5 million, and during the two years after Pearl Harbor, more than 1,000 GI grooms and their war brides went to the altar each day.[14]

The rush to the altar was accompanied by a baby boom. Some couples, like Melba and Sidney Winer of Detroit, decided to have a "goodbye baby" before the husband went overseas. Many other couples decided to have the children that they had put off during the depression but could no longer postpone, even for a war. The result was a sharp rise in the birthrate. For two decades preceding the war, the birthrate, like the marriage rate, had declined. But by 1943 the birthrate rose to its highest level in twenty years. During the 1930s, America's population had increased by only 3 million people, but during the war, the population soared by 6.5 million. The roots of the postwar baby boom are to be found in this wartime surge in births.[15]

Wartime Migration

The mobilization for war spurred a sluggish economy to new levels of industrial activity and stirred an unprecedented tide of family migration. There were 16 million people who left home for military service, and another 15.3 million civilians moved from city to city in search of higher-paying jobs in the thriving defense industries. Thousands of small businesses dissolved during the war years—300,000 failed in 1942 alone—and husbands and wives followed the flow of capital into new urban areas and new jobs. Laura Briggs, the daughter of a Jerome, Idaho, farmer, was only eleven years old when her father decided to sell everything, including the linoleum on the farmhouse floor, pack the family's black '41 Chevy, and move to Long Beach, California, to work in a defense plant. He was convinced that there was "big money" to be made manufacturing armaments, and so he sold most of the family's belongings and rented the farm to his brother.[16]

Other migrants were members of servicemen's families, who followed a uniformed husband or father from one base to another. Dellie Hahne followed her husband, a pilot, to Amarillo, Texas, and then to Panama City, Florida. "Following your husband was really difficult," she recalled. She moved from one strange town to another and would have to find a room to rent, a way to feed herself without ration coupons, and a way to support herself on a fifty-dollar allotment check. Her situation was duplicated by thousands of soldiers' wives clustering around military bases.[17]

This unprecedented reshuffling of the population caused enormous growth in coastal cities in the South and West, which were the centers of the nation's armaments industries and debarkation points for the armed forces, affecting the conditions of family life in both urban and rural America. In just three years, Vanport, Oregon, grew from a rural hamlet with a few hundred families to a city of 40,000. San Diego grew from a city of 203,000 to a much larger city of 400,000, excluding military personnel. The populations of Portland, Oregon; Norfolk, Virginia and Mobile, Alabama jumped 50 percent and 2 million people moved to six large cities, including Detroit, Los Angeles, and San Francisco. At the same time, other areas actually lost population. Boston lost 150,000 inhabitants, Pittsburgh 200,000, and the New York City metropolitan area 800,000. The most dramatic population losses occurred in rural areas as tens of thousands of inhabitants of the Dakotas, Minnesota, Kentucky, and Tennessee moved to California, Washington State, Oregon, Michigan, and Illinois.[18]

Wartime migration created severe problems of housing, health, and education—problems that were compounded by wartime shortages of construction materials, labor, and tax revenue. Housing presented the most immediate problem, with 98 percent of all cities reporting insufficient numbers of single-family houses and 90 percent lacking an adequate stock of apartments. Migrating workers crowded into squalid trailer camps, shantytowns, and "foxhole houses"—excavated basements covered with tar-paper roofs. A million and a half families were forced to share apartments or houses with relatives, friends, or strangers.[19]

The housing shortage was nationwide in scope. Young mothers in Leesville, Louisiana, paid $50 a month to live in converted chicken coops and barns. In one two-story house near the Willow Run aircraft factory, twenty-seven miles outside of Detroit, five men slept in the basement, a family of five lived on the first floor, four people lived on the second floor, nine men slept in the garage, and four families inhabited four trailers parked in the yard. In Brunswick, Maine, twenty-six people lodged and boarded in a local college professor's house. Noted one reporter: "People are living in old abandoned gas stations, chicken coops and tents." Finding apartments that would accept children was a particularly difficult task. Exclaimed one apartment hunter: "[Landlords] got all these rules: no children, no dogs, no cats. . . . Why I know one family that lived in a hotel room for two months—couldn't rent a thing—and had to board their kids out."[20]

Congestion and overcrowding were the order of the day. "It is not unusual," one observer noted, "to find children of all ages, including adolescents, either occupying the bedroom of the parents or sleeping together where no provision can be made for various sexes or age groups." To relieve overcrowding, the federal government spent $2.3 billion to build 832,000 housing units, but public housing was woefully inadequate to meet the growing demand. Elsie Rossio of Seneca, Illinois, remembered what life was like in her war apartment. "The walls were paper thin. . . . The first night we slept there. . . . I shook my husband and whispered someone was in our room. He turned on the light and then we realized it was next door."[21]

For black Americans, housing problems were especially acute. Seven hundred thousand blacks moved from the rural South to

Northern and Western cities, searching for jobs in defense industries. Each month Baltimore's black population grew by two thousand. Sixty thousand black Americans migrated to Detroit during the war years, doubling the city's black population. Restricted housing covenants kept blacks "virtual prisoners" in racial ghettoes, in the words of the *New York Times.* In Baltimore blacks were crowded ten persons to each house, and in Detroit more than half the city's black families lived in substandard dwellings.[22]

The shortage of housing for black and white families was the fuse that set off violent racial conflagrations during the war years. Cramped, crowded living conditions, frequent movement from one community to another, and inadequate recreational facilities created severe stress, and people vented their rage in racial conflicts. The worst erupted in Detroit in 1942, after blacks sought to enter a segregated public housing project set aside for them and a white mob, seeking the housing for itself, resisted. Violence sparked by this incident left forty dead. Other racial violence provoked by the congestion, confusion, and scarcity of adequate living conditions in wartime struck Mobile, Alabama; Beaumont, Texas; and Harlem. The government, struggling to adjust to the defense needs of the war effort, was not prepared for its social implications.[23]

Wartime Prosperity and Privation

When World War II erupted in Europe in September 1939, unemployment was still a critical problem in America. Jobless Americans numbered 10 million and countless more were underemployed. Average weekly earnings in industry and agriculture were actually lower in 1939 than they had been two years earlier. Even by the end of 1941, when the unemployment rate had fallen, there were still between 5 and 7 million men and women out of work.[24]

American participation in the war brought a sharp drop in joblessness. By mid–1943 full employment had been achieved, and as the jobless rate fell, incomes rose sharply. Just before the war, median income was approximately $2,000 a year, or $50 a week. Forty percent of all workers earned less than $1,000 annually. But the beginnings of war in Europe brought marked wage increases. Between 1938 and 1942, average family income in Boston jumped from $2,455 to $3,618; in Chicago, from $3,233 to $3,776. One black woman in Atlanta saw her earnings rise from just $460 a year as a domestic servant to $2,477 as a drill-press operator. All segments of the population gained, but the poorest American families gained the most. The poorest fifth of families saw their incomes rise 68 percent during the war; the family income of the next fifth climbed 59 percent. The result was a sharp reduction in income inequality.[25]

The wartime gains in employment and wages ushered in a revival of national confidence and a more optimistic outlook. William Peffley of Greencastle, Pennsylvania, recalls how exhilarating it felt suddenly to have money in his pocket: "Going to work in the navy yard after coming out of the machine shops in Pennsylvania, I felt like something had come down from heaven. I went from forty cents an hour to a dollar an hour. We had all the overtime we wanted."[26]

But if the war years were a period of relative prosperity for some American families, they were also years of critical shortages of food, clothing, gas, water, electricity, housing, and transportation for others. For many, the war was characterized by hardship and an erosion of living standards. Nominal wages rose, but the cost of living climbed sharply. Forced savings programs and higher taxes lowered incomes, and rationing limited the availability of many goods. Nine out of ten Americans surveyed in 1944 believed that they were living no better than they had before the war.[27]

Inflation cut deeply into wage gains. Between the beginning of the war and 1942, the general level of retail prices had climbed 27 percent. Food prices shot up 53 percent and clothing prices increased 28 percent. Apples sold for ten cents apiece; the price of a watermelon had soared to $2.50; a head of lettuce had reached an unprecedented 28 cents; and oranges were selling for an astonishing $1.00 a dozen.[28]

Many goods were unavailable regardless of price. In December 1941, the government halted production of cars. A month later, production of vacuum cleaners, refrigerators, radios, sewing machines, and phonographs ceased. Altogether, production of nearly three hundred items considered nonessential to the war effort was banned or curtailed, including coat hangers, waffle irons, beer cans, and toothpaste tubes. Even items that continued to be produced were scarce and expensive, including coffee, sugar, diapers, hair curlers, home heating oil and cigarettes. During the winter of 1942–1943, allocations of home heating oil were just two-thirds what they had been in 1941, and as a result wintertime indoor temperatures of 60 degrees became commonplace. Since silk was essential to the war effort, women substituted rayon hose and cotton socks or used makeup on their legs. In response to the shortage of coffee and sugar, drinkers rebrewed coffee grounds and began to use such sugar substitutes as saccharin and corn syrup. Even clothing styles shifted to meet the nation's needs. To conserve wool and cotton, dresses were limited to two inches of hem, blouses and shirts to one patch pocket; attached hoods and shawls were banned; no coat cuffs and belts were permitted to be wider than two inches, and no skirt was allowed be more than seventy-two inches around.[29]

Food shortages plagued many American families. By 1943 a quarter of all production of canned fruits and juices was being diverted to the armed forces. As a result, the amount of food on American's tables declined. In 1943 per capita food consumption declined 4 percent from the year before. Meat consumption dropped and consumption of fresh vegetables fell 11 percent. One housewife in four said that she was unable to buy all the food she needed for her family. Commented one woman: "My old man won't eat liver and stuff like that. You can't get pork. Don't know how I'll get enough meat for him."[30]

Family incomes went up—but higher taxes and war savings ate up part of the increase. Income taxes rose 50 percent during the war. In 1940 just 7.8 million people had to pay federal income taxes; in 1945 the number had climbed to 48 million. At the same time, families were encouraged to save a significant portion of their earnings, especially in the form of war bonds. Urged by Kate Smith and a host of Hollywood celebrities to support the boys at the front by investing in the war effort, Americans purchased more than $135 billion worth of War Bonds. This investment would fuel a spectacular postwar boom in consumer spending.[31]

For consumers, rationing was a major source of irritation. To stem the wartime rise in prices, the federal government instituted rationing and wage and price controls. In 1942, Congress gave the Office of Price Administration (OPA) authority to freeze prices and wages and control rents and to institute rationing of scarce items. The OPA initially applied price controls to groceries and then extended the program to bicycles, irons, used cars, and household appliances.[32]

The rationing of foodstuffs brought the war into every home across the nation. The first items to be rationed were sugar and coffee in 1942. Processed and canned foods were next, followed by meat, fish, dairy products, tires, and gasoline. Every month, each man, woman, and child in the country received two ration books—one for canned goods and one for meat, fish, and dairy products—and coupons from their local schools. Three billion ration stamps were passed out each month—red stamps for meat, butter and fats; blue stamps for canned foods; and black stamps for gasoline. Meat was limited to twenty-eight ounces per person a week; sugar, eight to twelve ounces; and coffee, a pound every five weeks.[33]

The burden of coping with shortages and rationing fell, largely, on the backs of America's homemakers. Government propaganda declared that each woman had to become "a general in her own kitchen," making do with her family's rations and saving valuable resources for the war effort. To compensate for the scarcity of meat, homemakers were encouraged to cook casseroles or meatless dishes. Many homemakers used horsemeat, which cost just twenty cents a pound and was unrationed, rather than beef which cost fifty-five cents a pound and was. To make up for the shortage of fresh vegetables, victory gardens sprouted on empty lots or in backyards, and families tended them with loving care. By 1943, twenty million victory gardens were growing 40 percent of the nation's vegetables, and homemakers were managing to keep greens on family dining tables.[34]

American housewives were bombarded with advice on how household conservation could help the military cause. A jar of kitchen fat, they were told, contained enough glycerine to make a pound of black powder, sufficient to fill six 75-mm shells or fifty .32-caliber bullets. If each family used just one less tin can a week, enough tin and steel would be saved to build five thousand tanks or thirty-eight Liberty ships. Thirty lipstick holders contained enough brass to make twenty rifle cartridges. Fifteen pairs of nylon stockings were enough to make a gun powder bag. 30,000 razor blades contained enough steel to make fifty machine guns. Those on the home front were expected to sacrifice for the war effort as well.[35]

One woman, Sheril Jankovsky Cunning, who lived in Long Beach, California, as a child during the war, vividly recalled how her family coped with wartime shortages. "I remember all the neighborhood women sitting around the kitchen table pooling and trading ration coupons. My grandmother raised chickens so we didn't need our meat coupons. And we made our own butter." One month her family would trade their meat and dairy coupons for sugar; the next, her mother would trade sugar for steak or stockings. By planting a Victory garden, raising chickens, cutting back on nonessential items, and finding substitutes for goods in short supply, her family and millions of others made do during the war.[36]

Women Workers

Few wartime developments had so great an impact on American life as did the rapid entry of women into the labor force. The removal of 16 million men to the armed forces led to a vast increase in the national demand for domestic labor and the number of women in the labor force soared from 14 to 19 million. Nearly half of all American women held a job at some point during the war.[37]

Suddenly women entered occupations that had traditionally been closed to them. In offices, factories, shipyards, and shops, women workers "manned" jobs traditionally reserved for men. There were 250,000 women working in plants manufacturing electrical equipment; 100,000 were on production lines producing ammunition; 300,000 constructed airplanes; and 150,000 worked as riveters, welders, and crane operators in shipyards.[38]

The war not only brought large number of women into the work force, it introduced a new kind of woman to work outside the home. Before the war, most women who took jobs outside the home were young and unmarried. World War II altered this pattern, unleashing married women's labor. Three-quarters of the increase in women's employment was made up of married women. Between 1940 and 1944, the number of mothers with young children in the labor force jumped by 76 percent to 1.47 million. For the first time in American history, more than half of all women workers were married. The middle-class taboo against a working wife or mother had been irrevocably repealed.[39]

The sharp increase in married women's employment gave rise to widespread public anxiety. Many wartime commentators expressed alarm that employment of women outside the home would generate marital friction. A social worker warned that employment of wives would undermine their husbands' self-images: "In our complicated society, with its traditional concept of employment as a masculine prerogative, a woman's working may have symbolic meaning for her husband and may be a threat to him if he is not altogether secure in his masculinity." Other observers worried that working would strip women of their femininity. Columnist Max Lerner feared that the war had created a "new Amazon" who would "outdrink, outswear, and outswagger the men."[40]

Throughout the war public attitudes toward married women working were characterized by deep ambivalence. On the one hand, women were repeatedly told by the federal government that victory could not be achieved without their entry into the labor force. On the other, the federal government declared, "Now, as in peacetime, a mother's primary duty is to her home and children." Despite official pronouncements discouraging mothers from working, economic necessity led nearly 1.5 million mothers of small children to enter the labor force during the war. The overwhelming majority of these women were members of families with incomes below the national average, who said that their primary motive for working was financial.[41]

Guidance counselors, child psychologists, and physicians feared that working mothers gave their offspring inadequate attention. They linked a vast array of social and psychological problems—ranging from truancy, sleeping and eating disorders, and regressive infantile forms of behavior (including thumb sucking, bed-wetting, and whining) to egocentric, introverted, or nonempathetic behavior and "slower mental development, social ineptness, weakened initiative, and . . . [an inability] to form satisfactory relationships"—to maternal neglect. By 1950, when John Bowlby published his enormously influential study of English children's reaction to the German bombings entitled *Maternal Care and Mental Health*, there was a growing consensus that having a mother at home full-time was indispensable to a child's normal development and that children who experienced the loss of fulltime maternal attention were prone to antisocial behavior and the inability to form intense emotional relationships with other people.[42]

Child care was a serious problem during the war. Nearly 1.5 million mothers with children under the age of ten joined the work force, but most were only able to make haphazard arrangements for child care. Most working parents left children in the care of neighbors or grandparents, but many children were left to fend for themselves. Newspaper reporters called these children "8-hour orphans" or "latch-key" children and predicted harmful social consequences from these instances of maternal neglect.[43]

Barbara De Nike of the Bronx remembers how difficult it was for wartime mothers to provide adequate child care. As the wife of a sailor, she was able to live in Navy housing. But whenever her husband received orders to report to a new base or to ship out on duty, she had just twenty-four hours to vacate her apartment. "I felt so buffeted about," she recalled. "All you could do was try to cope." Unwilling to subject her children to these interruptions in their family life, she sent them to visit with an aunt while she took temporary jobs and looked for new living quarters. Few landlords would rent to families with children, so she and her two children were forced to stay with another aunt in a one-room apartment. Her aunt could not cope with two little children, and Barbara was forced to place her children in a Catholic orphanage while she looked for another place to live. Women—who had to manage children, finances, and anxiety alone— found it difficult to do all these things effectively. Few public resources and little recognition were extended to wartime working women as they struggled to be both active citizens and breadwinners.[44]

Public child care facilities were inadequate. At the beginning of the war, the Federal War Manpower Commission had taken the position that mothers with young children not seek work until childless women had been employed. Despite this pronouncement, 1.5 million mothers of small children did enter the work force during the war. To assist these working mothers, the federal government spent nearly $52 million on 3,102 centers providing day care to about 105,000 children every work day—a tiny fraction of the children requiring such care.[45]

Most of these wartime child care centers were overcrowded, ill equipped, and poorly located. One wartime nursery near Baltimore was typical. Initially housed in a pair of trailers, the nursery was moved into a housing project administration building after the trailers were found to be in violation of health standards. In the new building, eighty preschoolers were cared for in a single room and had to share a single bathroom with the building's employees. Many centers were located in churches and in private residences, often lacking any out-door play space. Because of widespread belief that day care for the very young should be provided by their own mothers, no provision was made for children under the age of two.[46]

Despite the pressing need for child care, many wartime nurseries remained underutilized, in part because many mothers were opposed to the kinds of institutionalized child care provided by the government. The high fees war nurseries charged further limited the use of public child care. Daily fees typically ranged from fifty to seventy-five cents, or nearly a tenth of a day's wage, discouraging many poorer parents from making use of the centers.[47]

Compared to the efforts made by our wartime allies, the U.S. government did little to facilitate the entry of wives and mothers into the work force. The U.S. lagged far behind Britain, where the government constructed central kitchens, public nurseries, and rural retreats for working mothers and their children and required employers to give women workers an afternoon off each week to conduct the family shopping. In retrospect it appears that the government's failure to provide adequate support services had a detrimental effect on the war effort. Women workers in such cities as Baltimore, Buffalo, Detroit, Los Angeles, and San Diego changed jobs twice as often as men and were absent from work twice as much. The relatively high rate of job turnover and absenteeism during the war years may be attributed to the conflict many women faced between their roles as homemakers and wage earners.[48]

Public disapproval of women's ability to cope with the family in the absence of a father focused not only on maternal deprivation but on its mirror image, maternal oversolicitousness. Americans had been shocked by the number of men — more than five million—who were rejected for military service on the basis of physical or psychological deficiencies. Three million men were classified as emotionally unstable and many authorities blamed this on overprotective mothers. Dr. Edward A. Strecker, a psychiatric consultant to the Army and Navy, accused "America's traditional sweet, doting, self-sacrificing mom" of having "failed in the elementary mother function of weaning offspring emotionally as well as physically." Philip Wylie, author of the 1942 best-seller *A Generation of Vipers*, argued that psychological and emotional immaturity was caused by a combination of a dominant, overly protective mother and a passive or absent father.[49]

The specter of Nazism intensified concern about the impact of the war on mothering. Many experts believed that Nazism was a product of Germany's patriarchal family structure. Some mental health experts argued that German fathers had implanted within their children "the authoritarian attitude, the belittling of women, and the cult of aggressive masculinity" that furnished fertile soil for the growth of national socialism. Others blamed German mothers for creating an "authoritarian personality" by placing too much emphasis on obedience and exercising overly strict discipline during early childhood. If analysts agreed that repressive discipline had led to a totalitarian state, there was also a consensus that America's "democratic" family posed problems of its own. Lacking clearly defined roles or a status hierarchy, the formlessness of the American family meant that many homes were riven by intense emotional tensions deriving from weak fathers, dominating mothers, and bickering children. The results of an upbringing in such an unstructured domestic environment were reflected in high rates of psychological maladjustment and immaturity—the symptoms ranging from extreme passivity and introversion to intense hostility and competitiveness. The American family was being scrutinized in a new and personal way but in a large public arena.[50]

War's Children

Although it is uncertain whether juvenile delinquency, parental neglect, or child abuse represented greater problems in the United States in the 1940s than in the 1930s, there is a mass of evidence indicating that social workers, psychologists, and public leaders were deeply troubled by the impact of the war on the nation's young people. Popular magazines were filled with graphic depictions of the wartime plight of youth. The *Saturday Evening Post* described nine children chained to trailers in a southern California trailer camp while their parents labored, as well as four children locked in their mother's automobile while she worked the graveyard shift. There were stories of youth violence, such as the ruthless murder of a New York City schoolteacher by zoot-suited teenagers in 1942 or the more than 500 "conflict gangs" in the city, fighting with brass knuckles, blackjacks, broken bottles, ice picks, and guns made out of four-inch pieces of pipe. Most disturbing of all were reports of abuses in child labor, including stories of an eleven-year-old girl suffering a heart attack while performing farm labor, a fifteen-year-old boy dying from burns suffered while cleaning a food vat, and a sixteen-year-old boy losing an arm after catching it in a centrifugal dryer.[51]

Such events obviously do not give a typical picture of the life of young people during World War II. Yet these happenings were common enough to disturb the public about the problems the war posed for youth. Children lived in a society shaken and disrupted by war. Many were growing up in homes without fathers and with working mothers. Frequent migration subjected children to extreme social and psychological dislocation. School attendance and child labor laws were relaxed, and wartime excitement and stress were widespread. It is not surprising to discover that most observers believed that the war had weakened traditional controls on the young and intensified the problem of rearing responsible and well-adjusted young people.[52]

Wartime dislocations drastically altered the experience of the young. In increasing numbers, teenage boys and girls joined the labor force, entered the armed forces, married, and insisted on adult rights. Young people found these years a period of economic opportunity. The number of teenagers who worked rose by 1.9 million; the number attending school fell by 1.25 million. Four times as many fourteen- and fifteen-year-olds were working in 1945 as in 1941. At the same time that increasing numbers of young people joined the labor force, fewer went to school. In 1942 alone, more than two thousand schools failed to open, in part because of a lack of teachers but also because many young people were turning away from education. In Arkansas 10,000 children and 3,000 in Mobile, Alabama, were without school facilities. In the Detroit area, the school day for most children was cut to three hours, and in many other overcrowded areas, children were placed on half-day schedules.[53]

To permit children and teenagers to fulfill the labor needs of a nation at war, child labor statutes were weakened. Fourteen- and fifteen-year-olds were permitted in various states to work at night at such food processing tasks as peeling shrimp and packaging fresh fruits and vegetables. The state of Delaware relaxed its night-work prohibitions so that children as young as fourteen could work until midnight delivering milk. Florida permitted children as young as fourteen to work during school hours and allowed twelve-year-olds to take after-school jobs. In some states no age restrictions were placed on work in agriculture. Manpower was at a premium and young people were a valuable resource.[54]

Inevitable wartime exigencies and demands on families led to a relaxation of social restraints for all, including children. One serviceman's wife gave voice to a common concern, that the war had made it more difficult to discipline children: "The kids don't seem to mind as much as they did when he was home." Reports of teenage vice filled the newspapers. In New York City in 1943, a seventeen-year-old was convicted of running a prostitution ring comprising thirty young prostitutes aged twelve to fifteen. At big-city bus stations, teenage girls, called "khacky-whacky" girls or "V-girls," flirted with soldiers. Female youth gangs, known as "wolf packs," sprang up in big cities; a common initiation rite was sexual relations with male gang members. Frequent movement from one community to another, prolonged absence of fathers, the assumption of increased responsibilities, and a weakening of parental discipline all contributed to a sharp rise in wartime rates of premarital pregnancy, illegitimacy, and venereal disease.

In adjusting to wartime conditions, American youth, was developing a new sense of identity.[55]

Subject to public demands and criticism, American adolescents, began to assert themselves and create a distinctive teenage subculture with its own garb, hairstyles, dance music, language, and values. Teenage boys, particularly in poorer communities, showed their disdain for social conventions by donning zoot suits—loosely cut coats with wide, padded shoulders and pants flaring below the waist but tapered at the ankles. Combined with a wide-brimmed hat, a skin-tight T-shirt, and a ducktail haircut, such a uniform upset many adults with its aggressive flamboyance. Teenage boys also began to swing yo-yos, participate in "bull sessions," congregate around juke boxes, and sport penny loafers and blue jeans. Teenage girls, called "bobby-soxers" after the short socks they wore, held slumber parties, read new magazines like *Glamour, Mademoiselle,* and *Seventeen,* and swooned and shrieked over Frank Sinatra. All emphasized the shared interests and values of the peer group as distinct from the larger adult population.[56]

Before the war, adolescents were referred to as "youngsters" and were largely expected to share the outlooks and assumptions of their parents as well as subordinate their desires to them. Wartime, however, bred a new and distinctive social phenomenon: "teen culture." Whether in response to the threat of the adult world's war or the stress of family disruption, adolescents took on a new and distinctive social identity, independent of those of their families. Wartime jobs for teenagers allowed them to buy their own magazines, purchase records, attend movies, and wear clothing targeted exclusively at a teenage audience. Young people adopted their own dance styles, like the jitterbug, and generated their own customs, status symbols, and fads. More and more, their recreation took place outside the home, away from family. Increasingly, the peer group and the products of popular culture began to rival parents as influences on their behavior and aspirations.[57]

Varieties of Wartime Family Experience

Participation in the war took 16 million men away from their families and created "servicemen's families" with their own specific problems. Nearly one family out of every five—18.1 percent—lost one or more family members to the armed forces. The four to five million wives of servicemen experienced the pangs of separation with particular intensity. These women found that their lives were beset by severe strains, ranging from intense loneliness to the difficulties of raising children alone and anxious concern over the fate of loved ones overseas. Said one serviceman's wife: "I try not to worry and if I can't sleep at night I just take a sleeping pill. Life seems more like existing to me than living." Admitted another: "I smoke like a fiend and chew my nails like mad. I knit all the time and never finish anything. . . . I was nervous before but not that bad." Separated from husbands and kin, these women received little relief from the burdens of child care. Observed one wartime single parent: "When my husband was home he would stay in some nights and relieve me, but now I must carry all the responsibilities, worries, and work without any help."[58]

The difficulty of raising children without the assistance of a husband was compounded by the limited amount of money most "war widows" had to spend. During the war the federal government provided servicemen's dependents with $50 monthly allotment check, plus $20 per child, which was intended to meet only the basic necessities of life. This allowance was so inadequate that many servicemen's wives had to move in with parents or relatives, share dwellings in overcrowded service apartments, and take jobs. In one section of Chicago, more than half of all servicemen's wives, and nearly half of all mothers with children, lived with parents or other close relatives. Wives who "doubled up" frequently complained about a lack of privacy and a loss of independence. Said one: "I get along well with my mother, but I had my own home long enough to develop my own methods of keeping house, so Mother and I have altogether different ideas of how a house should be run."[59]

To supplement their meager government allowances, many servicemen's wives found it necessary to take jobs. They were three times as likely to do so as other married women. Taking a job also helped servicemen's wives cope with a problem even greater than lack of money—loneliness. At work they found companionship that they could not attain at home.[60]

No families on the home front were more deeply affected by the war than those of Japanese Americans. In the spring of 1942, 112,000 Japanese Americans—two-thirds of them U.S. citizens—were relocated from homes on the West Coast to detention camps located in barren and forbidding parts of Arizona, Arkansas, California, Colorado, Idaho, Utah, and Wyoming. Any individual who had one Japanese great-grandparent was liable to internment. The victims of racial prejudice, war hysteria, and economic jealousies, Japanese Americans suffered a gross violation of their civil liberties.[61]

For Japanese American families, internment meant severe economic hardship, physical dislocation, and a sharp reordering of family roles. Unable to store their personal property or sell it at a fair price, they suffered enormous income and property losses, estimated at $400 million in 1942 dollars. Most internees still have not received any restitution for their losses.[62]

The losses experienced by these families were not just financial but social and psychological as well. At the internment camps wintertime temperatures sometimes fell to 30 degrees below zero. Surrounded by barbed wire fences, the camps were patrolled from watchtowers by rifle-toting guards under orders to shoot anyone who approached within twenty feet of a fence. The wooden barracks, which were covered with tar paper, were partitioned into one-room family apartments eighteen by twenty feet in size, each containing six or seven persons. Furnishings were limited to cots, blankets, and a light bulb.[63]

Toilets, showers, and dining facilities were communal, precluding family privacy. Dining ceased to be a private family ritual, and strict parental control over children loosened. One young Japanese American described conditions in his family's camp: "The apartments, as the Army calls them, are stables . . . mud is everywhere . . . We have absolutely no fresh meat, vegetables or butter. Mealtime queues extend for blocks; standing in a rainswept line, feet in the mud, for scant portions of canned wieners and boiled potatoes, hash . . . or beans . . . and stale bread."[64]

The internment camps tended to invert traditional roles and relationships in the Japanese American family. Men and women, regardless of age, worked at interchangeable jobs paying $12 to $19 a month, undermining the father's traditional role as breadwinner. Within the camps, influence shifted away from the older generation, the Issei, who had been born abroad, to the younger generation, born in the United States, known as the Nisei. Positions as camp administrators were reserved for the Nisei, who held American citizenship and spoke fluent English. Further, most of the 17,000 Japanese Americans allowed to leave the camps to attend college, take jobs in the East or Midwest, or enter military service during the internment period were Nisei. Many of them fought in Nisei army battalions in Europe, further proving their loyalty to the United States. And finally, a disproportionate share of the individuals first released from the camps at the war's end were Nisei. For many Issei the social changes engendered by the war produced a deep sense of depression. While many American families experienced the war as a time of severe economic and psychological dislocation, it was the Issei who experienced the stress and strain of wartime in its most intense form.[65]

Problems of Postwar Adjustment

Early in 1946 a film entitled *The Best Years of Our Lives* appeared in the nation's movie theaters. Almost immediately, the film attracted large crowds, eager to understand the ways in which the war had changed American society. Inspired by a 1944 *Time* magazine article describing the ambivalent emotions with which 370 surviving members of the First Marine Division—the conquerors of Guadalcanal—returned home, the film examined the problems of readjustment faced by three soldiers as they resumed civilian life.

In the contrasting stories of their homecomings, the film explored the economic and social changes produced by the war. Middle-aged Al Stephenson, who had served as an infantry sergeant during the war, returned to his stuffy job as a bank executive with mixed emotions. He was repelled by the grasping materialism he found back home and felt uneasy about his long-postponed reunion with his wife and now grown-up daughter. Captain Fred Derry, who had been a soda jerk before becoming a bombadier, returned home bitter about his lack of postwar job prospects and his discovery that his wife, whom he had married on impulse before shipping out, had been unfaithful. Homer Parris, a sailor who had to learn to use prosthetic hooks to replace the hands blown off on D day, had to learn to deal with the pity and condescension he received from his own family.

Al Stephenson, Fred Derry, and Homer Paris were semifictional creations, but the problems they faced were by no means unusual. Of the 16 million men and 100,000 women who had served in the nation's armed forces, many faced problems of readjustment similar to those depicted on the screen. Like the men in *The Best Years of Our Lives*, they had risked their lives overseas only to return home to discover that the world they had left behind had changed in some disturbing, and some simply different, ways. After worrying for years about defeating the Axis, now they worried about the fidelity of their wives, their unfamiliarity with their children, their economic prospects, and finding a niche in the postwar world.

For many returning GIs and their wives, the stresses of adjustment were barely manageable, and as the war ended, these strains were reflected in a startling upsurge in the nation's divorce rate. Between 1940 and 1944 the divorce rate rose from sixteen per hundred marriages to twenty-seven per hundred. In 1945, 500,000 marriages were dissolved, and in early 1946, when only half the GIs had returned home, 200,000 were already involved in divorce proceedings. By 1950 as many as a million GIs were divorced. When combined with a relatively large number of divorces among Americans who had not gone to war, the result was an epidemic of divorces unprecedented in American history. Whereas, in 1940, one marriage in six had ended in divorce, by 1946 the figure had worsened to one in four.[66]

There was no single explanation for this dramatic rise in the number of broken marriages. Contributing factors include the haste with which couples had wed; the strains of wartime separation; and the shock of strangeness and disillusionment on being reunited. A former Army captain remembered how difficult it was to readjust to marriage after his return home: "Maria and I married right before I went into the service, and we had only a month or so together steadily. After that it was hurried weekends for six months, a day here or there, then overseas for three years. I can't tell you why it happened—I came home, and we looked at one another, and we knew right away we didn't want to stay married. Oh, we tried, and went through all the motions, but we just lost interest. When I finally moved out, it was no more significant than changing college roommates or finding a new apartment."[67]

The reality or suspicion of wartime adultery was a new and disturbing element in family life. Newspapers and magazines gave enormous publicity to stories of wives who had been unfaithful to their servicemen husbands. One of the most notorious cases involved a soldier from Chicago whose legs were amputated following a mine explosion. He returned from Germany to discover that his wife had left him for a forty-nine-year-old meat buyer she had met at work. Another widely publicized case involved a sailor who returned from the Pacific only to find another man wearing his old clothes, living with his wife and son. As a result of separation and female independence, World War II had, for the first time, made America's families vulnerable to infidelity on a large scale.[68]

Servicemen's wives were equally concerned about their husband's fidelity. Shirley Hackett of Wallingford, Connecticut, recalled a family dispute that erupted when she learned that her mother-in-law had told her husband that it "wasn't healthy" for soldiers "not to have sex" while apart from their wives. She particularly resented her mother-in-law's double standard of sexual morality. "If I mentioned I was going to the movies," she remembered, "[her mother-in-law] would always say, 'Who are you going with? What time are you going to get back?' All the time my husband was away, she watched me like a hawk." Shirley Hackett's anxieties about wartime infidelities were not hers alone. A poll of young women taken in 1943 indicated that almost half believed that their husbands had been unfaithful.[69]

Also contributing to the postwar flood of divorces was a new independence and self-sufficiency found among women who had lived alone and had earned an independent income during the war. Wartime experiences made many women more independent and had elevated their expectations and self-images. Sybil Lewis, a black woman from Sapulpa, Oklahoma, worked as a riveter in a Lockheed aircraft factory during the war. Like many other women workers, she believed that work outside the home had been a broadening experience. "The war years had a tremendous impact on women," she said. "I know for myself it was the first time I had a chance to get out of the kitchen and work in industry and make a few bucks." After the war was over, this new sense of independence sometimes collided with husbands' ideas of women's proper role. Shirley Hackett, who made ball bearings during the war, recalled a conflict that took place on her husband's return. "Immediately we began having discussions about handling the checkbook. I was paying the bills and he informed me right away that that wasn't women's work, that he would do it." Her husband's words infuriated her because she had been balancing a checkbook for four years "and all of a sudden I didn't know how to do anything."[70]

An added source of familial stress was the postwar housing shortage, which forced many couples to live with relatives or to occupy cramped one-room apartments. As early as October 1945, when only 3 million of 16 million GIs had returned home, 1.2 million families were doubling up. In Manhattan one desperate couple moved into a department store display window. In Englewood, Colorado, a Navy veteran evicted from an apartment dragged his sofa into city hall and moved in along with his wife and seven-month-old child. In Los Angeles an ex-Marine pitched a tent in a city park. In Portland, Oregon, the local newspaper ran an ad reading: "$6000 Family Home! Only $8350." In Washington, D.C., Idaho Senator Glen Taylor sat on the Capitol steps, strummed a guitar and sang: "Oh, give me a home,

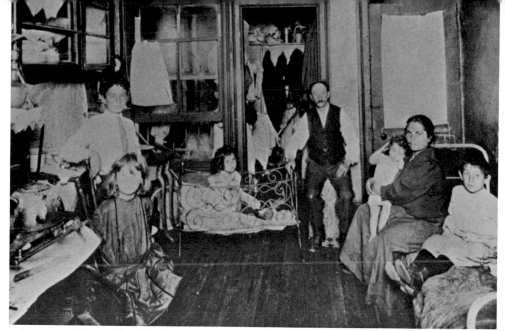

A Tenement Flat in New York City in 1910. During the quarter century following 1890, 18 million immigrants arrived in the United States. This photograph conveys the sense of crowding and impoverishment that characterized tenement life. Seven family members lived in a single room, approximately 250 feet square, which served as bedroom, living room, kitchen, and laundry. *Courtesy of the Museum of the City of New York.*

Three Generations of a Jewish Immigrant Family in Punxsutawney, Pennsylvania around 1880. Between 1880 and 1920, more than two million Jews from Russia and Poland fled Europe to escape political and religious persecution as well as economic hardship. Many members of the first generation retained traditional styles of dress and appearance long after arriving in the United States. In this photograph, the father's long beard and skull cap contrast sharply with the assimilated dress of the second generation. *Courtesy of Melba and Sidney Winer.*

Chinatown Children (1896–1908). As early as 1880, 100,000 immigrants from southern China had arrived in the United States. Like many other immigrant groups, these people attached great significance to the retention of ethnic customs and dress. Photograph by Arnold Genthe. *Courtesy of the Museum of Modern Art, New York.*

A Mexican-American Mother and Son in an Edinburgh, Texas, Carrot Field.
The rapid growth of large-scale commercial agriculture in Texas's lower Rio Grande valley, Arizona's Salt River valley, and California's Imperial and San Joaquin valleys drew thousands of Mexicans into the southwestern United States. *Courtesy of the Library of Congress.*

A Mother and Child in a Kitchenette, 1937. The plight of black Americans became increasingly desperate during the Depression. Most urban black families made their homes in kitchenettes, small rooms containing an ice box, a gas hot plate, and a single bed. To save space, this mother used a crate as a table and used the stove for boiling laundry and for ironing. Photograph by Arnold Rothstein. *Courtesy of the Library of Congress.*

Black Family, Gee's Bend, Alabama, 1937. In the rural South, black families lived in conditions of poverty that were abysmal. Their dwellings typically had dirt floors, no windows or screens, and almost no furniture. Their diet consisted almost entirely of salt pork, hominy grits, corn bread, and molasses. Photograph by Arnold Rothstein. *Courtesy of the Library of Congress.*

A Depression Migrant. During the Great Depression, a million tenant farmers and Dust Bowl refugees took to the nation's highways and railroads. The Southern Pacific Railroad boasted that it threw 683,000 vagrants off its trains in 1931. Free public flophouses and missions in Los Angeles provided beds for 200,000 of the uprooted. Photograph by Arnold Rothstein. *Courtesy of the Library of Congress.*

Mobilizing Women for War. The induction of 16 million men into military service during World War II left thousands of jobs unfilled at home. Many of these jobs were "manned" by women workers. Between 1941 and 1945, female employment increased a staggering 57 percent. These women workers were employed at the B-24 bomber plant at Willow Run, outside of Detroit. *Courtesy of the collections of Henry Ford Museum and Greenfield Village.*

Rosie the Riveter. The wartime need for workers allowed hundreds of thousands of women to take on jobs previously considered suitable for men only. This photograph shows a female employee at work at the B-24 bomber plant at Willow Run in 1943. *Courtesy of the collections of Henry Ford Museum and Greenfield Village.*

Since You Went Away. World War II subjected the nation's families to severe strains and dislocations. Family separation, an unprecedented tide of migration, and wartime rationing and shortages tested families with novel economic and psychological pressures. The deepest source of strain was worry about the troops fighting overseas. In this photograph, a "war widow" stares pensively into space. *Courtesy of the collections of Henry Ford Museum and Greenfield Village.*

The Stampede to the Suburbs. The rapid growth of suburbs was one of the most important social changes of the post-war era. By eliminating trim, adopting interchangeable designs, and utilizing assembly line techniques, developers like Arthur Levitt made single-family homes affordable for the families of veterans. Levittown, New York, shown here, had 17,477 new homes. *Courtesy of the National Archives, Washington, D.C.*

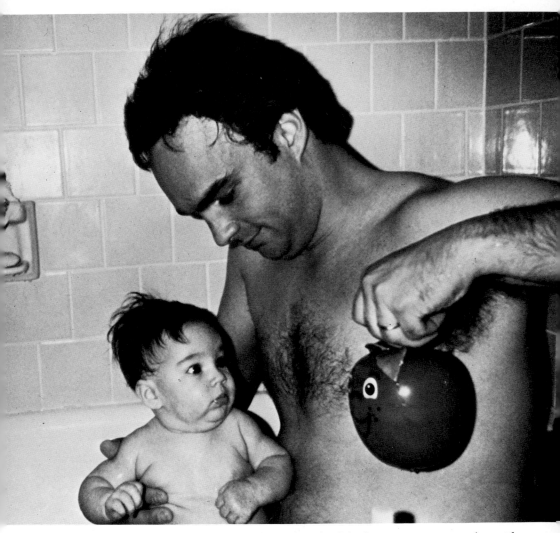

Father and Daughter—'80s Style. As a result of the feminist movement and a rapid influx of women into the workforce, fathers have become increasingly involved in their children's everyday lives. This shift in traditional roles reveals once more the resilience of the family in the face of changing social and economic patterns. *Courtesy of Eric Dodge and Teresa Byrne-Dodge.*

near the Capitol dome, with a yard where the children can play. Just one room or two, any old thing will do, we can't find a pla-a-ace to stay."[71]

By the end of 1945, 1.25 million men were being discharged from the military each month, and adequate housing was nearly impossible to find. Fourteen thousand families crowded into empty Army barracks, and over a million couples shared living quarters with relatives or other families. In North Dakota, grain bins were converted into housing, and in Atlanta the city bought a hundred trailers to house veterans' families. Chicago sold 250 street cars for conversion into living quarters.[72]

By eliminating some of the social stigma surrounding divorce, the dramatic postwar upsurge in divorce rates carried an important implication for the future. For growing numbers of men and women, divorce was no longer seen as a symbol of disgrace. Said one divorced woman in 1946: "I used to think that I'd cut off my head before I went back to Ohio and admitted that I made a bust of marriage. But now, so what? Of the first five girlfriends I made in New York, three are divorced, and I'm on my way. I'm not blasé about it, because it hurt. But I'm not wearing sackcloth and ashes either."[73]

War's Legacy

In 1942, Pulitzer Prize–winning author William Saroyan published an idyllic fable of wartime life in small-town California. In *The Human Comedy*, Saroyan told the story of the Macauleys, one of America's many fatherless wartime families. Set in the mythical town of Ithaca, which was modeled on Fresno, Saroyan's birthplace, the story followed the wartime experiences of Homer Macauley, age thirteen, who had taken a job as a postal messenger to support his family. (Homer's name and that of his four-year-old brother Ulysses are, of course, references to an earlier war and the brothers' odyssey of discovery). The story chronicles Homer's life as he works each day after school until midnight, carrying War Department telegrams to those Ithaca families whose sons have been killed in action. By carefully interweaving small but telling details of wartime sacrifice, ethnic conflict, and social and psychological dislocation, Saroyan succeeded in tracing the way that the war made itself felt nine thousand miles from the nearest battlefield.

World War II placed severe strains on the nation's families. During the war one-sixth of the nation's families suffered prolonged separation from sons, husbands, and fathers. Four to five million "war widows" had to cook, clean, launder, and bear and care for children alone. Wartime migration added even greater stress. Wartime families faced a shortage of adequate housing and a lack of schools, hospitals, and child care facilities. Frequent movement from one community to another weakened kinship ties, generated a sense of impermanence, and created severe problems of social and psychological adjustment. The widespread employment of women and teenagers, acute shortages of necessities and conveniences, and the relaxation of many customary social constraints made familial stress an inevitable by-product of the war abroad.

For many families the strains and tensions produced by the war proved unmanageable. The consequences were apparent not only in a dramatic upsurge in the divorce rate but also in severe problems of child welfare. Tens of thousands of unsupervised "latchkey" children, frequent reports of child abuse, and climbing rates of illegitimacy, juvenile delinquency, truancy, and runaways testified to an unprecedented breakdown of parental discipline and supervision.

For the most part, American families had to deal with the consequences of wartime disruption with little government assistance. Federal efforts to construct housing, schools, and child care centers were inadequate, and during the war many New Deal social welfare programs were dismantled or severely cut back, including the Civilian Conservation Corps and the free school lunch program. Ironically and wrongly, when psychologists, social workers, and family counselors assessed blame for wartime problems, they tended to point an accusing finger not at unsettled wartime conditions but at individual mothers. Both neglectful and overly protective mothers were accused of causing a host of social problems ranging from emotional instability in children to juvenile delinquency. In the end U.S. families, separated and buffeted by wartime stresses, were viewed as the cause of their own problems.

The next decade would witness a sharp reaction to the psychological and societal stresses of wartime. Many Americans, having postponed marriage or a family during the depression and World War II, finally had a chance to fulfill their wishes. They married at younger ages and had more children than preceding generations. Responding to the postwar housing shortage, millions of families moved to new single-family homes in the suburbs. And in a dramatic reversal of the wartime influx of women into the labor force, millions of women decided against acquiring a higher education and pursuing a career and instead concentrated on rearing their children and keeping house.

*A family picnics outside their new 1949 Ford station wagon.
Courtesy of the collections of Henry Ford Museum and
Greenfield Village.*

CHAPTER IX

The Golden Age:
Families of the 1950s

AT the end of her first year as a psychology graduate student at the University of California at Berkeley in 1944, Betty Naomi Goldstein was confronted with a choice that would change her life. She was offered a large fellowship that would support her through a doctorate, but her boyfriend demanded that she turn it down. "You can take that fellowship," she remembered him saying, "but you know I'll never get one like it. You know what it will do to us." Betty was faced with a serious dilemma: "Either I pursue my career or I sublimate my wishes to a man." Fearful of "becoming an old maid college teacher," she turned down the fellowship. Despite her sacrifice, the romance did not last.[1]

Betty subsequently moved to Greenwich Village, where she supported herself as a journalist. There she met Carl Friedan, a product of summer stock theater, and fell in love. Two months after their first date he moved into her apartment, and in 1947, after a whirlwind seven-month courtship, they married. Like thousands of other women, she gave birth, in rapid succession, to three children. And like many other post-war families, the Friedans moved from an apartment project to a house in the suburbs, overlooking the Hudson River. Betty continued to free-lance four or five articles a year for women's magazines, but she felt freakish for having a career and worried that she was neglecting her children. She devoted most of her time to child-care and entertaining, and on her census form, she listed her occupation as "housewife."[2]

In her decision to forego professional training and the pursuit of a professional career and devote her energies to child-rearing and homemaking, Betty Friedan was by no means alone. After the war many women who had joined the work force returned to being housewives. Managing a home in the suburbs and raising a family became the goal of most women during the 1950s.

To a generation economically strapped in the depression and sacrificing for the war effort in World War II, the opportunity to have a family and buy a suburban house, with a backyard barbecue and a living room teeming with children, filled a deep emotional need. For two decades American families had experienced unprecedented strain, and now they turned away from public concerns and sought in private life satisfactions available nowhere else. For those who could personally recall their family's struggle to make ends meet during the depression, and who, during the war, had experienced family separation, frequent movement from place to place, and anxiety about men and women fighting overseas, a house of their own and family togetherness was a promise of security and fulfillment. By "marrying at an earlier age, rearing larger families," and owning their own homes, young adults of the 1950s could, in the words of *McCall's* magazine, find their "deepest satisfaction."[3]

The Great Exception

In the memories of many Americans whose recollections of the decade are limited to faded magazine photographs, old movies, and television reruns, the 1950s stand out as the golden age of the American family, a reference point against which recent changes in family life can be measured. And indeed, compared to today, family life in the 1950s was, superficially, much more stable. Rates of divorce, single-parent families, and illegitimacy were half what they are today; birthrates were twice as high; and many more young adults married at young ages.[4]

The fact is, however, that the pattern of family life characteristic of the fifties differed dramatically from any that has been observed earlier in our history or since. Young adults of the 1950s married in unprecedented numbers. They married earlier than other twentieth-century Americans, and they had more children and bore them faster. At the same time, the rate of increase in divorce rates was slower than it had been for earlier or later American families.[5]

The high marriage and birthrates and relatively stable divorce rate of the 1950s were all sharply out of line with long-term demographic trends. Throughout the last century, the proportion of Americans marrying has remained relatively stable. During the 1940s and 1950s, however, that proportion shot upward. By the end of World War II, there were 2.5 million fewer single women than in 1940, and by the end of the 1950s, 70 percent of all women were married by the age of twenty-four, compared to just 42 percent in 1940 and 50 percent today. Marriage rates during the 1950s reached an all-time high.[6]

The age of marriage fell to a record low. Over the past century, young men have tended to marry in their mid- to late-twenties while young women have wed in their early or mid-twenties. In 1890 the median age of marriage for men was 26.7 years, and in 1900 fewer than half of young women under the age of 24 had been married. The 1950s, however, witnessed a sharp exception to this pattern. Young men and women both married much earlier than in the past. The average age of marriage for men dropped to just twenty-two; for women, to twenty. Although today it is often said that young people are delaying marriage to unusually late ages, in fact, the average age of marriage today is in line with historical averages. It was the young men and women of the fifties, reacting against the hardships and separations of depression and war, who married unusually early.[7]

Families of the 1950s were also distinctive in their large size. Since 1810 American birthrates have consistently declined, and average family size has consistently dropped. During the 1950s, however, this pattern reversed itself as women of childbearing age bore more children, spaced them closer together, and had them earlier and faster than had their mothers. The fertility rate rose 50 percent from 1940 to 1957—producing a population growth rate approaching that of India. The birthrate for third children doubled and for fourth children tripled. Nearly one-third of all American women had their first children before they reached their twentieth birthday.[8]

And finally, the stable divorce rate of the 1950s was out of line with long-term trends. Since the Civil War, the American divorce rate has risen consistently about 3 percent a decade. Here, too, the 1950s stand out as a glaring exception. After 1947 the divorce rate leveled off. By the late 1950s, the divorce rate was roughly the same as it had been in 1940, at ten divorces for every thousand married women. In 1940, 1.4 percent of the population had been divorced; twenty years later the figure had climbed to just 2.5 percent. The rate of increase in divorce was lower during the 1950s than in any other decade of this century.[9]

Renewed Emphasis on the Family

In its Easter 1954 issue, *McCall's*, the nation's most popular women's magazine, published a picture essay illustrating the life of the ideal postwar family. The article focused on Ed Richtscheidt, a paper mill executive, and his wife Carol, who lived in a suburban New Jersey gray-shingled split-level house. This couple "centered their lives almost completely around their children and their home." Together they shopped at the supermarket, decorated their house, and made breakfast. Ed was "ready and willing to do his share of bathing, feeding, comforting, [and] playing" with the children.[10]

According to the editors of *McCall's*, the defining characteristic of the ideal family was "togetherness," a "new and warmer way of life" in which women and men sought to achieve fulfillment "not as women alone or men alone, isolated from one another, but as a family sharing a common experience." Family togetherness quickly became a national ideal, seized upon by advertisers, ministers, and newspaper editors.[11]

Reacting against the poverty of the depression and the upheavals of World War II, the instability of international affairs, and the increasingly impersonal quality of social relations, couples placed a new emphasis on the family as the source of hopes and aspirations. As two contemporary observers explained: "The employee of a large, bureaucratic-type organization [finds that his job] offers little in the way of meaningful personal relationships. . . . In this mushrooming of size and anonymity, the family stands out as a haven of intimacy. . . . Children are seen as providing security."[12]

During the postwar period, marriage was seen as an essential ingredient for a full and happy life. Fewer than one American in ten believed that an unmarried person could be happy. A popular advice book summed up the consensus of opinion: "Whether you are a man or a woman, the family is the unit to which you most genuinely belong. . . . The family is the center of your living. If it isn't, you've gone far astray." In record numbers Americans rushed to marry. By the late 1950s, the average marriage age of women dropped to twenty years and fourteen million women were engaged by the age of seventeen.[13]

Marriage fever was accompanied by a baby boom. During the 1950s a million more children were born each year than during the 1930s. The birthrate, which had plunged to 18.7 percent in the depression year of 1935, climbed to over 25 percent by 1947 and stabilized at that level throughout the 1950s. When asked to state the ideal size for a family, three-quarters of the women surveyed answered three, four, or more children. Back in 1941, the largest number of women had replied two children.[14]

Growing numbers of women decided to forsake higher education or a career and achieve emotional fulfillment as wives and mothers. Young women began marrying immediately after high school. Nearly half of all women married while they were still teenagers. Instead of taking jobs or pursuing their education, more and more women considered being a housewife a full-time career. Two out of three women who entered college dropped out before graduating; 60 percent left college in order to marry or because they feared that a college education would hurt their chances of marrying. A 1952 advertisement for Gimbel's department store expressed the prevailing point of view. "What's college?" the ad asked. The answer: "That's where girls who are above cooking and sewing go to meet a man so they can spend their lives cooking and sewing." As a result of the general cultural imperative that woman's place was in the home, a declining proportion of college women prepared for careers as college professors, doctors, and lawyers or pursued advanced degrees.[15]

The popular literature and media of the decade reinforced the emphasis on family life. Psychologists, educators, and journalists frequently repeated the idea that marriage was necessary for personal well-being. Individuals who deviated from this norm were inevitably described as unhappy or emotionally disturbed. Novelist Philip Roth recalled the popular wisdom:

> A young college-educated bourgeois male of my generation who scoffed at the idea of marriage for himself, who would just as soon eat out of cans or in cafeterias, sweep his own floor, make his own bed, and come and go with no legal binding attachments . . . laid himself open to the charge of "immaturity," if not "latent" or blatant "homosexuality." Or he was just plain "selfish." Or was "frightened of responsibility."

Failure to marry was typically associated with "homosexuality," "emotional immaturity and infantile fixations," "unwillingess to assume responsibility," the "narcissistic pursuit of career ambitions," and "deviant physical characteristics."[16]

Educators, psychologists, women's magazines, and opinion shapers all echoed the view that women's primary responsibility was to manage the house and care for children. In 1955 Adlai E. Stevenson told the graduating women at Smith College that their role in life was to "influence us, man and boy," to "restore valid, meaningful purpose to life in your home," and to keep their husbands "truly purposeful." Women's magazines pictured housewives as happy with their tasks and depicted career women as neurotic, unhappy, and dissatisfied. Many educators echoed Margaret Pickel, dean of Barnard College,

who argued that women could not compete with men in the workplace, because they "had less physical strength, a lower fatigue point,
and a less stable nervous system." National magazines were saturated
with Freudian notions of "penis envy" and the sexual origins of
neurosis and argued that women could only achieve happiness by
accepting the roles of wife and mother and rejecting "masculine striv-
ings." One best-seller, *Modern Woman: The Lost Sex*, warned that careers and higher education would lead to the "masculinization of
women with enormously dangerous consequences to the home, the
children dependent on it, and the ability of the woman, as well as
her husband, to obtain sexual gratification."[17]

Postwar Economic Boom

The temper of the times was conducive to marital life and domestic
expansion. A postwar economic boom made it possible for Americans
to satisfy their desires for a stable, secure family life. Millions of young
adults ceased waiting to marry or to have a family and abandoned
cramped apartments for brick and frame houses located in America's
burgeoning suburbs.[18]

When Dwight Eisenhower rose for a final time, in January 1960,
to deliver the annual State of the Union Address, he used the occasion to hail the "well-being" of the American family. Since 1946, the
president noted, the real income of every man, woman, and child in
the country, corrected for inflation, had risen nearly 20 percent.
Houses and apartments—15 million of them—had been constructed,
eliminating the postwar housing shortage. And 31 million of the nation's 44 million families now owned their own home. In 1960 75
percent of the nation's families had a car, in contrast to just 54 percent
in 1948. Almost every kitchen had a refrigerator. Who could not
believe that the American family was indeed blessed, and the future
held even greater prosperity and stability.[19]

A hallmark of postwar prosperity was the suburban boom. Setting
up a separate household had at last become affordable. As late as
1940, half of all young adults between the ages of twenty and twenty-
four lived with their parents. After the war these young people married and increasingly moved to homes of their own.[20]

On the morning of March 7, 1949, builder William J. Levitt opened
a sales office for a new development of inexpensive single-family
homes in a potato field in the center of Nassau County on Long
Island. In bitter cold weather, more than a thousand young couples
crowded outside the sales office, waiting for a chance to buy a four-

room, 25- x 32-foot house for $6,999, government-financed, no money down. Some had camped out in tents for as long as four days.[21]

To build houses rapidly and inexpensively, Levitt used the method made famous by Henry Ford: the production line. Levitt broke down the construction of a home into twenty-six separate steps. Teams of construction workers, trained to execute specific steps, leveled the land, paved streets, poured concrete slabs, planted trees every twenty-eight feet, and installed plumbing and electrical wiring. A hundred houses were built at a time. Construction was governed by clockwork. By 8 A.M., trucks unloaded prefabricated siding at each house site; at 9:30 A.M., toilets arrived; at 10 A.M., sinks, tubs, and Sheetrock were delivered; at 11 A.M., flooring followed. To speed construction and trim costs, painters used spray guns instead of brushes and carpenters used power saws. Interior partitions, roof trusses, and door and window units were cut to the required shape before they left the factory.[22]

In order to give young couples a chance to buy an affordable house, Levitt cut costs by eliminating basements and giving all houses in his development the same floor plan. Interior and exterior painting was limited to a single two-tone color scheme. Critics derided the monotony and uniformity of this new suburban development. Nevertheless newlyweds caught in the postwar housing shortage flocked to Levittown by the thousands. When the first phase of consruction was completed, 17,500 families had moved in. A second massive development, near Philadelphia, housed 70,000 people.[23]

One of the most profound social changes of the postwar era was the rapid growth of the suburbs. Up until World War II, the best-educated, most prosperous Americans tended to live in the nation's cities. The country's largest manufacturing and commercial companies also concentrated their operations inside large cities. But after 1945, as the economy expanded, both people and businesses sought new spaces and places. Many members of the growing middle class scattered into sprawling suburbs and other outlying areas to find their ranch house and patch of lawn. Many of the nation's factories, outgrowing their city space, followed these people or dispersed their operations into rural areas. In the ten years following 1948, 13 million homes were built in the United States; 11 million—85 percent—were built in the suburbs. During the 1950s suburbs accounted for 64 percent of the nation's population growth. By 1960 as many Americans lived in the suburbs as in central cities, and the suburban way of life was shaping the patterns and rhythms of American families.[24]

The federal government had a great deal to do with the spread of the population into the suburbs, since it made mortgage money available at low interest rates through the Veterans Administration and the Federal Home Loan Mortgage Administration. This, combined with an abundance of cheap energy for automobile transportation and state and federal governmental policies that encouraged highway construction, propelled many middle-class Americans into the suburbs.[25]

The movement to the suburbs had a profound impact on the postwar family. Suburbanization reinforced the family orientation of postwar society. Most suburban residents were newlyweds or young couples between the ages of twenty-five and thirty-five and their chilren. Few suburban residents were single adults, young people in their late teens or early twenties, members of minority groups, the elderly, or the poor. The fact that fewer suburban wives and mothers worked than their urban counterparts underscored a family orientation. In the suburbs many postwar Americans sought to satisfy their desires for more living space and physical comfort, a private yard, compatible neighbors, clean air, a sense of privacy, and a chance to escape poor neighborhoods.[26]

During the middle and late 1950s, sociologists, psychologists, architectural critics, novelists, and popular social commentators generated a largely critical literature on family life in the suburbs. In such books as *The Organization Man*, *The Crack in the Picture Window*, *The Man in the Gray Flannel Suit*, *How the Bough Breaks*, *No Down Payment*, and *The Split-Level Trap*, they charged that the new suburbs fostered conformity, isolation, and matriarchy.[27]

According to the popular stereotype, families in the suburbs were child-centered and female-dominated. Because of the demands of commuting, a father had little time to spend with his family. Being so preoccupied with his role as breadwinner, he was unable to be the paternal authority and caring father to his children. The result was "a matriarchal society, with children who know men only as nighttime residents and weekend guests." The father's absence forced the mother to assume the roles of both parents. Not only was she responsible for playing with her children and disciplining them, she also had to chauffeur them to and from school, friends' homes, piano and dancing lessons, and the doctor. Deprived of stimulating contacts with other adults, the lives of suburban housewives were characterized by isolation, boredom, and loneliness. Quipped one humorist, a suburban housewife's life was "merely motherhood on wheels," delivering children first "obstetrically . . . and by car forever after."[28]

The suburban family was dominated to a great extent by the needs of children. "Filiarchy" had replaced traditional patriarchy. Suburban children "tend to be pampered as never before." They were coddled from birth, with their mother and father responding to their every whim. Explained one best-seller: "Mobile people have adopted the notion that you must eternally give to your children: otherwise you are not a loving parent." Children's daily lives, critics complained, were overorganized and overpressured, filled with lessons and club meetings, leaving them with little time for themselves. Mothers, deprived of outside interests, exerted too much pressure on their children to achieve and be popular.[29]

Transience and isolation were characteristics common to suburban family life. Population turnover in the new suburbs was extremely high, as families relocated as they climbed the corporate ladder, resulting in a lack of stability. In Levittown, one family in every six moved each year, and in the New York metropolitan area, less than 6 percent of the suburban population in 1960 was living in the same house as in 1955. Atlas Van Lines estimated that the typical corporate manager moved fourteen times during his lifetime. Frequent movement from one house to another accentuated the rootlessness of suburban families, isolating individual families from grandparents and relatives and friendly neighbors; weakening generational continuity; and undermining family networks. Frequent moving conditioned many to develop short-term affective relationships that were easy to relinquish. Their cost, however, was the undermining of a capacity for intimacy.[30]

Despite many popular stereotypes about suburban life, family life in the suburbs was varied and diverse. In the real world of mid-twentieth-century America, there were established, exclusive, upper-crust, Protestant suburbs like Grosse Pointe Farms, Michigan; treeless, potato-field tract developments, with sprawling acres of split-levels and ranches, like Levittown; and industrialized, racially and ethnically divided, working-class and lower-class suburbs like Milpitas or Compton, California. Many suburbanites spent no more time commuting to work than city dwellers. Many suburban fathers hurried home from work in order to take part in family life.[31]

Ethnic, religious, and class differences all persisted in the suburbs and made themselves felt in family patterns. Working-class families tended to diverge sharply from popular generalizations about life in the suburbs. Their households tended to be characterized by an especially marked sexual division of labor between husband and wife. Working-class families were much more likely to socialize with kinsfolk than with neighbors. Their characteristic approach to child rearing involved strict supervision and enforcement of rules, not coddling and permissiveness. However, the suburban way of life with its distinctive features had become a part of the American landscape and its contours continue, even today, to shape much of family life.[32]

Democratizing the Companionate Ideal of the Family

In 1951, Paul Michaelides, after a few years of floundering around running the family hardware store, was starting his sophomore year in college. Elaine Donald, who was not quite twenty years old, was studying child psychology at a local junior college. They met while both were at college, married the next year, and in rapid succession had six children. Paul explained their mutual attraction: "Very early on, I felt I could tell her about my disappointments, about anything that went wrong at school or at home. I didn't have to pretend, put on [a] kind of false facade. . . . From the beginning, I felt as though I could show her my weaknesses and tell her my worries—without ever being concerned that she would be critical or misunderstand."[33]

The middle-class suburban family of the 1950s was pursuing the "companionate" ideal of family life once held only by the well-to-do, upper-middle-class families of the 1920s. Back then, the affluent progressive marriage strove for unprecedented mutuality and intimacy. In the postwar economic boom, the luxury of mutual pleasure and companionship could be enjoyed by millions of Americans, like Paul and Elaine Donald Michaelides, in the privacy of their own homes. Marriage, wrote singer Pat Boone in a 1958 best-seller, was now "a fifty-fifty deal." The American housewife was now respected as a full and "active" partner in her marriage.[34]

In fact, partnership did not mean equality. A wife's primary role was to serve as her husband's ego massager, sounding board—and housekeeper. Explained one expert: "Her job is at once to understand him, to help him understand himself, to help him rise to his capacities." When one expert sought proof of the "twentieth century democratizing of the American home," he pointed to a study which had "strikingly shown" a sharp increase in husbands' participation in housework. Of eighteen major household tasks, the study showed, husbands performed three—they locked up at night, fixed broken things, and performed yardwork. Wives were responsible for the remaining household chores, such as cooking, dusting, vacuuming, washing dishes, chauffeuring children, changing diapers, laundering, and ironing.[35]

The fifties ideal of a marital partnership was based on the assumption of a wife's role as hostess and consort. This was essential for the smooth running of the household and for the promotion of her husband's career. Corporations began to scrutinze closely the wives of job applicants to ensure that they were sociable, contented, and willing to accept their husband's transfers. Commented one sociologist: "The socially retarded wife has become the great sorrow of the corporation, and partly its responsibility."[36]

An essential element in the family ideal of the 1950s was a carefree, child-centered outlook—with relaxed methods of child discipline, separate rooms for each child, and educational toys and music lessons. The figure most responsible for disseminating this orientation was Dr. Benjamin Spock. Looking back at his own childhood, Dr. Spock remembered his mother as "very tyrannical, very moralistic, very opinionated, although very dedicated to her children." He and his five brothers and sisters felt that their "mother had x-ray vision because she always could spot guiltiness." "We didn't realize," he explained, "that she instilled such a sense of guilt in us that it showed all over when we came in having done something naughty."[37]

When he came to write his own book on child rearing in 1946—targeted at war-weary parents scornful of the child-rearing homilies of their parents and grandparents—Dr. Spock counseled parents to dispense with the rigidities of traditional child rearing. Spock rejected the idea of strict feeding and bathing schedules that were the rule among pediatricians and told parents to pick up their babies and enjoy them. Spock's reassuring message was, "You know more than you think you do."[38]

During the 1960s Spock's book was often treated as a synonym for permissiveness in child rearing, but in fact the book always emphasized the importance of discipline. Spock stressed that children needed firm leadership, since this would not only produce a better behaved child but a happier one. But, he added, parental success in instilling discipline in children depended not on techniques formulated in psychology laboratories or on physical punishment or intimidation but upon the power of love, reason, and parental example. Spock's philosophy is best understood not as permissiveness but as psychoanalytic and Freudian. He taught parents that their actions carried enormous consequences for their children's future, that their children's needs and desires had as much legitimacy as their own, that parental authority should be flexible rather than arbitrary and absolute, and that children needed to be involved in the formulation of rules intended to govern their behavior. He placed particular emphasis on the importance of the mother-child bond, arguing that creative individuals owed their talents to "the inspiration they received from a particularly strong relationship with a mother who had especially high aspirations for her children."[39]

For Spock the key to successful child rearing was a mother's love. As he put it, "Children raised in loving families want to learn, want to conform, want to grow up. If the relationships are good, they don't have to be forced to eat, forced to learn to use the toilet." The ideal mother did not attempt to mold her children or rigidly structure their environment, as behaviorist psychologists of the 1920s had urged. Instead she sought to meet her children's needs for love, attention, and maternal care; and in fulfilling the needs of her children, she, in turn, would find fulfillment.[40]

Despite Dr. Spock's warm and comforting language, child care manuals of the 1950s were characterized by an undercurrent of anxiety. No previous generation of child care books had ever expressed so much anxiety and fear about children's health, safety, and happiness. A major source of concern was over children's physical health. The 1940s and early 1950s was the last period when large numbers of American children died or were left crippled by such dreaded childhood ailments as polio or meningitis. Because of the risk that even a minor ailment might grow into a more serious disease, parents were told to be watchful for even the slightest symptoms of these diseases, such as a sore throat, a headache, stomach cramps, a high fever, and stiffness of the neck and back.[41]

Prior to the introduction of the Salk vaccine in 1955, tens of thousands of American children were crippled by polio each year. Massive outbreaks of polio occurred in 1944, 1946, 1949, 1950, and 1951. In 1952, 58,000 Americans contracted polio—a record figure. Norma Jean Mason was one of the children to contract the disease. One Sunday the nine-year-old had a stomachache and felt a stiffness in her legs. Her father, a foreman at a lumber mill, put a heating pad on her legs and rubbed them. The next day she was running a slight fever and Norma's parents called a doctor, who tested her reflexes and muscles. Within about ten minutes, he determined that she had polio. One day Norma was healthy and active; a day later her parents had to consider the likelihood of her dying, being crippled, or being compelled to live in a mechanical respirator.[42]

Child care experts were anxious not only about children's physical health but also about their emotional and psychological well-being. As rates of infant and child mortality declined, child-rearing professionals became increasingly preoccupied with the role of childhood upbringing in shaping a child's mental health. Psychoanalysts, following the lead of René Spitz, traced childhood psychological disorders to defects in mothering, such as "overanxious permissiveness," "oscillation between pampering and hostility," and "maternal hostility consciously compensated." Throughout the period, there was public and professional concern over the problems that might result from having a mother who subconsciously directed her hostilities and frustrations toward her offspring. Children of such frustrated mothers might suffer severe emotional damage if the mother displaced her own frustrations and needs for independence and achievement onto her children. This pattern of child rearing was linked by such pscyhologists as Theodore Lidz, Irving Bieber, and Erik Erikson with schizophrenia, homosexuality, identity diffusion, and an inability to assume the commitments of adulthood. Betty Friedan accurately summarized the mood of the period:

> It was suddenly discovered that the mother could be blamed for everything. In every case history of the troubled child; alcoholic, suicidal, schizophrenic psychopathic, neurotic adult; impotent, homosexual male; frigid, promiscuous female; ulcerous, asthmatic, and otherwise disturbed American, could be found a mother. A frustrated, repressed, disturbed, martyred, never satisfied, unhappy woman. A demanding, nagging, shrewish wife. A rejecting, overprotecting, dominating mother.[43]

Parents and teachers were repeatedly reminded to be watchful for signs of maladjustment. One parent recalled a worrisome report she received about her son: "The teacher explained to me, that he was doing fine on his lessons but that his social adjustment was not as good as it might be. He would pick just one or two friends to play with, and sometimes he was happy to remain by himself."[44]

A major source of concern was that children, and particularly boys, were failing to develop an appropriate sex role identity. Because boys were brought up almost exclusively by women, and men were absent from the home most of the day, it was feared that they would identify with their mothers' behavior and fail to develop a firm sense of their masculinity. Therefore it was crucial that fathers play a proper role in child rearing. To encourage boys into a proper masculine identification, child care professionals encouraged fathers and sons to participate together in sports. To help girls to develop a proper feminine identity, Dr. Spock called on a father to do "little things . . . like complimenting her on her dress, or hair-do, or the cookies she's made." A father might occasionally help out with the dishes or set the table or cook or make the baby's formula, but, he was warned, he should not perform such tasks too often because this would only confuse his children. "Live your gender," stressed one advice writer, because children needed "manly men and womanly women" as proper role models.[45]

In retrospect it seems clear that the underlying source of the anxiety pervading child-rearing manuals during the postwar era lay in the fact that mothers were raising their children with an exclusivity and in an isolation without parallel in American history. Most mothers had little technical knowledge of child development other than their own memories of childhood; they received little support from neighbors, apart from coffee klatsches, or husbands; and thus they were largely dependent upon the expert advice provided by Dr. Spock and women's magazines. Psychological theories that stressed the critical importance of early childhood magnified the anxieties and uncertainties that many mothers felt. Responsibility for their children's character and achievements rested almost entirely on their shoulders. New burdens and expectations were being placed on the home, but in child rearing as in many other areas of family life, wives and mothers received little help as they tried to fulfill the family's expanding functions.[46]

The 1950s Family: Images and Realities

If the ideal family of the 1950s has come to represent a standard of comparison against which Americans look at family life today, it is because the popular media, particularly television, brought the fifties family into living rooms across the nation. In 1940 there had been just 3,785 TV sets in the United States. Two decades later nine homes in every ten had at least one television set. It was during the 1950s that television emerged as the nation's dominant form of entertainment. For the preceding generation of Americans, clothing styles, speech patterns, and even moral attitudes and political points of view had been shaped by the movies. For post–World War II Americans, television replaced the movies' dominant position as popular entertainment. This new medium reached audiences far larger than those attracted by motion pictures, and it projected images right into the home, where viewers could follow the pregnancy of Lucy Arnaz on the "I Love Lucy" show or laugh at the antics of Ralph Kramden on "The Honeymooners." Television programs conveyed cultural images as strong and as influential on the viewer as the commercials which financed the new medium. Each night on TV, screen stars projected conceptions of masculinity and femininity, parenthood, and childhood and adolescence to millions of viewers. The most popular television personalities tell us a great deal about family postwar U.S. ideals: Jerry Mather as the epitome of preteen mischief on "Leave It to Beaver," Robert Young as the embodiment of the wrinkle-browed, all-knowing middle-class parent on "Father Knows Best," and William Bendix as the henpecked, bumbling, postwar working-class father on "The Life of Riley."[47]

The images conveyed by television were certainly caricatures, but like many stereotypes, they contained elements of reality. Although few social commentators took television's depictions of family life seriously, in hindsight it is clear that they reflected underlying tensions and anxieties in the population. Television tended to present two contrasting images of the American family. One showed life in the affluent middle-class suburbs; the other focused on the problems of working-class family life. Class, not ethnicity, tended to be the defining variable. During the late 1940s and early 1950s, television briefly experimented with a series of situation comedies dealing with ethnic life, many of which had appeared previously on radio, including "The Goldbergs" (Jews in New York City); "I Remember Mama" (a Norwegian immigrant family in San Francisco); and "Life with Luigi" (Italians in Chicago). Emphasis quickly shifted to a new kind of less controversial domestic comedy, epitomized by "The Life of Riley," "Make Room for Daddy," "The Donna Reed Show," and "Father Knows Best." These new sit-coms were targeted at the growing number of blue-collar Americans who pursued the dream of joining the suburban middle class and leaving behind the problems of big city ethnic life.[48]

"The Honeymooners" personified the frustrations and aspirations of many postwar blue-collar couples as they struggled to make their way up the economic ladder. In the most typical episodes, Ralph Kramden, a loud-mouthed, quick-tempered, self-centered Brooklyn bus driver, and his friend Ed Norton, a clumsy, befuddled sewer worker, spent their time dreaming up get-rich-quick schemes (such as selling wallpaper that would glow in the dark, uranium mine speculation, or no-cal pizza) or else conspiring to outwit their wives so they could have some male-only fun. The image of marriage typically depicted was one of domestic bickering provoked by economic strain (in the serial Ralph's salary is only $62 a week). Ralph's constant ranting at his wife is depicted as a defense against his own sense of inadequacy and inability to make enough money. His wife Alice, in turn, plays on his sense of inadequacy by repeatedly taunting him for his failure to achieve greater success.[49]

Television shows like "The Honeymooners" contributed a number of lasting images to American views of post–World War II family life. The working-class husband as a bumbling, clumsy fool and dreamer, taunted by his wife, was a foolish but sympathetic hero. His prototype was Dagwood Bumstead of the "Blondie" comic strip of the 1930s, but he gained his greatest prominence in the 1950s on the television screen. The archetype first appeared on TV in 1951 with Desi Arnaz in "I Love Lucy," and reappeared with Stu Erwin in "The Trouble with Father," Ozzie Nelson in "The Adventures of Ozzie and Harriet," William Bendix in "The Life of Riley," Charles Farrell in "My Little Margie," and Danny Thomas in "Make Room for Daddy." It was an image of the father and husband as a man of arrested emotional development, wholly incompetent at domestic chores, but lovable and forgivable.[50]

The working-class wife was a flighty scatterbrain, whose life is confined to a separate domestic sphere but who longs to play a role outside the home. Lucille Ball epitomized this character, and many of the episodes of the "I Love Lucy" show revolve around her repeated attempts to become a part of her husband's nightclub act. Although the wife is portrayed as wacky, she is also wily enough to get her own way with her husband. And ultimately, it is she who is responsible for counteracting her husband's harebrained schemes by providing a bedrock of common sense.[51]

When television portrayed middle-class family life in "Leave It to Beaver," "Father Knows Best," or "The Donna Reed Show," a sharply contrasting image appeared. In the middle-class suburban household, the essential problem of family life was not how to make ends meet but how to raise children effectively. Indeed, in these TV shows, the realm of work, politics, and even community life is largely invisible. The fathers simply disappear from home during the work week and viewers never learn the details of their jobs, precisely because their real work lies in mowing the lawn, fixing up the house, and engaging in long heart-to-heart talks with their children.[52]

As in the working-class situation comedies, the wives are not employed in any paid work. Unlike the working-class wives, however, the suburban wives do not spend their time talking to neighbors. Their lives are spent as full-time mothers, looking after their children, straightening the house, and baking cookies. Any evidence of romance in their relationships with their husbands is lacking (note the ever-present twin beds in their bedroom), for their lives are totally wrapped up in their children and in their parental role.[53]

The typical episode centers on a particular child-rearing problem. The characteristic approach to child-rearing involves a mixture of permissiveness and calm, wholesome advice. The commonsense wisdom of Jim Anderson on "Father Knows Best" was typical of the advice disseminated by television. He allows his children to make their own mistakes and learn from experience. He advised his wife to stand back and simply watch the misadventures of their children. "Keep out of it and see what happens," he would comment. Then, when the children needed help, they would surely turn to their parents for advice.[54]

Superficially, the portrait of family life presented on motion picture screens differed profoundly from the upbeat comedies that appeared on television. The popular family melodramas of the 1950s—such as *Rebel Without a Cause*, *East of Eden*, and *Red River*—reveal a pattern of deeply troubled family relationships. These films depicted sexual frustration, anxious parents, bitter clashes between the generations, alienated children, insensitive or fretful fathers, defiant adolescents, and loveless marriages. In part this "obsession" with the theme of marriage and family life "as a kind of hell" reflected a popularized form of psychoanalytic thought, which offered simplistic formulas to explain human behavior. Films of the fifties laboriously repeated the theme that sexual frustration inevitably led to neurosis and that harsh, neglectful, or uncomprehending parents produce alienated children. It was a far cry from the soothing and funny fare available on TV.[55]

According to many of the popular films of the decade, the source of family woes lies in a lack of familial love. Love is the solution to problems ranging from juvenile deliquency to schizophrenia. Adolescents in films like *Splendor in the Grass* or *Tea and Sympathy* are rebellious because their parents "won't listen" and they crave more love and attention from their mothers and fathers. Husbands and wives drink or take drugs or stray sexually in such films as *The Man with the Golden Arm*, *The Catered Affair*, or *The Dark at the Top of the Stairs* because they cannot communicate adequately with their spouses. While the films of the 1950s appear to offer a critical and more ambivalent view of marriage, their underlying message was hopeful. Even the most severe family problems could be resolved by love. All it took was understanding, perseverance, and love.[56]

Undercurrents of Discontent

Every June during the 1950s, approximately 350,000 men and women were married. Between one-quarter and one-third of those marriages eventually ended in divorce. In addition, many marriages that were not legally dissolved were unsuccessful. Many couples who either could not or would not divorce separated. Altogether, nearly 2 million married men and women lived apart from their spouses during the 1950s. Moreover, many couples who continued to live together were unhappy. Public opinion polls indicated that approximately one-fifth of all couples considered themselves unhappy in marriage, and another fifth reported only "medium happiness." The image of domestic tranquility celebrated in the popular media was, in part, a myth.[57]

Betty Friedan said that her marriage was troubled from the start. Her husband's "vision of a wife was one who stayed home and cooked and stayed with the children. And one who didn't compete," she recalled. "I was not that wife. In some of those early years, I made more money a week than he did, and I took to doing stupid things like losing my purse so we wouldn't have a fight." Poet Sylvia Plath— like Friedan, a Smith College graduate—burned her poet husband's papers, left written curses on the ashes, and committed suicide after discovering that her husband, "the one man whom I can make into the best man the world has seen," had been unfaithful.[58]

Throughout the 1950s evidence accumulated that suggested that all was not well with the American family. On Long Island, police uncovered a call-girl ring of thirteen suburban housewives. Physicians reported excessive use of alcohol, barbiturates, and tranquilizers by Connecticut matrons. Stories surfaced about hundreds of couples in San Francisco's suburbs participating in "wife-swapping." A University of Colorado team identified 302 cases of battered children in a single year, in which 33 children had died.[59]

Social scientists attributed the instability of family life to the fact that traditional sex roles were rapidly being redefined. Today the

1950s are commonly associated with a clear and sharply delineated conception of sex roles and family roles. In fact in men, the prevailing moral code did value stability, responsibility, maturity, and a protective commitment toward women and children; and in women, a willingness to sacrifice their own individuality for their family's good. Yet, in the immediate postwar period, traditional sex roles seemed to be subject to extreme strain.[60]

Popular magazines ran a large number of articles focusing on "the restlessness of American women." A 1949 issue of *Life* magazine observed that "suddenly and for no plain reason the women of the United States [had been] seized with an eerie restlessness." "A mask of placidity," wrote one physician, "hides an inwardly tense and emotionally unstable individual seething with hidden aggressiveness and resentment." A 1956 issue of *Life* predicted that historians of the future would see this period as the "era of the feminist revolution."[61]

Several factors contributed to a widespread sense of discontent among American women. The closing off of employment opportunities and freedoms enjoyed during World War II frustrated women who had tasted the economic and personal independence of "men's work." A tension underlay women's needs for personal fulfillment and the sometimes conflicting demands of her family role. On the one hand, young women received the same education as men and were encouraged to develop their skills and intellectual abilities. On the other, women were pressured to maintain their "femininity" and to seek fulfillment as wives and homemakers, and they were cautioned against pursuing a career. The result was a deep sense of ambivalence and internal turmoil toward both homemaking and career.[62]

Adding to women's discontent was the lack of recognition accorded to the work they performed. During the 1950s home economists discovered that the contemporary American housewife devoted far more time to housework than had her mother or grandmother. A 1945 survey revealed that while the typical farm housewife spent sixty hours a week on housework, her big-city counterpart averaged over eighty hours a week. Despite the acquisition of such "labor-saving" appliances as automatic washing machines, clothes dryers, freezers, and electric mixers, contemporary housewives actually spent more time than their forebears washing clothes, cooking, and shopping.[63]

Men's roles, too, were subjected to extreme stress in the postwar United States. With chagrin, psychologists traced the decline of the traditional father and his replacement by a bumbling "dad" who seemed out of place in the family home. The patriarchal, autocratic father popularized in Clarence Day's 1939 play *Life With Father*—a father who feasted on lamb while his family ate stew—was contrasted with his contemporary counterpart, who spent much of his time commuting to and from his corporate office. Some considered the change basically positive. *McCall's* magazine rejoiced that the old-fashioned paterfamilias, "disciplinarian and bogeyman," had been "pretty well displaced by the father who's pal and participator." But more serious analysts worried that the father's role within the family had been weakened. One study indicated that most fathers believed that their family function had been largely reduced to that of full-time wage earner for their wives and children. Fatherhood, according to a popular conception of the 1950s, was increasingly characterized by psychological distance and part-time involvement. Popular culture was saturated with acute cravings for calm, decisive, strong, consistent, strict paternal authority, but real fathers seemed incapable of meeting these needs.[64]

The dilemmas facing postwar males received searching analysis in such works of fiction and nonfiction as David Riesman's *The Lonely Crowd*, William H. Whyte's *The Organization Man*, and Sloan Wilson's *The Man in the Gray Flannel Suit*. These books offered a cogent analysis of the psychological strains and pressures placed on men by the postwar shift of jobs from small businesses to the high-pressure, highly competitive world of the large bureaucratic corporation. The bureaucratization of work and the demands of corporate life bred "careerism"—a compulsive concentration on work to the exclusion of all other aspects of life. Men who found their family lives unsatisfying, problematic, or who were anxious about family finances often compensated by "losing themselves" in their work, subordinating everything to the pursuit of their careers. Such compulsive involvement with work was often both physically and emotionally debilitating. A growing number of physicians during the 1950s voiced concern that work-related stress was a major cause of peptic ulcers, high blood pressure, and heart attacks among upwardly mobile executives who were risking their lives in their efforts to get ahead. The "careerist" father was so drained by his work and his long commute that he had little energy left for his family and so became a "part-time father." His gradual withdrawal from all emotional commitment to his wife and children augured ill for the health of the family.[65]

The reverse of the careerist was the man who found work in the bureaucratic organization monotonous and demeaning and sought compensation for his troubled pride in focusing all his energies on his family. For these men compensation for the frustrations and inadequacies of work might be found in mowing the lawn, waxing the car, or the pursuit of hobbies. Richard Yates's popular 1961 novel, *Revolutionary Road*, was the story of one unhappy corporate employee who sought to compensate for all his unrealized ambitions by displacing his needs onto his wife and children. His family, however, proved incapable of providing the satisfactions he craved. The message was that men needed to experience success at work in order to feel secure at home.[66]

The postwar blue-collar male confronted an array of special strains and tensions. Facing more tenuous economic circumstances than did their white-collar counterparts, as a result of lower pay and less secure employment, these men clung more intently to old-fashioned distinctions between men's roles and women's place. Blue-collar men felt that their status and self-esteem were closely tied to their ability to support their family and keep their wife at home. Their refusal to allow their wives to work had the practical effect of accentuating economic stress. Blue-collar families had to move more frequently than did middle-class families, and they frequently lacked the economic resources to entertain in order to make new friends. The isolation of the working-class housewife, in turn, generated feelings of irritability and a desire for a job outside the home, leading to friction with her husband.[67]

Postwar social analysts tended to downplay the tensions and stresses in American family life, emphasizing instead how well suited the modern American family was to the demands of mid-twentieth-century society. The small, isolated, inward-turning American family, it was argued, conformed to the practical needs of a mobile, bureaucratized society. Cut off from wider kinship ties, the American famiy was able to change residences, status, occupations, and even child-rearing techniques without excessive resistance. In emphasizing the "goodness of fit" between the family and the needs and circumstances of postwar life, academic sociologists were heavily influenced by the writings of Harvard sociologist Talcott Parsons, who described social and familial change in terms of a differentiation of functions and a specialization of roles that occurred in more complex, industrialized countries. In the economic realm, Parsons argued, differentiation and specialization were geared toward increased productivity. The family, which had lost its traditional economic, educational, religious, and welfare functions, provided family members with emotional sustenance and support.[68]

In certain respects the companionate family was well suited to the needs and circumstances of postwar life—such as unprecedented social and geographical mobility, escalating incomes, and increased leisure. At the same time, however, unresolved tensions concerning gender roles, parent-child relations, and excessive expectations of marriage and family lay under the surface. Larger social and political changes were setting the stage for the upheavals that would rock family life during the 1960s.

According to current nostalgia, the 1950s were a decade when college students were referred to as the "silent generation" and intellectuals proclaimed the "end of ideology"—an era of Hula Hoops, 3-D movies, and college students stuffed into telephone booths. Little of larger social importance seems to have occurred. Yet it is clear that historical processes were under way that would radically alter the character of American family life. One such process was a revolutionary change in the character of women's lives. Because of the widespread use of contraceptives and the power to cease childbearing at an earlier age, a declining portion of married women's lives was devoted to caring for very young children. As a result, more and more married women entered the labor force during the 1950s. By 1960 the proportion of American wives working outside the home reached one out of three. Twice as many women worked in 1960 as in 1940, and the female employment rate was increasing at four times that rate of men. Most of these new women workers were over the age of thirty-five, and very few pursued careers. Most held part-time jobs, as salesclerks, secretaries, or bank tellers, and used their incomes to help their families, putting children through college, paying off a mortgage, or paying for a family vacation. By 1960 the stereotype of dad the full-time breadwinner and mom the full-time homemaker no longer applied to a significant number of families. A growing discrepancy had begun to appear between the image of womanhood popularized by advertisers, women's magazines, educators, and psychologists and the actual realities of many women's lives.[69]

Dramatic social transformations were under way. Beginning in 1957, the birthrate began to drop. (This decline cannot be attributed to the birth control pill, since it was not introduced until 1960.) Although a 1961 *Ladies Home Journal* poll of young women found that "most" wanted four children and "many" wanted five, a growing number of women had decided to have fewer children. The decline in birthrates was accompanied by a decision by an increasing proportion of women to postpone marriage. A dramatic upsurge also took place in the areas of women's education and employment. The proportion of bachelor's and master's degrees received by women rose from just 24 percent in 1950 to over 40 percent fifteen years later. The greatest area of change was in employment. By 1960 25 percent of all middle-class wives were in the labor force, compared to just 7 percent immediately after the end of World War II. Over half of all female college graduates were working. Clearly women were opting for new roles—work, college, and professions. Agendas were changing, and during the 1960s this would profoundly affect families.[70]

By 1960 what Betty Friedan would later call "the problem that has no name," had already burst into the public spotlight. CBS television presented a documentary on "The Trapped Housewife." The *New York Times* also reported evidence of widespread discontent: "Many young women—certainly not all—whose education plunged them into a world of ideas feel stifled in their homes. . . . Like shut ins, they feel left out." *Newsweek* echoed this refrain, claiming that the discontent of housewives "is deep, pervasive, and impervious to superficial remedies which are offered at every hand." *Redbook* magazine ran an article entitled "Why Young Mothers Feel Trapped" and asked for examples of this problem. It received 24,000 replies.[71]

At the same time that women were breaking away from a single identity as wife and mother, youth was becoming a group more separate and distinct from children and adults. For the first time in recent American history, a large proportion of young people from their teens into their twenties developed a separate existence, relatively free of the demands of adulthood and more independent of parental supervision than children, in a culture marked by distinctive dress, music, and life-styles. During the 1950s, youth culture evolved its own language, employing such terms as "cool," "with it," and "hip." It developed its own distinctive social roles, such as the "greaser," the "beatnik," the "frat rat," and the "hood." It created its own form of music, rock and roll. And in such figures as Holden Caulfield of *Catcher in the Rye* and actor James Dean, it had its own heroes and archetypes.[72]

What tied these disparate elements of youth culture together was a common orientation: alienation from adult roles and values. The central concerns of youth were mirrored in its vocabulary. To many young people, the word "cool" took on important symbolic overtones. To be "cool" was to show detachment, an absence of emotion, and a lack of commitment. Millions of teenagers identified with the vulnerable, sensitive, directionless youth who was unable to conform to the conventional adult values of suburban and corporate America.[73]

Americans bitterly debated how many young people actually participated in the new youth culture. Most of the popular magazines stressed the conservatism of the majority of young people. *Time* declared that "perhaps more than any of its predecessors, this generation wants a good secure job." *Collier's* agreed, calling it a "reassuring truth that the average young American is probably more conservative than you or your neighbor." Sociologist Edgar Z. Friedenberg, author of *The Vanishing Adolescent*, emphasized the political apathy, conformism, and adult orientation of most young people. Talcott Parsons took the position that youth culture was simply a means of facilitating the problematic transition to adulthood. But other social commentators viewed youth culture with less equanimity. They were deeply disturbed by what they regarded as a growing irresponsibility and aimlessness among young people, who derided achievers as "squares." In the view of many editorial writers, frat men, jocks, beats, delinquents, and rock and rollers were united by their moral laxity and their lack of commitment to constructive and collective goals and values.[74]

In retrospect it seems clear that the emergence of youth culture reflected the evolution of new patterns of age segmentation in American society. For longer and longer periods of their lives, young people were spending their time in the company of other young people within such specialized, youth-oriented institutions as schools, colleges, and sports facilities. New occupations had sprouted up to serve the new and growing market, including disk jockeys, adolescent psychologists, and orthodontists. Advertisers and industry were increasingly conscious of the enormous commercial potential of a separate youth market. With the average adolescent in the mid-1950s spending $555 annually "for goods and services, not including the necessities normally supplied by their families," manufacturers of record albums, cosmetics, comic books, and even training bras aimed at the expanding youth market. Publishers unleased a flood of books on the subject of youth gangs—such as Irving Shulman's *The Amboy Dukes* and *Cry Tough*—and Hollywood released movie after movie aimed at young audiences, ranging from juvenile delinquency films like *The Wild One* to science fiction thrillers like *Invasion of the Body Snatchers*. Even young children had their own special version of youth culture—complete with its own television shows, like "Howdy Doody" and the "Wonderful World of Disney," and its own heroes, like the coonskin-hatted Davy Crockett.[75]

Many adults, convinced that the youth culture posed a serious threat to traditional values, sought to break down the barriers it had erected between parents and children. *Look* magazine in 1957 hired a research company to define words commonly used by teenagers, such as "blast," "bread," and "raunchy." High-school authorities in San Antonio banned tight jeans and ducktail haircuts on the grounds that undisciplined dress encouraged undisciplined behavior. A city in Maryland declared that "going steady" was permitted only when practiced in a context of group dating, and the city of Houston, Texas, forbade young people under the age of eighteen to own a car, unless it was used exclusively for transportation to and from work.[76]

To many adults the most threatening aspect of youth culture was its association with sexual permissiveness. In slang the phrase "rock and roll" often referred to sexual intercourse, and sexuality was a basic element in the new music. The lyrics of many early rock and roll songs could hardly have been more sexually explicit: "Baby let me bang your box," or "Drill, daddy, drill." Rock and roll music, however, was only one of many developments of the 1950s that prefigured a shift in public attitudes toward sex. Hugh Hefner's *Playboy* magazine, which first appeared in 1953, urged men to regard women as delectable sex objects and to prefer an irresponsible bachelorhood to the responsibilities of marriage and a family. Even more influential in cutting through public taboos about sexuality was the publication in 1953 of Alfred Kinsey's *Sexual Behavior in the Human Female*, which emphasized the disparity between public attitudes toward female sexuality and actual behavior patterns. Half the women surveyed reported having engaged in sexual intercourse before marriage, a third with two or more men. And a quarter of the married women surveyed admitted to having had extramarital intercourse.[77]

The dramatic social transformations taking place in sexual values and in women's and young people's lives would, in the 1960s and 1970s, undermine the patterns of early marriage, large families, and stable divorce rates characteristic of the postwar era.

The Family (1962). Mixed media by Marisol. Courtesy of the
Museum of Modern Art, New York.

CHAPTER X

Coming Apart: Radical Departures Since 1960

A GENERATION ago Ozzie, Harriet, David, and Ricky Nelson epitomized the American family. Over 70 percent of all American households in 1960 were like the Nelsons: made up of dad the breadwinner,
mom the homemaker, and their children. Today, less than three decades later, "traditional" families consisting of a breadwinner father, a
housewife mother, and one or more dependent children account for
less than 15 percent of the nation's households. As American families
have changed, the image of the family portrayed on television
has changed accordingly. Today's television families vary enormously,
running the gamut from traditional families like "The Waltons" to
two-career families like the Huxtables on "The Cosby Show" or the
Keatons on "Family Ties"; "blended" families like the Bradys on "The
Brady Bunch," with children from previous marriages; two single
mothers and their children on "Kate and Allie"; a homosexual who
serves as a surrogate father on "Love, Sidney"; an unmarried couple
who cohabit in the same house on "Who's the Boss?"; and a circle of
friends, who think of themselves as a family, congregating at a Boston
bar on "Cheers."[1]

Since 1960 U.S. families have undergone a historical transformation as dramatic and far reaching as the one that took place at the
beginning of the nineteenth century. Even a casual familiarity with
census statistics suggests the profundity of the changes that have
taken place in family life. Birthrates plummeted. The average number
of children per family fell from 3.8 at the peak of the baby boom to
less than 2 today. At the same time, the divorce rate soared. Today
the number of divorces each year is twice as high as it was in 1966
and three times higher than in 1950. The rapid upsurge in the divorce
rate contributed to a dramatic increase in the number of single-parent

households, or what used to be known as "broken homes." The number of households consisting of a single woman and her children has doubled since 1960. A sharp increase in female-headed homes was accompanied by a steep increase in the number of couples cohabiting outside marriage; their numbers have quadrupled since 1960.[2]

Almost every aspect of family life seems to have changed before our eyes. Sexual codes were revised radically. Today only about one American woman in five waits until marriage to become sexually active, compared to nearly half in 1960 who postponed intercourse. Meanwhile, the proportion of births occurring among unmarried women quadrupled. At the same time, millions of wives entered the labor force. The old stereotype of the breadwinner-father and housewife-mother broke down as the number of working wives climbed. In 1950, 25 percent of married women living with their husbands worked outside the home; in the late 1980s the figure is nearly 60 percent. The influx of married women entering the labor force was particularly rapid among mothers of young children. Now more than half of all mothers of school-age children hold jobs. As a result, fewer young children can claim their mother's exclusive attention. What Americans have witnessed since 1960 are fundamental challenges to the forms, ideals, and role expectations that have defined the family for the last century and a half.[3]

Profound and far-reaching changes have occurred in the American family—in behavior and in values. Contemporary Americans are much more likely than their predecessors to postpone or forgo marriage, to live alone outside familial units, to engage in intercourse prior to marriage, to permit marriages to end in divorce, to permit mothers of young children to work outside the home, and to allow children to live in families with only one parent and no adult male present. Earlier family norms—of a working father, a housewife, and children—have undergone major alterations. The term "family" has gradually been redefined to include any group of people living together, including such variations as single mothers and children, unmarried couples, and gay couples.[4]

All these changes have generated a profound sense of uncertainty and ambivalence. Many Americans fear that the rapid decline in the birthrates, the dramatic upsurge in divorce rates, and the proliferation of loose, noncontractual sexual relationships are symptoms of increasing selfishness and self-centeredness incompatible with strong family attachments. They also fear that an increased proportion of working mothers has caused more children to be neglected, resulting in climbing rates of teenage pregnancy, delinquency, suicide, drug and alcohol abuse, and failure in school.[5]

Today fear for the family's future is widespread. In 1978 author Clare Boothe Luce succinctly summarized fears about the fragility of the family that continue to haunt Americans today:

> Today 50% of all marriages end in divorce, separation, or desertion. . . . The marriage rate and birth rate are falling. The numbers of one-parent and one-child families are rising. More and more young people are living together without benefit of marriage. . . . Premarital and extra-marital sex no longer raises parental or conjugal eyebrows. . . . The rate of reported incest, child molestation, rape, and child and wife abuse, is steadily mounting. . . . Run-away children, teenage prostitution, youthful drug addiction and alcoholism have become great, ugly, new phenomena.[6]

What are the forces that lie behind these changes in family life? And what are the implications of these transformations?

New Morality

The key to understanding the recent upheavals in family life lies in a profound shift in cultural values. Three decades ago most Americans shared certain strong attitudes about the family. Public opinion polls showed that they endorsed marriage as a prerequisite of well-being, social adjustment, and maturity and agreed on the proper roles of husband and wife. Men and women who failed to marry or who resented their family roles were denigrated as maladjusted or neurotic. The message conveyed by the broader culture was that happiness was a by-product of living by the accepted values of hard work and family obligation.[7]

Values and norms have shifted. The watchwords of contemporary society are "growth," "self-realization," and "fulfillment." Expectations of personal happiness have risen and collided with a more traditional concern (and sacrifice) for the family. At the same time, in addition to its traditional functions of caring for children, providing economic security, and meeting its members' emotional needs, the family has become the focus for new expectations of sexual fulfillment, intimacy, and companionship.[8]

Today a broad spectrum of family norms that prevailed during the 1950s and early 1960s is no longer widely accepted. Divorce is not stigmatized as it used to be; a large majority of the public now rejects the idea that an unhappily married couple should stay together for their children's sake. Similarly, the older view that anyone who rejected marriage is "sick," "neurotic," or "immoral" has declined sharply, as has the view that people who do not have children are "selfish." Opinion surveys show that most Americans no longer believe that a woman should not work if she has a husband who can support her, that a bride should always be a virgin when she marries, or that premarital sex is always wrong.[9]

Economic affluence played a major role in the emergence of a new outlook. Couples who married in the 1940s and 1950s had spent their early childhood years in the depression and formed relatively modest material aspirations. Born in the late 1920s or 1930s, when birthrates were depressed, they faced little competition for jobs at maturity and were financially secure enough to marry and have children at a relatively young age. Their children, however, who came of age during the 1960s and 1970s, spent their childhoods during an era of unprecedented affluence. Between 1950 and 1970, median family income tripled. Increased affluence increased opportunities for education, travel, and leisure, all of which helped to heighten expectations of self-fulfillment. Unlike their parents, they had considerable expectations for their own material and emotional well-being.[10]

In keeping with the mood of an era of rising affluence, philosophies stressing individual self-realization flourished. Beginning in the 1950s, "humanistic" psychologies, stressing growth and self-actualization, triumphed over earlier theories that had emphasized adustment as the solution to individual problems. The underlying assumptions of the new "third force" psychologies—a name chosen to distinguish them from the more pessimistic psychoanalytic and behaviorist psychologies—of Abraham Maslow, Carl Rogers, and Erich Fromm, is that a person's spontaneous impulses are intrinsically good and that maturity is not a process of "settling down" and suppressing instinctual needs but of achieving one's potential.[11]

Even in the early 1960s, marriage and family ties were regarded by the "human potential movement" as potential threats to individual fulfillment as a man or a woman. The highest forms of human needs, contended proponents of the new psychologies, were autonomy, independence, growth, and creativity, all of which could be thwarted by "existing relationships and interactions." Unlike the earlier psychology of adjustment, associated with Alfred Adler and Dale Carnegie, which had counseled compromise, suppression of instinctual impulses, avoidance of confrontations, and the desirability of acceding to the wishes of others, the new humanistic psychologies advised individuals to "get in touch" with their feelings and freely voice their opinions, even if this generated feelings of guilt.[12]

The impulse toward self-fulfillment and liberation was further advanced by the prophets of the 1960s counterculture and New Left, Norman O. Brown and Herbert Marcuse. Both Brown and Marcuse transformed Sigmund Freud's psychoanalytic insights into a critique of the constraints of liberal society. They were primarily concerned not with political or economic repression but rather with what they perceived as the psychological repression of the individual's instinctual needs. Brown located the source of repression in the ego mechanisms that controlled each person's instincts. Marcuse, in a broader social critique, believed that repression was at least partially imposed by society.[13]

For both Brown and Marcuse, the goal of social change was the liberation of eros, the agglomeration of an individual's pleasure-seeking life instincts, or, as Marcuse put it, the "free gratification of man's instinctual needs." Brown went so far as to challenge openly the basic tenets of "civilized sexual morality," with its stress on genital, heterosexual, monogamous sex, and extolled a new ideal of bisexualism and "polymorphous perversity" (total sexual gratification). For a younger affluent, middle-class generation in revolt against liberal values, the ideas of Brown and Marcuse provided a rationale for youthful rebellion.[14]

An even more thoroughgoing challenge to traditional family values was mounted by the women's liberation movement, which attacked the family's exploitation of women. Feminists denounced the societal expectation that women defer to the needs of spouses and children as part of their social roles as wives and mothers. Militant feminist activists like Ti-Grace Atkinson called marriage "slavery," "legalized rape," and "unpaid labor" and denounced heterosexual love as "tied up with a sense of dependency." The larger mainstream of the women's movement articulated a powerful critique of the idea that child care and housework was the apex of a woman's accomplishments or her sole means of fulfillment. Feminists uncovered unsettling evidence of harsher conditions behind conventional familial togetherness, such as child abuse and wife beating, wasted lives and exploited labor. Instead of giving the highest priority to their families, women were urged to raise their consciousness of their own needs and abilities. From this vantage point, marriage increasingly came to be described as a trap, circumscribing a woman's social and intellectual horizons and lowering her sense of self-esteem. Homemaking, which as recently as the early 1960s had been celebrated on such television shows as "Queen for a Day," came under attack as an unrecognized and unpaid form of work in contrast to more "serious" occupations outside the home. And, as for marital bliss forevermore, feminists warned that divorce—so common and so economically difficult for women—was an occurrence for which every married woman had to be prepared. In general the feminists awakened American women to what they viewed as the worst form of social and political oppression—sexism. The introduction of this new awareness would go far beyond the feminists themselves.[15]

The challenge to older family values was not confined to radical members of the counterculture, the New Left, or the women's liberation movement. Broad segments of society were influenced by, and participated in, this fundamental shift in values.

Although only a small minority of American women ever openly declared themselves to be feminists, there can be no doubt that the arguments of the women's movement dramatically altered women's attitudes toward family roles, child care, marital relationships, femininity, and housework. This is true even among many women who claim to reject feminism. Polls have shown a sharp decline in the proportion of women favoring large families and a far greater unwillingness to subordinate personal needs and interests to the demands of husbands and children. A growing majority of women now believe that both husband and wife should have jobs, both do housework, and both take care of children. This represents a stunning shift of opinion in a decade and a half. A new perception of woman in the family has taken hold. In extreme imagery she is a superwoman, doing a full-time job while managing her home and family well. The more realistic image is of the wife and mother who works and struggles to manage job and family with the help of spouse, day care, and employer. Thus, as women increasingly seek employment outside the home, the family itself shifts to adjust to the changing conditions of its members while striving to provide the stability and continuity it has traditionally afforded.[16]

During the 1960s a sexual revolution that predated the counterculture swept the nation's literature, movies, theater, advertising, and fashion. In 1962, Grossinger's resort in New York State's Catskill mountains introduced its first singles-only weekend, thereby publicly acknowledging couples outside marriage. That same year Illinois became the first state to decriminalize all forms of private sexual conduct between consenting adults. Two years later, in 1964, the first singles

bar opened on New York's Upper East Side; the musical *Hair* introduced nudity to the Broadway stage; California designer Rudi Gern-
reich created the topless bathing suit; and bars featuring topless wait-
resses and dancers sprouted. By the end of the decade, a growing
number of the nation's colleges had abolished regulations specifying
how late students could stay outside their dormitories and when and
under what circumstances male and female students could visit with
each other.[17]

One of the most important aspects of this latter-day revolution in
morals was the growth of a "singles culture"—evident in a proliferation of singles bars, apartment houses, and clubs. The sources of the
singles culture were varied and complex, owing as much to demographic shifts as to the ready availability of birth control, cures for
venereal diseases, and liberalized abortion laws. The trend toward
postponement of marriage, combined with increased rates of college
attendence and divorce, meant that growing numbers of adults spent
protracted periods of their sexually mature lives outside marriage. The
result was that it became far easier than in the past to maintain an
active social and sex life outside marriage. It also became more acceptable, as its patterns became grist for the popular media and imagina-
tion.[18]

Sexually oriented magazines started to display pubic hair and film-
makers began to show simulated sexual acts. *I Am Curious (Yellow)*
depicted coitus on the screen. *Deep Throat* released in the 1970s,
showed cunnilingus and fellatio. Other manifestations of a relaxation
of traditional mores included a growing public tolerance of homosexuality, a blurring of male and female sex roles, increasing public acceptance of abortion, the growing visibility of pornography, a marked
trend away from female virginity until marriage, and a sharp increase
in the proportion of women engaging in extramarital sex. Within one
decade the cherished privacy of sexuality had been overturned and
an era of public sexuality had been ushered in.[19]

Increasingly, values championed by the women's movement and
the counterculture were adopted in a milder form by large segments
of the American population. A significant majority of Americans
adopted permissive attitudes on such matters as premarital sex, cohabitation outside of marriage, and abortion. Fewer women aspired
to motherhood and homemaking as a full-time career and instead
joined the labor force as much for independence and self-fulfillment
as from economic motives. The preferred number of children declined
sharply, and to limit births, the number of abortions and sterilizations

increased sharply. A revolution had occurred in values and behavior.[20]

Black Families in Poverty

At the same time as the attitudes and behavior of middle-class white
Americans were transformed as a result of increasing affluence, the
impact of feminism, and a revolution in sexual mores, the circumstances of the black family also shifted, but in very different ways.
The situation of poor black families significantly worsened during the
1960s and 1970s. Illegitimate births increased dramatically, and the
proportion of young blacks living in poverty climbed steeply. Today,
half of all black children grow up in poverty, more than half are born
outside wedlock, and nearly half live in female-headed households.[21]

The plight of the black family came to public attention early in the
fall of 1965, when the federal government released a confidential report written by Daniel Patrick Moynihan, then an obscure assistant
secretary of labor, called *The Negro Family: The Case for National Action*. In his report Moynihan argued that the major obstacle to the
advancement of the black community lay in a vicious and self-perpet-
uating cycle of despair in the urban ghettos. "The fundamental problem," Moynihan maintained, was the breakdown of the black family.
"The evidence—not final, but powerfully persuasive—is that the Negro family in the urban ghettos is crumbling." The black middle class
had managed to create stable families, "but for the vast numbers of
the unskilled, poorly educated city working class, the fabric of conventional social relationships has all but disintegrated."[22]

To support his thesis, Moynihan cited startling statistics. Nearly 25
percent of all black women were divorced, separated, or living apart
from their husbands, compared to 7.9 percent of white women. Illegitimacy among blacks had risen from 16.8 percent in 1940 to 23.6
percent in 1963, while the white rate had only climbed from 2 to 3
percent. The proportion of black families headed by women had
climbed from 8 percent in 1950 to 21 percent in 1960, while the white
rate had remained steady at 9 percent. The breakdown of the black
family, Moynihan contended, had led to a sharp increase in welfare
dependency, delinquency, unemployment, drug addiction, and failure
in school.[23]

The Moynihan Report attributed the instability of the black family
to the effects of slavery, Reconstruction, poor education, rapid urbanization, and thirty-five years of severe unemployment, which had undermined the role of the black man in the family. Unable to support

their families, many black fathers simply disappeared, leaving the women to cope and rule. In Moynihan's view, children raised in female-headed families, deprived of a male role model and authority figure, tended to remain trapped in a cycle of poverty and disadvantage:

> From the wild Irish slums of the 19th-century Eastern seaboard, to the riot-torn suburbs of Los Angeles, there is one unmistakable lesson in American history; a community that allows a large number of men to grow up in broken homes, dominated by women, never acquiring any stable relationship to male authority, never acquiring any set of rational expectations about the future—that community asks for and gets chaos.[24]

The report concluded with a call for national action to strengthen the black family through programs of jobs, family allowances, and birth control. It did not support the belief that enforcement of civil rights laws would be sufficient to bring about equality. Only new and special efforts by the federal government could alleviate conditions within urban ghettos and strengthen the black family.[25]

Release of the Moynihan report in August 1965 unleashed a storm of public criticism. Critics feared that the report would reinforce white prejudice by suggesting that sexual promiscuity and illegitimacy were socially acceptable within the black community and that the instability of the black family was the basic cause of racial inequality. Others accused the report of diverting attention from the underlying problems of racism and poverty and of blaming the victims for their own distress.[26]

How accurate was Moynihan's assessment of the black family? On the one hand, he was prescient in identifying single-parenthood, illegitimacy, and poverty among children as major social issues. Indeed, these problems have so worsened since Moynihan wrote his report that they now affect the entire society and can no longer be addressed solely in terms of race. At the same time, however, in important respects Moynihan's analysis was flawed. The problems of illegitimacy and absent fathers were exaggerated, the strengths of the black family were ignored, and the differences between the black family and the white family were overestimated.[27]

Contrary to the impression conveyed by the report of the prevalence of "matriarchy," "deviance," and "family disorganization" among blacks, the overwhelming majority of black families during the 1960s, 1970s, and 1980s were composed of two spouses. In 1960, 75 percent of black children lived with two parents; a decade later, 67 percent did. Today six out of every ten black families have two parents, and two-parent families remain the norm in the black community. The report's discussion of illegitimacy also seriously distorted the facts. Far from increasing, as Moynihan implied, the black illegitimacy rate—the proportion of unmarried women bearing children—had actually been declining consistently since 1961 and has, in fact, continued to decline up until today. In 1960, ninety-eight out of every thousand single black women gave birth to a baby. In 1980 only seventy-seven did. The proportion of black births that were illegitimate increased, but this was the result of a sharp drop in the birthrate of married black women. The report further exaggerated the difference between black and white illegitimacy rates by ignoring the fact that white women were much more likely than black women to use contraceptives, to have premarital pregnancies terminated by abortion, or to put babies born out of wedlock up for adoption.[28]

Moynihan tended to downplay the role of unemployment and the welfare system in producing family instability. Low wages and the unstable, dead-end occupations available to black men contributed to a sense of frustration and powerlessness that prevented many lower-class men from becoming stable husbands and fathers. And the welfare system added to the breakup of families since in half the states welfare benefits could only begin after a father deserted his family.[29]

Much of the disparity between white and black family patterns—in 1965 and today—is simply a result of poverty. The statistical gap between the races largely disappears when one compares blacks and whites of the same economic level. Blacks with incomes above the poverty line differ little from white families in their proportion of female-headed households. Furthermore, a significant part of the disparity in family patterns is explained by the skewed sex ratio of the black population: The number of black men of marriageable age is significantly smaller than the number of black women of marriageable age. The 1970 census indicated that there were only 86 black males for every 100 black females aged twenty to twenty-four and just 84 black males for every 100 females aged twenty-five to thirty-four.[30]

Although many poor families do not conform in structure to middle-class norms, it is important not to underestimate the strength and durability of the lower-class black kinship system. By focusing on the instability, weakness, and pathology of lower-class black families, the Moynihan Report failed to recognize that lower-class black family patterns were a rational response to conditions of severe deprivation.

Moynihan underestimated the competence of black mothers in rearing and supporting their children and the support black families received from an extended kinship network. Although Moynihan regarded lower-class black families as "disorganized" and "father-deprived" because they failed to conform to middle-class ideals of the nuclear family, later researchers found an extensive network of kin and friends supporting and reinforcing the lower-class black family. In urban ghettos, destitution and the inability of individual households to fulfill basic needs led lower-class blacks to form "domestic networks," which tended to replace the nuclear family as the fundamental unit of social organization. Friends and relatives helped mothers, took the place of fathers, provided child care, and shared resources.[31]

When President Lyndon B. Johnson announced the War on Poverty in 1964, his diagnosis of the problem of poverty was profoundly influenced by the Moynihan Report. Drawing on Moynihan's argument that poverty and unemployment had undermined the black family and that family disorganization perpetuated social and economic inequality, President Johnson pledged that a primary goal of federal antipoverty programs would be "to strengthen the family and create conditions under which most parents will stay together." Unless the family was strengthened, the president declared, all other legislation "will never be enough to cut completely the circles of despair and deprivation." A unique political commitment to the family had been made by the federal government.[32]

When Lyndon Johnson left the presidency in 1969, he left behind a legacy of a transformed federal government. At the end of the Eisenhower presidency in 1961, there were only 45 domestic social programs. By 1969 the number had climbed to 435. Federal social spending, excluding Social Security, had risen from $9.9 billion in 1960 to $25.6 billion in 1968. Johnson's "Great Society" represented the broadest attack Americans had ever waged on the special problems facing poor and disadvantaged families. It declared decisively that the family-related problems of the poor—problems of housing, income, employment, and health—were ultimately a federal responsibility.[33]

During the 1960s the federal government showed an increasing commitment to improving the welfare of the nation's poor families. To improve their economic status, government greatly expanded public assistance programs. In 1959 there was essentially only a single welfare program providing public assistance to the poor—Aid to Families with Dependent Children (AFDC). Payments were small, amounting to only about a quarter of the median income, and relatively few poor families participated in the program. During the 1960s and early 1970s, AFDC rolls grew rapidly as a result of a sharp increase in the number of female-headed families and changes in eligibility requirements, including a 1961 law that allowed states to grant assistance to families containing an unemployed father and a 1968 Supreme Court ruling that it was unconstitutional for states to deny AFDC benefits to households containing a live-in adult male.[34]

To assure adequate health care coverage to persons receiving federally supported public assistance, in 1965 Congress established Medicaid and in 1968 enacted the Child Health Improvement and Protection Act providing for prenatal and postnatal care. To combat hunger and malnutrition among the poor while disposing of surplus agricultural commodities, the federal government created the Food Stamp program in 1961 and subsequently added school breakfast and lunch programs. To address the problems of crowded and dilapidated housing, Congress in 1961 began to subsidize builders of low-income housing and in 1965 made rent supplements available to poor families. To reduce infant and maternal mortality, the numbers of unwanted children, and physical and mental handicaps among the poor, Congress in 1967 extended Medicaid coverage to include family planning services and required that they be provided to AFDC mothers. To train poorer Americans for new and better jobs, Congress adopted the Manpower Development and Training Act in 1962 and the Economic Opportunity Act in 1964 to provide vocational training, basic education, and summer employment for disadvantaged youth. To encourage adult AFDC recipients to enroll in job-training programs and seek work, Congress in 1967 required states to provide day care or child development facilities for the children of such women. To promote education in 1964 Congress established Head Start, a program of compensatory preschool education for poor children.[35]

Johnson promised to reduce poverty, alleviate hunger and malnutrition, expand community medical care, provide adequate housing, and enhance the employability of the poor. When he left office in 1969, he could legitimately argue that he had kept his promise. Contrary to the widespread view that "in the war on poverty, poverty won," substantial progress had been made. During the 1960s the incidence of poverty was reduced, infant mortality was cut, and blighted housing was demolished. In 1960, 40 million persons, 20 percent of the population, were classified by the government as poor. By 1969, their number had been reduced to 24 million, 12 percent of the population. Infant mortality among the poor, which had barely declined between 1950 and 1965, fell by one-third in the decade after 1965 as a result of the expansion of federal medical and nutritional programs. Implementation of Medicaid and Medicare helped to improve the health of the poor. Before 1965, 20 percent of the poor had never been examined by a physician; by 1970 the figure had been cut to 8 percent. The proportion of families living in substandard housing— usually defined as housing lacking indoor plumbing—also declined steeply, from 20 percent in 1960 to 11 percent a decade later.[36]

Few questions of public policy have evoked greater controversy than the impact of government welfare programs on the families of the poor. Political conservatives have generally argued that public assistance, food subsidies, health programs, and child care programs weakened poorer families. President Ronald Reagan voiced a common conservative viewpoint when he declared, "There is no question that many well-intentioned Great Society-type programs contributed to family breakups, welfare dependency, and a large increase in births out of wedlock."[37]

Belief in a causal connection between increased government welfare expenditures and family breakdown rests on a close chronological correlation between rising welfare spending and dramatic increases in female-headed households and illegitimacy among the poor. Back in 1959, just 10 percent of low-income black Americans lived in a single-parent household. By 1980 the figure had climbed to 44 percent. It was during the late 1960s, a time of rapid economic growth and increasing antipoverty expenditures, that the prevalence of two-parent black families declined most steeply, from 72 percent in 1967 to 69 percent in 1968 to just 63 percent in 1973. Today 59 percent of black families have two parents present. At the same time, the number of illegitimate births among the poor grew substantially. Had the number of single-parent families remained at the 1970 level, the number of poor families in 1980 would have been 32 percent lower than it was.[38]

What was the impact of massive federal intervention on the families of the poor? Did the expansion of state services contribute to rising rates of illegitimacy and single-parent families? The answers to these questions are still uncertain. On the one hand, there is little empirical evidence that welfare policies encourage family breakup. Statistical studies have found no correlation between the level of AFDC benefits and the proportion of black children in single-parent households. What other studies have shown is that increases in wages produce a sharp drop in female-headed households, reinforcing the view that low wages and unstable employment are major contributors to family instability.[39]

It seems clear that some of the apparent deterioration in black family patterns is illusory. The dramatic increase in black single-parent families living on welfare is not so much a result of a dramatic increase in the number of unmarried women having illegitimate babies as that fewer unmarried mothers live with their parents or other relatives than was the case in the past. Nearly two-fifths of the increase in female-headed households between 1950 and 1972 is explained by the movement of existing single-parent families out of households of parents or other relatives. Public assistance allowed female heads of poor families greater opportunity to set up independent homes. If female-headed families made up a growing proportion of the poor, this partly reflected a sharp reduction in poverty among other groups. One of the consequences of government policy was to alter dramatically the profile of the poor. Increases in Social Security payments dramatically reduced the incidence of poverty among the elderly. The Supplemental Social Security program introduced in 1973 sharply reduced poverty among the disabled. As a result of reductions in poverty among the elderly and disabled and increases in the number of single-parent, female-headed households, poverty has been increasingly feminized.[40]

The Feminization of Poverty

Today families headed by women are four and a half times as likely to be poor as families headed by males. Teenagers who have children out of wedlock are seven times as likely to be in poverty. Although female-headed families constitute only 15 percent of the U.S. population, they account for over 50 percent of the poor population. Teenagers and women in their early twenties who bear illegitimate children constitute a large segment of the population that remains poor and dependent on welfare for long periods of time.[41]

And yet the picture is not quite so bleak as it might seem at first glimpse. Although a majority of poor families are female-headed, it is no longer true that most female-headed families are poor. Over the past two decades, the poverty rate of female-headed families has declined steeply, as women have succeeded in obtaining better-paying jobs in the labor force. Back in 1960 50 percent of all female-headed families lived in poverty. By 1970 the figure had fallen to 38 percent

and down to 19 percent in 1980. Meanwhile, few female-headed families remain in poverty for very long. Most mothers who receive public
assistance are self-supporting individuals who have recently experienced a sudden divorce or separation. Most of these women leave
the welfare rolls within two years. And finally, many poor women
eventually marry, leaving poverty. Nearly three-quarters of young
black women who bear a child out of wedlock marry by the age of
twenty-four, usually ending their poverty.[42]

Still, there can be little doubt that the nation's welfare policies
actually provide incentives to the poor to avoid marriage. Under present law, if an AFDC mother marries, the stepfather assumes financial
responsibility for supporting her children, which may deter the couple
from marrying. In twenty-nine states, unemployed fathers are ineligible for assistance, which may encourage an unemployed father to desert his family so that his wife and children can obtain AFDC benefits.
The discouragement of marriage in American welfare law contrasts
sharply with European policies. In such countries as France, Hungary,
Sweden, and East and West Germany, which have adopted explicit
"family policies," the national government subsidizes families in a variety of ways, including the provision of family allowances to supplement parents' income and direct cash payments to parents when they
have children.[43]

Children in a New Age

Along with a mounting federal commitment to shore up the nation's
poor families came another domestic revolution, a radical new self-
consciousness about child rearing. Over the past quarter century,
Americans have grown progressively more concerned about the plight
of the nation's young people. Alarmed by sharp increases in delinquency, alcohol and drug abuse, pregnancy, and suicides among children and adolescents, parents became uneasy about the proper way
to raise children. They also worried about the effects of day care, the
impact of divorce, and the consequences of growing up in a permissive
society in which premarital sex, abortion, and drugs are prevalent.

The past two decades have witnessed significant changes in the
experience of childhood and adolescence. Since 1960 the proportion
of children growing up in "traditional families" in which the father is
the breadwinner and the mother is a full-time homemaker has fallen
dramatically while the number growing up in single-parent, female-
headed households or in two-worker, two-parent households has

risen steeply. Before 1960 divorce was an occurrence experienced by relatively few children. Of children born during the 1970s, in contrast, 40 percent will experience a divorce before their sixteenth birthdays, and nearly 50 percent will spend at least part of their childhood in a single-parent home.[44]

At the same time as marriages grew less stable, unprecedented changes took place within families. The proportion of married women with preschoolers who were in the labor force jumped from 12 percent in 1950 to 45 percent in 1980. Families grew smaller and, as a result, children have fewer siblings. Families also became more mobile, and hence children have less and less contact with relatives outside the immediate family. According to one estimate, just 5 percent of American children see a grandparent regularly. Young children spend more of their time in front of the television set or in the care of individuals other than their parents—in day-care centers, preschool programs, or the homes of other families—and more and more teenagers take part-time work.[45]

Each of these changes has evoked anxiety for the well-being of children. Many adults worry that a high divorce rate undermines the psychological and financial security of children. Others fear that children who live with a single female parent will have no father figure with whom to identify or to emulate and no firm source of guidance. Many are concerned that two-career parents with demanding jobs substitute money for affection, freedom for supervision, and abdicate their parental roles to surrogates. Still others fret that teenage jobs undermine school attendance and involvement and leave young people with too much money to spend on clothing, records, a car, or drugs. Today's children and adolescents, many believe, are caught between two difficult trends—decreasing parental commitment to child nurture and an increasingly perilous social environment saturated with sex, addictive drugs, and alcohol—that make it more difficult to achieve a well-adjusted adulthood.[46]

According to many Americans, children have paid a high price for the social transformations of the 1960s and 1970s—spiraling divorce rates, the rapid influx of mothers into the work force, a more relaxed attitude toward sex, and the widespread use of television as a form of child care. They are afraid that these patterns have eroded an earlier ideal of childhood as a special, protected state—a carefree period of innocence—and that today's permissive culture encourages a "new precocity" that thrusts children into the adult world before they are mature enough to deal with it. They worry about the deleterious effects of divorce, day care, and overexposure—through television, movies, music, and advertisement—to drugs, violence, sex, and pornography. They are concerned that parents have absorbed a far too egalitarian view of their relationship with their children and have become incapable of exercising authority and discipline.[47]

Giving credence to these fears are a variety of social indicators that appear to show an erosion in the parent-child bond and a precipitous decline in children's well-being. Public opinion polls indicate that two-thirds of all parents believe that they are less willing to make sacrifices for their children than their parents were. Other social statistics—ranging from college entrance examination results to teenage suicide rates—suggest that the decline in parental commitment to children has been accompanied by a sharp increase in problems among young people. Since 1960 the high-school dropout rate has increased until roughly one student in four drops out before graduation; juvenile delinquency rates have jumped 130 percent; the suicide rate for young people fifteen to nineteen years old has more than tripled; illegitimate births among white adolescent females have more than doubled; and the death rate from accidents and homicides has grown sixteenfold. Half a million adolescent females suffer from such eating disorders as anorexia nervosa or bulimia. American teenagers have the highest pregnancy rate of any industrialized nation, a high abortion rate and a high incidence of such venereal diseases as syphilis, gonorrhea, and genital herpes.[48]

Of course, it is easy to exaggerate the depravity of today's youth. Such problems as drug abuse, illegitimacy, and suicide affect only a small fraction of young people, and millions of others are raised in strong, caring homes by supportive and loving parents. Despite this, however, there is a widespread perception that American society is experiencing great difficulty in preparing children for adulthood.[49]

To a growing number of Americans, parenthood has become an increasingly frightening prospect. Fathers who once drag raced in hot rods and guzzled beer illegally are frightened by the idea of their children using drugs. Mothers who once made out with their boyfriends in parked cars are alarmed by statistics showing that teenage girls run a 40 percent chance of becoming pregnant and run three times the risk of contracting venereal disease that they did. One result is that parents have become progressively more self-conscious, anxious, and guilt-ridden about child rearing; fearful that even a single mistake in parenting might inflict scars that could last a lifetime. To address parents' mounting anxiety, a veritable torrent of child-rearing manuals has appeared.[50]

Although most discussions of child rearing in the 1960s and 1970s dwell on Dr. Benjamin Spock, his era of influence was even then coming to an end. Until 1960, American child-rearing literature was dominated by a handful of manuals, notably Spock's *Baby and Child Care* and the publications of Dr. Arnold Gesell and the Yale Child Development Clinic, which traced the stages of children's physical, cognitive, and emotional development. The arena rapidly grew more crowded and confused during the 1960s with the publication of a spate of new child-rearing books. By 1981 more than 600 books were in print on the subject of child development. These new manuals tended to convey a sense of urgency absent in earlier child care books, rejecting the easy going approach championed by Dr. Spock. One child care expert, Dr. Lee Salk, addressed the subject in words typical of the new child-rearing literature: "Taking parenthood for granted can have disastrous results."[51]

As the number of child-rearing books multiplied during the 1960s, a fundamental schism became increasingly apparent. At one pole were those echoing concerns voiced by Vice President Spiro T. Agnew that overpermissiveness—that is, too much coddling of children and over-responsiveness to their demands—resulted in adolescents who were anarchic, disrespectful and undisciplined. An extreme example of this viewpoint could be found in James Dobson's *Dare to Discipline*, which called on parents to exercise firm control of their children through the use of corporal punishment. At the other pole were writers like Mark Gerzon, author of *A Childhood for Every Child*, who took the position that the characteristic American child-rearing techniques stifled creativity, generated dependence, instilled sexist biases, and produced repressed and conformist personalities. Authors like Gerzon called on parents to reject control through power and authority and to foster an environment based on warmth and understanding. Most child-rearing books, however, fell between the two, calling on parents to balance firmness and love and to adapt their methods to the unique temperament, needs, and feelings of each child.[52]

Although the authors of the burgeoning new child-rearing literature disagreed vehemently on such specific issues as the desirability of day care or whether mothers of young children should work outside the home, they did agree that successful child raising presents a much more difficult challenge today than it did in the past, noting that even parents with a deep commitment to their offspring confront difficulties that their parents did not have to face.[53]

Among the most potent new forces that intrude between parents and children is television. The single most important caretaker of children in the United States today is not a child's mother or a baby-sitter or even a day-care center but the television set in each child's home. Young children spend more time watching television than they do in any other activity other than sleep. The typical child between the ages of two and five spends about thirty hours a week viewing television, nearly a third of the child's waking time. Older children spend almost as much time in front of the TV. Indeed, children aged six to eleven average twenty-five hours a week watching TV, almost as much time as they spend in school. Since 1960 the tendency has been for children to become heavier and heavier television viewers.[54]

The debate about television's impact on children has raged furiously since the early 1950s. Critics are worried about parents' use of the television set as a baby-sitter and pacifier and as a substitute for an active parental role in socialization. They argue that excessive television viewing is detrimental because it encourages passivity and inhibits communication among family members. They express concern that children who watch large amounts of television tend to develop poor language skills, an inability to concentrate, and a disinclination to read. Moreover, they feel that television viewing tends to replace hours previously devoted to playtime either alone or with others. And, most worrisome, they believe that violence on TV provokes children to emulate aggressive behavior and acquire distorted views of adult relationships and communication.[55]

Research into the impact of television on children has substantiated some of these concerns and invalidated others. Television does appear to be a cause of cognitive and behavioral disturbances. Heavy television viewing is associated with reduced reading skills, less verbal fluency, and lower academic effort. Exposure to violence on television tends to make children more willing to hurt people and more aggressive in their play and in their methods of resolving conflicts. Time spent in front of the TV set does displace time previously spent on other activities and, as a result, many games and activities—marbles, jacks and trading cards, for example—are rapidly disappearing from American childhood.[56]

However, television also introduces children to new experiences easily and painlessly and stimulates interest in issues to which they might not otherwise be exposed. For many disadvantaged children, it provides a form of intellectual enhancement that deprived homes lacking books and newspapers could not afford. And, for many children, television programs provide a semblance of extended kinship attachments and outlets for their fantasies and unexpressed emotions.[57]

While some television shows, such as *Sesame Street* and *Mr. Rogers' Neighborhood*, do appear to improve children's vocabularies, teach them basic concepts, and help them verbalize their feelings, overwhelming evidence suggests that most television programs convey racial and sexual stereotypes, desensitize children to violence, and discourage the kinds of sustained concentration necessary for reading comprehension. On balance, it seems clear that television cannot adequately take the place of parental or adult involvement and supervision of children and that the tendency for it to do so is a justifiable reason for increased public concern.[58]

The single most profound change that has taken place in children's lives since 1960 is the rapid movement of millions of mothers into the labor force. In the space of just twelve years, the number of mothers of children five or under who work outside the home tripled. Today nearly half of all children under the age of six have a mother who works. Many factors have contributed to this trend, including a rising cost of living and a declining rate of growth in real family income; increased control of fertility through contraception and abortion, which has meant that careers are less likely to be disrupted by unplanned pregnancies; and women's rising level of educational achievement, which has led many women to seek work not only as a way of getting a paycheck but as a way of obtaining personal independence and intellectual stimulation.[59]

The massive movement of mothers into the work force presented a major social problem: How should young children be cared for when their mothers work outside the home? This question gave rise to more controversy than almost any other family-related issue during the late 1960s and early 1970s.[60]

The event that first precipitated this debate was the publication in 1964 of a Department of Labor study that found almost one million latchkey children in the United States, unsupervised by adults for significant portions of the day. As the number of working mothers climbed in the late 1960s, many family experts advocated day care as a necessary response to the lage number of mothers who had gone to work. At first the national debate focused on the child care problems of single mothers—widowed, divorced, and unmarried—and on whether they should be encouraged to enter the labor force.[61]

Liberals, led by Senator Walter Mondale, argued on behalf of a national system of comprehensive child development and day-care centers. Building on the model of the Head Start program, Mondale proposed in 1971 that the federal government establish a national system of services that included day-care programs, nutritional aid for pregnant mothers, medical and dental care, and after-school programs for teenagers. President Richard Nixon vetoed the bill in a stinging message that called the proposal fiscally irresponsible, administratively unworkable, and a threat to "diminish both parental authority and parental involvement with children." The president warned against committing "the vast authority of the national government to the side of communal approaches to child rearing over against the family-centered approach."[62]

Following the presidental veto, congressional support for a federally funded system of day care evaporated. Nevertheless the actual number of children enrolled in nursery schools or group day-care centers grew dramatically. At the time of the president's veto, less than one-third of all mothers with children one year old or younger held jobs. Today half of such women work, three-quarters of them full-time. As a result a majority of all children now spend some of their preschool years in the care of someone other than their mother.[63]

The trend is toward formal group day-care programs. Back in 1970 just 21 percent of all three- and four-year-olds were cared for in day-care centers or nursery schools. But between 1970 and 1983 the proportion virtually doubled, climbing to 38 percent. Today over two-thirds of all three- to four-year-olds are in a day-care, nursery school, or prekindergarten program.[64]

The single largest provider of day care now is the federal government, which offers child care, health, and educational services to some 400,000 low-income children through the Head Start program and which subsidizes private day-care facilities through child care tax credits, state block grants, and tax breaks for employers who subsidize day-care services. Nonetheless, the great majority of preschool child care arrangements in the United States are private, ranging from informal baby-sitting arrangements to private day-care centers run by national chains. Today two-thirds of all children are cared for in private facilities, and day care is an eleven-billion-dollar industry. The largest private corporation, Kinder-Care, has more than a thousand centers licensed to care for as many as a hundred thousand children.[65]

The drive for expanded day-care programs has its principal roots in the growing number of working mothers, the proliferation of single-parent homes, and the belief that access to day care is necessary to guarantee women's equal right to pursue a career. But the trend has also been fueled by new theories of child development, which emphasize the psychologically beneficial effects of a stimulating peer environment, by mounting evidence that children can assimilate information earlier than previously thought, and by research that has shown that disadvantaged children who participated in Head Start were more likely to graduate from high school, enroll in college, and obtain self-supporting jobs and were less likely to be arrested or register for welfare than were other children from low-income families.[66]

As formal child care programs proliferated, parents, educators, and social scientists began to examine the impact of day care on children's social and psychological growth, their intellectual development, and their emotional bond with their mother. The effects of day care remain the subject of intense controversy. Expert opinion varies widely, from those who fear that such programs provide an inadequate and unsatisfactory substitute for the full-time care and devotion of a mother to those who stress the resilience and adaptability of children. On one side, Jerome Kagan, a Harvard developmental psychologist, concludes that recent research reveals "that group care for young children does not seem to have much effect, either facilitating or debilitating, on the cognitive, social or affective development of most children." On the other side of the debate, Michael Rutter, a child psychologist at London's Institute for Psychiatry, states that "although day care for very young children is not likely to result in serious emotional disturbance, it would be misleading to conclude that it is without risks or effects."[67]

At present, knowledge about the impact of day care in children's intellectual, social, and emotional development remains limited. Research has suggested that quality day care has "neither salutary nor adverse effects on the intellectual development of most children"; that early entry into full-time day care may interfere with "the formation of a close attachment to the parents"; and that children in group day care are somewhat more aggressive, more independent, more involved with other children, more physically active, and less cooperative with adults than mother-raised children.[68]

The most pressing problem for parents at the moment is an inadquate supply of quality day care. The quality of day-care centers varies widely. The nature of care ranges from family day care, in which a woman takes children into her home for a fee, and cooperatives staffed or administered by parents, to on-site company nurseries, instituted by approximately one hundred corporations, and child care chains. High-quality centers, which can charge as much as $500 a month to care for a child, usually enroll only a small group of children and provide a great deal of individual attention. Low-quality centers, in contrast, tend to have a high ratio of children to caretakers, a high level of staff turnover, a low level of parental involvement, and a high noise level.[69]

Another serious problem is the lack of access to day care on the part of poorer children. Access to day care varies enormously according to family income. Seventy-five percent of all children from families with incomes of more than $25,000 a year participate in day-care or preschool program by the age of six, compared to just a third of children from families with incomes of less than $15,000. Today, as a result of limited public funding, just a fifth of all eligible children are enrolled in Head Start. Children from poorer families are also less likely to participate in programs with an educational component.[70]

The United States lags far behind major European nations in assuming public responsibility for children's welfare. Today most European countries offer a variety of programs designed to assist working mothers, including paid maternity and paternity leaves for mothers and fathers who hold jobs, financial allowances for families with children, and subsidized public nurseries and kindergartens. Finland and Hungary go even further, paying mothers who stay at home with their children. The United States, with its long tradition of private-sector approaches to public problems and ingrained hostility toward state intervention in the family, has yet to come to terms with the problems presented by the massive influx of mothers into the workplace. The burden of coping with child care remains with the individual family.[71]

Of all the dramatic changes that have taken place in children's lives in recent years, the one that has aroused the deepest public concern is the spiraling divorce rate. Since 1960 the number of children involved in divorce has tripled, and in every year since 1972, more than a million children have had their homes disrupted by divorce. Of the children born in the 1970s, 40 percent will experience the dissolution of their parents' marriage before they themselves are sixteen. As one expert noted, "Children are becoming less and less of a deterrent to divorce."[72]

As divorce became a more pervasive part of the American scene, researchers began to ask penetrating questions about the psychological and emotional implications of divorce for children. Back in the 1920s, authorities on the family, using the case-study method, had concluded that children experienced the divorce of their parents as a devastating blow that stunted their psychological and emotional growth and caused maladjustments that persisted for years. Beginning in the late 1950s and continuing into the early 1970s, a new generation of researchers argued that children were better off when their parents divorced than when they had an unstable marriage; that divorce disrupted children's lives no more painfully than the death of a parent, which used to break up families just as frequently; and that the adverse effects of divorce were generally of short duration.[73]

Recent research has thrown both of these points of view into question. On the one hand, it appears that conflict-laden, tension-filled marriages have more adverse effects on children than divorce. Children from discordant homes permeated by tension and instability are more likely to suffer psychosomatic illnesses, suicide attempts, delinquency, and other social maladjustments than are children whose parents divorce. As of now, there is no clear-cut empirical evidence to suggest that children from "broken" homes suffer more health or mental problems, personality disorders, or lower school grades than children from "intact" homes.[74]

On the other hand, it is clear that divorce is severely disruptive, at least initially, for a majority of children, and a significant minority of children continue to suffer from the psychological and economic repercussions of divorce for many years after the breakup of their parents' marriage. It is also apparent that children respond very differently to a divorce and to a parent's death. When a father dies children are often moody and despairing. During a divorce, many children, and especially sons, exhibit anger, hostility, and conflicting loyalties.[75]

Children's reactions to divorce vary enormously, depending on their age and gender and, most important of all, their perception of their parents' marriage. Children who viewed their parents' marriage as unhappy tend to adjust more easily to divorce than those who regarded their home life as basically happy.[76]

For many children initial acceptance of their parents' separation is followed by a deep sense of shock. Although some children react calmly on learning that their parents are divorcing, a majority of children of all ages are vulnerable to feelings of pain, anger, depression, and insecurity. Family breakups often result in regressive behavior and developmental setbacks that last at least a year.[77]

Studies that followed children five years after a divorce found that a majority of children show resilience and increased maturity and independence. But, for a significant minority, the emotional turmoil produced by divorce proves to be long standing, evident in persistent feelings of hostility, depression, sexual anxiety, and concern about being unloved. Among a minority of children, the apparent consequences of divorce include alcohol and drug abuse, outward-directed despair and aggression, and sexual promiscuity.[78]

Clearly, divorce is an extremely stressful experience for children, whose economic and emotional costs continue to run high long after the parents' separation. Economic disruption is the most obvious consequence of a divorce. In the immediate aftermath of a divorce, the income of the divorced woman and her children falls sharply, by 73 percent in the year following divorce, while the father's income rises by 42 percent. Adding to the financial pressures facing children of divorce is that fact that a majority of divorced men evade court orders to support their children. Recent surveys indicate that only 40 percent of support orders are fully complied with during the first year after a divorce and that by the tenth year after separation, the figure falls to 13 percent.[79]

Other sources of stress result from the mother's new financial responsibilities as her family's breadwinner, additional demands on her time as she tries to balance economic and child-rearing responsibilities, and, frequently, adjustment to unfamiliar and less comfortable living arrangements. Burdened by her new responsibilities as head of her household, a mother often devotes less time to child rearing, forcing her to rely more heavily on neighbors, relatives, and older children.[80]

The emotional and psychological upheavals caused by divorce are often aggravated by a series of readjustments children must deal with, such as loss of contact with the noncustodial parent. Many children of divorce have to deal with feelings of abandonment by their natural fathers. More than nine of every ten children are placed in their mother's custody, and recent studies have found that two months following a divorce fewer than half the fathers see their children as often as once a week and, after three years, half the fathers do not visit their children at all.[81]

Further complicating children's adjustment to their parents' divorce is the impact of remarriage. Roughly half of all mothers are remarried within approximately two years of their divorce, thus many children of divorce live only briefly in single-parent homes. Today there are over 4 million households—one of every seven with children—in which one parent has remarried and at least one child is from a previous union. These reconstituted families often confront jealousies and conflicts of loyalty not found in families untouched by divorce, leading a number of investigators to conclude that "homes involving steprelationships proved more likely to have stress, ambivalence, and low cohesiveness" than did two-parent homes. At the same time, other researchers have found that most children of divorce favored remarriage.[82]

Today's children are growing up in an unstable and threatening environment in which earlier sources of support have eroded. They live in a permissive culture that exposes them from an early age to drugs, sex, alcohol, and violence. The increasing divorce rate, the entry of many mothers into the full-time work force, high rates of mobility, and the declining importance of the extended family all contribute to a decline in support and guidance. As a society the United States has largely failed to come to grips with the major issues facing children, such as the need for quality care while parents work and the need for a stable emotional environment in which to grow up.[83]

Revolution in Family Law

As the nation's families have changed, America's courts have become increasingly embroiled in disputes that pit wives against husbands and children against parents. Today nearly half of all civil court cases in the United States involve questions of family law. The courts are struggling with such questions as whether, in cases of divorce, the mother should be presumed to be the parent best suited to rear young children or whether grandparents should be granted visitation rights to a grandchild whose parents have divorced. The courts have also had to decide whether a husband can give the couple's children his surname over his wife's objections, whether husbands and wives should be permitted to sue each other, and whether children have a right to "divorce" their parents or to choose where they will live, independent of their parents' wishes.[84]

A revolution has taken place in the field of family law, and equally sweeping changes have occurred in divorce law. State legislatures, responding to the sharp upsurge in divorce rates during the 1960s and 1970s, radically liberalized their divorce statutes, making it possible to end a marriage without establishing specific grounds, and, in many states, allowing one spouse to terminate a marriage without the consent of the other. As the number of divorces mounted, every state adopted reforms designed to reduce the acrimony and shame that accompanied the divorce process.[85]

Until 1970, when California adopted the nation's first "no-fault" divorce law, a basic legal assumption was that marital relationships could only be ended for serious cause. Under fault statutes, divorce could only be granted on such grounds as desertion, nonsupport, cruel and abusive treatment, adultery, alcoholism, or a long prison term, and the division of property in a divorce was to reflect the share of guilt attributed to each partner. A man who wanted a divorce was expected to pay lifetime alimony to his wife, the purpose of which was to reward the woman's devotion to her family and to punish the husband who would abandon his wife.[86]

Within a span of just five years, all but five states adopted the principle of no-fault divorce. Today every state except South Dakota has enacted some kind of no-fault statute. Under no-fault divorce laws, a couple can institute divorce proceedings without first proving that either was at fault for the breakup. Rather than sue the other marriage partner, a husband or wife can obtain a divorce simply by mutual consent or on such grounds as incompatibility, living apart for a specified period, or "irretrievable breakdown" of the marriage. In complete no-fault states, a single partner can obtain a divorce unilaterally, without regard for the wishes of the other partner.[87]

The goal of no-fault divorce was to provide couples with a way to avoid long, acrimonious legal battles over who was to blame for a failed marriage and how marital property was to be divided. In an effort to reduce the bitterness associated with divorce, many states changed the terminology used in divorce proceedings, substituting the term "dissolution" for the word "divorce" and eliminating any terms denoting fault or guilt.[88]

Recently courts have also sought to overturn the so-called "tender years" doctrine that a young child is better off with the mother unless the mother is proved to be unfit. The current trend is for the courts not to presume in favor of mothers in custody disputes over young children. Most judges now only make custody awards after considering psychological reports and the wishes of the children. To spare children the trauma of custody conflict, many judges award divorced parents joint custody, in which both parents have equal legal rights and responsibilities in decisions affecting the child's welfare.[89]

Likewise, courts have moved away from the concept of alimony and replaced it with a new concept called "spousal support" or "maintenance." In the past, courts regarded marriage as a lifelong commitment and, in cases in which the husband was found guilty of marital misconduct, held that the wife was entitled to lifelong support. Now maintenance can be awarded to either the husband or the wife, and it can be granted for a limited time to permit a spouse to go to school, acquire skills, and become self-supporting.[90]

As the legal system has moved away from the principle of lifelong alimony, growing attention has been placed on the distribution of a couple's assets at the time of divorce. One state, Mississippi, still awards property on the basis of the name of the title to the property. Four "community property" states divide property acquired during the marriage equally, while the remaining states allow judges to award property "equitably." In dividing up property, a majority of states now require the courts to place monetary value on the wife's contribution as homemaker and mother and require judges to consider such sources of family wealth as insurance policies, pensions, deferred income, and licenses to practice a profession.[91]

Today many women's groups, which initially favored no-fault divorce, are calling for sharp modifications of such laws. They maintain that under present law "divorce is a financial catastrophe for most women." Legal rules that treat men and women equally, critics argue, tend to deprive women of the financial support they need. Under no-fault laws, many older women, who would have been entitled to lifelong alimoney or substantial child support payments under the old fault statutes, find it extremely difficult to support their families. Today, the courts award only 15 percent of divorced women alimony, and in most cases the amount are small (averaging approximately $250 a month) and granted temporarily until a wife reenters the work force. Also, courts, following the principle of equality, generally require ex-husbands to pay only half of what is needed to raise the children, on the assumption that the wife will provide the remainder. To make matters worse, many men are remiss on court-ordered alimony or child support payments.[92]

Another problem results from the expectation that women will reenter the labor force. Courts generally assume that a woman will be able to support herself following a divorce. In reality, however, the earning capacity of many divorced women is quite limited, especially if they have been longtime housewives and mothers. According to one study, only about one-third of wives worked regularly before the divorce, many part-time or sporadically for relatively low incomes. Many of these women find it difficult or impossible to obtain jobs that will allow them to maintain a standard of living approaching the one they had while married.[93]

Cases in which husbands and wives are pitted against each other have increasingly found their way onto the nation's court dockets.

Among the issues facing the courts are these: Can a husband be criminally prosecuted for raping his wife? Can a husband give his children his surname over his wife's objections? Can an expectant mother obtain an abortion despite her husband's opposition? Until recently the law considered the father to be "head and master" of his family. His surname became his children's surname, his residence was the family's legal residence, he was immune from lawsuits instituted by his wife, and he was entitled to sexual relations with his spouse. Today the nation's courts have called all of these legal presumptions into question. The Massachusetts Supreme Court has ruled that husbands and wives can sue each other, the supreme courts of Massachusetts and New Jersey have said that husbands can be prosecuted for raping their wives, and the California Supreme Court has ruled that a husband cannot give his children his surname without his wife's agreement.[94]

Another dramatic change in the field of family law is the courts' tendency to grant legal rights to minor children. In the past, parents enjoyed wide discretionary authority over the details of their children's upbringing. More recently the nation's court have held that minors do have independent rights that can override parental authority. The issues being brought before the courts include these:

Should an unmarried fifteen-year-old Utah girl be able to obtain an abortion without her parents' knowledge?

Should a twelve-year-old Ukrainian boy and a fifteen-year-old Cuban girl have a right to choose where they will live, even if this means living apart from their natural parents?

Should a fifteen-year-old Washington State girl, unhappy with her parents' restrictions on her smoking, dating, and choice of friends, be allowed to have herself placed in a foster home against her parents' wishes?

Should children be encouraged to turn in their parents for drug use, as in a recent California case?[95]

In deciding such cases, the courts have sought to balance two conflicting traditions: the historic right of parents to to control their childrens' upbringing and the right of all individuals, including children, to privacy, due process, and equal rights. In some cases the courts have sided with the parents; in other cases they have supported children; in still others the ruling have been mixed. The U.S. Supreme Court has struck down state laws that give parents an absolute veto

over whether a minor girl can obtain an abortion but upheld a Utah
statute that required doctors to notify parents before performing an
abortion. The Court ruled in the Utah case that a compelling state
interest in maintaining the integrity of the family was more important
than the girl's right to privacy. Two states—Iowa and Utah—have
enacted laws greatly expanding minors' rights. These states permit
children to seek temporary placement in another home if serious conflict exists between the children and their parents, even if the parents
are not guilty of abuse or neglect.[96]

Recent decisions in family law have been characterized by two
seemingly contradictory trends. On the one hand, courts have modified or struck down many traditional infringements on the right to
privacy. They have prohibited laws regulating consenting sexual relations between spouses and restricting the right of parents to obtain
contraceptive information or pass it on to their children. Since 1970,
twenty states have decriminalized all forms of private sexual conduct
between consenting adults, and in four other states, judicial decisions
have invalidated statutes making such conduct a crime.[97]

On the other hand, courts have permitted government intrusion
into areas traditionally regarded as bastions of family autonomy.
Shocked by reports of abuse against children, wives, and the elderly,
state legislatures have strengthened penalties for domestic violence
and sexual abuse. Courts have reversed traditional precedents and
ruled that husbands can be prosecuted for raping their wives. A 1984
federal law gave states new authority to seize property, wages, divi-
dends, and tax refunds from parents who fail to make court ordered
child support payments. Other court decisions have relaxed traditional prohibitions against spouses testifying against each other.[98]

What links these two apparently contradictory trends is a growing
sensitivity on the part of the courts toward the individual and individual rights even when family privacy is at stake. Many recent court
decisions are consistent with a greater regard for the autonomy of the
individual. Thus, in recent cases, the courts have held that a husband
cannot legally prevent his wife from having an abortion, since it is
the wife who must bear the burden of pregnancy, and have also ruled
that a wife's legal domicile is not necessarily her husband's home.
Court decisions on marital rape reflect a growing recognition that a
wife is not her husband's property.[99]

One ironic effect of these legal decisions has been a gradual erosion
of the traditional conception of the family as a legal unit. In the colli-
sion between two set of conflicting values—individualism and the fam-

ily—the courts have tended to stress individual rights. For example, the Supreme Court recently struck down a Wisconsin law that forbids remarriage by divorced spouses until they have made arrangements for the financial care of their children on the grounds that it would encourage the birth of children out of wedlock, discriminate against the poor, and violate rights to personal freedom. Earlier in time the law was used to reinforce relationships between spouses and parents and children, but the current trend is to emphasize the separateness and autonomy of family members. The Supreme Court has repeatedly overturned state laws that require minor children to receive parental consent before obtaining contraceptive information or an abortion, and the lower courts have been unwilling to grant parents immunity from testifying against their own children. Similarly, state legislatures have weakened or abolished earlier laws that made children legally responsible for the support of indigent parents, while statutes that hold parents accountable for crimes committed by their minor children have been ruled unconstitutional.[100]

The nation's courts did not choose to become involved in family questions. The current legal ferment is a legacy of dramatic changes that have occurred in the nature of family life as divorce rates have soared, family patterns have grown less uniform, and the bonds connecting parents and children have loosened. These changes have resulted in novel disputes that have found their way into lawyers' offices. What is clear is that in a wide range of areas—including child custody, children's rights, spousal support, and property division—the nation's courts will continue to wrestle with a host of problems spawned by America's changing families.[101]

The Pro-Family Movement

Recent changes in family life have produced bewilderment, apprehension, and alarm, and many Americans believe that the consequences of these changes have been disastrous. A Gallup poll conducted in 1977 found that almost half of all Americans surveyed believed that family life has deteriorated in recent years. This sense of unease has generated a political crusade among Americans who fear that climbing rates of divorce, working mothers, and single parents represent a breakdown of family values. These people, who have adopted the label "pro-family," have built a powerful political coalition out of a series of disparate elements including religious conservatives, such as the Moral Majority, the Religious Roundtable, and Christian Voice; traditional political conservatives; and single-issue groups concerned about a variety of family-related issues such as legalized abortion, ratification of the Equal Rights amendment to the Constitution, feminism, access of teenagers to contraception, sex education in schools, homosexuality, pornography, school busing for racial integration, and eroticism on television.[102]

Although the pro-family movement has drawn support from men and women of every social and economic background, it has appealed largely to women of lower economic and educational status who hold strong religious beliefs, whose self-esteem and self-image are bound up with being mothers and housewives, and who want to ensure that women who devote their lives to the family are not accorded lower status than women who work outside the home.[103]

Despite many disagreements in strategy and belief, the pro-family movement is united in its assessment of blame for the purported deterioration of family life. The issues that ignite the most passionate outrage on the part of the pro-family movement include feminism, which is viewed as primarily responsible for encouraging women to work outside the home; "secular humanism," believed to be responsible for eliminating all traces of religious values in public life; and the youth movement of the 1960s, which is held responsible for propagating a gospel of erotic experimentalism and self-gratification, sanctioning any form of behavior no matter how unconventional. The pro-family movement is also united in agreement on how the beleaguered American family can be helped. Among other things, the movement has sought the restoration of prayer in schools, screening of textbooks, limits on teenagers' access to contraceptives, and reversal of the Supreme Court's decisions on abortion.[104]

The pro-family movement has waged political battles on several fronts. One part of its strategy has been an effort to overturn the landmark 1973 *Roe* v. *Wade* ruling, in which the Supreme Court declared that the decision to have an abortion was a private matter of concern to a woman and her physician, and that only in the later stages of pregnancy could the government limit the right to abortion. Opposition to abortion has taken many forms, from calls for a constitutional amendment that would declare that from the moment of conception a fetus is a full human being entitled to constitutional protections, to efforts to restrict the use of government funds for abortions, to lobbying for local statutes limiting access to abortion by requiring waiting periods before abortions could be performed and parental consent for abortions for minors. The major legislative success of the "right to life" movement was adoption by Congress of the so-called Hyde amendment, which permitted states to refuse to fund abortions for indigent women. Despite this legislative effort, some fifteen states and the District of Columbia continue to fund abortions for poorer women.[105]

Another goal of the pro-family movement is to limit teenagers' access to contraceptive information. One proposal, put forward by the Reagan administration, was the "squeal rule," which would require family planning agencies that receive federal funds to notify the parents of minor children of requests for contraceptives. Another battle has been fought over the Equal Rights Amendment. Those who oppose the amendment have argued that it poses a threat to the family because it would eliminate all discrimination on the basis of sex, including the prohibition of marriages between persons of the same sex, and guarantee access to abortion and family planning services.[106]

The major legislative aim of the pro-family movement has been enactment of the Family Protection Act, which combines the disparate concerns of the movement into a single piece of legislation. This act would prohibit the use of legal aid funds in cases dealing with abortion, divorce, and gay rights and would restore prayer to the public schools.[107]

Arguments between the pro-family movement and its critics reached a peak in 1978, when President Jimmy Carter convened a White House Conference on Families to develop coherent policies to assist American families. The conference quickly became a battleground over such issues as legalized abortion, the Equal Rights Amendment, and gay rights and revealed the deep schism of values that had developed around family issues. The pro-family movement charged that feminists and ethnic minorities had won a disproportionate share of slots at the conference and accused the delegates of a bias against "traditional Judeo-Christian values concerning the family." At the conclusion of the conference, the White House issued a report recommending ways that government could strengthen American family life. Among the proposals were calls for the ratification of the Equal Rights Amendment, the right to abortion, and sex education in the schools, but, because of the opposition spearheaded by the pro-family movement, implementation of these measures proved impossible.[108]

A Deep Sense of Ambivalence

As the 1978 White House Conference on Families dramatically illustrated, American society today is deeply divided by conflicting conceptions of what constitutes a family and how government can best strengthen families to deal with contemporary problems. Yet, despite the furor generated by these disputes, an important point should not be missed. Public opinion polls indicate that while only a minority of Americans supports the legislative proposals of the pro-family movement, a large majority agrees with their belief that the family is an institution in deep trouble.[109]

Recent transformations in American family life have left Americans with a deep ambivalence about their familial roles. A substantial majority of Americans today say that they are less willing to make sacrifices for their children than their parents were and believe that unhappy parents should not remain married simply for the sake of the children. Yet, at the same time, an almost equal majority believes that "parents now have a reduced commitment to their children and their children to them" and want "a return to more traditional standards of family life." Unable to assimilate fully the domestic revolution of the past two decades, Americans are struggling to find a fair way to juggle individual, familial, and social demands.[110]

The American family today, like the family at the end of the eighteenth century and again at the end of the nineteenth, is in the midst of a profound historical transformation. Older assumptions—such as the idea that marriage is a lifetime commitment and that a proper family contains a breadwinner father and a housewife mother—have eroded. The older definition of the paternal role that equated a "real man" with a "good provider" who single-handedly supported his family has increasingly given way to a new ideal—honored as much in the breach as in the observance—that he should take an active role in family life, child care, and housework. Similarly, the older ideal of womanhood that defined a "real woman" as a good mother, wife, and hostess has been diluted by a sharp decline in the number of children in each family and women's growing participation in the world of wage work. Meanwhile, new notions of "children's rights" have challenged traditional assumptions that parents should, rightly or wrongly, dictate important decisions in their children's lives.[111]

• Ours is an age of transition. Our families have grown less stable and uniform; traditional family role definitions and expectations have been thrown into question. And, like earlier ages of transition, ours is also an age of conflict. This includes conflicts between groups that hold competing ideals of a proper family but also deep internal conflicts that rage within individuals. Today a large majority of Americans feel torn between a continuing commitment to and nostalgia for older ideals of family life, stressing lifelong marriage and full-time mothering of children, and a newer, more flexible but less dependable conception of the family that allows for greater freedom and self-absorption.[112]

There is little point in looking nostalgically to the past for a solution to current problems. The 1950s pattern of family life—characterized by high rates of marriage, high fertility, and stable rates of divorce—which many continue to regard as an ideal, was the product of a convergence of an unusual series of historical, demographic, and economic circumstances unlikely to return again. Every barometer indicates that families in the future will be small, fragile, and characterized by late marriage and low birthrates. Today about half of all married women with minor children participate in the labor force. Today most working wives are part-time workers; in the future, many more will be likely to be full-time workers, as families become increasingly dependent on a wife's income.[113]

The challenge facing Americans in the years to come is not to hope wistfully for a return to the "normality" of the 1950s—which was actually inconsistent with long-term trends—but a much more difficult and much more concrete predicament. This challenge is to institute new social arrangements that will help moderate the effects of women's entry into the work force, of divorce, and of women's increasing need for autonomy. Possible solutions lie before us. These range from flexible working arrangements to enable employees to be effective parents to adequate supplies of affordable quality substitute care when parents work, maternity and paternity leaves to assist parents who are starting families, revision of welfare policies that encourage the flight of husbands, custody and visitation agreements that will facilitate continuing contact between divorced parents and their children, legal guarantees that children of divorce will receive an adequate and secure income, and monetary incentives for parents who stay home with their children. Americans agree on the desirability of strong families; the ultimate question is whether the nation has the political will to create conditions that will foster stronger families.[114]

*Children in daycare. Photograph by Dan Richardson.
Courtesy of the University of Houston.*

The Politics of the Family: The 1980s and Beyond

EACH recent decade has witnessed explosive public controversy over questions of sex and the family. It was during the 1960s that the family became the focus of an angry and ongoing public debate. Environmentalists warned of the dangers posed by a worldwide "population explosion"; feminists called for abortion law reform, day care centers, and shelters for battered wives; mounting campus unrest generated fears about a "generation gap"; and government policymakers debated whether poverty and street crime were related to "family disorganization." In the 1970s public controversy swirled around a new set of issues raised by the sexual revolution, the increasing divorce rate, and the growing number of working mothers, such as day care, abortion, single parenthood, and gay rights.[1]

During the 1980s, as anxiety mounted over the consequences of the sexual and social revolution that reshaped family life in recent years, public debate has focused on new issues. Milk cartons, subway billboards, and utility bills began to carry pictures of missing children, abducted by strangers or a noncustodial parent after a divorce. Big-city high schools opened clinics to dispense contraceptives in an attempt to reduce teenage pregnancy and out-of-wedlock births.

Television stations started to broadcast advertisements for condoms in order to slow the spread of AIDS (Acquired Immune Deficiency Syndrome) and other sexually transmitted diseases. New terms—such as "test-tube baby," "genetic engineering," "surrogate motherhood," and "safe sex"—became a part of public discourse, and abused children, pregnant teenagers, and battered wives became subjects of television documentaries and miniseries.

State legislators, shocked by reports of abducted and abused children, strengthened child pornography laws, increased penalties for sexual abuse, set up registries of missing children, and required applicants for jobs in day care centers to undergo checks for criminal records. Other legislation allowed wages and income tax refunds to be withheld from parents who fell too far behind on child support. A host of family problems, until recently considered private matters, became public political issues.[2]

During the 1980s the "family" became a buzzword, invoked by politicians of both parties to advance their agendas. Conservatives used the term as a synonym for "traditional social values" and as a way of expressing opposition to the growth of government and liberal welfare policies. Liberals, in turn, used the word as a synonym for "compassion" and as a way of defending government programs designed to help individuals suffering from poverty, abuse, and other problems. For both Democrats and Republicans, the concept of "family" became a symbol of two divergent views of the role and responsibilities of government.[3]

In the 1980 presidential campaign, Ronald Reagan tried to stake out the family issue for conservatives. "Family, work, and neighborhood" were at the top of his rhetorical agenda. In his campaign speeches he argued that federal programs that were supposed to provide family services had, in actuality, promoted "acceptance of indolence, promiscuity, easy abortion, casual attitudes toward marriage and divorce, and maternal indifference to child-rearing responsibilities." In many former Democrats and religious activists—concerned over abortion, school prayer, and pornography as well as by sharp increases in illegitimacy and single-parent families—the call for a return to traditional family values struck a responsive chord.[4]

In office President Reagan launched a counterrevolution against the New Deal, the Fair Deal, the New Frontier, and the Great Society. He halted the growth of social welfare programs and limited benefits to those he called the "truly needy." Although the president repeatedly said that he reduced only the rate of growth in social spending, not the actual level, spending was in fact curtailed in a variety of social welfare programs. Between 1981 and 1984, spending on AFDC was reduced 13 percent; food stamps, 13 percent; child nutrition, 28 percent; job training for young people, 53 percent; programs to prevent child abuse, 12 percent; and mental health services, 26 percent. The Reagan administration also eliminated cash welfare assistance for the working poor, reduced federal subsidies for child care services for low income families, and cut grants used to pay for the regulation of child care programs. At the same time that the Reagan administration tried to cut the role of government, it also attempted to use the power of government to encourage citizens to live by "traditional" family values. To this end, the administration supported legislation that would deny federal funding to any program that allowed unmarried teenagers to obtain contraceptives and abortions without their parents' knowledge.[5]

Following Reagan's election, Democrats began to emphasize family questions. In part the Democrats embraced family issues as a way of demonstrating that they were still in touch with the concerns of mainstream middle-class Americans, but the new emphasis on families also reflected the increasing number of baby-boomers who were marrying and having children. The Democrats declared that the president's concern about the family was hypocritical and that the Reagan administration's cuts in social spending seriously harmed children and families. They called for concrete programs—such as flexible work hours, maternity and paternity leaves, federal financial support and uniform standards for child care, increased spending on nutrition and health care for poor children, and federal enforcement of court-ordered child support payments—to strengthen families and to assist parents in caring for their children.[6]

In the 1984 presidential election, the Democrats unsuccessfully attempted to wrest the family issue away from the Republicans. Democrats used the family issue to dramatize such issues as poverty, federal budget deficits, and child care. Conservative Democrats focused on the family issue as a way to emphasize the sharp increase in federal budget deficits under the Reagan administration. The nation's $2 trillion debt was, they declared, a threat to the well-being of future generations of families. Jesse Jackson used the metaphor of family to describe the need to build a sense of community to replace the inward-looking individualism associated with the years of the Reagan presidency. New York Senator Pat Moynihan focused attention on a new generation of poor children and adolescents—accounting for nearly one-quarter of all Americans under eighteen—growing up in single-parent households and mired in a cycle of poverty.[7]

A common theme uniting the Democratic arguments was that government had a responsibility to help meet the needs of the nation's families. The Democratic view of society as a family that should share benefits and burdens was expressed most eloquently at the 1984 Democratic National Convention by New York Governor Mario Cuomo. "We believe in a government strong enough to use the words 'love' and 'compassion,'" Cuomo declared. "We must be the family of

America, recognizing that at the heart of the matter we are bound to one another."[8]

Today the angry controversy that surrounded child care and family issues in the late 1970s and early 1980s has quieted as both political parties have pledged support for the American family. Yet, beneath the surface calm, serious differences of opinion remain. While abstract support for pro-family policies is widespread, the electorate remains deeply divided over such specific issues as abortion, provision of family planning materials to adolescents, tax treatment of working mothers, and federal funding of day care. These policy disagreements, in turn, reflect divergent moral judgments of such issues as women's rights, the prerogatives of parents, the authority of husbands, adolescent sexuality, the rights of children, and mother-centered versus public approaches to child care. The result has been a national deadlock on family issues.[9]

As the stalemate drags on, family-related problems continue to grow. In particular, liberal and conservative politicians will have to address three major family-related issues in the years ahead. One unsolved problem involves the growing number of children who live in poverty as a result of family breakups. Today nearly half of all marriages end in divorce, and many others end in legal separation or desertion. At the same time, an increasing number of mothers are not married. As a result, an enormous number of children are living with a single parent, and all too frequently their economic plight is grave. There are now 12 million children who live in poverty. Since 1968 the number of poor American children has increased by 3 million while the real value of assistance through AFDC has declined by one-third.[10]

Another set of problems grows out of the continuing influx of mothers of young children into the work force. Families today face hard choices as they try to reconcile their children's need for quality care and young mothers' needs to work outside the home to help support their families. Since 1977 the number of children five years old or younger whose mothers are employed has increased by more than 50 percent to nearly 10 million. Today more than 50 percent of all mothers of children six or younger have jobs outside the home. Despite the explosive growth in women's employment, more than 60 percent of women have no right to get their jobs back if they take time off during pregnancy or following childbirth. And, decent, reliable, and affordable child care remains in short supply.[11]

Other changes such as new reproductive technologies—like artificial insemination, in vitro fertilization, embryo transfer, and surrogate mothering—that enable people who could not otherwise have babies to have them raise perplexing ethical and legal issues. With infertility increasing—as a result of venereal disease, exposure to dangerous chemicals, use of intrauterine birth control devices, and the growing number of couples waiting until their thirties or later to start a family—and adoption growing more difficult as the number of the most desired babies has dropped—many prospective parents have turned to artificial techniques of reproduction. These techniques present a wide range of dilemmas, from the rights of children to know their biological parents and the rights of egg or sperm donors to know their children to the question of responsibility if a child is born with a handicap. Surrogate mothering, in which a woman is artificially inseminated with the semen of another woman's husband or has the couple's embryo implanted in her uterus, has aroused particularly bitter controversy. Among the issues it has raised are the right of a surrogate mother to change her mind about relinquishing a child and the question of whether women should be encouraged to carry a child for financial gain.[12]

History offers no simple solutions to the problems facing today's families, but it does offer a bit of reassurance as we look toward the future. Ours is not the first generation of Americans to worry about a loosening of family bonds or to complain that parents are growing more selfish and irresponsible or that children are becoming more defiant of adult authority. History reminds us that American families have been through periods of crisis before and that despite recurrent fears for the impending demise of the family, the institution as such has not disappeared.

The history of American family life suggests that we need not be disturbed by change in and of itself, because change—and not stability—has been the norm. American families have repeatedly had to change in order to adapt to novel circumstances—from the challenges of New World colonization to the commercial and industrial revolutions, enslavement, immigration, depression, and war—and the changes that have taken place in family structure, roles, and conceptions have been so far reaching that they might be considered revolutions. Nor do we need to worry obsessively about the increasing diversity of family arrangements, since ethnic, religious, and economic diversity has always been a defining characteristic of American family life. Instead of focusing our attention on the futile question of whether the family will survive, we would do better as a society to confront the concrete problems that face families today, such as problems of employment, income, and child care and issues raised by changing legal norms and technologies.

The difference between our predicament and past concerns is that unlike earlier Americans, who relied upon the family as a valuable resource in adapting to difficult circumstances, many Americans today tend to regard familial responsibilities as an impediment to individual self-fulfillment. We have failed to take the steps necessary to resolve the tensions between our domestic arrangements and changing social and economic circumstances, and the results are apparent in the growing number of poor families and the declining well-being of children.

For nearly four centuries, the family has been our primary unit of nurture and emotional sustenance in the United States. Whether it can continue to perform these functions effectively will ultimately depend on whether we take the steps necessary to help the institution adapt to the unique conditions of our time.

Historical Perspectives
on the Family

THE systematic study of the history of the American family traces its roots back to the second half of the nineteenth century, when pioneering anthropologists discovered that while family and kinship relationships are rooted in biology, their particular forms vary according to culture and historical time period. One of the first researchers to examine family and kinship systematically was Lewis Henry Morgan, a Rochester, New York, lawyer. He studied the kinship terminology of the Iroquois Indians and found that the Iroquois categorized kin in ways that diverged sharply from the kinship system of other Americans. Morgan discovered that kinship terminology could provide insight into a group's residence patterns, marriage rules, and descent system. At the same time, legal historians, led by Sir Henry Maine, traced changes in the law of marriage, property, and inheritance in order to describe changes in the institution of the family. Maine's efforts to describe such changes led him to construct a model in which relationships based on status gave way to relations based on contract. These early evolutionary theorists (also including Friedrich Engels), argued that systems of marriage and the family passed through successive stages of development and that the modern family was the result of a prolonged cultural-evolutionary process.

In the early twentieth century, the evolutionary framework lost favor, largely in reaction to fruitless debates over the matriarchal or patriarchal origins of the family, and was supplanted by "functionalist" and "interactionist" forms of analysis. Functionalists focused on the family's roles and functions, and interactionists studied domestic roles and family dynamics. While both schools viewed evolutionary perspectives as unproductive and differed in their primary objects of concern, they did share implicit assumptions about the long-term direction of changes in family structure. In their view urbanization, industrialization, and the emancipation of women created a family type fundamentally different from those that had predominated in the past. Extended family ties supposedly disintegrated in an urban setting, the family unit was reduced to a nuclear core, and the traditional "institutional" functions of families and kinship groups were transferred to impersonal public institutions. Over the long term, the family was transformed "from institution to companionship."

After World War II, Harvard sociologist Talcott Parsons played a central role in defining the issues that inform the study of the family. His ambition was to construct a theory—built around the concepts of social equilibrium, socialization, specialization, and differentiation of functions and roles—that would subsume both Marxism and Freudian psychoanalysis. According to Parsons, the distinguishing feature of socioeconomic modernization in the public realm was specialization and differentiation in the interests of increased economic efficiency. In the private realm, the family, having surrendered its earlier educational, economic, and protective functions to public institutions, was free to specialize in child rearing and emotional sustenance. In a modern urban and industrial setting, Parsons maintained, the nuclear family was isolated from wider kinship groups and the world of work and carried primary responsibility for satisfying emotional needs for love, security, and loyalty. He argued further that the nuclear family was better suited than extended families to the demands of an urban and industrial environment. In his view such small and isolated families could easily move to follow new job opportunities and readily make the social and psychological adjustments required by changing lifestyles.

Over the past quarter century, professional historians have sought to refine and modify sociological models of the history of the family. The growth in historians' interest in the family has many sources. In part it represents a reaction to the increased rates of divorce and remarriage, the growing number of female-headed households, and the influx of married women into the labor force. But it also reflects a broader shift in historical research toward the study of social history—the study of how ordinary people lived their lives in the past. One reason why the history of the family has become an intellectual growth industry is that the family provides a bridge between two fundamental domains of human life and experience—social processes and psychological processes. As a primary agent of socialization, the family provides a vehicle for studying the transmission and adaptation of cultural patterns from one generation to the next. As a social institution, the family provides a vehicle for studying the transmission of property, gender roles, and the impact of economic and cultural change.

Methods of Study

The field of family history has exploded in the past decade, as hundreds of dissertations, books, and articles have reported on new sources, methods, and theories. The historical study of the family has been dominated by three methodological approaches. Demographic historians—drawing on census schedules, church records, government documents, and probate records—have used quantitative analysis to trace changes in residence patterns, household size, the age of marriage, fertility and mortality rates, life expectancy, the spacing of births, age relations within the family, and the developmental cycle of households (that is, changes in family and household composition over time). Demographic historians have borrowed from French demographer Louis Henry the technique of "family reconstitution," which involves the reconstruction of the genealogical history of families out of church records. Other historians, inspired by the work of English historian Peter Laslett and the Cambridge Group for the History of Population and Social Structure, have utilized aggregate data and genealogical histories to reconstruct the organizational structure of families and households, kinship networks, inheritance systems, and migration patterns.

These "new" social historians have found that from an early date, long before industrialization, most Western European families lived in nuclear households and differed from families elsewhere in the late age at which women married; the large proportion of men and women who never married or bore children; the emphasis placed on the conjugal tie between husband and wife; the religious emphasis placed on free and mutual consent in marriage and hostility toward endogamous marriages, polygamy, and concubinage; and the early adoption, beginning in the eighteenth century, of effective methods of contraception. These historians have argued that the decisive shifts in family history have been structural, involving decreasing family size, declining rates of mortality and fertility, prolonged residence of children in their parents' home, and more uniform timing of the life stages (such as marriage, starting to work, leaving home, and bearing children within marriage).

Cultural historians have focused not on changes in demographic structure and form but on the values, expectations, roles, and functions assigned to the family. Building on the pioneering work of the influential French cultural historian Philippe Aries in the early 1960s, scholars employing this cultural approach have made their primary aim the study of patterns of child rearing, sexual conduct, gender roles, marriage practices, death rituals, and public ideologies of the family in order to reconstruct the complex and contradictory texture of family life in the past. These historians have traced the rise, beginning in the sixteenth century, of a new conception of marriage, emphasizing mutual affection and companionship among spouses, growing permissiveness in childrearing, and a growing emphasis on privacy within the home.

A third school has examined changes in the economy and ecology to explain shifts in family and household structures. These historians, using theories and techniques derived from such contemporary social anthropologists as J. R. Goody, focus on the "strategies" families use to earn an income or acquire property, transmit land, maintain an adequate labor force, sustain or improve a standard of living, or strengthen and preserve kinship ties. The allocation of domestic roles, the choice of marriage partners, the bearing of a specific number of children, and the adoption of specific inheritance practices are each viewed as methods that families employ to achieve specific ends.

Analytical Strategies

A major problem confronting historians of the family is to find a conceptual framework to explain changes in family patterns over time. Scholars have adopted various approaches to synthesis. One widely used schema uses techniques derived from the discipline of demography to periodize changes in family structure. Measurable shifts in the ages at which men and women marry, in the order in which children marry, in family size and composition, in life expectancy and the duration of marriage, in residence patterns, and in fertility and death rates can provide concrete indices of the timing of changes in values and behavior, such as the decline in parental control over courtship, the substitution of romantic love for marriages contracted for property considerations, and the increasing isolation of the family from the kinship group and the world of work.

One problem with conceptual frameworks rooted strictly in demography is that there has always been significant variation in American

demographic patterns on the basis of region, social class, and ethnicity. This problem is clearly illustrated by regional contrasts in the
American colonies during the seventeenth century. In late-seventeenth-century New England, migration in family groups, a healthful
climate, and a prospering economy contributed to a rapid rate of natural population increase; in the Chesapeake region, in marked contrast, epidemic disease, a sharply skewed sex ratio, a high proportion
of recent immigrants in the population, and delayed marriage among
indentured servants resulted in a population unable to reproduce its
numbers naturally. Obviously it is not possible to speak of a typical
American pattern. Another problem with a strictly demographic
framework lies in the difficulty of inferring changes in attitudes and
beliefs from demographic changes. In the absence of written records,
demography can provide valuable clues to changes in family structure
and behavior, but it can only provide indirect evidence about changes
in emotions and sentiments or the nature of family relationships.

Another model of family history is drawn from modernization theory, which, in its simplest forms, contrasts "traditional" ways of life
with modern patterns, folk society with urban society, *Gemeinschaft*
with *Gesellschaft*, and "instrumental" with "affective" forms of family
relationships. Simpler models of modernization have largely been rejected because of their tendency to draw overly sharp dichotomies
between premodern and modern modes of behavior and to overem-
phasize the importance of such historical watersheds as industrialization. Contrary to such simpler theories, significant changes in the
family (such as a weakening of patriarchal authority) predated industrialization, and in many centers of early manufacturing, industrialization and urbanization actually reinforced kinship ties rather than undermined them.

While explicitly rejecting crude unilinear theories of historical development, more sophisticated modernization models—associated
with structual functionalist sociology—tend to assume that modernization entails certain specific transformations in the family, such as
a growing mutuality and emotional intimacy between spouses, the
development of a concept of romantic love as the basis for marriage,
and a shift in child-rearing practices from authoritarianism to a more
affectionate and permissive style in which children are rewarded by
parental affection or punished by threats of the withdrawal of love.
Modernization theory thus implies that the inexorable transformations in the family promote autonomy, independence, and affectivity
and fit hand in glove with industrial modes of work organization.

Other scholars have approached the problems of periodization and conceptualization from the perspective of women's history. Historians of women have argued convincingly that the most profound changes in the institution of the family—most notably the declining birthrate, the emergence of motherhood as a self-conscious vocation, and the upward trend in divorce—are closely intertwined with changes in the economic roles and status of women.

Still others have conceptualized the history of the family from a life-cycle perspective. The life-course approach to family history has three major aims: to trace historical changes in the stages of life, to reconstruct the developmental cycle of families and households, and to locate individual experience in the context of birth cohorts. Emphasis is placed on age groupings, such as childhood, adolescence, middle age, and old age, and on the timing of such key life-course transitions as the age of marriage, establishing an independent household, and bearing children. Such investigations can cast fresh light on changing conceptions of the life stages. The study of child-rearing practices can raise important questions about the impact of shifting patterns of socialization. The historical study of patterns of courtship, marriage, inheritance, and mobility can permit us to chart historical changes in the transition to adulthood. Comparisons of the experience of birth cohorts can offer insight into the power of a specific economic, social, and historical context to shape the nature, timing, and form of problems of individual development.

Each of these conceptual models has obvious strengths and limitations. The demographic perspective gains explanatory power if linkages are drawn to changes in women's roles and status, in public ideologies of the family, and in the family's emotional and power relationships. Conceptions of modernization grow more comprehensive if they take account of changes in the nature and timing of the life stages and broader shifts in the economy. Only a view of family change that draws on each perspective can do justice to the complexity of the family's history.

APPENDIX II

The Language
of Family History

STUDENTS of the family have developed a technical terminology and idiom that are useful in describing the structure and organization of family types. Because this jargon can pose a obstacle to clear comprehension, one would do well to understand the major social science concepts and terms used by family historians. Such words as "family," "household," and "kinship" have technical meanings that differ from their popular usage.

In popular parlance the word "family" is used broadly and loosely. It can refer to any group of persons of a common ancestry, to any group of individuals residing under one roof, and to a unit composed of one or more adults living together and cooperating in the care and rearing of their own or adopted children. In an effort to give the term "family" a more rigorous and formal meaning, social scientists have sought to disentangle its diverse definitions. In the first place, scholars distinguish "family" from "household." "Family" is defined as a kinship and legal unit based on affinal or biological relatedness (that is, relationships based on marriage or parent-child linkages), while "household" refers to a residential unit, the group of kin and nonkin who share a common residence.

Students of the family draw further distinctions based on the organizational structure of families. The nuclear or conjugal family is the unit composed of a husband, a wife, and their dependent children living in an independent household. Other types of families include the "consanguineal" family, which is the unit made up of a single parent and children, and various kinds of "complex" families, that is, units that are based on generational ties (such as three-generation households) and lateral ties (such as households containing two married siblings, their spouses and children).

251

Recent scholarship on the family has placed special emphasis on the concept of the "developmental cycle"—the idea that the size, composition, membership, and organizational structure of a particular family vary over time. As individual family members experience such key life-course events as the establishment of an independent household, formation of a marriage, birth, and death, family size and household structure change. The timing of such life stages as the age of marriage, the entrance into employment, the age of childbearing, or the spacing of children are not, of course, simply individual decisions. A particular historical and cultural context shapes such decisions as the proper age to marry or whether a family of a specific class should take in boarders or lodgers, thus ordering the developmental sequence of households.

By "kinship," social scientists refer to genealogical relationships among groups of families. Americans often use the term "extended family" to refer to a large group of relatives who are not coresident. In small-scale societies, kinship-based groups carry out significant cultural and social functions. In fact, kinship provides the fundamental organizing principle in many small-scale societies. Kinship groups are generally charged with responsibility for residence, social control, welfare, socialization, and economic activity and often hold specific political powers.

Kinship groups can be structured in a variety of ways. In small-scale societies descent group structures—patrilineal or matrilineal (based on ties through the father or mother) and cognatic (based on ties through either or both)—form the basis of the society's organizational patterns. Patri- or matrilineal or cognatic descent groups structure family and religious life as well as politics and economics. In large-scale societies, such as modern industrial societies, many functions traditionally assigned to kinship groups are taken over by impersonal public institutions and the economic marketplace. Still, extended family ties remain important even in urban and industrial societies. "Kindred" (relatives on a person's mother's or father's side) help fellow kin carry out a variety of tasks, particularly care of children, and provide a source of mutual aid and assistance in times of emergency.

Notes

EXPLANATORY NOTE: In order to prevent the text from being cluttered by citation numbers, each note covers all quotations and sources in a paragraph. For readers who wish to trace the source of a particular quotation, the sequence of sources cited corresponds with the sequence of quotations.

CHAPTER I

1. On Plymouth Colony, see William Bradford, *A History of Plymouth Plantation, 1620–1647*, ed. Charles F. Adams, 2 vols. (New York, 1968); George Langdon, *Pilgrim Colony: A History of Plymouth, 1620–1691* (New Haven, 1966); John Demos, *A Little Commonwealth: Family Life in Plymouth Colony* (New York, 1970).

2. The best introductions to the family in colonial New England are Edmund Morgan, *The Puritan Family: Religion and Domestic Relations in Seventeenth-Century New England* (1944; reprint, New York, 1966), esp. 43–46, 65–108, 114–22, 139, 142–50, Demos, *Little Commonwealth;* Demos, "The American Family in Past Time," *American Scholar,* 43 (1974), 424–25; Demos, "Images of the American Family, Then and Now," in *Changing Images of the Family,* eds. Virginia Tufte and Barbara Myerhoff (New Haven, 1979), 46–47; Daniel Blake Smith, "The Study of the Family in Early America: Trends, Problems, and Prospects," *William and Mary Quarterly,* 3rd ser., 34 (1982), 3–28; John M. Murrin, "Review Essay," *History and Theory,* 11 (1972), 226–75; Bernard Bailyn, *Education in the Forming of American Society: Needs and Opportunities for Study* (Chapel Hill, N.C., 1960), 15–36.

3. On diary-keeping and Puritan introspection, see Lawrence Stone, *The Family, Sex and Marriage in England, 1500–1800* (New York, 1977), 226–28, 264.

4. Peter Gregg Slater, *Children in the New England Mind: In Death and in Life* (Hamden, Conn., 1977), 16, 33; Arthur W. Calhoun, *A Social History of the American Family from Colonial Times to the Present* (New York, 1945), I, 106; Stone, *Family, Sex and Marriage in England,* 173–74, 212.

5. Calhoun, *Social History of the American Family,* I, 108–09, 118; Stone, *Family, Sex and Marriage in England,* 173–74, 212.

6. Calhoun, *Social History of the American Family*, I, 54; Willystine Goodsell, *A History of the Family as a Social and Educational Institution* (New York, 1915), 358–60; David Hackett Fischer, *Growing Old in America* (New York, 1977), 57–58.

7. Goodsell, *History of the Family as a Social and Educational Institution*, 347, 360–63; Calhoun, *Social History of the American Family*, I, 57, 59.

8. On the Puritan image of the family as a microcosm of the larger social and political world, see Demos, "American Family in Past Time," 423–24; Demos, "Images of the American Family, Then and Now," 46–47; Barbara Laslett, "The Family as a Public and Private Institution: An Historical Perspective," *Journal of Marriage and the Family*, 35 (1973), 480–92.

9. Morgan, *Puritan Family*, 27, 143, 144.

10. On rates of intermarriage and the blurring of familial and community ties, see Stephanie Grauman Wolf, *Urban Village: Population, Community, and Family Structure in Germantown, Pennsylvania, 1683–1800* (Princeton, N.J., 1976), chs. 7, 8, esp. 332. On kinship ties, see Morgan, *Puritan Family*, 150–60.

11. On the social and economic significance of kinship ties, see Bernard Farber, *Guardians of Virtue: Salem Families in 1800* (New York, 1972), 75–89, 96–108; Bernard Bailyn, *The New England Merchants in the Seventeenth Century* (Cambridge, Mass., 1955), 87–89, 101–2.

12. Refer to note 11.

13. On the kinship group and politics, see Kevin M. Sweeney, "River Gods in the Making: The Williamses of Western Massachusetts," in *The Bay and the River: 1600–1900, The Dublin Seminar for New England Folklife, Annual Proceedings, 1981*, ed. Peter Benes (Boston, 1982), 101–16; Randolph Shipley Klein, *Portrait of an Early American Family: The Shippens of Pennsylvania Across Five Generations* (Philadelphia, 1975), 2, 5–7, 55–58, 151, 200–203.

14. On the Puritan family's role in the social order, see Gerald F. Moran and Maris A. Vinovskis, "The Puritan Family and Religion: A Critical Reappraisal," *William and Mary Quarterly*, 3rd ser., 39 (1982); James Axtell, *School Upon a Hill: Education and Society in Colonial New England* (New Haven, 1974), 219; Morgan, *Puritan Family*, 19–20, 26–28, 134–36.

15. On the Puritan family's "public" functions, see Demos, *Little Commonwealth*, 182–84.

16. Ibid.

17. On the use of government to reinforce the authority of the Puritan family, see Demos, "American Family in Past Time," 424; Demos, "Images of the American Family, Then and Now," 47; Morgan, *Puritan Family*, 27, 57, 66, 78, 79, 113–14, 145–49.

18. On the older view of the evolution of the American family, see Murrin, "Review Essay," 228–29; Bailyn, *Education in the Forming of American Society*, 15–36. On the reinterpretation of the sixteenth- and seventeenth-century English family, see Keith Wrightson, *English Society, 1580–1680* (London, 1982), 66–118; Stone, *Family, Sex and Marriage in England*, 42–82; John R. Gillis, *For Better, For Worse: British Marriages, 1600 to the Present* (New York, 1985), 9–105; Randolph Trumbach, *The Rise of the Egalitarian Family: Aristocratic Kinship and Domestic Relations in Eighteenth-Century England* (New York, 1978).

19. Michael Walzer, *The Revolution of the Saints* (Cambridge, Mass., 1965).

20. Ibid.

21. Philip J. Greven, Jr., *Four Generations: Population, Land, and Family in Colonial Andover, Massachusetts* (Ithaca, N.Y., 1970), 72–99; Bailyn, "American Society in the Seventeenth Century," 104; John Demos, *Entertaining Satan: Witchcraft and the Culture of Early New England* (New York, 1982), 63.

22. Refer to note 21. Also see Robert V. Wells, *Revolutions in Americans' Lives* (Westport, Conn., 1982), 57–58.

23. Refer to notes 20 and 21. Also see John W. Adams and Alice Bee Kasakoff, "Migration and the Family in Colonial New England: The View from Genealogies," *Journal of Family History*, 9 (1984), 33.

24. Lyle Koehler, *A Search for Power: The Weaker Sex in Seventeenth-Century New England* (Urbana, Ill., 1980); Demos, *Little Commonwealth*, ch. 5.

25. On the legal rights of women, see Richard B. Morris, "Women's Rights in Early American Law," *Studies in the History of American Law with Special Reference to the Seventeenth and Eighteenth Century Colonies*, 2nd ed. (Philadelphia, 1959), 126–300; Marylynn Salmon, "Equality or Subversion? Feme Covert Status in Early Pennsylvania," in *Women of America: A History*, eds. Carol Ruth Berkin and Mary Beth Norton (Boston, 1979), 92–111; John R. Gunderson and Gwen Victor Gampel, "Married Women's Legal Status in Eighteenth Century New York and Virginia," *William and Mary Quarterly*, 3rd Series, 39 (1982), 114–34.

26. On the Puritan view of marriage, see Morgan, *Puritan Family*, 26–64.

27. Ibid., 55–59, 81–86, 151.

28. On the ideal wife, see Morgan, *Puritan Family*, 43–47, 161; Koehler, *Search for Power*, 136–37.

29. On marital love, see Morgan, *Puritan Family*, 47–54, 59–64, 161–62. On marital friction, see Koehler, *Search for Power*, 136–65.

30. On abusive husbands, see Koehler, *Search for Power*, 137–42.

31. On women's resistance to abuse, see Koehler, *Search for Power*, 142–46, 152–56.

32. Ibid., 142–46.

33. On the realities of married women's lives, see Laurel Thatcher Ulrich, *Good Wives: Image and Reality in the Lives of Women in Northern New England, 1650–1750* (New York, 1982), 9–10, 15, 23, 28, 50–51, 70–71; Alice Morse Earle, *Colonial Dames and Good Wives* (Boston, 1895).

34. On childbirth, see Demos, *Entertaining Satan*, 72, 124, 155, 204; Edward Shorter, *A History of Women's Bodies* (New York, 1982), ch. 4; Catharine M. Scholten, "'On the Importance of the Obstetrick Art': Changing Customs of Childbirth in America, 1760 to 1825," *William and Mary Quarterly*, 3rd ser., 34 (1977), 426–45; Scholten, *Childbearing in American Society: 1650–1850* (New York, 1985), chs. 1, 2; Judith Walzer Leavitt, *Brought to Bed: Childbearing in America, 1750–1950* (New York, 1986), 13–35, 64–86; Richard W. Wertz and Dorothy C. Wertz, *Lying-In: A History of Childbirth in America* (New York, 1977), 1–73.

35. Shorter, *History of Women's Bodies*, ch. 5.

36. Demos, *Little Commonwealth*, 133; Demos, *Entertaining Satan*, 204; Robert V. Wells, "Quaker Marriage Patterns in Colonial Perspective," *William and Mary Quarterly*, 3rd ser., 29 (1972), 440–41; Daniel Blake Smith, *Inside the Great House: Planter Family Life in Eighteenth-Century Chesapeake Society* (Ithaca, N.Y., 1980), 27.

37. Demos, *Little Commonwealth*, 192–93; Demos, *Entertaining Satan*, 24, 50.

38. On the experience of widowhood, see Ulrich, *Good Wives*, 7; Alexander Keyssar, "Widowhood in Eighteenth-Century Massachusetts: A Problem in the History of the Family," *Perspectives in American History*, 8 (1974), 83–119.

39. On death in childhood, see Slater, *Children in the New England Mind*, 16, 33. On the extent of orphanhood, see Murrin, "Review Essay," 231–32.

40. On the care and treatment of Puritan children, see Demos, *Little Commonwealth*, chs. 6, 7; Demos, *Entertaining Satan*, 127, 207. On legal and religious views of childhood and youth, see Ross W. Beales, Jr., "In Search of the Historical Child: Miniature Adulthood and Youth in Colonial New England," *American Quarterly*, 27 (1975), 379–98; Sandford Fleming, *Children and Puritanism: The Place of Children in the Life and Thought of the New England Churches, 1620–1847* (New Haven, 1933), 16, 60, 66–67, 153, 158; Monica Kiefer, *American Children Through Their Books* (Philadelphia, 1948), 1, 94, 225.

41. On the moral upbringing of Puritan children, refer to note 40; Morgan, *Puritan Family*, 66, 67, 71–78, 87–108, 136–39, 148, 172; Demos, *Entertaining Satan*, 207; Slater, *Children in the New England Mind*, 102–05.

42. On the practice of fostering out young children, see Morgan, *Puritan Family*, 68–78, 87–88, 120–22.

43. *Ibid.*; Demos, *Little Commonwealth*, 69, 134–46, 138–40, 142, 146, 182; Demos, "Developmental Perspectives on the History of Childhood," *Journal of Interdisciplinary History*, 2 (1971), 315–27; Demos, "American Family in Past Time," 428; Demos, *Entertaining Satan*, 156; Karin Calvert, "Children in American Family Portraiture," *William and Mary Quarterly*, 3rd ser., 39 (1982), 97.

44. On the transition from childhood to adulthood, refer to note 43. Also see Beales, "In Search of the Historical Child," 379–98; Calhoun, *Social History of the American Family*, I, 285–98; Goodsell, *History of the Family*, 395–97.

45. Murrin, "Review Essay," 228–32, 240–42; Demos, *Entertaining Satan*, 157.

46. Murrin, "Review Essay," 228–32, 240–42.

47. On the purported deterioration of the Puritan family, see Bailyn, *Education in the Forming of American Society*, 15–36.

48. On the enactment of ever more stringent laws relating to family government, see Bailyn, *Education in the Forming of American Society*, 15–36; Morgan, *Puritan Family*, 27, 57, 66, 78, 79, 113–14, 145–49.

49. Bailyn, *Education in the Forming of American Society*, 15–36; Bailyn, "American Society in the Seventeenth Century," 87–89, 105–108.

50. James A. Henretta, *The Evolution of American Society, 1700–1815: An Interdisciplinary Analysis* (Lexington, Mass., 1973), 12, 28–30.

51. *Ibid.*

52. Christopher M. Jedrey, *The World of John Cleaveland: Family and Community in Eighteenth-Century New England* (New York, 1979), 58–94.

53. Henretta, *Evolution of American Society*, 133–34; Daniel Scott Smith, "Parental Power and Marriage Patterns: An Analysis of Historical Trends in Hingham, Massashusetts," in *The American Family in Social-Historical Perspective*, ed. Michael Gordon, 3rd ed. (New York, 1983), 255–68; Greven, *Four Generations*, 222–23; Robert Gross, *The Minutemen and Their World* (New York, 1976), 211, 235.

54. Smith, "Parental Power and Marriage Patterns," 259–65.

55. *Ibid.*; James Deetz, *In Small Things Forgotten: The Archeology of Early American Life* (New York, 1977), 127.

56. Henretta, *Evolution of American Society,* 133–34; Daniel Scott Smith, "Parental Power and Marriage Patterns: An Analysis of Historical Trends in Hingham, Massachusetts," 255–68; Greven, *Four Generations,* 222–23; Gross, *The Minutemen and Their World,* 211, 235.

57. Refer to note 56. Also see Murrin, "Review Essay," 228–32, 240–42.

58. Slater, *Children in the New England Mind,* chs. 1, 2; Moran and Vinovskis, "The Puritan Family and Religion," 49–62; David E. Stannard, *The Puritan Way of Death: A Study in Religion, Culture, and Social Change* (New York, 1977); Maris A. Vinovskis, "Angels' Heads and Weeping Willows: Death in Early America," *American Antiquarian Society Proceedings,* 86 (1976), 273–302; Deetz, *In Small Things Forgotten,* ch. 4; Karen Halttunen, *Confidence Men and Painted Women* (New Haven, 1983), 125.

59. Jay Fliegelman, *Prodigals and Pilgrims: The American Revolution Against Patriarchal Authority, 1750–1800* (Cambridge, England, 1982), 1–2, 9–12, 33, 38, 51, 126, 170, 182, 193, 267; Kiefer, *American Children Through Their Books,* 1, 94, 225; Joseph F. Kett, *Rites of Passage: Adolescence in America, 1790 to the Present* (New York, 1977), 14–37. For comparative perspectives, see J.H. Plumb, "The First Flourishing of Children's Books," in Charles Ryskamp, ed., *Early Children's Books and Their Illustrations* (Boston, 1975), xvii; Plumb, "The New World of Children in Eighteenth Century England," *Past and Present,* 67 (1975), 88.

60. Kevin M. Sweeney, "Furniture and the Domestic Environment in Wethersfield, Connecticut, 1639–1800," *Connecticut Antiquarian,* 36 (1984), 10–39.

61. Ibid., 11–14; Deetz, *In Small Things Forgotten,* 55–58, 99–100, 104, 121–22, 151; Ulrich, *Good Wives,* 17–18, 26; Carole Shammas, "The Domestic Environment in Early Modern England and America," in Gordon, ed., *American Family in Social-Historical Perspective,*113–35.

62. Sweeney, "Furniture and the Domestic Environment," 11–14; Deetz, *In Small Things Forgotten,* 121–22.

63. Sweeney, "Furniture and the Domestic Environment," 27–34; Deetz, *In Small Things Forgotten,* 111–17.

CHAPTER II

1. On the diversity of the colonial population, see Maldwyn Allen Jones, *American Immigration* (Chicago, 1960), 39.

2. Ibid.

3. The anthropological literature on the American Indian peoples is so immense that it is only possible to suggest the most comprehensive and authoritative sources of information. The best recent bibliography is W. R. Swagerty, ed., *Scholars and the Indian Experience: Critical Reviews of Recent Writing in the Social Sciences* (Bloomington, Ind., 1984).

4. On geographical variation in Native American cultural patterns, see Harold E. Driver, *Indians of North America* (2nd rev. ed., Chicago, 1969); Fred Eggan, *The American Indian* (Chicago, 1966); Alice Kehoe, *North American Indians: A Comprehensive Account* (Englewood Cliffs, N.J., 1981); A. L. Kroeber, *Cultural and Natural Areas of Native North America* (1939; reprint, Berkeley, 1963); Robert F. Spencer and Jesse D. Spencer, *The Native Americans: Ethnology and Backgrounds of the North American Indians* (New York, 1977); Bruce G. Trigger, *Handbook of*

North American Indians, Vol. 15: The Northeast (Washington, D.C., 1978); and Clark Wissler, Indians of the United States (rev. ed., New York, 1966). Native American social organization is surveyed in Fred Eggan, ed., Social Anthropology of North American Tribes, 2nd ed. (Chicago, 1955) and styles of life are treated in James Axtell, The Indian Peoples of Eastern America: A Documentary History of the Sexes (New York, 1981).

Historical background is provided by Francis Jennings, The Invasion of America: Indians, Colonialism and the Cant of Conquest (New York, 1975); Eleanor B. Leacock and N. O. Lurie, eds., North American Indians in Historical Perspective (New York, 1971); Paul S. Martin, George I. Quimby, and Donald Collier, Indians Before Columbus (Chicago, 1947); Gary B. Nash, Red White and Black: The Peoples of Early America (Englewood Cliffs, N.J., 1974); Ruth M. Underhill, Red Man's America (Chicago, 1953); and Wilcomb Washburn, The Indian in America (New York, 1975), which can be supplemented by detailed studies of specific Native Americans and geographical areas such as William A. Haviland and Marjory W. Powers, The Original Vermonters (Hanover, 1981); Cornelius Jaenen, Friend and Foe: Aspects of French-Amerindian Cultural Contact in the Sixteenth and Seventeenth Centuries (New York, 1976); Howard S. Russell, Indian New England Before the Mayflower (Hanover, 1980); Neal Salisbury, Manitou and Providence: Indians, Europeans, and the Making of New England, 1500–1643 (New York, 1982); and Bruce Trigger, The Children of Aataentsic: A History of the Huron People to 1660 (Montreal, 1976).

5. General accounts of the Native Americans of the Eastern Woodlands include George T. Hunt, The Wars of the Iroquois (Madison, Wisc., 1940); Frederick Johnson, ed., Man in Northeastern North America (New York, 1946); and Robert E. Ritzenthaler, The Woodland Indians of the Western Great Lakes (Garden City, N.Y., 1970).

6. The peoples of the Southeastern Woodlands are the subject of Charles Hudson, The Southeastern Indians (Knoxville, Tenn., 1976) and J. Leitch Wright, Jr., The Only Land They Knew (New York, 1981).

7. On the Plains peoples, see Robert H. Lowie, Indians of the Plains (Garden City, N.Y., 1963).

8. Edward P. Dozier, The Pueblo Indians of North America (New York, 1970); Fred Eggan, The American Indian, ch. 5 (Chicago, 1966) and Social Organization of the Western Pueblos (Chicago, 1950); Clyde Kluckhohn and Dorothea Leighton, The Navaho (Cambridge, Mass., 1946); and Edward H. Spicer, Cycles of Conquest (Tucson, 1962) survey different aspects of aboriginal life in the Southwest.

9. Useful introductions to the peoples of California are Jack Forbes, Native Americans of California and Nevada (Healdsburg, Calif., 1968); Robert F. Heizer and Alan Almquist, The Other Californians (Berkeley, 1971); R. F. Heizer and M. A. Whipple, eds., California Indians, 2nd ed. (Berkeley, 1971); A. L. Kroeber, Handbook of the Indians of California (2nd ed., Berkeley, 1953).

10. Valuable overviews of the peoples of the Northwest Coast can be found in Phillip Drucker, Indians of the Northwest Coast (Garden City, N.Y., 1963) and Drucker, Cultures of the North Pacific Coast (New York, 1965).

11. On perceptions of Native American cultures, see Calvin Martin, Keepers of the Game (Berkeley, 1978); Robert F. Berkhofter, Jr., The White Man's Indian: Images of the American Indian from Columbus to the Present (New York, 1978).

12. On variations in Native American kinship and family systems, refer to notes 4–10.

13. On the American Indian family, family roles, and the family life cycle, refer to notes 4–10. A particularly valuable source on the American Indian families of the Eastern Woodlands is Axtell, *Indian Peoples of Eastern America: A Documentary History of the Sexes*, xv-xxi.

14. Axtell, *Indian Peoples of Eastern America*, 3–4, 14, 25–26. For information on specific tribes, refer to notes 5–10.

15. Ibid., 31–33. For information on specific tribes, refer to notes 5–10.

16. Ibid.

17. Ibid., 51–69. For information on specific tribes, refer to notes 5–10.

18. Axtell, *op cit.*, 71–76. For information on specific tribes, refer to notes 5–10.

19. Axtell, *op. cit.*, 76–102. For information on specific tribes, refer to notes 5–10.

20. On the impact of contact on kinship and family patterns, see James Axtell, *The European and the Indian: Essays in the Ethnohistory of Colonial North America* (New York, 1981); Gary C. Goodwin, *Cherokees in Transition: A Study of Changing Culture and Environment Prior to 1775* (Chicago, 1977); Edward McM. Larrabee, "Recurrent Themes and Sequences in North American Indian-European Contact," *Transactions of the American Philosophical Society* 66 (1976), 3–52; James H. Merrell, "Cultural Continuity Among the Piscataway Indians of Colonial Maryland," *William and Mary Quarterly*, 3rd ser., 36 (1979), 548–70.

21. Refer to note 20.

22. On the impact of contact on the Iroquois, see Anthony Wallace, *Death and Rebirth of the Seneca* (New York, 1972), 21–48, 239–302; Lewis Henry Morgan, *League of the Ho-De-No-Sau-Ne or Iroquois* (1851; reprint, New Haven, 1954).

The five member tribes of the Iroquois Confederacy—the Cuyuga, Mohawk, Oneida, Onondaga, and Seneca—which constituted the most highly developed Indian political confederation north of Mexico, lived in matrilineal societies. In such societies, access to land and membership in the political system were traced through the mother's family. The critical importance of women in the kinship system was accompanied by high status for women in other realms of Iroquois life. Women controlled the Iroquois system of housing, the "longhouses," the large, wood-framed, bark-covered structures in which a number of matrilineally-related families lived. Husbands, on marriage, were required to move into their wives' longhouse. Women also played a valued role in the Iroquois economic system, by raising corn, beans, squash, and other food crops. Although women could not become chiefs on the intertribal council, they did hold key roles in selecting council members, and they did participate in meetings in which tribal and village decisions were made.

While women were responsible for cultivating fields, gathering wild plants, cooking, rearing children, and making clothing, men served as warriors and hunters, roles that often took them away from their villages. For weeks at a time, men left the longhouses to hunt wild game or to fish or to go to war. As a result of these long separations, Iroquois marriages tended to be quite fragile and transient. Frequent changes of marital partners were fairly common.

23. Wallace, *Death and Rebirth of the Seneca*, 277–337; Wallace, "Handsome Lake and the Decline of the Iroquois Matriarchate," in *Kinship and Culture*, ed. Francis Hsu (Chicago, 1971), 367–76.

On the impact of contact upon the Algonquian, see Kehoe, *North American Indians*, 216–44; Eleanor Leacock, "Matrilocality in a Simple Hunting Economy," *Southwestern Journal of Anthropology*, 11 (1955), 31–34, 46; Frank Speck,

"Social Structure of the Northern Algonkian," *American Sociological Society,* 12 (1917), 90–98.

24. On the number of blacks in seventeenth-century America, see David Brion Davis, *Slavery and Human Progress* (New York, 1984), 51, 75–77; Nash, *Red, White, and Black,* 164.

25. On the status of blacks in early colonial America, see Nash, *Red, White, and Black,* 164–66; Edmund S. Morgan, *American Slavery, American Freedom: The Ordeal of Colonial Virginia* (New York, 1975), 311–12, 332–33.

26. On the experience of blacks in the Northern colonies, see Nash, *Red, White, and Black,* 176; Lorenzo J. Greene, *The Negro in Colonial New England* (New York, 1942), ch. 8.

27. On the experience of blacks in the Chesapeake colonies, see Nash, *Red, White, and Black,* 164–66; Morgan, *American Slavery, American Freedom,* 311–12, 332–33.

28. On the lack of opportunities to establish stable families, see Peter Wood, *Black Majority: Negroes in Colonial South Carolina from 1670 through the Stono Rebellion* (New York, 1974), 140–41, 150–55, 159–65; John B. Boles, *Black Southerners, 1619–1869* (Lexington, Ky., 1983), 35; Nash, *Red, White, and Black,* 208.

29. On demographic impediments to a stable family life, refer to note 28.

30. On sex ratios among colonial slaves, see Wood, *Black Majority,* 140–41, 159–65; Nash, *Red, White, and Black,* 208.

31. On the increase in the number of slaves at the end of the seventeenth century, see Wood, *Black Majority,* ch. 6; Robert W. Fogel and Stanley L. Engerman, "Recent Findings in the Study of Slave Demography and Family Structure," *Social Science Research,* 63 (1979), 567–75; Allan Kulikoff, "A 'Prolific' People: Black Population Growth in the Chesapeake Colonies, 1700–1790," *Southern Studies,* 16 (1977), 391–428; Kulikoff, "The Beginnings of the Afro-American Family in Maryland," in *Law, Society, and Politics in Early Maryland,* eds. Aubrey Land, Lois Green Carr, and Edward C. Papenfuse (Baltimore, 1977, 171–96; Kulikoff, "The Origins of Afro-American Society in Tidewater Maryland and Virginia, 1700–1790," *William and Mary Quarterly,* 3rd ser., 35 (1978), 226–59; Russell R. Menard, "The Maryland Slave Population, 1658 to 1730: A Demographic Profile of Blacks in Four Counties," *William and Mary Quarterly,* 3rd ser., 32 (1975), 29–54; John B. Boles, *Black Southerners,* 31–33, 35, 38–39.

32. On the upsurge in slave fertility, refer to note 31.

33. On the factors contributing to higher rates of fertility, refer to note 31.

34. Refer to note 31.

35. On the similarities in demographic patterns found among Southern black and white women, see Fogel and Engerman, "Recent Findings in the Study of Slave Demography," 567–75.

36. On the success of slaves in fashioning a strong system of family and kinship prior to the Revolution, see Mary Beth Norton, Herbert G. Gutman, and Ira Berlin, "The Afro-American Family in the Age of Revolution," in *Slavery and Freedom in the Age of the American Revolution,* eds. Ira Berlin and Ronald Hoffman (Charlottesville, Va., 1983), 177–83, 187–91.

37. On slave sexual mores, refer to note 36.

38. On the demographic contrasts between the Chesapeake and New England colonies, see Daniel Blake Smith, "The Study of the Family in Early Colonial America: Trends, Problems, and Prospects," *William and Mary Quarterly,* 3rd

ser., 39 (1982), 9; Smith, "Mortality and the Family in the Colonial Chesapeake," *Journal of Interdisciplinary History,* 8 (1978), 403–27; Wells, *Revolutions in Americans' Lives,* 23, 28–29; Morgan, *American Slavery, American Freedom,* 158–62; Lois Greene Carr and Lorena Walsh, "The Planter's Wife: The Experience of White Women in Seventeenth Century Maryland," in *A Heritage of Her Own,* eds. Nancy F. Cott and Elizabeth H. Pleck (New York, 1979), 25, 29–30, 33, 39; Walsh, "'Till Death Us Do Part': Marriage and Family in Seventeenth Century Maryland," in *The Chesapeake in the Seventeenth Century: Essays on Anglo-American Society,* eds. Thad W. Tate and David Ammerman (Chapel Hill, N.C., 1979), 126–52; Darrett B. and Anita H. Rutman, *A Place in Time: Middlesex County, Virginia, 1650–1750* (New York, 1984), 76, 78, 100–03, 114, 179. A growing body of scholarship has begun to suggest that the contrast between the Chesapeake and New England may be overdrawn and that mortality and mobility rates in New England might be significantly higher than the study of such small, stable communities as Andover, Massachusetts, appear to indicate. See, for example, Christine Heyrman, *Commerce and Culture: The Maritime Communities of Colonial Massachusetts, 1690–1750* (New York, 1984).

39. Refer to note 38.

40. Refer to note 38.

41. On the characteristics of the migrants to the Chesapeake colonies, see Morgan, *American Slavery, American Freedom,* 158–62.

42. On the paucity of older inhabitants, refer to note 41. Also see Carr and Walsh, "The Planter's Wife," 29–30, 33; Smith, "The Study of the Family in Early Colonial America," 9; Smith, "Mortality and the Family in the Colonial Chesapeake," 403–27; Wells, *Revolutions in Americans' Lives,* 23, 28–29; Morgan, *American Slavery, American Freedom,* 158–62; Walsh, "'Till Death Us Do Part,'" 126–52; Rutman, *A Place in Time,* 76, 78, 100–103, 114, 179.

43. Refer to note 42.

44. Refer to note 42.

45. On geographic isolation, see Carr and Walsh, "The Planter's Wife," 29–30, 33.

46. On contrasts in family patterns in the Chesapeake and New England colonies, see Carr and Walsh, "The Planter's Wife," 39.

47. On the importance of kinship ties, see Rutman, *A Place in Time,* 76, 78, 100–103, 114, 179.

48. On George Washington's family background, see James Thomas Flexner, *Washington: The Indispensable Man* (New York, 1984), 1–7; Douglas Southhall Freeman, *George Washington: A Biography* (New York, 1948), vol. 1: 15–72, 95–96, 190–258.

49. On Middlesex county, Virginia, see Rutman, *A Place in Time,* 47–51, 95–127, 220–21, 245.

50. Ibid., 70–79, 116–19, 237.

51. On the rights of widows, see Carr and Walsh, "The Planter's Wife," 34–39.

52. On the changes that occurred in the Chesapeake at the end of the seventeenth century, see Carr and Walsh, "The Planter's Wife," 42–43; Smith, "The Family in Early America," 9–10.

53. On persistent differences between the Chesapeake and New England colonies, see Daniel Blake Smith, *Inside the Great House: Planter Family Life in Eighteenth-Century Chesapeake Society* (Ithaca, N.Y. 1980), 175–230.

54. Jan Lewis, *The Pursuit of Happiness: Family and Values in Jefferson's Virginia* (Cam-

bridge, England, 1983), 28–38, 180–81, 212, 217–19; Michael Zuckerman, "William Byrd's Family," *Perspectives in American History*, 12 (1979), 255–311.

55. Lewis, *Pursuit of Happiness*, 99–103, 180–81, 205–06, 212–29.

CHAPTER III

1. On Alexis de Tocqueville's ideas about the American family, see Tocqueville, *Democracy in America*, ed. Phillips Bradley (New York, 1945), vol. 1: 315, vol. 2: 202–4; David Brion Davis, "The American Family and Boundaries in Historical Perspective" in *From Homicide to Slavery: Studies in American Culture* (New York, 1986), 166–83; Davis, *Homicide in American Fiction, 1798–1860: A Study in Social Values* (Ithaca, N.Y., 1957), 180–81, 183, 200.

2. Carl N. Degler, *At Odds: Women and the Family in America from the Revolution to the Present* (New York, 1980), 8–25 outlines the defining characteristics of the new kind of middle class family that emerged between 1770 and 1820.

3. On the changing image of the family, see John Demos, "The American Family in Past Time," *American Scholar*, 43 (1974), 432–39; Demos, "Images of the American Family, Then and Now," in *Changing Images of the Family*, eds. Virginia Tufte and Barbara Myerhoff (New Haven, 1979), 49–52; Kirk Jeffrey, "The Family as Utopian Retreat from the City," *Soundings*, 55 (1972), 21–41; Barbara Laslett, "The Family as a Public and Private Institution: An Historical Perspective," *Journal of Marriage and the Family*, 35 (1973), 480–92; William E. Bridges, "Warm Hearth, Cold World: Social Perspectives on Household Poets," *American Quarterly*, 21 (1969), 767.

4. Refer to note 3.

5. Refer to note 3.

6. Refer to note 3.

7. Refer to note 3.

8. On changes in family functions and expectations, see Steven Mintz, *A Prison of Expectations: The Family in Victorian Culture* (New York, 1983), 18–19.

9. On the role of advice books, philosophic treatises, and fiction in popularizing new ideas about the family, see Jay Fliegelman, *Prodigals and Pilgrims: The American Revolution Against Patriarchal Authority, 1750–1800* (Cambridge, England, 1982), esp. ch. 2. Another pioneering attempt to view ideas about the family in relationship to the cultural and intellectual history of the seventeenth and eighteenth centuries is Edwin G. Burrows and Michael Wallace, "The American Revolution: The Ideology and Psychology of National Liberation," *Perspectives in American History*, 6 (1972), 287.

10. Fliegelman, *Prodigals and Pilgrims*, chs. 5 and 6.

11. On the increasing emphasis attached to romantic love, see Fliegelman, *Prodigals and Pilgrims.*, ch. 5; Herman Lantz et al., "Pre-Industrial Patterns in the Colonial Family in America: A Contents Analysis of Colonial Magazines," *American Sociological Review*, 33 (1968), 414.

12. Fliegelman, *Prodigals and Pilgrims*, ch. 5; Lawrence Stone, *The Family, Sex and Marriage in England, 1500–1800* (New York, 1977), ch. 8.

13. On changing attitudes toward children, see Fliegelman, *Prodigals and Pilgrims*, 93–105, 114–16, 160–61, 260–65; Peter Gregg Slater, *Children in the New England Mind: In Death and In Life* (Hamden, Conn., 1977); Monica Kiefer, *American*

Children Through Their Books (Philadelphia, 1948); Philip J. Greven, Jr., *The Protestant Temperament: Patterns of Childrearing, Religious Experience, and the Self in Early America* (New York, 1977); Anne Kuhn, *The Mother's Role in Childhood Education* (New Haven, 1947); Bernard Wishy, *The Child and the Republic: The Dawn of Modern American Child Nurture* (Philadelphia, 1968); Robert Sunley, "Early Nineteenth Century American Literature on Child Rearing" in *Childhood in Contemporary Cultures*, eds. Margaret Mead and Martha Wolfenstein (Chicago, 1955). Comparative perspectives can be found in J.H. Plumb, "The First Flourishing of Children's Books," in *Early Children's Books and their Illustrations*, ed. Charles Ryskamp (Boston, 1975), xvii; Plumb, "The New World of Children in Eighteenth Century England," *Past and Present*, 67 (1975), 88; Peter Conveney, *Image of Childhood* (Baltimore, 1967), 29, 80.

14. Willard Sterne Randall, *A Little Revenge: Benjamin Franklin and His Son* (Boston, 1984); Claude-Anne Lopez and Eugenia W. Herbert, *The Private Franklin: The Man and His Family* (New York, 1975).

15. On the new emphasis attached to domesticity, see Mintz, *Prison of Expectations*, 11–20, 39. For an English comparison, see Walter E. Houghton, *The Victorian Frame of Mind, 1830–1870* (New Haven, 1957), 341–48.

16. On the changing attitude toward marriage, see Mary Beth Norton, *Liberty's Daughters: The Revolutionary Experience of American Women, 1750–1800* (Boston, 1980), 230–35, 238; Degler, *At Odds*, 26–51.

17. On shifting attitudes toward children, see Degler, *At Odds*, 66–110; Slater, *Children in the New England Mind*, 93–164; Kiefer, *American Children Through Their Books*; Wishy, *Child and the Republic*. For comparative perspectives, see Plumb, "The First Flourishing of Children's Books," xvii; Plumb, "The New World of Children in Eighteenth Century England," 88.

18. Degler, *At Odds*, 8–9, 191–95, 307, 329; Nancy F. Cott, *The Bonds of Womanhood: "Woman's Sphere" in New England, 1780–1835* (New Haven, 1977); Gerda Lerner, "The Lady and the Mill Girl: Changes in the Status of Women in the Age of Jackson," *Mid-Continental American Studies Journal*, 10 (1969), 5–15; Joseph F. Kett, *Rites of Passage: Adolescence in America, 1790 to the Present* (New York, 1977), 14–37, 111–43.

19. Local case studies that document the changing economic functions of the family include Paul Johnson, *A Shopkeeper's Millennium: Society and Revivals in Rochester, New York, 1815–1837* (New York, 1978); Susan E. Hirsch, *Roots of the American Working Class: The Industrialization of Crafts in Newark, 1800–1860* (Philadelphia, 1978), 5, 15, 22–23, 53, 58, 60–62, 71–76, 94, 136; Mary E. Ryan, *Cradle of the Middle Class: The Family in Oneida County, New York, 1790–1865* (Cambridge, England, 1981), 21–31, 43–65, 138, 141, 155–57, 162–79, 203–09; Stuart M. Blumin, *The Urban Threshold: Growth and Change in a Nineteenth Century American Community* (Chicago, 1976), 39–42, 162, 168–71, 187–88, 192–93, 218, 19, 244 n. 18, 253 n. 28. More general overviews of the family's changing economic roles can be found in Stephan Thernstrom, *A Social History of the American People* (San Diego, 1984), 227–28; Kenneth Keniston and the Carnegie Commission on Children, *All Our Children: The American Family Under Pressure* (New York, 1977), 3–23.

20. Refer to note 19.

21. On "putting-out" systems of production and cottage industries, see Ryan, *Cradle of the Middle Class*, 21–31, 43–51, 61–65, 138, 141, 176.

22. Johnson, *Shopkeeper's Millennium*, 43–48, 59; Hirsch, *Roots of the American Working Class*, 5, 15, 22–23, 53, 58, 60–62, 71–76, 94, 136; Ryan, *Cradle of the Middle*

Class, 21–31, 43–65, 138, 141, 155–57, 162–79, 203–9; Blumin, *Urban Threshold*, 39–42, 162, 168–71, 187–88, 192–93, 218, 19, 244 n. 18, 253 n. 28.

23. Cott, *Bonds of Womanhood*, chs. 1, 2; Hirsch, *Roots of the American Working Class*, 15.

24. On the fall in birthrates, see Robert V. Wells, "Family History and the Demographic Transition," *Journal of Social History*, 9 (1975); Wells, "Quaker Marriage Patterns in a Colonial Perspective," *William and Mary Quarterly*, 3rd ser., 29 (1972), 439–41; Wells, "Family Size and Fertility Control in Eighteenth Century America: A Study of Quaker Families," *Population Studies*, 25 (1971), 73–82; Degler, *At Odds*, 178–248; Susan Bloomberg et al., "A Census Probe into Nineteenth Century Family History: Southern Michigan, 1850–1880," *Journal of Social History*, 5 (1971), 28; Wendell H. Bash, "Changing Birth Rates in Developing America: New York State, 1840–1875," *Millbank Memorial Fund Quarterly*, 41 (1963), 163, 180–81; Maris A. Vinovskis, "Recent Trends in American Historical Demography: Some Methodological and Conceptual Considerations," *Annual Review of Sociology*, 4 (1978), 603–27.

25. Refer to note 24.

26. Maris A. Vinovskis, "Socioeconomic Determinants of Fertility," *Journal of Interdisciplinary History*, 6 (1976), 375–96; Tamara K. Hareven and Maris A. Vinovskis, "Patterns of Childbearing in Late Nineteenth Century America: The Determinants of Marital Fertility in Five Massachusetts Towns in 1880," in *Family and Population in Nineteenth Century America*, eds. Hareven and Vinvoskis (Princeton, 1978), 85–125; Vinovskis, "Recent Trends in American Historical Demography," 603–27.

The fall in birthrates was not simply a result of a trend toward urbanization. As late as 1860, less than a fifth of the national population lived in communities with 2,500 or more inhabitants, and although birthrates fell most rapidly in urban areas, the largest contribution to a decline in fertility came from rural areas.

Neither is there any simple economic explanation of the decline in fertility. A number of economists have postulated that the decreasing availability of farmland in settled regions helped reduce birthrates by increasing the difficulty of establishing new households, decreasing the value of children's labor, and raising the cost of furnishing children with sufficient land to establish their own households. The attempts to prove or disprove this hypothesis have been inconclusive.

27. On the transformation of children's role within the middle-class family, see Kett, *Rites of Passage*, 14–37, 111–43.

28. Degler, *At Odds*, 201–9; Daniel Scott Smith, "Family Limitation, Sexual Control, and Domestic Feminism in Victorian America," in *Clio's Consciousness Raised*, eds. Mary Hartman and Lois Banner (New York, 1974), 119–36.

29. Refer to note 28.

30. On the popular public image of the family a century ago, see Barbara Welter, "The Cult of True Womanhood, 1820–1860," *American Quarterly*, 18 (1966), 131–75.

31. Demos, "Images of the Family, Then and Now," 49–52; Demos, "American Family in Past Time," 432–34, 439; Kathryn Kish Sklar, *Catharine Beecher, A Study in American Domesticity* (New Haven, 1973), 151–67, 193–94.

32. Refer to note 31. Also see Tocqueville, *Democracy in America*, vol. 1: 315, vol. 2: 202–4, 209–14, 222–25.

33. On tensions within the nineteenth-century middle-class home, see Mintz, *Prison of Expectations*, 38–39, 59–87; Demos, "Images of the Family, Then and Now," 53–54.

34. On the weakness of paternal authority, see Arthur W. Calhoun, *A Social History of American Family Life from Colonial Times to the Present* (New York, 1917), vol. 2: 51–78.

35. On the ideology of patriarchy in the seventeenth century, see Edmund Morgan, *The Puritan Family: Religion and Domestic Relation in Seventeenth-Century New England* (1945; reprint, New York, 1966), 29–64; Gordon J. Schochet, *Patriarchalism in Political Thought: The Authoritarian Family and Political Speculations and Attitudes Especially in Seventeenth-Century England* (Oxford, England, 1975).

36. Norton, *Liberty's Daughters*, 230–35, 243–46.

37. Ibid.; Tocqueville, *Democracy in America*, vol 2: 202–4. For a comparative perspective, see Nigel V. Lowe, "The Legal Status of Fathers: Past and Present," in *The Father Figure*, eds. Lorna McKee and Margaret O'Brien (London, 1982), 26–42, and Trevor Lummis, "The Historical Dimension of Fatherhood: A Case Study, 1890–1914," in *Father Figure*, 43–56. Also see John Demos, "The Changing Face of Fatherhood," *Past, Present, and Personal: The Family and the Life Course in American History* (New York, 1986), 11–67.

38. Mintz, *Prison of Expectations*, 59–101.

39. Leonard Benson, *Fatherhood: A Sociological Perspective* (New York, 1968), 38, 43–44, 46–47, 55, 58–61, 73–85, 166, 323; Lorna McKee and Margaret O'Brien, "The Father Figure: Some Current Orientations and Historical Perspectives," in *Father Figure*, 3–25; Sklar, *Catharine Beecher*, 153, 265.

40. On nineteenth-century images of the female role and gender distinctions, see Welter, "The Cult of True Womanhood, 1820–1860," 131–75; Sklar, *Catharine Beecher*, 84–85, 174–75, 211–13; Nina Baym, *Women's Fiction: A Guide to Novels By and About Women in America, 1820–1870* (Ithaca, N.Y., 1978); Demos, "American Family in Past Time," 433–34; Patricia M. Alexander, "The Creation of the American Eve: The Cultural Dialogue on the Nature and Role of Women in Late Eighteenth Century America," *Early American Literature*, 9 (1975), 252–66; Ruth H. Block, "American Feminine Ideals in Transition: The Rise of the Moral Mother, 1785–1815," *Feminist Studies*, 4 (1978), 101–26.

41. Norton, *Liberty's Daughters*, 155–299; Norton, "'What an Alarming Crisis Is This': Southern Women and the American Revolution," in *The Southern Experience in the American Revolution*, eds. Jeffrey J. Crow and Larry Tise (Chapel Hill, N.C., 1978); Linda K. Kerber, *Women of the Republic: Intellect and Ideology in Revolutionary America* (Chapel Hill, N.C., 1980).

42. Linda K. Kerber, "Daughters of Columbia: Educating Women for the Republic, 1787–1805," in Stanley Elkins and Eric McKitrick, eds., *The Hofstadter Aegis: A Memorial* (New York, 1974); Ann D. Gordon, "The Young Ladies Academy of Philadelphia, in *Women of America: A History*, eds. Carol Ruth Berkin and Mary Beth Norton (Boston, 1979), 68–91; Kenneth Lockridge, *Literacy in Colonial New England* (New York, 1974); Maris A. Vinovskis and Richard M. Bernard, "Beyond Catharine Beecher: Female Education in the Antebellum Period," *Signs: Journal of Women and Culture in Society*, 3 (1978); Degler, *At Odds*, 150, 154–56, 267–89, 392–93.

43. Tocqueville, *Democracy in America*, vol. 1: 315, vol. 2: 209–14, 222–25.

44. On courtship and marriage, see Ellen K. Rothman, *Hands and Hearts: A History of Courtship in America* (New York, 1984); Cott, *Bonds of Womanhood*, 80–83;

Demos, "Images of the Family, Then and Now," 53–54. On the ideological responsibilities assigned to nineteenth-century women, see Sklar, *Catharine Beecher*, 84–85, 96–97, 174–75.

45. Ann Douglas, "The Road to Marriage," *New Republic* (October 8, 1984), 36–41; Cott, *Bonds of Womanhood*, 80–83; Sklar, *Catharine Beecher*, 28, 60, 193–95.

46. Mintz, *Prison of Expectations*, 16–18, 59, 117–18, 193, Degler, *At Odds*, 42–43, 52–53, 83–85, 91, 99, 158, 379.

47. On reform and the family, see Ryan, *Cradle of the Middle Class*, 89–91, 105–44.

48. Ross W. Beales, Jr., "In Search of the Historical Child: Miniature Adulthood and Youth in Colonial New England," *American Quarterly*, 27 (1975), 379–98, questions whether colonial children were in fact viewed as miniature adults. He notes that New Englanders drew distinctions between the legal responsibilities of different age groups and that the Puritan religion treated children and youth differently from the middle aged. The opposing view that colonial Americans, while recognizing the immaturity of children, assigned them a variety of adulthood responsibilities can be found in Kiefer, *American Children Through Their Books*, 1, 94, 225; Michael Zuckerman, *Peaceable Kingdoms: New England Towns in the Eighteenth Century* (New York, 1970), 73; Sandford Fleming, *Children and Puritanism: The Place of Children in the Life and thought of the New England Churches, 1620–1847* (New Haven, 1933), 16, 60, 66–67, 153, 188; John Demos, *A Little Commonwealth: Family Life in Plymouth Colony* (New York, 1970), 69, 134–46, 138–40, 142, 146, 182; Demos, "Developmental Perspectives on the History of Childhood," *Journal of Interdisciplinary History*, 2 (1971), 315–27; Demos, "American Family in Past Time," 428; Joseph F. Kett, "Adolescence and Youth in Nineteenth-Century America," *Journal of Interdisciplinary History*, 2 (1971), 285–86.

   Beales advances an argument for colonial New England similar to that made in Kett, *Rites of Passage*, 36, concerning the early nineteenth century: that the period of protected dependency was much shorter in the past than it is today, but that the transition to full adulthood independence took longer than it does now. Colonial youth achieved economic independence, established separate households, married, and attained political rights over a much longer period of time than is the case today.

49. Sunley, "Early Nineteenth-Century American Literature on Childrearing," 159–60, 162; Wishy, *Child and the Republic*, 42–49; Kuhn, *Mother's Role in Childhood Education*, 1–190; Degler, *At Odds*, 86–110.

50. Mintz, *Prison of Expectations*, 12–13, 18–19, 28–30, 39; Kett, *Rites of Passage*, 113–21; Sklar, *Catharine Beecher*, ch. 11.

51. On the emergence of a modern conception of adolescence, see Kett, *Rites of Passage*, 111–43.

52. Ibid.

53. Ann Foner, "Age Stratification and the Changing Family," *American Journal of Sociology* (1978 supplement), S345, S349, S356–57.

54. Kett, *Rites of Passage*, 111–43.

55. Lynne Carol Halem, *Divorce Reform: Changing Legal and Social Perspectives* (New York, 1980), 9–26; Davis, *Antebellum American Culture*, 7–8, 95–97.

56. On the history of divorce, see Nelson Manfred Blake, *The Road to Reno: A History of Divorce in the United States* (New York, 1962); Halem, *Divorce Reform*, 9–26; Nancy F. Cott, "Eighteenth Century Family and Social Life Revealed in Massachusetts Divorce Records," *Journal of Social History*, 10 (1976), 32; Cott, "Divorce

and the Changing Status of Women in Eighteenth Century Massachusetts," *William and Mary Quarterly*, 3rd ser., 33 (1976), 586–614; Robert L. Griswold, *Family and Divorce in California, 1850–1890: Victorian Illusions and Everyday Realities* (Albany, N.Y., 1982).

57. Refer to note 56; Davis, *Antebellum American Culture*, 7–8, 95–97.

58. On married women's property rights, see Norma Basch, *In the Eyes of the Law: Women, Marriage, and Property in Nineteenth Century New York* (Ithaca, N.Y., 1982).

59. On changes in the law of child custody, see Michael Grossberg, "Who Gets the Child? Custody, Guardianship, and the Rise of a Judicial Patriarchy in Nineteenth-Century America," *Feminist Studies*, 9 (1983), 235–60.

60. On the relationship between family structure and the social and economic needs of nineteenth century society, see Demos, "Images of the American Family, Then and Now," 53; Jeffrey, "The Family as Utopian Retreat from the City," 21–41.

61. Tocqueville, *Democracy in America*, vol. 1: 315, vol. 2: 202–4; Degler, *At Odds*, 8–9, 18–19, 26–51, 174–75, 191–95, 307, 329. Demos, "Images of the American Family, Then and Now," 53–54, develops a somewhat similar analysis of "goodness of fit" and "built-in contradictions" in the nineteenth-century American middle class family. For a particularly perceptive analysis of the inherent stresses, contradictions, and "developmental discontinuities" of the contemporary American family, see Kenneth Keniston, *The Uncommitted: Alienated Youth in American Society* (New York, 1965), 289–308.

62. Mintz, *Prison of Expectations*, 50–51, 61–62, 186, 196–98.

63. Demos, "Images of the Family, Then and Now," 54; Kett, *Rites of Passage*, 14–37, 111–43; Foner, "Age Stratification and the Changing Family," s345, s349, s356–57; Michael Katz, *The People of Hamilton, Canada West* (Cambridge, Mass., 1975), 303–05; Johnson, *A Shopkeeper's Millennium*, 43–48, 59; Karen Halttunen, *Confidence Men and Painted Women* (New Haven, 1983), 12–13.

64. In the South a somewhat different domestic ideal predominated. A distinguishing characteristic of white Southern family life was the persistence of a "code of honor," a code that attached greater significance to the importance of hierarchy, duty, and family allegiance than did the new code of domesticity and respectability in the North. During the early nineteenth-century, white Southerners were much more likely than their Northern counterparts to marry at extremely early ages, intermarry with cousins or other near kin, and openly to acknowledge pragmatic reasons for marriage, such as fear of spinsterhood or financial advantage. Southerners were also more likely to use family names as first or middle names or to name sons after their fathers (tendencies illustrated by such names as Jefferson Davis, Langdon Cheves, and Preston Brooks). Unlike Northerners, who increasingly substituted guilt-inducing punishments for physical discipline, Southerners were more likely to administer corporal punishment publicly. Older notions of patriarchy remained more important in the South, evident in the Southern conception of womanhood, defined in terms of purity, leisure, and subordination; in the custom of women coming to the dining table only after men had been served; and in statutes declaring that Southern wives did not have first claim on their own children in cases of death or divorce.

    On the distinctive Southern view of marriage and on contrasting regional definitions of the family circle, see Catharine Clinton, *Plantation Mistress: Woman's World in the Old South* (New York, 1982), 36–58, 60; Bertram Wyatt-Brown, *Southern Honor: Ethics and Behavior in the Old South* (New York, 1983), 120–25, 138–61, 241. On the continuing significance of the code of honor, see

Wyatt-Brown, *Southern Honor*, 149–74. On the ideal of Southern womanhood, see Anne Frior Scott, *The Southern Lady: From Pedestal to Politics, 1830–1930* (Chicago, 1970), 5–21.

Most case studies of nineteenth century Southern families have focused on the planter elite. These include such valuable works as Robert Manson Myers, *The Children of Pride* (New Haven, 1972); Carol K. Bleser, *The Hammonds of Redcliffe* (New York, 1981); Jane Turner Censer, *North Carolina Planters and Their Children, 1800–1860* (Baton Rouge, La., 1984), as well as a series of recent dissertations, such as Russell L. Blake, "Ties of Intimacy: Social Values and Personal Relationships of Ante-bellum Slaveholders" (University of Michigan, Ann Arbor, 1978); Ann Williams Boucher, "Wealthy Planter Families in Nineteenth Century Alabama" (University of Connecticut, Storrs, 1978); and Steven Stowe, "All the Relations of Life: A Study in Sexuality, Family, and Social Values in the Southern Planter Class" (State University of New York at Stony Brook, 1979).

On communitarian experiments in nineteenth-century America, see Arthur Bestor, *Backwoods Utopias: The Sectarian and Owenite Phases of Communitarian Socialism in America, 1663–1829* (Philadelphia, 1950); Maren L. Carden, *Oneida: Utopian Community to Modern Corporation* (New York, 1969); Donald D. Egbert and Stow Persons, *Socialism and American Life* (Princeton, 1952); Michael Fellman, *The Unbounded Frame: Freedom and Community in Nineteenth Century American Utopianism* (Westport, Conn., 1973); Ivor Grattan-Guinness, *Joseph Fourier, 1768–1830* (Cambridge, Mass., 1972); J.F.C. Harrison, *Quest for the New Moral World: Robert Owen and the Owenites in Britain and America* (London, England, 1969); Mark Holloway, *Heavens on Earth: Utopian Communities in America, 1680–1880* (New York, 1951); Richard W. Leopold, *Robert Dale Owen* (New York, 1940); Raymond Lee Muncy, *Sex and Marriage in Utopian Communities: Nineteenth Century America* (Bloomington, Ind., 1973); Robert A. Parker, *A Yankee Saint* (1935; reprint, Hamden, Conn., 1973); William H. Pease, *Black Utopia: Negro Communal Experiment in America* (Madison, Wisc., 1963); Sidney Pollard and John Salt, eds., *Robert Owen: Prophet of the Poor* (Cranbury, N.J., 1971); William Wilson, *The Angel and the Serpent* (Bloomington, Ind., 1964).

65. On the history of the Mormons and the practice of polygamy, see Julie Roy Jeffrey, *Frontier Women: The Trans-Mississippi West, 1849–1880* (New York, 1978), 164–75; Leonard J. Arrington, *Great Basin Kingdom* (Lincoln, Neb., 1958); Fawn M. Brodie, *No Man Knows My History: The Life of Joseph Smith* (New York, 1945); Robert B. Flanders, *Nauvoo: Kingdom on the Mississippi* (Urbana, Ill., 1965); Norman F. Furniss, *The Mormon Conflict, 1850–1859* (New Haven, 1960); Marvin S. Hill and James B. Allen, eds., *Mormonism and American Culture* (New York, 1972); Thomas F. O'Dea, *The Mormons* (New Haven, 1957); Kimball Young, *Isn't One Wife Enough* (Westport, Conn., 1954).

66. For evidence of public concern about the early nineteenth century American family, see David Brion Davis, *Homicide in American Fiction: A Study in Social Values* (Ithaca, N.Y., 1957), 148, 151–54. Also see Walters, *Antislavery Appeal*, 93. On contemporary English anxieties about the family and domestic morality, see Houghton, *The Victorian Frame of Mind*, 359–72.

CHAPTER IV

1. Quoted in Leon F. Litwack, *Been in the Storm So Long: The Aftermath of Slavery* (New York, 1979), 204.

2. Ronald Walters, *The Antislavery Appeal: American Abolitionism After 1830* (Baltimore, 1976), 93.

3. Herbert G. Gutman, *The Black Family in Slavery and Freedom, 1750–1925* (New York, 1976), 327–60; James D. Anderson, "Black Conjugations," *American Scholar*, 46 (Summer, 1977), 386, 388.

4. Refer to note 3.

5. Norton, Gutman, and Berlin, "Afro-American Family in the Age of Revolution," 175–91.

6. Gutman, *Black Family in Slavery and Freedom*, 327–60.

7. *Ibid.*, 344.

Southern slavery differed from slavery elsewhere in the Western Hemisphere in the slaves' ability to establish a strong and durable family life. This was the result of the demographic fact that only in the American South was the ratio of male slaves to female slaves roughly equal. In the Caribbean and throughout Latin America, female slaves constituted significantly less than half the black population. In Cuba in 1860, for instance, there were 156 male slaves for every 100 female slaves. In the United States in 1850, there were 98 female slaves for every 100 male slaves. In fact, the ratio of male to female slaves was actually more equal than the sex ratio among Southern whites.

On comparative slave sex ratios, see John W. Blassingame, *The Slave Community: Plantation Life in the Antebellum South* (New York, 1979), 149–50; Carl N. Degler, *Neither Black Nor White: Slavery and Race Relations in Brazil and the United States* (New York, 1971), 61–62.

8. On the strength and adaptability of the slave kinship system, see Gutman, *Black Family in Slavery and Freedom*, 13, 102, 260–62, 304–5, 308, 345–46.

In certain superficial respects, the demographic characteristics of slave family life closely resembled those of Southern white families. Although the birthrate among Southern slaves was much higher than the rate of slaves elsewhere in the New World, it was not significantly different from the rate among Southern whites. Southern slave women, like Southern white women, spaced their children closely together, because of a short period of breast-feeding, which averaged just one year against two or three in the West Indies. Both Southern slave and Southern white women experienced a high degree of childlessness (15–20 percent of slave women who had completed their childbearing years bore no children, compared to just 3.8 percent of Northern white women). And like Southern white women, slave women began to reduce their fertility rate prior to the Civil War, although among slaves the decline began somewhat later and occurred less rapidly.

Southern white and black family lives differed in two important respects. First, slave women began to bear children nearly two years earlier than white women, apparently because slaves did not have to delay marriage for financial and property reasons. Second, slave women, particularly on smaller farms and plantations, were much more likely to live apart from their spouses. On farms with fifteen or fewer slaves, only one-fifth of all slave households had two parents present.

On differences between white and black Southern family patterns, see Robert W. Fogel and Stanley L. Engerman, "Recent Findings in the Study of Slave Demography and Family Structure," *Social Science Research*, 63 (1979), 575–77; John B. Boles, *Black Southerners, 1619–1869* (Lexington, Ky., 1983), 100–101; Richard Sutch, "The Care and Feeding of Slavery," in *Reckoning with Slavery: A Critical Study in the Quantitative History of American Negro Slavery*, ed. Paul A. David et al. (New York, 1976), 283–92. On similarities in Southern black and white birthrates and child spacing, see Fogel and Engerman, "Recent Findings," 575. On differences in Southern black and white marriage and childrearing patterns, see Fogel and Engerman, "Recent Findings," 572–75. For a differing view, see Gutman, "The World Two Cliometricians Made," *Journal of Negro History*, (1975), 63–64. On differences in Southern black and white residential patterns within marriage, see Fogel and Engerman, "Recent Findings," 579; Boles, *Black Southerners*, 75–76, 107; Gutman, "The World Two Cliometricians Made," 62.

9. On the slave family's lack of legal protections, see Gutman, *Black Family in Slavery and Freedom*, 52, 293–96, 556 n. 4. Abream Scriven, quoted in Gutman, *Black Family in Slavery and Freedom*, 35–36, 238.

10. On disruption of families with children, see Gutman, *Black Family in Slavery and Freedom*, 146–9, 319, 570 n. 7. Nancy Gardner, quoted in Robert Fogel and Stanley Engerman, *Time on the Cross: The Economics of American Negro Slavery* (Boston, 1974), 143.

11. Gutman, *Black Family in Slavery and Freedom*, 317–19, 354–59; Gutman, "Slave Family and Its Legacies," 195–97; Engerman, "Commentary," in Michael Craton, ed., *Roots and Branches: Current Directions in Slave Studies* (Toronto, 1979), 206; Engerman, "The Realities of Slavery," 57–58.

12. On the residence of slave husbands and wives on separate plantations, see Gutman, *Black Family in Slavery and Freedom*, 131, 135–38, 141–42, 284–85. Quotations from Litwack, *Been in the Storm So Long*, 235.

13. On unusual age combinations in slave marriages, see Herbert G. Gutman and Richard Sutch, "Victorians All? The Sexual Mores and Conduct of Slaves and their Masters," in *Reckoning with Slavery: A Critical Study in the Quantiative History of American Negro Slavery*, ed. Paul A. David et al. (New York, 1976), 146–48. On proportions of slaves marrying, see Fogel and Engerman, "Recent Findings," 575–77.

14. Eugene D. Genovese, *Roll, Jordan, Roll: The World the Slaves Made* (New York, 1974), 482–501; Jacqueline Jones, *Labor of Love, Labor of Sorrow: Black Women, Work, and the Family From Slavery to the Present* (New York, 1985), 4–5, 12–13, 29–43; Gutman, *Black Family in Slavery and Freedom*, 59–60, 86, 189–91, 307, 346; Deborah White, *A'r'nt I a Woman: Female Slaves in the Plantation South* (New York, 1985).

15. On the role of slave parents, see Gutman, *Black Family in Slavery and Freedom*, 59–60, 86, 189–91, 307, 346; Litwack, *Been in the Storm So Long*, 238; Willie Lee Rose, "Childhood in Bondage" in *Slavery and Freedom*, ed. William H. Freeling (New York, 1982), 37–48.

16. Rose, "Childhood in Bondage," 37–48; John B. Boles, *Black Southerners*, 151–53; Lawrence W. Levine, *Black Culture and Black Consciousness: Afro-American Folk Thought From Slavery to Freedom* (New York, 1977); Thomas L. Webber, *Deep Like the Rivers: Education in the Slave Quarter Community, 1831–1865* (New York, 1978).

17. On slave courtship and marriage, see Blassingame, *Slave Community*, 156–70; Gutman, *Black Family in Slavery and Freedom*, 269–77, 281–84; Litwack, *Been in the Storm So Long*, 239–40.

18. Refer to note 17.

19. On slave childbearing, see Gutman, *Black Family in Slavery and Freedom*, 50, 60–61, 76–77, 163; Fogel and Engerman, "Recent Findings," 572, 574–75.

20. On the induction of slave children into the labor force, see Gutman, *Black Family in Slavery and Freedom*, 142, 207–09, 366, 402–12.

21. On older slaves, see Gutman, *Black Family in Slavery and Freedom*, 594–95, 597 n. 28; Gutman and Sutch, "Victorians All?" 148–53.

22. On differences in Southern black and white mortality rates, Fogel and Engerman, "Recent Findings," 576–77; Boles, *Black Southerners*, 100–101; Sutch, "The Care and Feeding of Slaves," 283–92.

23. On slave rations, see Lee and Passell, *New Economic View of American History*, 189–91; Sutch, "Care and Feeding of Slaves," 231–65. On nutritional deficiencies, see Boles, *Black Southerners*, 91–96; Sutch, "Care and Feeding of Slaves," 268–82; Todd L. Savitt, *Medicine and Slavery: The Diseases and Health Care of Blacks in Antebellum Virginia* (Urbana, Ill., 1978).

24. On the physical conditions of slave life, see Boles, *Black Southerners*, 88; Susan Previant Lee and Peter Passell, *A New Economic View of American History* (New York, 1979), 189–91, Sutch, "Care and Feeding of Slaves," 231–65. On the lack of sanitation in the slave quarters, see Boles, *Black Southerners*, 89–90.

25. On slave cabins, see Lee and Passell, *New Economic View of American History*, 191–92; Sutch, "Care and Feeding of Slaves," 292–98.

26. Genovese, *Roll, Jordan, Roll*, 529.

27. On the abolitionist critique of sexual mores under slavery, see Walters, *Antislavery Appeal*, 74–76, 95.

28. On miscegenation and the sexual abuse of slave women, see Walters, *Antislavery Appeal*, 80, 83–86, 392–93, 399–402; Fogel and Engerman, *Time on the Cross*, 132; Stanley L. Engerman, "The Realities of Slavery: A Review of Recent Evidence," *International Journal of Comparative Sociology*, 20 (1979), 58; Gutman and Sutch, "Victorians All?," 149–53; Blassingame, *Slave Community*, 154–55; Litwack, *Been in the Storm So Long*, 239.

29. On slave breeding, see Calhoun, *Social History of the American Family*, vol. 2: 243–46; Boles, *Black Southerners*, 69; Gutman and Sutch, "Victorians All?" 154–61.

30. On premarital sexual activity, see Gutman, *Black Family in Slavery and Freedom*, 60–75, 80–86, 385–402. Also see Genovese, *Roll, Jordan, Roll*, 459–60, 471, 475.

31. On slave sexual mores, see Gutman, *Black Family in Slavery and Freedom*, 8–9, 25–27, 60, 386–87, 536, 636 n. 13; Genovese, *Roll, Jordan, Roll*, 459–60, 471, 475. Quotation is from Litwack, *Been in the Storm So Long*, 243.

32. Gutman quoted in *Time* (February 14, 1977), 76–77. On the strains the Civil War inflicted on the slave family, see Jones, *Labor of Love, Labor of Sorrow*, 46–51; Gutman, *Black Family in Slavery and Freedom*, 19–28, 227, 268–69, 321–24, 367–75, 551–52 n. 29, 546–47 n. 11.

33. Litwack, *Been in the Storm So Long*, 229, 230, 239, 246–47; Jones, *Labor of Love, Labor of Sorrow*, 50–57; Gutman, *Black Family in Slavery and Freedom*, 8–9, 18–24, 34–37, 139–43, 204–7, 366–85.

34. Litwack, *Been in the Storm So Long*, 240.

35. Ibid., 227.

36. On sharecropping and freed families, see Jones, *Labor of Love, Labor of Sorrow*, 58–68; Gutman, *Black Family in Slavery and Freedom*, 167–68, 442, 626 n. 5.

37. Litwack, *Been in the Storm So Long*, 244.

38. Ira Berlin, *Slaves Without Masters: The Free Negro in the Antebellum South* (New York, 1974), 15–132.

39. Ibid., 217–340.

40. On the plight of antebellum free blacks, refer to notes 38 and 39. Also see Leonard P. Curry, *The Free Black in Urban America, 1800–1850* (Chicago, 1981), 81–

95; Davis, *Antebellum American Culture*, 212–13, 273–76. The lives of free black women in antebellum Virginia are carefully examined in Suzanne Lebsock, *The Free Women of Petersburg: Status and Culture in a Southern Town, 1784–1850* (New York, 1984).

41. On historiographical treatment of free blacks and urban slaves, see Kenneth L. Kusmer, "Black Urban History in the United States: Retrospect and Prospect," *Trends in History*, 3 (1982), 57–69.

42. On living conditions of free blacks, see Curry, *Free Black in Urban America*, 49–54, 143; Kenneth L. Kusmer, *A Ghetto Takes Shape: Black Cleveland, 1870–1930* (Urbana, Ill., 1976), 12–13.

43. On the prevalence of two-parent households among free blacks, see Elizabeth H. Pleck, "The Two-Parent Household: Black Family Structure in Late Nineteenth Century Boston," *Journal of Social History*, 6 (1972), 3–31; Pleck, *Black Migration and Poverty in Boston, 1865–1900* (New York, 1979); Theodore Hershberg, "Free Blacks in Antebellum Philadelphia: A Study of Ex-Slaves, Freeborn and Socioeconomic Decline," *Journal of Social History*, 5 (1971), 186; Paul Lammermeir, "The Urban Black Family Structure in the Ohio Valley, 1859–1880," *Journal of Marriage and the Family*, 35 (1973), 454; James Oliver Horton and Lowes E. Horton, *Black Bostonians: Family Life and Community Struggle in the Antebellum North* (New York, 1979), 19–20; Crandell A. Shifflet, "The Household Composition of Rural Black Families: Louisa County, Virginia, 1880," *Journal of Interdisciplinary History*, 6 (1975), 235–60. In contrast to her earlier article, which was based on analysis of a single census and which stressed the prevalence of two-parent families, Pleck's book, which traces the same families longitudinally, discovers a great deal of marital instability.

44. On proportion of free blacks living in female-headed households, see Frank F. Furstenberg, Jr., Theodore Hershberg, and John Modell, "The Origins of the Female-Headed Black Family: The Impact of the Urban Experience," in *Philadelphia: Work, Space, Family, and Group Experience in the Nineteenth Century, Essays Toward an Interdisciplinary History of the City*, ed. Theodore Hershberg (New York, 1981). Lebsock, *Free Women of Petersburg*, emphasizes the high number of female-headed households among free black women in Petersburg, Virginia.

    For the demographic characteristics of free black families, see Horton and Horton, *Black Bostonians*, 16–17, 21, 24. On the economic contribution of married black women to the family economy, see Pleck, "A Mother's Wage," 3–31.

45. B.M. Kuyk, "Seeking Family Relationships," *Negro History Bulletin*, 42 (July 1979), 60.

46. On older view of the matriarchal slave family, see E. Franklin Frazier, *The Negro Family in the United States* (New York, 1939), 341. Critical examinations of the older view can be found in Gutman, "The Slave Family and Its Legacies," 183, 186–90; Gutman, *Black Family in Slavery and Freedom*, 13, 102–06, 558–59, 602–3, 633–34.

47. On the continuing importance of the extended kinship network, see Gutman, *Black Family in Slavery and Freedom*, 434–39; Nell Irvin Painter, *Exodusters: Black Migration to Kansas After Reconstruction* (New York, 1976); Carol Stack, *All Our Kin: Strategies for Survival in a Black Community* (New York, 1974).

CHAPTER V

1. Margaret Byington, *Homestead: The Households of a Mill Town* (1910; reprint, Pittsburgh, 1974), 3.

2. Ibid., 1–2, 36–37; Melvyn Dubovsky, *Industrialism and the American Worker, 1865–1920* (Arlington, Ill., 1975), 3, 12–15, 19.

3. Samuel P. Hayes, "Homestead Revisited," introduction to Byington, *Homestead*, xxxvi; Byington, *Homestead*, 36–37; David Brody, *Workers in Industrial America: Essays on the Twentieth Century Struggle* (New York, 1980), 16.

4. Byington, *Homestead*, 30, 38–41, 63, 74–80, 107–09, 125–26, 138–44, 201.

5. Ibid., 131, 135–43.

6. On the essential facts of working class life, see Dubovsky, *Industrialism and the American Worker*, 2–3, 9–22; Stephan Thernstrom, *Poverty and Progress: Social Mobility in a Nineteenth Century City* (Cambridge, Mass., 1971), 18, 20, 22, 136; Leslie Woodcock Tentler, *Wage-Earning Women: Industrial Work and Family Life in the United States, 1900–1930* (New York, 1979), 87, 88. Alexander Keyssar, *Out of Work: The First Century of Unemployment in Massachusetts* (Cambridge, England, 1986), the first historical attempt to investigate systematically the human costs of unemployment, estimates that during the hardest times, upwards of 40 percent of all Massachusetts workers and over 60 percent of all workers in some blue-collar industries, were out of a job for part of the year, usually for four months or more. Even when the economy was healthy, about one in four workers, and much higher proportions of industrial workers, could expect to be unemployed for three months a year.

7. On the conditions of the working class, see Foster Rhea Dulles, *Labor in America: A History* (New York, 1964), 79.

8. Edward C. Kirkland, *A History of American Economic Life* (New York, 1941), 336, 337–38.

9. On Patrick Kennedy, see Peter Collier and David Horowitz, *The Kennedys: An American Drama* (New York, 1984), 21–22; James MacGregor Burns, *Edward Kennedy and the Camelot Legacy* (New York, 1976), 20–21. On Irish immigration, see Cecil Woodham-Smith, *The Great Hunger* (New York, 1962); Oscar Handlin, *Boston's Immigrants: A Study in Acculturation* (Cambridge, Mass., 1941).

10. Maldwyn Allen Jones, *American Immigration* (Chicago, 1960); Philip Taylor, *The Distant Mirror: European Migration to the United States of America* (New York, 1971); Marcus L. Hansen, *The Atlantic Migration, 1607–1860* (Cambridge, Mass., 1940); Norman J. Ware, *The Industrial Worker, 1840–1860* (Boston, 1924); Herbert G. Gutman, *Work, Culture, and Society in Industrializing America* (New York, 1976); James West Davidson and Mark Hamilton Lytle, *After the Fact: The Art of Historical Detection* (New York, 1982), 205–29.

11. Refer to note 10.

12. Caroline Golab, "The Impact of the Industrial Experience on the Immigrant Family: The Huddled Masses Reconsidered" in *Immigrants in Industrial America, 1850–1920*, ed. Richard L. Ehrlich (Charlottesville, Va., 1977), 17; Jerome Karabel, "Why There Is No Socialism in America," *New York Review of Books* (February 8, 1979), 24.

13. A. Gordon Darroch, "Migration in the Nineteenth Century: Fugitives or Families in Motion?," *Journal of Family History*, 6 (1981), 257–77; Tamara K. Hareven, *Family Time and Industrial Time: The Relationship Between Family and Work in a New England Industrial Community* (Cambridge, England, 1982), 2, 109, 115–19, 165, 363–65.

14. Refer to note 13.

15. In the new land, age roles often appeared to be inverted, since children often had to assist adults, who had greater difficulty mastering language skills and American customs.

On the problems encountered by immigrants, see Virginia Yans McLaughlin, "Patterns of Work and Family Organization: Buffalo's Italians," *Journal of Interdisciplinary History*, 2 (1971), 299–314; Rudolph Vecoli, "Contadini in Chicago: A Critique of the Uprooted," *Journal of American History*, 51 (1964), 404–16; Handlin, *Boston's Immigrants*, 25–123.

16. Extract from Rocco Corresco, "Biography of a Bootblack," The *Independent*, 56 (1902), 2863ff., quoted in Ginzberg and Berman, *American Worker in the Twentieth Century*, 82–85.

17. Tamara Hareven, *Family Time and Industrial Time*, 2, 101–2, 109, 115–19, 165, 219, 363–65; Darroch, "Migration in the Nineteenth Century," 257–77. For the earlier view on the destructive impact of industrialization, see Ronald L. Howard, *A Social History of American Family Sociology* (Westport, Conn., 1981), 51, 53, 62, 66, 68, 77, 80, 87–88.

18. Hareven, *Family Time and Industrial Time*, 101–02, 109, 219, 364–66; Michael Anderson, *Approaches to Family History, 1750–1914* (London, England, 1980), 75–83; Susan J. Kleinberg, "The Systematic Study of Urban Women" in *Class, Sex, and the Woman Worker*, eds. Milton Cantor and Bruce Laurie (Westport, Conn., 1977), 20–42.

19. On the persistence of the working-class family economy, see Tamara Hareven, "Review Essay: Origins of the Modern Family in the United States," *Journal of Social History*, 17 (1983), 341–42. On living costs, see Garraty, *New Commonwealth*, 129, 133, 137. On women and children working, see Hareven, *Family Time and Industrial Time*, 208; Elizabeth H. Pleck, "A Mother's Wage: Income Earning Among Married Italian and Black Women, 1896-1911," in *A Heritage of Her Own*, eds. Nancy F. Cott and Elizabeth H. Pleck (New York, 1979), 367–92; Carol Groneman, "'She Earns as a Child—She Pays as a Man'—Women Workers in a Mid-Nineteenth-Century New York City Community," in *Immigrants in Industrial America*, ed. R. L. Ehrlich, 35, 38, 40.

20. On the role of the working-class housewife, see Hays, "Homestead Revisited" in Byington, *Homestead*, xxiii-xxv. On boarders, see Carl N. Degler, *At Odds: Women and the Family in America from the Revolution to the Present* (New York, 1980), 393–94; Susan Strasser, *Never Done: A History of American Housework* (New York, 1982), 148–51; Myfanwy Morgan and Hilda H. Golden, "Immigrant Families in an Industrial City: A Study of Households in Holyoke, 1880," *Journal of Family History*, 4 (1979), 59–68; A. Gordon Darroch, "Migration in the Nineteenth Century: Fugitives or Families in Motion?" *Journal of Family History*, 6 (1981), 257–77; Michael Anderson, "Family and Class in Nineteenth Century Cities," *Journal of Family History*, 2 (1977), 139–49; Claudia Goldin, "Family Strategies and the Family Economy in the Late Nineteenth Century: The Role of Secondary Workers" in *Philadelphia: Work, Space, Family, and Group Experience in the Nineteenth Century, Essays Toward an Interdisciplinary History of the City*, ed. Theodore Hershberg (New York, 1981), 292.

21. On outwork, see Susan E. Hirsch, *Roots of the American Working Class: The Industrialization of Crafts in Newark, 1800-1860* (Philadelphia, 1978), 15, 22–23; Leslie Woodcock Tentler, *Wage-Earning Women: Industrial Work and Family Life in the United States, 1900-1930* (New York, 1979), 142–43.

22. On housework, see Ruth Schwartz Cowan, *More Work for Mother: The Ironies of Household Technology* (New York, 1983), 24, 26, 48; Susan Strasser, *Never Done*, 11–124; Naomi Bliven, "Review," *New Yorker* (September 6, 1982), 104–6.

23. On shifting standards of cleanliness, see Barbara Ehrenreich and Dierdre English, *For Her Own Good* (Garden City, N.Y., 1978), 128–31; Cowan, *More Work for Mother*, 36, 40–41, 53, 63–66; Strasser, *Never Done*, 22, 29, 34–35.

24. On child labor see, Goldin, "Family Strategies and the Family Economy in the Late Nineteenth Century," 284, 289; Theodore Hershberg, *Philadelphia: Work, Space, Family and Group Experience in the Nineteenth Century,* 235, 236; John Modell, Frank F. Furstenberg, Jr., Theodore Hershberg, "Social Change and Transitions to Adulthood in Historical Perspective," in *Philadelphia: Work, Space, Family and Group Experience in the Nineteenth Century,* ed. T. Hershberg, 335.

25. On the breakdown of the apprenticeship system, see Sean Wilentz, *Chants Democratic: New York City and the Rise of the American Working Class, 1788-1850* (New York, 1984), 33, 48, 50, 52, 119; Joseph F. Kett, *Rites of Passage: Adolescence in America, 1790 to the Present* (New York, 1977), 145-52, 169.

26. On the economic contribution of child laborers, see Goldin, "Family Strategies and the Family Economy in the Late Nineteenth Century," 277-305.

27. Ibid.; Tentler, *Wage-Earning Women,* 89-93.

28. Edward C. Kirkland, *History of American Economic Life,* rev. ed. (New York, 1941), 348; Foster Rhea Dulles, *Labor In America: A History* (New York, 1969), 78.

29. Kirkland, *History of American Economic Life,* 348.

30. Michael R. Haines, "Poverty, Economic Stress, and the Family in a Late Nineteenth-Century American City: Whites in Philadelphia, 1880," in *Philadelphia: Work, Space, Family and Group Experience in the Nineteenth Century,* 258; Kett, *Rites of Passage,* 151.

31. On the family life cycle and economic hardship, see Tentler, *Wage-Earning Women,* 88; Hareven, *Family Time and Industrial Time,* 208; Garraty, *The New Commonwealth,* 129, 133, 137; Haines, "Poverty, Economic Stress, and the Family," 242, 256. On the hardships of old age, see Hareven, *Family Time and Industrial Time,* 88; Garraty, *New Commonwealth,* 129, 133, 137; Kett, *Rites of Passage,* 151; Hershberg, *Philadelphia: Work, Space, Family and Group Experience,* 238; Haines, "Poverty, Economic Stress, and the Family," 262.

32. On the significance of property ownership, see Richard L. Bushman, "Family Security in the Transition from Farm to City, 1750-1850, *Journal of Family History,* 6 (1981), 238-56.

33. On the importance attached to ownership of a house, refer to note 32; Goldin, "Family Strategies and the Family Economy in the Late Nineteenth Century," 292.

34. On the similarities between working-class and middle-class families, see Hareven, "Review Essay," 341-42; Degler, *At Odds,* ch. 6. On differences among ethnic groups and between working-class and middle-class families, see Hareven, "Review Essay," 341-42; Golab, "The Impact of the Industrial Experience on the Immigrant Family," 1-32; Groneman, "'She Earns as a Child—She Pays as a Man,'" 33-46; Stanley Lieberson, *A Piece of the Pie: Blacks and White Immigrants Since 1880* (Berkeley, 1980), 1, 10-14, 21-24, 41-47, 173-78, 193-98.

35. On differences in housing patterns, see Taylor, *Distant Mirror,* 205-6.

36. On ethnic differences in female and child labor, see Golab, "The Impact of the Industrial Experience on the Immigrant Family," 19; Hershberg, *Philadelphia: Work, Space, Family, and Group Experience,* 237; Pleck, "A Mother's Wages," 367-92; Goldin, "Family Strategies and the Family Economy in the Late Nineteenth Century," 284.

37. On intermarriage, see Taylor, *Distant Mirror,* 210-11, 232. On the decline in fertility among immigrant groups, see W.F. Ogburn, "Eleven Questions Concerning American Marriage," in *The Family: Source Materials for the Study of*

Family and Personality, ed. Edward Byron Reuter and Jessie Ridgway Runner (New York, 1931), 183–91; Ogburn, "Factors Affecting Marital Status," in Reuter and Runner, eds., *Family,* 191–200; Louis I. Dublin, "The Measurement of Family Well-being," in *Family,* 176–83.

38. Kirkland, *History of American Economic Life,* 334.

39. On manufacturers' efforts to adapt the organization of the factory to familial values, see Kirkland, *History of American Economic Life,* 334, 337–38; Thomas Dublin, *Women at Work: The Transformation of Work and Community in Lowell, Massachusetts, 1826–1860* (New York, 1979), 3–22.

40. On women and families within early factories, see Dublin, *Women and Work.*

41. On heightened family cohesiveness, see Hirsch, *Roots of the American Working Class,* 53, 58–60, 65–66.

42. On the continuing importance of kinship ties in the workplace, see Hareven, *Family Time and Industrial Time,* 38–40, 47, 62, 89, 123.

43. On the importance of scientific management techniques in circumscribing the role of the extended kinship group, see Hareven, *Family Time and Industrial Time,* 363–66.

44. U.S. Bureau of the Census, *Statistical History of the United States from Colonial Times to the Present* (New York, 1965), 2, 4, 9, 14.

45. John Mack Faragher, *Women and Men on the Overland Trail* (New Haven, 1979), 4, 11, 16, 18, 21–22.

46. Faragher, *Women and Men on the Overland Trail,* 4, 11, 16, 18, 21–22. Other important sources of information on the pioneer family can be found in Julie Roy Jeffrey, *Frontier Women: The Transmississippi West, 1840–1880* (New York, 1979); Sandra L. Myres, *Westering Women and the Frontier Experience, 1800–1915* (Albuquerque, N. Mex., 1982); Lillian Schlissel, *Women's Diaries of the Westward Journey* (New York, 1982); Joanna Stratton, *Pioneer Women* (New York, 1982).

47. Faragher, *Women and Men on the Overland Trail,* 32–33, 37–39.

48. Ibid., 71–84.

49. On gender roles and pioneering, see Faragher, *Women and Men on the Overland Trail,* 66, 69, 71–84, 106, 136–43; Jeffrey, *Frontier Women,* 25–50.

50. Stratton, *Pioneer Women,* 33–45; Myres, *Westering Women,* 98–139; Schlissel, *Women's Diaries of the Westward Journey,* 19–158; Jeffrey, *Frontier Women,* 25–50.

51. Everett Dick, *The Sod House Frontier, 1854–1890* (Lincoln, Nebr., 1954), 1–2; Robert Caro, *The Years of Lyndon Johnson: The Path to Power* (New York, 1983), 8–14.

52. Caro, *Years of Lyndon Johnson,* 3–18.

53. Ibid., 110–17.

54. Ibid.

55. For a firsthand account of the hardships of prairie life, see John Ise, *Sod and Stubble: The Story of a Kansas Homestead* (New York, 1936). Also see Joan M. Jensen, ed., *With These Hands: Women Working on the Land* (New York, 1981) and *Loosening the Bonds: Mid-Atlantic Farm Women, 1750–1850* (New Haven, 1986).

56. On time spent on farm housework, see Joann Vanek, "Work, Leisure, and Household Roles: Farm Households in the United States, 1920–1955," *Journal of Family History,* 5 (1980), 422–31; Garraty, *New Commonwealth,* 74.

57. Gilbert C. Fite, "Daydreams and Nightmares: The Late Nineteenth-Century Agricultural Frontiers," *Agricultural History*, 40 (1966), 285–91.

58. Ibid., 290–92.

59. Ibid., 291.

60. Octavius T. Howe, *Argonauts of '49* (Cambridge, Mass., 1923), 181–82.

61. On the agricultural revolution, see John L. Shover, *First Majority, Last Minority: The Transforming of Rural Life in America* (DeKalb, Ill., 1976), 4, 116; Garraty, *New Commonwealth*, 74; Susan Parvient Lee and Peter Passell, *A New Economic View of American History* (New York, 1979), 241–60, 263, 271–74, 292–301, 318–22; William L. Bowers, *The Country Life Movement in America, 1900–1920* (Port Washington, N.Y., 1974), 7–14.

62. On declining rural birthrates, see John Mack Faragher, "History From the Inside-Out: Writing the History of Women in Rural America," *American Quarterly*, 33 (1981), 547–48.

63. On rural out-migration, see Bowers, *Country Life Movement*, 13–16, 65–70; Hal S. Barron, *Those Who Stayed Behind: Rural Society in Nineteenth Century New England* (Cambridge, England, 1984), 112–31.

64. On the familial orientation of rural areas, see Barron, *Those Who Stayed Behind*, 54, 87, 100, 105–06, 127–29, 133–35, 155–56; Faragher, "History from the Inside-Out," 552–53.

65. On inheritance practices, see Mark Friedberger, "The Farm Family and the Inheritance Process: Evidence from the Corn Belt, 1870–1950," *Agricultural History*, 57 (1983), 1–13; Ronald Howard, *Social History of American Family Sociology*, 74–78; Bowers, *Country Life Movement*, 13–16, 65–72.

66. Peter Roberts, *Anthracite Coal Communities: A Study of the Demography, the Social, Educational and Moral Life of the Anthracite Regions* (New York, 1904); David Alan Corbin, *Life, Work, and Rebellion in the Coal Fields: The Southern West Virginia Miners, 1880–1922* (Urbana, Ill., 1981)

67. Roberts, *Anthracite Coal Communities*, 114, 346; *Testimony before the Industrial Commission*, ed. Benjamin Jones (Washington, D.C., 1899, vol. 12: 138 ff.) quoted in *American Worker in the Twentieth Century*, eds. Ginzberg and Berman, 51–65.

68. Garraty, *New Commonwealth*, 132–33, 154–55.

69. Corbin, *Life, Work, and Rebellion in the Coal Fields*, 40–42.

70. Roberts, *Anthracite Coal Communities*, 76–81, 87–95.

71. Ibid., 264, 269.

72. On the early age of marriage and high fertility rates in mining areas, see Michael R. Haines, "Fertility, Marriage, and Occupation in the Pennsylvania Anthracite Region, 1850–1880," *Journal of Family History*, 2 (1977), 28–55.

73. On the importance of supplementary income, see Roberts, *Anthracite Coal Communities*, 175, 181, 362; Corbin, *Life, Work, and Rebellion in the Coal Fields*, 15–16.

74. On role of women in coal-mining areas, see Corbin, *Life, Work, and Rebellion in the Coal Fields*, 33–34, 55.

75. On the frequency of premature death, irregular employment, disabling accidents, low wage scales, and inadequacy of public welfare mechanisms, see Dubovsky, *Industrialism and the American Worker*, 14–22; Thernstrom, *Poverty and Progress*, 18, 20, 22, 136.

76. On high death rates, see Peter Uhlenberg, "Changing Configurations of the Life Course," in *Transitions: The Family and the Life Course in Historical Perspective,* ed. Tamara K. Hareven (New York, 1978), 94–95.

77. On hours of work, see *Statistical History of the United States from Colonial Times to the Present,* 15, 82, 83, 91–93, 409; Dubovsky, *Industrialism and the American Worker,* 19; on the prevalence of accidents, see Dubovsky, *Industrialism and the American Worker,* 19; on housing conditions, see Garraty, *New Commonwealth,* 130–31.

78. On changes in 1920s, see James Patterson, *America's Struggle Against Poverty, 1900–1930* (Cambridge, Mass., 1981), 14–19.

CHAPTER VI

1. For information on the divorce of Claude H. Harman and Jessie Harman, see Harman v. Harman, Sup. Ct. of Cal., 198 *Cal.* 695, 247 *Pac.* 194; Lynne Carol Halem, *Divorce Reform: Changing Legal and Social Perspectives* (New York, 1980), 136.

2. On California divorce law, see Halem, *Divorce Reform,* 136; Elaine Tyler May, *Great Expectations: Marriage and Divorce in Post-Victorian America* (Chicago, 1980), 5–6, 30, 104.

3. On the changing functions and expectations assigned to the middle class family, see David Brion Davis, "The American Family and Boundaries in Historical Perspective," in *From Homicide to Slavery: Studies in American Culture* (New York, 1986), 166–83; John Demos, "Images of the Family, Then and Now," in *Changing Images of the Family,* eds. Virginia Tufte and Barbara Myerhoff (New Haven, 1979), 56–59.

4. On the turn-of-the-century crisis of the family, see Christopher Lasch, *Haven in a Heartless World: The Family Besieged* (New York, 1977), 8–9; Robert Briffault, ed., *Marriage: Past and Present* (Boston, 1956), 26; Peter Gabriel Filene, *Him/ Her/Self: Sex Roles in Modern America* (New York, 1976), 36–39.

5. On the rising turn of the century divorce rate, Lasch, *Haven in a Heartless World,* 8; May, *Great Expectations,* 2–5; J.P. Lichtenberger, *Divorce: A Social Interpretation* (New York, 1931), 154–86.

6. On the shrinking middle-class birthrate, see Lasch, *Haven in a Heartless World,* 8–9; David Kennedy, *Birth Control in America: The Career of Margaret Sanger* (New Haven, 1971), 42–44.

7. On the alarm sparked by the changing position of women, see Lasch, *Haven in a Heartless World,* 8–9; Frederick Lewis Allen, *Only Yesterday: An Informal History of the Nineteen-Twenties* (New York, 1931), 89, 92–93, 103–8. On the changes taking place in women's lives, see Sallie Westwood, *All Day, Every Day: Factory and Family in the Making of Women's Lives* (Urbana, Ill., 1985). On the revolution in morals and manners, see James G. McGovern, "The American Woman's Pre-World War I Freedom in Manners and Morals," *Journal of American History* 55 (1968), 315–33; Allen, *Only Yesterday,* 90–91, 100–101, 115; Henry F. May, *The End of American Innocence: A Study of the First Years of Our Own Time, 1912–1917* (New York, 1959), 340–47; John C. Burnham, "The Progressive Era Revolution in American Attitudes Toward Sex," *Journal of American History,* 59 (1972), 885–908.

8. On turn-of-the-century efforts to tighten divorce laws, see May, *Great Expecta-*

tions, 4–7; Lichtenberger, *Divorce*, 154–86; Morton Keller, *Affairs of State: Public Life in Late Nineteenth Century America* (Cambridge, Mass., 1977), 471.

9. On the trend toward increasingly stringent divorce procedures, refer to note 8.

10. On the ineffectuality of changes in divorce laws, see Lichtenberger, *Divorce*, 154–86; May, *Great Expectations*, 4–7.

11. On the falling birthrate and its impact on women's lives, see William F. Ogburn, "The Family as an Institution in Modern Society," in *The Family: Source Materials for the Study of Family and Personality*, eds. Edward Byron Reuter and Jessie Ridgway Runner (New York, 1931), 185; Filene, *Him/Her/Self*, 10.

12. On public fears of "race suicide," see Kennedy, *Birth Control in America*, 42, 44, 45, 123, 237; Lasch, *Haven in a Heartless World*, 8–9.

13. On legal responses to falling birth rates, see James Mohr, *Abortion in America: The Origins and Evolution of National Policy 1800–1900* (New York, 1978), 200–25; Kennedy, *Birth Control in America*, 218.

14. On changes in women's dress, see Eric Hobsbawm, *The Age of Capital* (London, England, 1975), 232–37; Filene, *Him/Her/Self*, 6–7, 68–71; Allen, *Only Yesterday*, 89, 103–08.

15. On the flapper, see McGovern, "American Woman's Pre-World War I Freedom in Manners and Morals," 322–33; May, *End of American Innocence*, 340–47. On women's increasing participation in roles outside the home, see Filene, *Him/Her/Self*, 20–29.

16. On changes in women's employment, see Alice Kessler-Harris, *Out to Work: A History of Wage-Earning Women in the United States* (New York, 1982), 217–49; Carl N. Degler, *At Odds: Women and the Family in America from the Revolution to the Present* (New York, 1978), 362–417. On the shifting boundaries of women's sphere, see Filene, *Him/Her/Self*, 5–35.

17. On the revolution in manners, see McGovern, "American Woman's Pre-World War I Freedom," 322–33; May, *End of American Innocence*, 340–47; Allen, *Only Yesterday*, 90–91, 100–101, 117. On vice films, see Robert Sklar, *Movie-Made America: A Cultural History of American Movies* (New York, 1975), 23.

18. On the purity crusade and the repeal of sexual reticence, see Nathan G. Hale, Jr., *Freud and the Americans: The Beginnings of Psychoanalysis in America* (New York, 1971), 252; James Reed, *From Private Vice to Public Virtue: The Birth Control Movement and American Society* (Princeton, 1983), 57; Burnham, "Progressive Era Revolution in American Attitudes Toward Sex," 885–908.

19. On changes in sexual conduct, see Sidney Ditzion, *Marriage, Morals and Sex in America* (New York, 1969), 393; William O'Neill, *Everyone Was Brave: A History of Feminism in America* (Chicago, 1974), 296–304, 312–18; Hale, *Freud and the Americans*, 475–76; Kennedy, *Birth Control in America*, 136.

20. On the problematic prospects of the American family, see Arthur Calhoun, *Social History of the American Family from Colonial Times to the Present* (New York, 1945), vol. 3: 323–32.

21. On efforts to reassert Victorian values, see Allen, *Only Yesterday*, 92–93.

22. On the emergence of a new companionate ideal of the family, see Lasch, *Haven in a Heartless World*, 37–43; Paula S. Fass, *The Damned and the Beautiful: American Youth in the 1920's* (New York, 1977), 71–95; Demos, "Images of the American Family, Then and Now," 56–69.

23. On social theory and the crisis of the family, see Halem, *Divorce Reform*, 56–66;

Fass, *Damned and the Beautiful*, 95–118; Lasch, *Haven in a Heartless World*, 29–36.

24. On shifting ideals of marriage, womanhood, and childhood, see Filene, *Him/Her/Self*, 5–35.

25. On the debate over the proper nature of marriage, see Ditzion, *Marriage, Morals and Sex in America*, 196–97, 224–25, 278–79, 355–70, 381–83.

26. On the companionate ideal of marriage, see Ben B. Lindsey and Wainwright Evans, *The Revolt of Modern Youth* (New York, 1925); Charles Larson, "Introduction" to Lindsey and Evans, *The Companionate Marriage*, ed. Charles Larson (1927; reprint, New York, 1972), n.n.; Fass, *Damned and the Beautiful*, 71–95.

27. On the impact of the new companionate ideal, see Fass, *Damned and the Beautiful*, 71–95; Kennedy, *Birth Control in America*, 138, 140, 160.

28. On the sexualization of marriage, see Fass, *Damned and the Beautiful*, 70–78.

29. On extent of sexual ignorance and the drive for sex education, see Edward Westermarck, *The Future of Marriage in Western Civilization* (New York, 1937), 49.

30. On the drive for birth control information, see Reed, *From Private Vice to Public Virtue*, 62.

31. On the psychological gulf separating husbands and wives, see Caplow et al., *Middletown Families*, 18–19. On the role of the father, see Mintz, *A Prison of Expectations*, ch. 4; John Higham, "Reorientation of American Culture in the 1890s" in *Origins of Modern Consciousness*, ed. John Weiss (Detroit, 1966), 25–32; Barbara Ehrenreich, "A Feminist's View of the New Man," *New York Times Magazine* (May 20, 1984), 36ff.

32. On the causes of the shift in the role of father, see Higham, "Reorientation of American Culture in the 1890s," 25–32; Ehrenreich, "A Feminist's View of the New Man," 36ff.

33. On the changing role of the father in Jewish families, see Sholem Asch, *Mother* (New York, 1937); Henry Roth, *Call It Sleep* (New York, 1934); Anzia Yesierski, *The Bread Givers* (New York, 1925); Abraham Cahan, *Yekl* (New York, 1896).

34. On the democratization of family relations, see Bronislaw Malinowski, "Parenthood, The Basis of Social Structure," in *The New Generation*, eds. V.F. Calverton and S.D. Schmalhausen (New York, 1930), 113–68; Fass, *Damned and the Beautiful*, 53–55, 83–95.

35. Malinowski, "Parenthood, The Basis of Social Structure," 113–68; Fass, *Damned and the Beautiful*, 55, 83–95.

36. Fass, *Damned and the Beautiful*, 88, 93, 289.

37. On the emergence of a separate youth subculture, see Joseph F. Kett, *Rites of Passage: Adolescence in America, 1790 to the Present* (New York, 1977), 252, 257, 258, 260; Fass, *Damned and the Beautiful*, 55, 83–95, 118–221.

   The first sociological studies of parent-child relations showed that relations between parents and children were emotionally closer in "modern" urban households than in traditional "rural" households, but that urban children also experienced greater "independence" than their rural counterparts. A systematic comparison of rural and urban households conducted for a White House Conference on Child Health and Protection in 1934 indicated that urban children confided in their parents more frequently, were punished less often, and were more likely to display filial affection openly. But urban children were less likely to be assigned specific household chores or take part in joint family activities like going to church. Surveys also found young people spending increasing amounts of time with age-mates and apart from their parents. Less than half the urban boys and two-thirds of the urban girls studied spent as many as four evenings a week at home.

38. On public fears of declining parental authority, Fass, *Damned and the Beautiful*, 83–95; Allen, *Only Yesterday*, 90–91, 93.

   The early twentieth century witnessed the formulation of a new conception of adolescence, which was associated with drastic swings in mood, inner turmoil, sensitivity, and generational conflict with parents. A Clark University psychology professor, G. Stanley Hall, in his classic work *Adolescence* in 1904, argued that the "storm and stress" of adolescence was a by-product of physiological maturation and was critical in helping teens to deal with the problems of growth, development, and the achievement of meaningful lives.

   On the reasons for rise of a new conception of adolescence, see Hale, *Freud and the Americans*, 29; Fass, *Damned and the Beautiful*, 120–29; Kett, *Rites of Passage*, 171–72, 215–44; Dorothy Ross, *G. Stanley Hall: The Psychologist as Prophet* (Chicago, 1972), 319, 333, 337. Note that more and more young people irrespective of class continued to live at home with their parents during their teens and to attend high school. Enrollment in high schools shot up 750 percent between 1880 and 1900 and jumped another 650 percent between 1900 and 1930. This meant that adolescents of different social classes shared a common experience and environment for part of each weekday.

39. On early-twentieth-century efforts to help the family adapt to modern conditions, see Lasch, *Haven in a Heartless World*, 29–43; Fass, *Damned and the Beautiful*, 95–118, Halem, *Divorce Reform*, 56–66, 156.

40. For an insightful overview of Progressivism, see Robert H. Wiebe, *The Search for Order, 1877 to 1920* (New York, 1966).

41. On changes in child-birth procedures, see Shorter, *History of Women's Bodies*, chs. 3–7; Leavitt, *Brought to Bed*, chs. 5–8; Wertz and Wertz, *Lying-In*, 109–73.

42. On demands for anesthesia, see Reed, *From Private Vice to Public Virtue*, 60.

43. On the shift from home delivery to hospital delivery and the rise of caesarian birth, see Shorter, *History of Women's Bodies*, 141–49, 156–64, 175–76.

44. On the transformation of child-rearing techniques, see Martha Wolfenstein, "Fun Morality: An Analysis of Recent American Childrearing Literature," in *Childhood in Contemporary Cultures*, eds. Margaret Mead and Martha Wolfenstein (Chicago, 1955), 168–78; Celia B. Stendler, "Psychologic Aspects of Pediatrics: Sixty Years of Child Training Practices," *Journal of Pediatrics*, 36 (1950), 122–34; Clark E. Vincent, "Trends in Infant Care Ideas," *Child Development*, 22 (1951), 199–209 Richard J. Bernstein, *John Dewey* (Atascadero, Calif., 1966), 38–40, 142; Elizabeth M.R. Lomax, Jerome Kagan and Barbara G. Rosenkrantz, *Science and Patterns of Child Care* (San Francisco, 1978); Ross, *G. Stanley Hall*, 125, 279–308.

45. On childrearing ideas in the 1890s, see Lomax, Kagan, and Rosenkrantz, *Science and Patterns of Child Care*, 19–44; Stendler, "Psychologic Aspects of Pediatrics," 126–28.

46. On the growth of the idea of "scientific mothering," see Stendler, "Psychologic Aspects of Pediatrics," 128–29; Ehrenreich and English, *For Her Own Good*, 173–89; Ross, *G. Stanley Hall*, 125, 279–308; Lomax, Kagan, and Rosenkrantz, *Science and Patterns of Child Care*, 19–44.

47. On turn-of-the-century trends in child-rearing advice, see Lomax, Kagan, and Rosenkrantz, *Science and Patterns of Child Care*, 19–44; Stendler, "Psychologic

Aspects of Pediatrics," 128–29. Also see Sheila M. Rothman, *Woman's Proper Place: A History of Changing Ideals and Practices, 1870 to the Present* (New York, 1980).

48. On the Children's Bureau Infant Care bulletin, see Wolfenstein, "Fun Morality," 169. On the persistence of such ideas, see Mary Catherine Bateson, *With a Daughter's Eye: A Memoir of Margaret Mead and Gregory Bateson* (New York, 1984), 29.

49. On the behaviorist psychology of John B. Watson, see Fass, *Damned and the Beautiful*, 100–107, 116, 117; Stendler, "Psychologic Aspects of Pediatrics," 129–30; Lomax, Kagan, and Rosenkrantz, *Science and Patterns of Child Care*, 109–50.

50. On psychoanalysis and the increasing emphasis on personality development, see Lomax, Kagan, and Rosenkrantz, *Science and Patterns of Child Care*, 63, 73–76; Halem, *Divorce Reform*, 103–8; Willystine Goodsell, *Problems of the Family*, rev. ed. (New York, 1928), 459–87; Stendler, "Psychologic Aspects of Pediatrics," 130–32.

51. On the increasing emphasis attached to personality development, see Lomax, Kagan, and Rosenkrantz, *Science and Patterns of Child Care*, 63, 73–76; Stendler, "Psychologic Aspects of Pediatrics," 130–32.

52. On the shift toward "permissiveness" in child-rearing, see Stendler, "Psychologic Aspects of Pediatrics," 132–34; Lomax, Kagan, and Rosenkrantz, *Science and Patterns of Child Care*, 36–38, 62–63.

53. On domestic service during the nineteenth century, see Daniel E. Sutherland, *Americans and their Servants: Domestic Service in the United States from 1800 to 1920* (Baton Rouge, La., 1981), 10, 45; Susan Strasser, *Never Done: A History of American Housework* (New York, 1982), 151; Faye E. Dudden, *Serving Women: Household Service in Nineteenth Century America* (Middletown, Conn., 1983), 5, 12, 75; David M. Katzman, *Seven Days a Week: Domestic Service in Industrializing America* (Urbana, Ill., 1978), 151.

54. On the declining availability of domestic servants after 1900, see Katzman, *Seven Days a Week*, 7–24, 110–15, 122–27, 138–39, 273; Sutherland, *Americans and their Servants*, 30, 61, 190.

55. On the Mother's Movement, see Filene, *Him/Her/Self*, 39–43; Barbara Ehrenreich and Dierdre English, *For Her Own Good: 150 Years of Experts Advice to Women* (New York, 1978), 127–48.

56. On public policy and housework, refer to note 55.

57. On the introduction of "labor-saving" household appliances, see Ehrenreich and English, *For Her Own Good*, 145–48; Joann Vanek, "Time Spent in Housework," *Scientific American* (November 1974), 116–20.

58. On early-twentieth-century social scientists and the historical evolution of the family, see Halem, *Divorce Reform*, 56–66; Fass, *Damned and the Beautiful*, 95–118.

59. On the legal regulation of marriage, see Keller, *Affairs of State*, 463–65.

60. On the legal restriction of marriage, refer to Keller, *Affairs of State*, 463–65.

61. On resistance to legal regulation of marriage, see Joseph Kirk Folsom, *The Family: Its Sociology and Social Psychiatry* (New York, 1934), 346–54.

62. On assumptions guiding divorce laws, see Maggie Scharf, "Review of Lenore Weitzman, *The Divorce Revolution*," *New Republic* (April 21, 1986), 35–37.

63. On early-twentieth-century innovations in the legal approach to divorce, see Halem, *Divorce Reform*, 116–57.

64. On the establishment of family courts, see Halem, *Divorce Reform*, 116–20.

65. On the trend toward increasingly liberal interpretations of divorce statutes, see Halem, *Divorce Reform*, 134–36.

66. On questions of custody, see Halem, *Divorce Reform*, 141–49.

67. On alimony and property division, Halem, *Divorce Reform*, 149–53.

68. On the need for instruction in marriage skills, see Lasch, *Haven in a Heartless World*, 11–12.

    Marriage counseling emerged as a distinct profession after World War I. The first centers providing advice on sexual and marital problems were established in Austria, Denmark, Germany, and Sweden in the early 1920s. In the United States, the first college courses on marriage were taught in 1924 and the first marriage consultation centers was opened in New York City in 1929 by Drs. Hannah and Abraham Stone.

    On the emergence of marriage counseling as a profession, see Emily Harshorne Mudd, *The Practice of Marriage Counseling* (New York, 1951); Clark E. Vincent, ed., *Readings in Marriage Counseling*, part 1 (New York, 1957).

69. On the government's increasingly active role in "child saving," see Keller, *Affairs of State.*, 464–67; Robert M. Mennel, *Thorns and Thistles* (Hanover, N.H., 1973); Steven Schlossman, *Love and the American Delinquent* (Chicago, 1977); Joseph M. Hawes, *Children in Urban Society: Juvenile Delinquency in Nineteenth-Century America* (New York, 1971); Anthony M. Platt, *The Child Savers: The Invention of Delinquency* (Chicago, 1969). Also see Sheila M. Rothman, *Woman's Proper Place.*

70. On changes in parents' legal responsibility toward children, see Keller, *Affairs of State*, 463–64.

    Reversing the traditional common law rule that a parent had only a moral obligation to support his children in return for their "service," a majority of state courts had held by 1900 that parents had a legal obligation to support their children regardless of whether they were providing service or not.

71. On the increasing number of working mothers, see Tentler, *Wage-Earning Women*, 138, 165. On arrangements for childcare used by working mothers, see Tentler, *Wage-Earning Women*, 153–60.

72. On pioneering efforts to provide day nurseries for children of working mothers, see Tentler, *Wage-Earning Women*, 161–65.

73. On early efforts to provide public assistance to mothers and dependent children, see Goodsell, *Problems of the Family*, 192–202.

74. On the inadequacy of early welfare legislation, see Tentler, *Wage-Earning Women*, 161–65.

75. On public support for prenatal and obstetrical care, see Goodsell, *Problems of the Family*, 213–17; J. Stanley Lemons, *The Woman Citizen: Social Feminism in the 1920s* (Urbana, Ill., 1975).

76. On early-twentieth-century demographic changes in family patterns, see Peter Uhlenberg, "Death and the Family, *Journal of Family History*, 5 (1980), 313–20; Uhlenberg, "Cohort Variations in Family Life Cycle Experiences of United States Females," *Journal of Marriage and the Family*, 36 (1974), 284–92; Uhlenberg, "A Study of Cohort Life Cycles: Cohorts of Native-Born Massachusetts Women, 1830–1920," *Population Studies*, 23 (1969), 407–20.

    Whereas 60 percent of all families lost at least one child in 1900, only 16 percent did forty years later. Whereas 25 percent of all children lost a parent in 1900, in 1940 just 10 percent did.

77. On the costs and benefits of familial change, see Tamara Hareven, "American

Families in Transition: Historical Perspectives on Change," in *Family in Transition*, ed. Arlene S. Skolnick, 3rd ed. (Boston, 1980), 87.

CHAPTER VII

1. Russell Baker, *Growing Up* (New York, 1982), 21, 22, 80, 84. Russell Baker now writes columns of political commentary and humor for the *New York Times*.

2. Dixon Wecter, *Age of the Great Depression* (New York, 1948), 16–18, 27, 39; *Time* (February 1, 1982), 22; Glen Elder, Jr., *Children of the Great Depression: Social Change in Life Experience* (Chicago, 1974), 20; Lester V. Chandler, *America's Greatest Depression* (New York, 1970), 34, 35.

3. Robert S. McElvaine, *The New Deal: America, 1929–1941* (New York, 1984), 171; Chandler, *America's Greatest Depression*, 34.

4. Wecter, *Age of the Great Depression*, 17–18, 27, 39; Elder, *Children of the Great Depression*, 20.

5. Frederick Lewis Allen, *The Big Change, 1900–1950* (New York, 1952), 127–28.

6. Chandler, *America's Greatest Depression*, 27; Theodore Caplow et al., *Middletown Families: Fifty Years of Change and Continuity* (Minneapolis, 1982), 91; Caroline Bird, *The Invisible Scar* (New York, 1966), 37; Ruth Shonle Cavan and Katherine Howland Ranck, *The Family and the Depression: A Study of One Hundred Chicago Families* (Chicago, 1938), 22.

7. Alexander Keyssar, *Out of Work: The First Century of Unemployment in Massachusetts* (Cambridge, England, 1986).

8. Chandler, *America's Greatest Depression*, 62, 73, 194.

9. Ibid.; James Patterson, *America's Struggle Against Poverty, 1900–1980* (Cambridge, Mass., 1981), 41.

10. Theda Skocpol and John Ikenberry, "The Political Formation of the American Welfare State In Historical and Comparative Perspective," *Comparative Social Research*, 6 (1983), 87–148.

11. Susan Ware, *Holding Their Own: American Women in the 1930s* (Boston, 1982), 8, 9; Caplow et al., *Middletown Families*, 66, 105, 120; Wecter, *Age of the Great Depression*, 31–32.

12. Refer to note 11; Samuel A. Stouffer, *Research Memorandum on the Family in the Depression* (New York, 1937), 69; Francis Merrill, *Social Problems on the Home Front* (New York, 1948), 35.

13. William Leuchtenberg, *The Perils of Prosperity* (Chicago, 1958), 249; Bird, *Invisible Scar*, 284; Ware, *Holding Their Own*, 6, 7; Elder, *Children of the Great Depression*, 206; Winona L. Morgan, *The Family Meets the Depression* (Minneapolis, 1939), 14; Wecter, *Age of the Great Depression*, 29; Merrill, *Social Problems on the Home Front*, 35; Stouffer, *Research Memorandum on the Family in the Depression*, 69.

14. Cavan and Ranck, *Family and the Depression*, 51.

15. Wecter, *Age of the Great Depression*, 26–27; Lois Scharf, *To Work and to Wed: Female Employment, Feminism and the Great Depression* (Westport, Conn., 1980), 147, 148.

16. Scharf, *To Work and to Wed*, 147, 148.

17. Ibid., 149, 150; Wecter, *Age of the Great Depression*, 30, 32; Caplow et al., *Middletown Families*, 105.

18. Scharf, *To Work and to Wed*, 152, 153.

19. On the impact of the Great Depression on the father's role, see Ware, *Holding Their Own*, 15–16; Jeanne Westin, *Making Do: How Women Survived the '30s* (Chicago, 1976), 4, 5; Scharf, *To Work and to Wed*, 140–41.

20. Caplow et al., *Middletown Families*, 18; Ware, *Holding Their Own*, 21, 24–25, 29; Scharf, *To Work and To Wed*, 139–46; Lorine Pruette and Iva Lowther Peters, *Women Workers Through the Depression* (New York, 1934), 102, 119.

21. Ware, *Holding Their Own*, 11–12, 30.

22. Bird, *Invisible Scar*, 293; Wecter, *Age of the Great Depression*, 18.

23. Chandler, *America's Greatest Depression*, 35–38. Public recognition of the special problems of older Americans dates back to the Progressive Era, when the first public commission on aging was established (in Massachusetts in 1909), the first federal old age pension bill was introduced (also in 1909), the first survey of the economic conditions of the elderly was conducted (in Massachusetts in 1910), and the first old age pension system was enacted (in Arizona in 1915). It was during this period that old age became increasingly associated with such problems as dependency, physical disability, mental debility, and a host of character problems including depression, bitterness, hypochondria, and an inability to absorb new ideas.

Recognition of the problems of the elderly did not, however, lead to public action. Public and private responses to the problems of old age came far later in the United States than in Europe. Germany established the first compulsory old age insurance system in 1889, Austria in 1906, England in 1908, France in 1910, and Sweden in 1913. There was one area, however, where the United States did create a large public pension system for the aged: For Civil War veterans and their dependents, on which the federal government spent five billion dollars between the Civil War and World War I. See David Hackett Fischer, *Growing Old in America* (New York, 1978), 157, 160, 174; Andrew Achenbaum, *Old Age in the New Land: The American Experience Since 1790* (Baltimore, Md., 1978), 110–12, 121–22; Patterson, *America's Struggle Against Poverty*, 72; Wecter, *Age of the Great Depression*, 200–201; Caplow et al., *Middletown Families*, 94.

24. Wecter, *Age of the Great Depression*, 183; Chandler, *America's Greatest Depression*, 35–39.

25. Refer to note 24.

26. Elder, *Children of the Great Depression*, 28, 96, 98, 99, 114–15. One characteristic of the Great Depression that struck many observers was the width of the generation gap separating parents and children. "It is our impression," sociologists Robert and Helen Lynd wrote in 1935, "that no two generations of Americans have ever faced each other across as wide a gap in their customary behavior as have American parents and children since the World War. And this disjunction, we believe, has been increased by the Depression." A new word would enter the American vocabulary in the wake of the 1930s to describe and set apart young people: "teenager."

A major factor contributing to the growing gulf between generations was the rapid increase in enrollment in secondary schools. Especially after 1934, when National Recovery Administration rules barring child labor began to be strictly enforced, enrollment in junior and senior high schools shot upward. Where only half of young Americans between the ages of fourteen and eighteen attended high school in 1930, three-quarters did in 1940.

The rise of the high school carried a number of important implications for the lives of young people. Schools took on increasing responsibility for the development of children. The expansion of the high school can also be seen as an index of the growing need for credentials in an increasingly bureaucratized and professionalized society. Perhaps the most important implication of increased schooling was to further the development of a peer culture existing separate and apart from the family. In high school, young people encountered a culture of their peers, which helped influence attitudes and set standards of behavior, independent of parents or churches. See Caplow et al., *Middletown Families*, 20, 157; Scharf, *To Work and to Wed*, 72–73; Ware, *Holding Their Own*, 56.

27. James Agee and Walker Evans, *Let Us Now Praise Famous Men: Three Tenant Families* (Boston, 1941).

28. To discourage the influx of migrants, thirty-nine states denied relief to anyone who failed to meet stringent residence requirements. Most states lengthened residence requirements to two or three years, but a number of states instituted five-year and even ten-year requirements. Wecter, *Age of the Great Depression*, 163–64, 174, 183–85; Chandler, *America's Greatest Depression*, 40, 45–47; Caro, *The Years of Lyndon Johnson*, 243; Patterson, *America's Struggle Against Poverty*, 60–62; Allen, *Since Yesterday*, 160–61.

29. Vacuum cleaners and cloth dust mops replaced older cleaning implements made of cornbroom, a major Midwestern crop. As a result farmers turned to wheat, but huge crop surpluses drove prices to record lows. In northeastern New Mexico, southeastern Colorado, southwestern Kansas, Oklahoma, and the Texas panhandle, yearly rainfall declined from an average of twenty-eight inches between 1914 and 1923 to just seventeen inches during the 1930s. The introduction of a new kind of plow—the "one-way" plow—allowed farmers to work more acres than ever before, but it also broke down the soil structure, making the land highly vulnerable to wind erosion. See Paul Bonnifield, *The Dust Bowl: Men, Dirt, and Depression* (Albuquerque, N. Mex. 1979), 2, 10, 20, 27, 74, 188; Chandler, *America's Greatest Depression*, 40–41.

30. Allen, *Since Yesterday*, 160–61.

31. Raymond Wolters, *Negroes and the Great Depression* (Westport, Conn., 1970).

32. James H. Jones, *Bad Blood: The Tuskegee Syphilis Experiment* (New York, 1981), 61–65, 85–86, 218–19; Patterson, *America's Struggle Against Poverty*, 39–40.

33. Bird, *Invisible Scar*, 19, 44, 208; William J. Brophy, "Black Texans and the New Deal" in *The Depression in the Southwest*, ed. Donald W. Whisenhunt (Port Washington, N.Y., 1980), 117; Wecter, *Age of the Great Depression*, 162.

34. St. Clair Drake and Horace R. Cayton, *Black Metropolis: A Study of Negro Life in a Northern City* (New York, 1945), 8–9, 512–19, 573–77, 608–60.

35. Ibid.

36. Ibid., 203, 577–78, 612–53, 663–68.

37. Milton Meltzer, *Brother Can You Spare a Dime? The Great Depression, 1929–1933* (New York, 1969), 57, 99; Wechter, *Age of the Great Depression*, 162, 164; Brophy, "Black Texans and the New Deal," 117, 119, 123.

38. Abraham Hoffman, *The Repatriation of Mexican Nationals from the United States During the Great Depression* (Ann Arbor, Mich., 1971), 36–37; Hoffman, *Unwanted Mexican Americans in the Great Depression: Repatriation Pressures, 1929–1939* (Tucson, Ariz., 1974).

39. Hoffman, *Repatriation of Mexican Nationals*, 6–17.

40. Douglas Earl Foley, *From Peones to Politicos: Ethnic Relations in a South Texas Town, 1900–1977* (Austin, Tex., 1977), 116–32.

41. Hoffman, *Repatriation of Mexican Nationals*, 124–26.

42. Bird, *Invisible Scar*, 252–53; Leuchtenberg, *Perils of Prosperity*, 247, 252; Chandler, *America's Greatest Depression*, 31.

43. Skocpol and Ikenberry, "The Political Formation of the American Welfare State," 120–41.

44. Ibid., 88–119.

45. Chandler, *America's Greatest Depression*, 45, 49–51, 194; Patterson, *America's Struggle Against Poverty*, 56–57; Caro, *Years of Lyndon Johnson*, 244.

46. Caro, *Years of Lyndon Johnson*, 502–13.

47. Ibid., 519–22.

48. Chandler, *America's Greatest Depression*, 142; Wecter, *Age of the Great Depression*, 145, 148, 149.

49. Ibid.; Allen, *Since Yesterday*, 165–66.

50. Allen, *Since Yesterday*, 165–66; Wecter, *Age of the Great Depression*, 178–80; Ware, *Holding Their Own*, 104–5; Stouffer, *Research Memorandum on the Family*, 137.

51. Bird, *Invisible Scar*, 52; Ware, *Holding Their Own*, 9–10; Margaret Jarman Hagood, *Mothers of the South: Portraiture of the White Tenant Farm Woman* (1939; reprint, New York, 1977), 120–24.

52. Refer to note 51.

53. Skocpol and Ikenberry, "The Political Formation of the American Welfare State," 120–41. The explanation for the heightened concern with the elderly was twofold. First, the number of older Americans increased sharply. In the ten years after 1925, the number of people over sixty-five climbed from just 5.7 million to 7.8 million. Back in 1860 just one American in forty was sixty-five or over; by 1940 the ratio had been reduced to one in fifteen. The other reason for growing public concern was the fact that financial dependency among the elderly increased. The proportion of the aged who were self-supporting dropped sharply, while the number wholly or partly dependent on public relief, private charity, or friends and relatives shot upward. In 1890, when those over the age of sixty-five made up 3 percent of the population, only 25 percent were without jobs, because most were self-employed farmers. As late as 1910, 87 percent of the elderly were self-supporting. By 1930, before the full impact of the Depression had been felt, this figure had declined to 60 percent. The phrase "old at forty" described a disturbing reality. An employer in Muncie, Indiana, commented that forty to forty-five was the age limit for production work; men over that age were only hired as sweepers or to do similar jobs. See David Hackett Fischer, *Growing Old in America* (New York, 1978), 157, 160, 174; Achenbaum, *Old Age in the New Land*, 110–12, 121–22; Patterson, *America's Struggle Against Poverty*, 72; Wechter, *Age of the Great Depression*, 200–201; Caplow et al., *Middletown Families*, 94.

54. Fischer, *Growing Old in America*, 184; Wecter, *Age of the Great Depression*, 207–8.

55. Skocpol and Ikenberry, "The Political Formation of the American Welfare State," 120–41.

CHAPTER VIII

1. Frankie Cooper's oral history is printed in Mark Jonathan Harris, Franklin D. Mitchell, and Steven J. Schechter, *The Homefront: America During World War II* (New York, 1984), 35–37.

2. Ibid.

3. Ibid.

4. Ibid.

5. Useful overviews of the impact of World War II on the home front include Richard Polenberg, *War and Society: The United States, 1941–1945* (Philadelphia, 1972); John Morton Blum, *V Was for Victory: Politics and American Culture During World War II* (New York, 1976); Allan M. Winkler, *Home Front U.S.A.: America during World War II* (Arlington Heights, Ill., 1986); Richard R. Lingeman, *Don't You Know There's a War Going On? The American Home Front, 1941–1945* (New York, 1970); Geoffrey Perrett, *Days of Sadness, Years of Triumph: The American People, 1939–1945* (New York, 1973); Ronald H. Bailey, *The Home Front: U.S.A.* (Alexandria, Va., 1978).

6. Perrett, *Days of Sadness, Years of Triumph*, 137; Winkler, *Home Front U.S.A.*, 33; Bailey, *Home Front*, 147–48.

7. Polenberg, *War and Society*, 144–50.

8. Elliot Johnson's oral history is quoted in Harris et al., *The Homefront*, 186–87.

9. On the dramatic increase in the number of hasty and impulsive marriages, see Francis E. Merrill, *Social Problems on the Home Front: A Study of Wartime Influences* (New York, 1948), 27–29; Bailey, *Home Front*, 51; *New York Times*, May 1, 1943, I, 3; *NYT*, March 14, 1943, IV, 14.

10. Bailey, *Home Front*, 51.

11. William Manchester, *The Glory and the Dream* (Boston, 1974), 427.

12. Bailey, *Home Front*, 51.

13. On "Allotment Annies," see Bailey, *Home Front*, 51.

14. On the dramatic increase in wartime marriage rates, see Bailey, *Home Front*, 51; *NYT*, May 1, 1943, I, 21; *NYT*, March 14, 1943, IV, 14.

15. William Fielding Ogburn, "Marriages, Births, and Divorces," *Annals*, 229 (1943), 20–29; D'Ann Campbell, *Women at War with America: Private Lives in a Patriotic Era* (Cambridge, Mass., 1984), 206–7; *NYT*, May 6, 1948, 32: 8.

16. On wartime mobility, see *NYT*, December 8, 1946, VI, 18; Winkler, *Home Front U.S.A.*, 43–44; Bailey, *Home Front*, 142–44. Laura Briggs's oral history is given in Harris et al., *The Homefront*, 32–35.

17. Dellie Hahne's oral history is printed in Harris et al., *The Home Front*, 179–80.

18. On wartime population shifts, see *NYT*, December 8, 1946, VI, 18; Winkler, *Home Front U.S.A.*, 43–44; Bailey, *Home Front*, 142–44; Polenberg, *War and Society*, 139–41.

19. On wartime housing shortages, see Bailey, *Home Front*, 143; Polenberg, *War and Society*, 141–44; Winkler, *Home Front U.S.A.*, 44–45.

20. Merrill, *Social Problems on the Home Front*, 33–35; *NYT*, December 8, 1946, VI, 16; *NYT*, June 17, 1945, VI, 14; Campbell, *Women at War with America*, 169–70, 195, 198; Polenberg, *War and Society*, 141–44; Bailey, *Home Front*, 143.

21. *NYT*, December 8, 1946, VI, 16; *NYT*, June 17, 1945, VI, 14; Campbell, *Women at War with America*, 69, 95, 107, 133, 169–72, 179, 184–86, 190, 195–98, 207; Polenberg, *War and Society*, 141–44; Bailey, *Home Front*, 143; Winkler, *Home Front U.S.A.*, 44–45. Elsie Rossio's oral history is quoted in Harris et al., *The Homefront*, 41–44.

22. On impact of the war on black Americans, see Merrill, *Social Problems on the*

Home Front, 32–33; Neil A. Wynn, *The Afro-American and the Second World War* (New York, 1976).

23. Refer to note 22.

24. Perrett, *Days of Sadness, Years of Triumph*, 327.

25. *Ibid.*, 354; *NYT*, August 3, 1943, I, 18; *NYT*, October 10, 1943, I, 5; Campbell, *Women at War with America*, 168–69, 218.

26. William Peffley's oral history is given in Harris et al., *The Homefront*, 39–41.

27. *NYT*, August 3, 1943, I, 18; *NYT*, October 10, 1943, I, 5; Campbell, *Women at War with America*, 168–69, 218.

28. Refer to note 27; Faith M. Williams, "The Standard of Living in Wartime," *Annals*, 229 (1943), 117–27.

29. *NYT*, December 12, 1943, VI, 12; *NYT*, May 13, 1945, VI, 16; Bailey, *Home Front*, 156, 162; Campbell, *Women at War with America*, 76, 122–24, 170–77, 181–83.

30. Campbell, *Women at War with America*, 76, 122–24, 170–77, 181–83.

31. *Ibid.*; Williams, "The Standard of Living in Wartime," 117–27.

32. Winkler, *Home Front U.S.A.*, 37–43; Bailey, *Home Front*, 110–12, 156, 162.

33. Refer to note 32; Williams, "Standard of Living in Wartime," 125–26; Manchester, *Glory and the Dream*, 422; *NYT*, March 13, 1941, I, 38; *NYT*, May 1, 1943, I, 21.

34. *NYT*, December 12, 1943, VI, 12: *NYT*, May 13, 1945, VI, 16; Winkler, *Home Front U.S.A.*, 37–43; Bailey, *Home Front*, 110–12, 156, 162.

35. *NYT*, December 12, 1943, VI, 12; *NYT*, May 13, 1945, VI, 16.

36. Sheril Jankovsky Cunning's oral history is printed in Harris et al., *The Homefront*, 70.

37. On the entry of women into the paid labor force, see *NYT*, July 18, 1943, VI, 18; *NYT*, May 5, 1946, VI, 21; *NYT*, April 29, 1945, VI, 16; Winkler, *Home Front U.S.A.*, 49–57; Polenberg, *War and Society*, 146.

38. Karen Anderson, *Wartime Women: Sex Roles, Family Relations, and the Status of Women During World War II* (Westport, Conn., 1981), 91, 124. Also see Susan M. Hartmann, *The Homefront and Beyond: American Women in the 1940s* (New York, 1982) and Maureen Honey, *Creating Rosie the Riveter: Class, Gender, and Propaganda During World War II* (Amherst, Mass., 1984).

39. Anderson, *Wartime Women*, 122–46; Henry L. Zucker, "Working Parents and Latchkey Children," *Annals*, 236 (1944), 47. It would be a mistake to exaggerate the novelty of women's wartime employment or the extent to which married women entered the labor force. Many of the women who joined the wartime work force had already worked for wages earlier in their lives. More than nine out of every ten urban women born in 1915 had held a job before the war. The Women's Bureau of the Department of Labor estimated that no more than 26 percent of American wives worked for pay during the war, though many served as volunteers in selling war bonds, staffing charitable agencies, and staging collection drives. Least likely to take jobs outside the home were mothers of children under six. Just 12 percent of these women joined the labor force. Older women, and particularly the wives of GIs, were more likely to take a job than other married women. See Merrill, *Social Problems on the Home Front*, 31; Zucker, "Working Parents and Latchkey Children," 43; Campbell, *Women at War with America*, 72; *NYT*, April 29, 1945, VI, 16.

40. Anderson, *Wartime Women*, 77; Polenberg, *War and Society*, 146–47.

41. On government policy and women's employment, see Winkler, *Home Front U.S.A.*, 49–57. On the socioeconomic characteristics of working mothers, see Zucker, "Working Parents and Latchkey Children," 47.

42. On the problem of "maternal neglect," see Merrill, *Social Problems on the Home Front*, 55–59, 66; Barbara Ehrenreich and Deirdre English, *For Her Own Good: 150 Years of Experts' Advice to Women* (Garden City, N.Y., 1978), 206–8; Peter Steinfels and Margaret O'Brien Steinfels, "What Are Families Really For?," *New Republic* (May 16, 1983), 32–33.

43. Zucker, "Working Parents and Latchkey Children," 43–50.

44. Barbara De Nike's oral history is quoted in Harris et al., *The Homefront*, 194.

45. Zucker, "Working Parents and Latchkey Children," 43–50; Anderson, *Wartime Women*, 131–34, 138–41.

46. Refer to note 45.

47. Refer to note 45.

48. For comparative perspectives on wartime social services for working mothers, see William Chafe, *The American Woman: Her Changing Social, Economic, and Political Roles, 1920–1970* (New York, 1972), 158–72.

49. On "momism," see Ehrenreich and English, *For Her Own Good*, 208–11; *NYT*, April 28, 1945, I, 11.

50. *NYT*, March 18, 1944, I, 10; *NYT*, December 1, 1946, I, 21; *NYT*, March 17, 1946, VI, 11; *NYT*, August 18, 1948, I, 11.

51. On the wartime plight of children, see Willard Waller, "The Family and Other Institutions," *Annals*, 229 (1943), 109–10; Anderson, *Wartime Women*, 97–101; Eleanor Boll, "The Child," *Annals*, 229 (1943), 73–74; *NYT*, December 10, 1944, VI, 16.

52. Perrett, *Days of Sadness, Years of Triumph*, 347–50.

53. Elizabeth S. Magee, "Impact of the War on Child Labor," *Annals*, 229 (1943), 103–4; Waller, "The Family and Other Institutions," 109–10.

54. Beatrice McConnell, "Child Labor in Agriculture," *Annals*, 236 (1944), 83–91; Gertrude Follis Zimand, "Changing Picture of Child Labor," *Annals*, 236 (1944), 92–100; Magee, "Impact of the War on Child Labor," 104–7; Merrill, *Social Problems on the Home Front*, ·78–85, 93–94; Boll, "The Child," 69–78.

55. Perrett, *Days of Sadness, Years of Triumph*, 348–50; Merrill, *Social Problems on the Home Front*, 145–68; Campbell, *Women at War with America*, 226–27; Manchester, *Glory and the Dream*, 419–20; *NYT*, December 10, 1944, VI, 16: *NYT*, February 27, 1944, VI, 8; *NYT*, July 25, 1943, VI, 19.

56. Refer to note 55; Bailey, *Home Front*, 147–49.

57. Refer to notes 55 and 56. Prior to the late 1930s, the word "teenager" referred not to young people but to "brushweed used for fences and hedges."

58. On family separation during wartime, see Merrill, *Social Problems on the Home Front*, 49–51; Anderson, *Wartime Women*, 124; Campbell, *Women at War with America*, 101–37, 163–86, 190–92.

59. Campbell, *Women at War with America*, 189–90, 195, 198.

60. Ibid., 198–99.

61. Blum, *V Was for Victory*, 155–67; Harry H. Kitano, *Japanese Americans: The Evolution of a Subculture* (2nd ed., Englewood Cliffs, N.J., 1976), 75–80.

62. Refer to note 61.

63. Refer to note 61; Perrett, *Days of Sadness, Years of Triumph*, 216–30, esp. 224. The 277,000 Japanese Americans who lived in the United States in 1941 were a relatively recent immigrant group. Japanese migration to the United States began in the 1860s and by the turn of the century, their numbers had reached approximately 100,000. The overwhelming majority of these early migrants were male—in 1890, seven out of every eight Japanese immigrants were male—and like most immigrants of the period, many viewed their sojourn in America as temporary. Of the 160,000 Japanese who arrived in America between 1908 and 1924, 70,000 returned to Japan. The sexual imbalance in the immigrant population gradually diminished as a result of a "Gentlemen's Agreement" between the U.S. and Japan in 1908 which reduced Japanese migration by a third but permitted the wives and children of resident Japanese to join their husbands and fathers.

    As a result of immigration restrictions adopted by Congress in 1924 and delayed marriage on the part of the first generation of immigrants, the Japanese American population's age structure was sharply skewed. Among the roughly 47,000 Issei, who were born in Japan, the average age in 1941 of men was 56, and of women, 47. Among the 80,000 Nisei, born in the United States, the average was only 18. Other generational differences included language—most Issei spoke Japanese and little English—and religion—three-quarters of the Issei were Buddhist, half the Nisei were Christian. See Kitano, *Japanese Americans*, 75–80; Thomas Sowell, *Ethnic America* (New York, 1981), 164–68; Blum, *V Was for Victory*, 157.

64. Perrett, *Days of Sadness, Years of Triumph*, 224.

65. Lingeman, *Don't You Know There's a War Going On?*, 339–40; Sowell, *Ethnic America*, 172–75; Kitano, *Japanese Americans*, 75–80; Blum, *V Was for Victory*, 161–62.

66. On the rising divorce rate, see Bailey, *Home Front*, 147; Geoffrey Perrett, *A Dream of Greatness: The American People, 1945–1963* (New York, 1979), 64.

67. Joseph C. Goulden, *The Best Years, 1945–1950* (New York, 1976), 42.

68. Goulden, *The Best Years*, 42–43.

69. Shirley Hackett's oral history is given in Harris et al., *The Homefront*, 195–98, Bailey, *Home Front*, 147.

70. Sybil Lewis's and Shirley Hackett's oral histories are printed in Harris et al., *The Homefront*, 230–31, 251–52.

71. Goulden, *The Best Years*, 132–33; Perrett, *A Dream of Greatness*, 28, 37.

72. Manchester, *The Glory and the Dream*, 430.

73. Joseph C. Goulden, *The Best Years*, 42.

CHAPTER IX

1. For biographical material on Betty Friedan, see *McCalls* (May 1971), 84ff.; Paul Wilkes, "Mother Superior to Women's Lib," *NYT*, November 29, 1970, VI, 27ff.

2. Refer to note 1.

3. Betty Friedan, *The Feminine Mystique* (New York, 1963), 41–42; Andrew J. Cherlin, "The 50's Family and Today's," *NYT*, November 18, 1981, I, 31.

4. Andrew J. Cherlin, "Changing Family and Household: Contemporary Lessons

from Historical Research," *Annual Review of Sociology,* 9 (1983), 58–60; Cherlin, "The 50's Family"; Cherlin, *Marriage, Divorce, Remarriage* (Cambridge, Mass., 1981).

5. Refer to note 4.

6. Refer to note 4; William H. Chafe, *The Unfinished Journey: America Since World War II* (New York, 1986), 123.

7. Refer to notes 4 and 6.

8. Refer to notes 4 and 6; Godfrey Hodgson, *America in Our Time* (Garden City, N.Y., 1976), 50–51.

9. Cherlin, "Changing Family and Household," 58–60; Cherlin, "The 50's Family"; Cherlin, *Marriage, Divorce, Remarriage.*

10. Friedan, *Feminine Mystique,* 42–43.

11. Ibid., 41–43.

12. John Brooks, *The Great Leap: The Past Twenty-Five Years in America* (New York, 1966), 140.

13. Douglas T. Miller and Marion Nowak, *The Fifties: The Way We Really Were* (Garden City, N.Y., 1977), 147; Friedan, *Feminine Mystique,* 12.

14. Hodgson, *America in Our Time,* 50–51; *NYT,* November 19, 1961, VI, 89.

15. Miller and Nowak, *The Fifties,* 160; Chafe, *Unfinished Journey,* 123; Friedan, *Feminine Mystique,* 12.

16. Ehrenreich, *Hearts of Men,* 14–28.

17. Chafe, *Unfinished Journey,* 124; Chafe, *The American Woman: Her Changing Social, Economic, and Political Roles, 1920–1970* (New York, 1972), 177, 199–210; *NYT,* November 30, 1977, I, 1.

18. Cherlin, "The 50's Family."

19. *NYT,* January 21, 1960, I, 17.

20. Mary Jo Bane, *Here to Stay: American Families in the Twentieth Century* (New York, 1976), 40–49.

21. William Manchester, *The Glory and the Dream: A Narrative History of America, 1932–1972* (Boston, 1974), 431–32; *Houston Chronicle,* March 30, 1986, V, 18; Joseph C. Goulden, *The Best Years, 1945–1950* (New York, 1976), 11, 138–39, 427; Miller and Nowak, *The Fifties,* 133–34, 136, 198–99; Perrett, *Dream of Greatness,* 71–72.

22. Refer to note 21.

23. Refer to note 21.

24. Mintz, "The American City in Transition" in W.W. MacDonald et al., *Conflict and Change: America, 1939 to the Present* (St. Louis, Mo., 1983), 77–79; Hodgson, *America in Our Time,* 51; Manchester, *The Glory and the Dream,* 431–32; *NYT,* July 31, 1983, VI, 32; Richard Polenberg, *One Nation Divisible: Class, Race, and Ethnicity in the United States Since 1938* (New York, 1980), 127–39; Chafe, *Unfinished Journey,* 117–22.

25. Mintz, "The American City in Transition," 77–79.

26. On suburban family patterns, see Larry H. Long and Paul C. Glick, "Family Patterns in Suburban Areas: Recent Trends," in *The Changing Face of the Suburbs,* ed. Barry Schwartz (Chicago, 1976), 39–67.

27. Scott Donaldson, *The Suburban Myth* (New York, 1969), 1–22.

28. On women in the suburbs, see Chafe, *Unfinished Journey*, 123–24; Donaldson, *Suburban Myth*, 14–15, 123–24.

29. On "filiarchy," see Donaldson, *Suburban Myth*, 15, 126–28; Chafe, *Unfinished Journey*, 123.

30. Edith Sonn Oshin, "Here Today—But Where Tomorrow?," *NYT*, March 5, 1967, VI, 89ff.; *NYT*, August 26, 1962, VI, 15; December 29, 1973, 18: 1; Manchester, *The Glory and the Dream*, 781. Each year during the 1950s, approximately one-quarter of the U.S. population moved. President John F. Kennedy would later refer to these individuals as the "reverse freedom riders." Despite the highly publicized migration of blacks from the South, a higher proportion of whites moved each year from one county to another (6.8 percent as against 4 percent).

31. Donaldson, *Suburban Myth*, 45–48, 117–26.

32. On working-class suburban families, see Bennet M. Berger, *Working-Class Suburb: A Study of Auto Workers in Suburbia* (Berkeley, 1968), esp. ch. 5; Herbert J. Gans, *The Levittowners: Ways of Life and Politics in a New Suburban Community* (New York, 1967), 24, 61–65, 160, 163–67.

33. Benita Eisler, *Private Lives: Men and Women of the Fifties* (New York, 1986), 22–23, 46–47, 178–79, 186, 199–200, 204, 211, 218, 241–47, 365–66. The names are pseudonyms.

34. Perrett, *A Dream of Greatness*, 65; Miller and Nowak, *The Fifties*, 157.

35. Miller and Nowak, *The Fifties*, 156–57; Perrett, *A Dream of Greatness*, 294.

36. Perrett, *A Dream of Greatness*, 294–95.

37. For biographical information on Dr. Benjamin Spock, see *Parents* (September 1986), 70.

38. By 1973, *Baby and Child Care* had gone through 201 printings and sold 23, 445, 781 copies. It had been translated into twenty-nine languages and was the worldwide best-selling title written by an American. For two decades it sold about a million copies a year. *NYT*, December 25, 1969, I, 37; *NYT*, September 11, 1973, I, 50; Christopher Jencks, "Is It all Dr. Spock's Fault?" in *The Contemporary American Family*, ed. William J. Goode (New York, 1971), 189–91.

39. *NYT*, September 19, 1977, I, 35; *NYT*, January 21, 1976, I, 25; *NYT*, June 27, 1976, VI, 26; *NYT*, January 12, 1974, I, 39; *NYT*, January 23, 1974, I, 23; *NYT*, January 7, 1973, VII, 2; *NYT*, October 13, 1973, I, 30; *NYT*, February 16, 1969, VII, Pt. 2, 4; *NYT*, November 8, 1968, I, 54; *NYT*, August 27, 1967, VI, 63; *NYT*, November 13, 1966, VI, 179; *NYT*, April 14, 1974, VII, 3; Jencks, "Is It all Dr. Spock's Fault?" 189–91.

40. Ehrenreich and English, *For Her Own Good*, 198.

41. Eisler, *Private Lives*, 31.

42. Fred Davis, *Passage Through Crisis: Polio Victims and Their Families* (Indianapolis, 1963), 15–17.

43. Ehrenreich and English, *For Her Own Good*, 204–5.

44. Eisler, *Private Lives*, 34.

45. Ehrenreich and English, *For Her Own Good*, 214–39. Early editions of *Baby and Child Care* take it for granted that fathers will not participate to any great degree

in child care: "Of course, I don't mean that the father has to give just as many bottles, or change just as many diapers as the mother. But it's fine for him to do these things occasionally. He might make the formula on Sunday." Also see Eisler, *Private Lives*, 236.

46. Kenneth Keniston, *The Uncommitted: Alienated Youth in American Society* (New York, 1965), 290–91.

47. Harry Cattleman and Walter J. Podrazik, *Watching TV: Four Decades of American Television* (New York, 1982), 105, 119–20; Horace Newcomb, *TV: The Most Popular Art* (Garden City, N.Y., 1974), ch. 2.

48. Cattleman and Podrazik, *Watching TV*, 105, 119–20.

49. Ibid.

50. Muriel G. Cantor, *Prime Time Television: Content and Control* (Beverly Hills, Calif., 1980), 39–43; *NYT*, May 17, 1982, I, 22; *NYT*, August 25, 1974, VI, 10; *NYT*, March 21, 1965, VI, 79.

51. Refer to note 50.

52. Phyllis Lee Leven, "Putting Down Father," *NYT*, March 21, 1965, VI, 79: Cattleman and Podrazik, *Watching TV*, 119–20.

53. Refer to note 52.

54. Refer to note 52; a University of Illinois study found that children during the 1950s craved strong paternal authority. See Brooks, *The Great Leap*, 146.

55. Nora Sayre, *Running Time: Films of the Cold War* (New York, 1982), 101–49.

56. Ibid.

57. *NYT*, June 24, 1956, reprinted in *The Family*, ed. Gene Brown (New York, 1979), 172.

58. *NYT*, November 29, 1970, VI, 27ff.; Eisler, *Private Lives*, 336, 337, 344–50.

59. Donaldson, *The Suburban Myth*, 118; Friedan, *Feminine Mystique*, 291–92.

60. Perrett, *A Dream of Greatness*, 69–70; Ehrenreich, *The Hearts of Men*, 169.

61. Leila J. Rupp, "The Survival of American Feminism: The Women's Movement in the Postwar Period," in *Reshaping America: Society and Institutions, 1945–1960*, eds. Robert H. Bremner and Gary W. Reichard (Columbus, Ohio, 1982), 38.

62. Chafe, *Unfinished Journey*, 125–26; Chafe, *The American Woman*, 210–15. Also see Eugenia Kaledin, *Mothers and More: American Women in the 1950s* (New York, 1984).

63. Friedan, *Feminine Mystique*, 227–46; Barbara Ehrenreich and Deirdre English, "The Manufacture of Housework," *Radical America*, 26 (1975), 5ff. Some analysts explain the increased amount of time spent on housework as a way in which housewives were able to prove that they were contributing to the family economy.

64. Levin, "Putting Down Father," *NYT*, March 21, 1965, VI, 79; *NYT*, May 17, 1982, I, 22; Robert H. Bremner, "Families, Children, and the State," in *Reshaping America*, eds. Bremner and Reichard, 7.

65. David Riesman, *The Lonely Crowd* (New Haven, 1950), 129–31; William H. Whyte, *The Organization Man*; Keniston, *The Uncommitted*, 295–300; Perrett, *A Dream of Greatness*, 294–95.

66. Refer to note 65.

67. Mirra Komarovsky, *Blue Collar Marriage* (New York, 1964); *NYT*, August 25, 1974, VI, 10 ff.

68. Talcott Parsons and Robert F. Bales, *Family, Socialization, and Interaction Process* (Glencoe, Ill., 1953); Keniston, *The Uncommitted*, 273–81; Mintz, *A Prison of Expectations: The Family in Victorian Culture* (New York, 1983), 190–93.

69. Miller and Nowak, *The Fifties*, 3–5; Chafe, *Unfinished Journey*, 126–28.

70. Ehrenreich and English, *For Her Own Good*, 256; Jo Freeman, *The Politics of Women's Liberation* (New York, 1975), 28–31; Chafe, *Unfinished Journey*, 126–27.

71. Ehrenreich and English, *For Her Own Good*, 255; Friedan, *Feminine Mystique*, 17–20, 59.

72. Keniston, *The Uncommitted*, 394–406; Jeffrey Hart, *When the Going Was Good! American Life in the Fifties* (New York, 1982), 130–36.

73. Refer to note 72.

74. James Coleman, *The Adolescent Society* (Glencoe, Ill., 1961); F. Elkin and W. A. Westley, "The Myth of Adolescent Culture," *American Sociological Review*, 20 (1955), 680–84; Edgar Z. Friedenberg, *The Vanishing Adolescent* (Boston, 1959); Keniston, *The Uncommitted*, 491–92; James Gilbert, *A Cycle of Outrage: America's Reaction to the Juvenile Delinquent in the 1950s* (New York, 1986), 127–42; Miller and Nowak, *The Fifties*, 275.

75. Manchester, *The Glory and the Dream*, 722–25.

76. Gilbert, *A Cycle of Outrage*, 15–16; Brooks, *The Great Leap*, 146.

77. Hart, *When the Going Was Good!*, 9, 11–16, 51–52, 130–36; Alfred C. Kinsey et al., *Sexual Behavior in the Human Female* (Philadelphia, 1953).

CHAPTER X

1. The statistics on changes in family composition can be found in Daniel Yankel-ovich, *New Rules: Search for Self-Fulfillment in a World Turned Upside Down* (New York, 1981), xiv-xv.

2. Stephen L. Klineberg made a similar argument in a public lecture "American Families in Transition: Challenges and Opportunities in a Revolutionary Time" delivered at Rice University, February 15, 1983. Also see Andrew Hacker, *The End of the American Era* (New York, 1971), 174; James J. Lynch, *The Broken Heart: The Medical Consequences of Loneliness* (New York, 1977), 8–10; *Time* (December 2, 1985), 41; *NYT*, June 27, 1979, I, 1; *NYT*, May 26, 1981, I, 1.

It must be emphasized that despite the dramatic changes that have taken place, the institution of the family is not an endangered species. Today, commitment to marriage remains strong and 90 percent of young Americans marry. Despite rising divorce rates, the majority of marriages do not end in divorce, most divorced individuals remarry, and only a small percentage marry more than twice. Even when divorces occur, they do not necessarily produce grave social problems. Forty percent of all divorces occur within four years of marriage and usually involve no children. At the same time, the desire to have children remains as high as ever. Today only 1 percent of American women say that the ideal number of children in a family is none. And despite concern about the fragility of family ties, the increase in the divorce rate has been largely offset by a decline in death rates. As a result, marriages today are only slightly more likely to be disrupted by divorce, desertion, or death than they were earlier in the century. Indeed, even with the rising divorce rate, fewer children today are raised in institutions or by relatives or by mothers barely able to support them than formerly. In spite of the rising divorce rate, the prevalence of single-parent households has not increased markedly among the middle class because women today are much more likely to remarry after a divorce.

Even in the controversial areas of child care and sexuality, behavior has changed less than newspaper headlines suggest. Today most preschoolers are cared for by full-time mothers or mothers who work part-time. Most mothers of young children accommodate their work schedules to the needs of their children. Continuity is also apparent in sexual behavior. Despite the increasing incidence of premarital sex and widespread public discussion of swinging, wife swapping, and illegitimacy, the overwhelming majority of women who have premarital sex have just one or two partners, usually a fiance or a steady date. Nor has the proportion of unmarried white women having babies increased dramatically. In 1950, 99.5 percent of white teenage women did not have illegitimate births; thirty years later, 98.1 percent of this group did not. See Mary Jo Bane, *Here to Stay: American Families in the Twentieth Century* (New York, 1976), 12–13, 30; Sar A. Levitan and Richard S. Belous, *What's Happening to the American Family?* (Baltimore, 1981), 21, 63; Mary Jo Bane et al., "Child Care Settings in the United States" in *Child Care and Mediating Structures*, eds. Brigitte Berger and Sidney Callahan (Washington, D.C., 1979), 19; Carol Tavris and Carole Offir, *The Longest War: Sex Differences in Perspective* (New York, 1977), 64–69.

3. Tavris and Offir, *The Longest War*, 64–69; Peter Uhlenberg and David Eggebeen, "Declining Well-Being of American Adolescents," *The Public Interest* (Winter 1986), 32–33; Lynch, *Broken Heart*, 8–10; *Time* (December 2, 1985), 41; *NYT*, June 27, 1979, I, 1; *NYT*, May 26, 1981, I, 1; *NYT*, March 16, 1986, I, 18.

4. The impact of these changes is most readily apparent in the lives of a key "pace-setting" segment of the population: educated career women. These women are four times less likely to marry than women of lower economic and educational status and 50 percent more likely to divorce. See Andrew Hacker, "Goodbye to Marriage," *New York Review of Books* (May 3, 1979), 23–27. Peter Clecak, *America's Quest for the Ideal Self: Dissent and Fulfillment in the 60s and 70s* (New York, 1983), 93–94.

5. Yankelovich, *New Rules*, 104, 184.

It is easy to exaggerate the significance of rising rates of divorce, working mothers, and single parent households and to conclude that these changes are bad for the family. But it is also possible to view these developments in a more favorable light. Declining birthrates mean that Americans are less likely to bear children by accident or because it is socially expected than earlier Americans, while rising divorce rates mean that people today are less willing to tolerate unhappy and empty marriages. See Klineberg, "American Families in Transition."

6. Ben J. Wattenberg, *The Good News is the Bad News is Wrong* (New York, 1985), 290–91.

7. Joseph Veroff, Elizabeth Douan, and Richard A. Kulka, *The Inner American: A Self Portrait from 1957 to 1976* (New York, 1981), 191, 192, 194, 196; Yankelovich, *New Rules*, 5, 68, 97, 99.

8. Yankelovich, *New Rules*, 5. The rapid rise in the divorce rate is clearly a legacy of changing social values. When individuals are asked why they have decided to get a divorce, a new set of reasons predominates. A survey conducted by the Family Service Association found that the major source of conflict in marriages involved "communications." Conflict over sex was another reason commonly cited in explanations of divorce. More traditional areas of conflict, such as disputes over children or family finances, lagged far behind. See *NYT*, January 3, 1974, I, 16.

It should be noted, however, that the best predictors of a marital breakup remain what they have always been: a teenage marriage, a wife pregnant before marriage, and a low level of family income. Psychological stress continues to be a leading cause of divorce, since many marriages fail following an acutely stressful experience, such as an unexpected death in the family, revelation of an infidelity, or loss of a job. See Arthur J. Norton and Paul C. Glick, "Marital Instability in America: Past, Present, and Future," in *Divorce and Separation: Context, Causes, and Consequences*, eds. George Lebinger and Oliver C. Moles, (New York, 1979), 6–19; Bane, *Here to Stay*, 22, 32–33, 36.

Traditional causes of marital stress were aggravated by social and legal changes during the 1970s. Economic instability produced conditions conducive to high divorce rates. Instability in a husband's employment or earnings is a major source of strain in the marriages of poorer couples, producing friction because of the husband's inability to fulfill his family's expectations. Divorce is more likely as well when a wife's earnings are higher than her husband's, in part because independent earnings add to a woman's sense of self-esteem and in part because this contributes to the husband's sense of insecurity. As more wives entered the labor force after 1970, this factor became a growing source of marital strain. Increased rates of social mobility across ethnic, religious, and geographical lines also contributed to the rising rates of marital instability. Census statistics disclose that more and more people are marrying partners who come from outside their ethnic or religious group or their area of birth. After marriage an increasing number of couples pull up stakes and move to new parts of the country, particularly to the Sunbelt, disrupting ties with family and friends. Divorce statistics show that the twelve metropolitan areas with the highest divorce rates are all located in Southern and Western states. Victor R. Fuchs, *How We Live* (Cambridge, Mass., 1983), 147–50; *NYT*, November 13, 1981, I, 12.

Changes in law also contributed to the rising number of divorces. Legal changes that made it easier to obtain a divorce included enactment of no-fault divorce laws in every state except South Dakota, "do-it-yourself" divorce kits that allow couples to dissolve a marriage without the help of a lawyer, a tendency toward lower alimony awards, and a trend toward making property settlements less contingent on who was at fault in breaking up the marriage. *NYT*, January 5, 1974, I, 16; *NYT*, March 19, 1975, I, 33; *NYT*, February 7, 1983, I, 1; Joan Anderson letter, *NYT*, December 5, 1981, I, 24; Lenore J. Weitzman and Ruth B. Dixon, "The Transformation of Legal Marriage Through No-Fault Divorce: The Case of the United States," in *Marriage and Cohabitation in Contemporary Societies: Areas of Legal, Social, and Ethical Change*, eds. John M. Eekelaar and Sanford N. Katz (Toronto, 1979), 143–53; Lynne Carol Halem, *Divorce Reform: Changing Legal and Social Perspectives* (New York, 1980), 233–83.

Finally, the current upsurge in divorces may be a product of the early marriages contracted during World War II and the early postwar period, when an unprecedented number of very young couples were joined together in wedlock. The high number of divorces during and after the World War II may have contributed to the high divorce rate during the 1970s, because the children of divorce face a substantially higher risk than others of having their own marriages fail. Norton and Glick, "Marital Instability in America," 6–19; *NYT*, November 27, 1977, I, 1; *NYT*, April 13, 1982, C1.

9. Veroff, Douan, and Kulka, *The Inner American.*, 191, 192, 194, 196; Yankelovich, *New Rules*, 5.

10. Richard A. Easterlin, "The American Baby Boom in Historical Perspective" Occasional Paper no. 79 (Washington, D.C., National Bureau of Economic

Research, 1962); "Relative Economic Status and the American Fertility Swing," in *Social Structure, Family Life Styles, and Economic Behavior*, ed. Eleanor B. Sheldon (Philadelphia, 1972); Easterlin, "The Conflict Between Aspirations and Resources," *Population and Development Review*, 2 (September/December 1972), 417–26; Arthur A. Campbell, "Baby Boom to Birth Dearth and Beyond," *Annals*, 435 (January 1978), 52–53.

11. Russell Jacoby, *Social Amnesia: A Critique of Conformist Psychology from Adler to Laing* (Boston, 1975); Ehrenreich, *Hearts of Men*, 89–98, 122, 147, 164–65; Yankelovich, *New Rules*, 235.

12. Refer to note 11. For an example of the new viewpoint on marriage and divorce, see a popular textbook *Essentials of Life and Health* (New York, 1972): "Far from being a wasting illness, divorce is a healthful adaptation, enabling monogamy to survive in a time when patriarchal powers, privileges and marital systems have become unworkable; far from being a radical change in the institution of marriage, divorce is a relatively minor modification of it. . . . "; quoted in Lynch, *The Broken Heart*, 10.

13. Allen J. Matusow, *The Unraveling of America: A History of Liberalism in the 1960s* (New York, 1984), 277–80, 321–23.

14. Refer to note 13. If a single term gave expression to the growing influence of young people during the 1960s, it was the phrase the "generation gap." It referred to the appearance among the young of a separate culture, a distinct language, and a distinctive outlook, apart from the world of adults. A shift in generational experience may have contributed to the perceived gulf between old and young. Young people of the 1960s, unlike their parents, had escaped the years of hardship, austerity, and sacrifice of the depression and World War II. Also contributing to a generation gap was the rising level of education attained by younger Americans. Many studies conducted during the 1960s concluded that those who had attended college were generally more liberal in their social, religious, and moral attitudes than those who had not.

It would be a mistake, however—a mistake made by many social commentators—to exaggerate the dimensions of the generation gap during the 1960s. Little persuasive evidence was uncovered during the sixties showing extensive alienation between adolescents and their parents. Survey research found a deep cleavage within the younger generation itself, dividing young college students from those who had entered blue collar jobs directly from high school, who were reportedly appalled "by the collapse of patriotism and respect for the law." Altogether, little evidence was found to indicate that younger Americans had abandoned traditional moral frameworks. Even in the most controversial and highly publicized areas of change—sex and drug-taking—truly dramatic shifts would have to wait for the 1970s. Studies of sexual behavior in the late 1960s detected only a modest liberalization in sexual practices compared to findings of twenty years before, while surveys of drug use found that only about 10 percent of young Americans had experimented with marijuana.

A number of influential studies of college students also argued that younger people's rejection of the strict norms that prevailed in the 1950s did not constitute a generation gap. According to these studies, students were simply giving expression to suppressed elements in their parents' lives. See Yankelovich, *New Rules*, 174; Kenneth Keniston, *Young Radicals* (New York, 1968; *NYT*, February 4, 1971, I, 1; *NYT*, January 17, 1972, I, 33; *NYT*, August 18, 1977, C13; *NYT*, December 1, 1968, VI, 129; *NYT*, November 2, 1969, VI, 32ff.; *NYT*, January 18, 1970, VI, 10.

15. Manchester, *Glory and the Dream*, 1221, 1355, 1463–68. The literature on the

women's movement is vast. A useful introduction is William H. Chafe, *Women and Equality: Changing Patterns in American Culture* (New York, 1977). On the ideology of feminism, see Barbara Sinclair Deckard, *The Women's Movement: Political, Socioeconomic, and Psychological Issues* (New York, 1975); Sara Evans, *Personal Politics: The Roots of Women's Liberation in the Civil Rights Movement and the New Left* (New York, 1979); Jo Freeman, *The Politics of Women's Liberation: A Case of an Emerging Social Movement and Its Relation to the Public Policy Process* (New York, 1975); Judith Hole and Ellen Levine, *Rebirth of Feminism* (New York, 1971); *Radical Feminism*, eds. Anne Koedt, Ellen Levine, and Anita Rapone (New York, 1973); Gayle Graham Yates, *What Women Want: The Ideas of the Movement* (Cambridge, Mass., 1971).

16. On the impact of feminism, see Judith M. Bardwick, *In Transition: How Feminism, Sexual Liberation, and the Search for Self-Fulfillment Have Altered America* (New York, 1979); Chafe, *Women and Equality*, ch. 5; Cynthia Fuchs Epstein, "Ten Years Later: Perspectives on the Women's Movement," *Dissent*, 22 (Spring 1975), 169–76; Janet Giele, *Women and the Future: Changing Sex Roles in Modern America* (New York, 1978); Elinor Lenz and Barbara Myerhoff, *The Feminization of America: How Women's Values Are Changing Our Public and Private Lives* (Los Angeles, 1985); Jane de Hart Mathews, "The New Feminism and the Dynamics of Social Change," in *Women's America: Refocusing the Past*, eds. Linda Kerber and Jane de Hart Mathews (New York, 1981), 397–421.

17. Manchester, *Glory and the Dream*, 1035–36. On the sexual revolution, see "Sex and the Contemporary American Scene," *Annals of the America Academy of Political and Social Science*, 376 (March 1968).

18. *NYT*, February 10, 1971, I, 48. On the growth of a "singles culture," see *NYT*, January 3, 1974, I, 16; *NYT*, April 21, 1977, C1. Homosexual rights ordinances were adopted in Ann Arbor, Michigan; Berkeley, California; Columbus, Ohio; Detroit, Michigan; Minneapolis, Minnesota; San Francisco, California; Seattle, Washington; and Washington, D.C., between 1972 and 1974. In 1973, the American Psychiatric Association removed homosexuality from its list of mental disorders.

19. Manchester, *Glory and the Dream*, 1035–36; "Sex and the Contemporary American Scene," *Annals of the America Academy of Political and Social Science*, 376 (March, 1968); *NYT*, February 10, 1971, I, 48; *NYT*, January 3, 1974, I, 16; *NYT*, April 21, 1977, C1.

20. Yankelovich, *New Rules*, xiv, 88, 97, 99, 100, 103, 104.

21. Daniel Patrick Moynihan, *Family and Nation: The Godkin Lectures, Harvard University* (San Diego, 1986); *NYT*, September 27, 1977, reprinted in *The Family*, ed. Gene Brown (New York, 1979), 353. For a helpful discussion of factors that have prompted concern for the family, see Nathan Glazer, "The Rediscovery of the Family," *Commentary* (March 1978), 49–56.

22. Lee Rainwater and William L. Yancey, *The Moynihan Report and the Politics of Controversy* (Cambridge, Mass., 1967), includes the full text of *The Negro Family: The Case for National Action* as well as responses to the report by government policymakers, journalists, civil rights leaders, and academic social scientists. For other responses to the report, see *NYT*, July 19, 1965 and April 28, 1967, reprinted in Brown, ed., *The Family*, 356–57.

23. Rainwater and Yancey, *Moynihan Report and the Politics of Controversy*, 51–60, 75–91.

24. Ibid., 75–80. For the comparison with Irish immigrants, see Moynihan, *Family and Nation*, 27–28.

25. Rainwater and Yancey, *Moynihan Report and the Politics of Controversy*, 93–94.

26. Ibid., 133–215; Andrew Billingsley, *Black Families in White America* (New York, 1968); R. Farley and A.I. Hermalin, "Family Stability: A Comparison of Trends Between Blacks and Whites," *American Sociological Review*, 36 (1971); J. Heiss, "On the Transmission of Marital Instability in Black Families," *American Sociological Review*, 37 (1972), 82–92; Robert B. Hill, *Strengths of Black Families* (New York, 1971); Joyce Ladner, *Tomorrow's Tomorrow* (Garden City, N.Y., 1972); R. Staples, "Toward a Sociology of the Black Family: A Theoretical and Methodological Assessment," *Journal of Marriage and the Family* 33 (1971), 119–38.

27. *NYT*, April 7, 1985, I, 1.

28. Thomas Meehan, "Moynihan of the Moynihan Report," *NYT*, July 31, 1966, VI, 5; *NYT*, July 29, 1971, I, 16; Rainwater and Yancey, *Moynihan Report and the Politics of Controversy*, 347–49.

The debate over the sources of difference in white and black illegitimacy rates remains shrouded in controversy. The Kinsey Institute studies of human sexuality, conducted in the 1940s and 1950s, suggested that black women tended to become sexually active at a somewhat earlier age than white women. At the age of fifteen, Kinsey reported, 50 percent of all non-college-educated black women had had premarital intercourse, compared to ten to fifteen percent of white women of similar educational backgrounds. Kinsey also reported that young black women had a greater frequency of intercourse, which he suggested could account for one-third to one-half of the difference in illegitimacy rates.

Other studies attributed the difference in illegitimacy rates to the fact that a higher proportion of black women spent their child-rearing years in an unmarried state, reflecting higher rates of nonmarriage, divorce, desertion, and widowhood. Other researchers suggested that higher black illegitimacy rates reflected the greater use of contraceptives and greater resort to abortion by unmarried white women, underreporting of white illegitimate births, and the greater prevalence of "shotgun" marriages among whites.

What studies have found is that white women were more likely to legitimate children conceived before marriage. In 1971, 34 percent of white children were born within eight months of marriage compared to 26 percent of black children. Research found that the proportion of women who legitimate children by shotgun marriages correlates closely with education. When the education factor is controlled for, the same proportion of black and white women who have a premarital pregnancy marry before the child's birth. Other studies indicate that black women were more likely to have unplanned or unwanted births because they were less likely to use contraceptives or abortions. Kinsey found that three times as many non-college educated unmarried white women had abortions as similarly situated black women. Black women were also less likely to put children up for adoption. In 1971, two-thirds of illegitimate white children were put up for adoption or placed into foster care, as opposed to 7 percent of illegitimate black children. See Sar A. Levitan, William B. Johnston, and Robert Taggart, *Minorities in the United States: Problems, Progress, and Prospects* (Washington, D.C., 1975), 38; Rainwater and Yancey, *Moynihan Report and the Politics of Controversy*, 223–35, 348–49.

29. Rainwater and Yancey, *Moynihan Report and the Politics of Controversy*, 219, 235, 354–68, 436–37, 454.

30. Thomas Meehan, "Moynihan of the Moynihan Report," *NYT*, July 31, 1966, 6, 5; *NYT*, July 29, 1971, I, 16; Rainwater and Yancey, *Moynihan Report and the Politics of Controversy*, 318–20.

31. Carol B. Stack, *All Our Kin: Strategies for Survival in a Black Community* (New York, 1974); *The Extended Family in Black Societies*, eds. Demitri B. Shimkin, Edith M. Shimkin, and Dennis A. Frate (Chicago, 1978), especially essays by Bert N. Adams, Regina E. Holloman and Fannie E. Lewis, Lenus Jack, Jr., Kiyotaka Aoyagi, and Vera M. Green; Hill, *Strengths of Black Families*, 5–8.

32. Rainwater and Yancey, *Moynihan Report and the Politics of Controversy*, 1–3.

33. *NYT*, December 9, 1968, I, 1.

34. Charles Murray, "No, Welfare Isn't Really the Problem," *Public Interest*, no. 84 (Summer 1986), 5–6; Sar A. Levitan, *Programs in Aid of the Poor*, 5th ed. (Baltimore, Md., 1985), 34.

35. Levitan, *Programs in Aid of the Poor*, 1–154; Levitan, *The Great Society's Poor Law: A New Approach to Poverty* (Baltimore, Md., 1969); Levitan and Robert Taggart, *The Promise of Greatness* (Cambridge, Mass., 1976); *On Fighting Poverty: Perspectives from Experience*, ed. James L. Sundquist (New York, 1969); *The Great Society: Lessons for the Future*, eds. Eli Ginzburg and Robert M. Solow (New York, 1974).

36. Levitan, *Programs in Aid of the Poor*, 5–6; John E. Schwartz, *America's Hidden Success: A Reassessment of Twenty Years of Public Policy* (New York, 1983), 32–50; Sheldon H. Danziger and Daniel H. Weinberg, eds., *Fighting Poverty: What Works and What Doesn't* (Cambridge, Mass., 1986).

37. Sar A. Levitan and Clifford M. Johnson, *Beyond the Safety Net: Reviving the Promise of Opportunity in America* (Cambridge, Mass., 1984), 60–61.

38. *Ibid.*; Charles Murray, *Losing Ground: American Social Policy, 1950–1980* (New York, 1984), 129–33.

39. Government studies have found that a 10 percent increase in AFDC benefits was associated with a 2 percent increase in the number of female-headed families, while a 10 percent increase in male wages was accompanied by an 8 percent decline in female-headed families. Levitan and Johnson, *Beyond the Safety Net*, 64; Robert Lerman, "The Family, Poverty, and Welfare Programs: An Introductory essay on Problems of Analysis and Policy," in U.S. Congress, Joint Economic Committee, *Studies in Public Welfare* (Washington, D.C.: U.S. Government Printing Office, 1974), 18–19; Marjorie Honig, "The Impact of Welfare Payment Levels on Family Stability," in *Studies in Public Welfare*, 37–53. See essays on poverty and family structure by Mary Jo Bane, William Julius Wilson, and Kathryn M. Neckerman in *Fighting Poverty*, eds. Danziger and Weinberg. For a contrasting view, see Murray, *Losing Ground*, 124–33.

40. *Progress Against Poverty: A Review of the 1964–1974 Decade*, eds. Robert D. Plotnick and Felicity Skidmore (New York, 1975), 13, 62–63, 104–5; Levitan and Taggart, *The Promise of Greatness*, 49, 51; *NYT*, July 18, 1971, IV, 12.

41. Levitan, *Programs in Aid of the Poor*, 13–14, 34–38, 94–95.

42. Welfare mothers divide into at least two identifiable groups. Most single women on welfare are older women seeking temporary assistance while recovering from the loss of a spouse through divorce, desertion, or death. These women account for 85 to 90 percent of all single women who ever go on welfare. Another group of single women on welfare are younger, less-educated mothers, particularly those who bore an illegitimate child during their teens or early twenties, who are more likely to remain dependent on public assistance for long periods. Roughly 10 to 15 percent of the people who ever go on welfare remain on public assistance for eight years or more; they constitute more than half of the people on welfare at any one time. See Mickey Kaus, "Welfare and Work: A

Symposium," *New Republic* (October 6, 1986), 22; *NYT*, September 25, 1986, I, 26. Ben J. Wattenberg, *The Good News is the Bad News is Wrong* (New York, 1985), 191, 240, 243.

43. Sar A. Levitan, *Programs in Aid of the Poor for the 1970s* (Baltimore, Md., 1969), 29; Sheila B. Kamerman and Alfred J. Kahn, eds., *Family Policy: Government and Families in Fourteen Countries* (New York, 1978), 428–503.

44. Sheila B. Kamerman and Cheryl D. Hayes, eds., *Families That Work: Children in a Changing World* (Washington, D.C., 1982), 12–36; Joan Beck, "Growing Up in America is Tough," *Houston Chronicle* (April 2, 1986), A10; Glazer, "Rediscovery of the Family," 50.

Growing anxiety over children and adolescents was, of course, related to the postwar baby boom. Census statistics showed an explosion in the number of young Americans during the 1960s. The number of young people aged fourteen to twenty-four jumped 47 percent in a decade, reaching forty million in 1970. At the end of the 1960s, young people accounted for 20 percent of the American population, a third more than in 1960. Because teenagers and young adults constituted a growing proportion of the population, as a result of depressed birthrates during the 1930s followed by the postwar baby boom, young people exerted a disproportionate influence on public opinion.

The 1960s witnessed major gains in income, education, and employment by teenagers. Teenagers were far more likely to finish high school or attend college than were their parents. The proportion of young Americans receiving college degrees tripled in the three decades after 1940—climbing from 6 to 16 percent—while the proportion receiving high school diplomas doubled—from 38 percent to 75 percent. *NYT*, February 4, 1971, I, 1; *NYT*, January 17, 1972, I, 33; *NYT*, August 18, 1977, C13.

45. Today, as many as two-thirds of all American high school junior and seniors hold part-time paying jobs. See Ellen Greenberger and Laurence Steinberg, *When Teenagers Work: The Psychological and Social Costs of Adolescent Employment* (New York, 1986), 3–46.

46. Joan Beck, "Growing Up in America is Tough," *Houston Chronicle* (April 2, 1986), A10.

47. Marie Winn, *Children Without Childhood* (New York, 1983); David Elkind, *The Hurried Child: Growing Up Too Soon* (Reading, Mass., 1981); Vance Packard, *Our Endangered Children: Growing Up in a Changing World* (Boston, 1983). Similar fears were already being voiced in the 1950s. See Eda LeShan, *The Conspiracy Against Childhood* (New York, 1967).

48. Peter Uhlenberg and David Eggebeen, "The Declining Well-Being of American Adolescents," *Public Interest*, no. 85 (Winter 1986), 25–38.

49. While it is true that the suicide rate for white male adolescents increased 260 percent between 1950 and 1976, the illegitimacy rate of illegitimate births among white adolescent females increased 143 percent over the same period, and the rate of death by homicide among white adolescent males increased 177 percent between 1959 and 1976, actual rates remained at low levels. The white male adolescent homicide rate rose from 3 per 100,000 in 1959 to 8 per 100,000 in 1976; the white male adolescent suicide rate climbed from 4 per 100,000 in 1950 to 13 per 100,000 in 1976; and illegitimacy among white teenage women rose from 5.1 per 1,000 to 12.4 per 1,000. It is also easy to exaggerate drug usage. Seventeen percent of all high school seniors have tried cocaine once in their life; 54 percent have tried marijuana at least once. See Ira S. Steinberg, *The New Lost Generation: The Population Boom and Public Policy* (New York,

1982), 7–19; Adam Paul Weisman, "I Was a Drug-Hype Junkie," *New Republic* (October 6, 1986), 14–17.

50. *NYT*, October 26, 1969, I, 57; *NYT*, April 2, 1967, VI, 112ff.

51. *NYT*, September 11, 1973, I, 50; *NYT*, December 25, 1969, I, 37.

52. *NYT*, April 14, 1974, VII, 3; *NYT*, November 8, 1968, I, 54; *NYT*, January 7, 1973, I, 22, 23; *NYT*, February 16, 1969, VII, Pt. 2, 4; *NYT*, June 27, 1976, VI, 26ff.; *NYT*, December 3, 1973, I, 54; *NYT*, March 16, 1981, II, 8; *NYT*, September 11, 1973, I, 50.

53. *NYT*, December 3, 1973, I, 54; *NYT*, March 16, 1981, II, 8; *NYT*, September 11, 1973, I, 50.

54. Fuchs, *How We Live*, 51, 55–56, 69–71; Bane, *Here to Stay*, 15; John P. Murray, *Television and Youth: 25 Years of Research and Controversy* (Stanford, Wash., 1980), 67.

55. Marie Winn, *The Plug-In Drug* (New York, 1977); Murray, *Television and Youth*, 18–57.

56. Murray, *Television and Youth*, 18–57; *NYT*, January 6, 1959, March 2, 1969, September 18, 1969, September 28, 1969, September 4, 1971, January 11, 1972, April 20, 1980, reprinted in *Childhood, Youth and Society*, ed. Gene Brown (New York, 1980), 70–94.

57. Refer to note 56.

58. Refer to note 56.

59. Fuchs, *How We Live*, 126–33, 150, 166, 169, 173–74, 190, 204; *NYT*, November 30, 1977, I, 1. One set of factors that propelled married women into the labor force was a rising cost of living and a declining rate of growth in real family income. Income, adjusted for inflation, rose 38 percent during the 1950s and 33 percent in the 1960s, but dropped 9.2 percent between 1973 and 1982. At the same time that real income fell, other costs, especially for housing, climbed steeply. Back in 1971, it took an income of just $6,770 to afford a median-price house, which then cost just $24,800. Actual median income that year was $10,300, 51.9 percent more than was required. A decade later, the median price of a house had climbed to over $70,000 and a family that earned the median family income was unable to afford such a house. Other economic factors that led many married women to seek a paycheck included rising real wages for women workers, which increased the attractiveness of work outside the home and the growth of service industries, such as retail trade, education, and health. Such service jobs have traditionally offered more opportunities to women than other occupations because they do not rely on physical strength, their work hours are usually flexible, and the workplace is often located in residential areas.

60. Sheila Kamerman and Alfred Kahn, "The Day-Care Debate: A Wider View," *Public Interest*, no. 54 (1979), 76–93.

61. *NYT*, November 30, 1970, I, 1; *NYT*, April 1, 1973, IV, 9; *NYT*, January 9, 1976, I, 18.

62. Edward B. Fiske, "Early Schooling is Now the Rage," *NYT*, April 13, 1986, XII, 24–30; *NYT*, December 10, 1971, and April 30, 1972, in *The Family*, ed. Gene Brown, 337–43.

63. Fiske, "Early Schooling," 25; Kamerman and Kahn, "The Day-Care Debate," 76–93.

64. Fiske, "Early Schooling," 25.

65. Ibid., 25–26. A 1985 Conference Board study estimated that 120 companies and 400 hospitals and public agencies sponsored daycare centers at or near their facilities. Another 2,500 firms provide financial support for child care. *NYT,* June 21, 1985, 25: 2.

66. Fiske, "Early Schooling," 25–26.

67. Packard, *Our Endangered Children,* 137–38; Jerome Kagan, "The Effects of Infant Day Care on Psychological Development, *The Growth of the Child* (New York, 1978), 78.

68. Packard, *Our Endangered Children,* 139–41, 146, 166–72; Jay Belsky and Laurence D. Steinberg, "The Effects of Day Care: A Critical View," *Child Development,* 49 (1978), 929–49; Belsky and Steinberg, "What Does Research Teach Us About Day Care?" *Children Today* (July-August, 1979); Sally Provence, Audrey Naylor and June Patterson, *The Challenge of Day Care* (New Haven, 1977).

69. Packard, *Our Endangered Children,* 144–58.

70. Fiske, "Early Schooling," 30.

71. Sheila B. Kamerman and Alfred J. Kahn, eds., *Family Policy: Government and Families in Fourteen Countries* (New York, 1978), 428–503; *NYT,* June 9, 1979, 17: 2; Packard, *Our Endangered Children,* 162–66; *Houston Chronicle,* March 2, 1987, A7.

 Ten states—California, Connecticut, Hawaii, Illinois, Kansas, Massachusetts, Minnesota, New Hampshire, Ohio, and Washington—currently require employers to grant special leaves to pregnant women and to reinstate them in their jobs or comparable positions when they return. In all other states, maternity policies are governed by the 1978 federal Pregnancy Discrimination Act, which made it illegal to discriminate on the basis of pregnancy or childbirth in hiring, reinstatement, termination, and disability benefits.

 Five states—California, Hawaii, New Jersey, New York, and Rhode Island—provide temporary disability insurance, which provides half the wage the female worker earned during a six to ten week maternity leave.

72. Packard, *Our Endangered Children,* 185; Uhlenberg and Eggebeen, "The Declining Well-Being of American Adolescents," 37.

73. Levitan and Belous, *What's Happening to the American Family?,* 69–72; Halem, *Divorce Reform,* 191–93.

74. Packard, *Our Endangered Children,* 189–201; Halem, *Divorce Reform,* 174–81; Levitan and Belous, *What's Happening to the American Family?,* 69–72; Judith S. Wallerstein and Joan B. Kelley, *Surviving the Breakup: How Children and Parents Cope With Divorce* (New York, 1980); Cynthia Longfellow, "Divorce in Context: Its Impact on Children" in *Divorce and Separation,* 287–306.

75. Refer to note 74.

76. Refer to note 74.

77. Refer to note 74.

78. Refer to note 74.

79. Fuchs, *How We Live,* 73–75, 149–50, 214; Levitan and Belous, *What's Happening to the American Family?,* 72–75; *NYT,* April 2, 1974, I, 34; Lenore Weitzman, *The Divorce Revolution: The Unexpected Social and Economic Consequences for Women and Children* (New York, 1985).

80. Refer to note 79.

81. *NYT,* May 22, 1983, VI, 48–57; *NYT,* November 23, 1980, I, 28.

82. Packard, *Our Endangered Children*, 294; Halem, *Divorced Reform*, 187–91; Levitan and Belous, *What's Happening to the American Family?*, 70, 74.

83. Winn, *Children Without Childhood*; Elkind, *The Hurried Child*; Packard, *Our Endangered Children*.

84. *NYT*, May 3, 1981, IV, 9.

85. Weitzman and Dixon, "The Transformation of Legal Marriage Through No-Fault Divorce," 143–53; Halem, *Divorce Reform*, 233–83; Andrew Hacker, "Post-Marital Economics," *Fortune* (December 23, 1985), 167, 170.

Hacker divides divorces into three classifications. One group, comprising about 40 percent of all divorces, involves marriages dissolved within four years of a wedding. Usually, these marriages involve no children. A second group, comprising another 40 percent of divorces, occurs when a woman is in her mid-to-late-thirties. Most of these divorces involve children. The remaining 20 percent of divorces involve long-term marriages with wives typically in their 40s and 50s.

86. Refer to note 85.

87. Refer to note 85; *NYT*, February 7, 1983, A14; *NYT*, January 3, 1974, I, 16.

88. Refer to note 85; *NYT*, March 19, 1975, I, 33.

89. *NYT*, February 7, 1983, A14; *NYT*, April 18, 1982, C1.

90. Mary Ann Glendon, *The New Family and the New Property* (Toronto, 1981), 47, 52, 54–55; *NYT*, February 7, 1983, A14.

91. Glendon, *New Family and the New Property*, 57; *NYT*, March 31, 1978, F11; *NYT*, November 3, 1972, I, 24; *NYT*, March 17, 1974, IV, 7; *NYT*, March 5, 1979, I, 1. The four community property states are California, Idaho, Louisiana, and New Mexico.

92. Weitzman, *Divorce Revolution*; Hacker, "Post-Marital Economics," 167–76.

93. Refer to note 92.

94. *NYT*, May 3, 1981, IV, 9.

95. *NYT*, October 11, 1980, I, 21; *NYT*, May 3, 1981, IV, 9; *NYT*, October 6, 1980, II, 8.

96. Refer to note 95; *NYT*, January 15, 1975, I, 71. A new source of contention lies in the conflict between the rights of a pregnant mother and the rights of the fetus she is carrying. Several courts have ruled that the state has the power to require a woman to give birth by cesarean section or to have a blood transfusion in order to save a fetus. One court, in Maryland, required a pregnant woman who was taking narcotics to enter a drug rehabilitation program and undergo weekly urine tests to prevent the birth of an addicted infant. The difficult question that the courts are being forced to resolve is the extent to which government can intervene to protect a fetus against maternal negligence in order to ensure the birth of a healthy baby. Among the questions stirring controversy is whether protection of a fetus would justify laws barring the sale of alcohol to pregnant women or statutes requiring genetic testing, like amniocentesis, of pregnant women who are at risk of giving birth to a child suffering from a condition such as Tay-Sachs disease, sickle-cell anemia, or Down's syndrome. See *Wall Street Journal*, April 12, 1985, II, 1.

97. G. Sidney Buchanan, *Morality, Sex, and the Constitution* (Lanham, Md., 1985); Glendon, *New Family and the New Property*, 43.

98. *NYT*, May 3, 1981, IV, 9.

99. Glendon, *New Family and the New Property,* 43.

100. Ibid., 11, 38, 49, 71–73.
    One area in which the nation's courts have recently shown increasing sensitivity to "informal" familial relationships involves the custody rights of stepparents. Today, one American child in five lives in a stepfamily, and six states have adopted statutes providing visitation rights for stepparents. In states without such statutes, divorce agreements have provided for visits between children and stepparents, awards of custody to stepparents, and, in a few instances, financial support for stepchildren. See *NYT,* March 2, 1987, I, 1.

101. Glendon, *New Family and the New Property,* 61; *NYT,* February 7, 1983, 1: 4.

102. *NYT,* June 3, 1980, II, 12.

103. Kristin Luker, *Abortion and the Politics of Motherhood* (Berkeley, 1984), 126–215; Glazer, "Rediscovery of the Family," 50.

104. *NYT,* January 15, 1983, I, 18.

105. Ibid.

106. *NYT,* January 7, 1980, IV, 8; *NYT,* March 26, 1980, III, 18; *NYT,* June 6, 1980, II, 4; *NYT,* June 9, 1980, III, 16; *NYT,* June 22, 1980, I, 24; *NYT,* July 14, 1980, I, 12.

107. Refer to note 106.

108. Gilbert Y. Steiner, *The Futility of Family Policy* (Washington, D.C., 1981).

109. Andrew Hacker, "Goodbye to Marriage," *New York Review of Books* (May 3, 1979), 23–27.

110. Yankelovich, *New Rules,* 103, 104.

111. Ibid., 101, 103.

112. Ibid., 104, 131.

113. George Masnick and Mary Jo Bane, *The Nation's Families, 1960–1990* (Boston, 1980); *NYT,* May 23, 1980, I, 18.

114. For proposals to strengthen the family, see Packard, *Our Endangered Children,* 343–63; Kenneth Keniston and the Carnegie Council on Children, *All Our Children: The American Family Under Pressure* (New York, 1977), 216–21.

EPILOGUE

1. *NYT,* December 25, 1969, I, 37.

2. *NYT,* March 24, 1985, IV, 5; *NYT,* July 8, 1985, I, 1; *NYT,* March 15, 1987, V, 1.

3. *NYT,* August 20, 1984, C15.

4. *Ibid.; NYT,* September 28, 1986, I, 1. On the conservative critique of federal family initiatives, see Steiner, *Futility of Family Policy,* 17.

5. *NYT,* October 20, 1984, I, 18; *NYT,* October 24, 1984, I, 13; *NYT,* August 20, 1984, C15; *NYT,* September 28, 1986, I, 1.

6. *NYT,* September 1, 1985, I, 37.

7. *Newsweek* (February 17, 1986), 31; Laura Gellott, "Staking Claim to the Family," *Commonweal* (September 20, 1985), 488ff.

8. Refer to note 7.

9. Andrew Hacker, "Farewell to the Family," *New York Review of Books* (March 18, 1982), 37ff.; Steiner, *Futility of Family Policy*, 20, 50.

10. On the new generation of poor Americans, see *NYT*, October 20, 1985, I, 1; *NYT*, February 6, 1987, I, 30; *NYT*, February 19, 1987, I, 12; Barbara Bergmann, *The Economic Emergence of Women* (New York, 1986).

   In three states, California, Maine, and Wisconsin, maximum AFDC benefits for a family of four remained stable between 1970 and 1985. In all other states, the value of benefits declined. In Texas the decline was 59 percent; in Massachusetts, 46 percent; in New York City, 38 percent. See Moynihan, *Family and Nation*, 15.

   One proposed solution to the exploding rate of child poverty is strict enforcement of court-ordered child support payments. Unfortunately, the average court-ordered payment is so low—$2,460 a year, or roughly $47 a week—that it is unlikely to make a major difference in the actual lives of poor children. See *NYT*, (Carol E. Curtis letter), February 17, 1987, I, 28.

   Although the most rapid growth in the number of poor children has occurred in single-parent families, it needs to be stressed that half of all poor families contain both a husband and a wife. While there is no generally accepted explanation for the increase in single-parent families, there can be little doubt that a major contributor is the increasing number of men unable to support a family. Over the past decade, 80 percent of the new jobs created were in the service sector of the economy, and most of these jobs have gone to women. Today half the young black males between the ages of sixteen and twenty-four have never held a job. See *NYT* (Jane J. Young letter), February 27, 1987, I, 34; Richard B. Freeman and Harry J. Holzer, *The Black Youth Employment Crisis* (Chicago, 1986), 3–18.

11. On child-rearing dilemmas of working mothers, see *NYT*, March 11, 1985, C11; *NYT*, September 2, 1984, I, 1; *NYT*, September 4, 1984, B11.

   On January 13, 1987, the U.S. Supreme Court upheld a California law that gave women up to four months unpaid disability leave for pregnancy. In a related decision, issued January 21, 1987, the Court ruled that states can deny unemployment benefits to anyone who leaves a job for reasons unrelated to work, including pregnancy.

   Many women today are forced to choose between their job and their child. No more than 40 percent of the nation's 49 million working women have job-protected, paid maternity leaves of at least six weeks duration. Ten states have adopted laws that guarantee workers jobs after they return from maternity leave. Five states provide temporary disability insurance to replace income lost during a maternity leave. In contrast, at least 75 other countries guarantee women the right to leave work for a specified period to care for a baby and provide job guarantees and cash payments to compensate for time lost from work because of pregnancy or childbirth. See *NYT*, March 11, 1985, C11 and refer to note 71, chapter 10.

12. On new reproductive techniques, see *NYT*, February 15, 1987, E22; *NYT*, October 1, 1986, C1; *NYT*, February 11, 1986, C1; *NYT*, March 20, 1985, III, 8; *NYT*, November 16, 1984, A20, A21.

Index